The Ambivalence of Power in the Twenty-First-Century Economy

FRINGE

Series Editors
Alena Ledeneva and Peter Zusi, School of Slavonic and East European Studies, UCL

The FRINGE series is a platform for cross-disciplinary analysis and the development of 'area studies without borders'. FRINGE is an acronym standing for Fluidity, Resistance, Invisibility, Neutrality, Grey zones, and Elusiveness – categories fundamental to the themes that the FRINGE Centre supports. The oxymoron in the notion of a 'FRINGE Centre' expresses our interest in (1) the tensions between 'area studies' and more traditional academic disciplines; and (2) social, political, and cultural trajectories from 'centres to fringes' and inversely from 'fringes to centres'. The series pursues an innovative understanding of the significance of grey zones and patterns of social and cultural complexity. We aim to develop forms of analysis of those elements of complexity that are resistant to articulation, visualization or measurement.

Alena Ledeneva is Professor of Politics and Society at the School of Slavonic and East European Studies of UCL.

Peter Zusi is Associate Professor at the School of Slavonic and East European Studies of UCL.

The Ambivalence of Power in the Twenty-First-Century Economy

Cases from Russia and beyond

Edited by Vadim Radaev and Zoya Kotelnikova

First published in 2022 by
UCL Press
University College London
Gower Street
London WC1E 6BT

Available to download free: www.uclpress.co.uk

Collection © Editors, 2022
Text © Contributors, 2022
Images © Contributors, 2022

The authors have asserted their rights under the Copyright, Designs and Patents Act 1988 to be identified as the authors of this work.

A CIP catalogue record for this book is available from The British Library.

Any third-party material in this book is not covered by the book's Creative Commons licence. Details of the copyright ownership and permitted use of third-party material is given in the image (or extract) credit lines. If you would like to reuse any third-party material not covered by the book's Creative Commons licence, you will need to obtain permission directly from the copyright owner.

This book is published under a Creative Commons Attribution-Non-commercial Non-derivative 4.0 International licence (CC BY-NC-ND 4.0). This licence allows you to share, copy, distribute and transmit the work for personal and non-commercial use provided author and publisher attribution is clearly stated. Attribution should include the following information:

Radaev, V. and Kotelnikova, Z. (eds). 2022. *The Ambivalence of Power in the Twenty-First-Century Economy: Cases from Russia and beyond.* London: UCL Press. https://doi.org/10.14324/111.9781800082687

Further details about Creative Commons licences are available at http://creativecommons.org/licenses/

ISBN: 978-1-80008-270-0 (Hbk)
ISBN: 978-1-80008-269-4 (Pbk)
ISBN: 978-1-80008-268-7 (PDF)
ISBN: 978-1-80008-272-4 (epub)
ISBN: 978-1-80008-271-7 (mobi)
DOI: https://doi.org/10.14324/111.9781800082687

Contents

List of figures	vii
List of tables	ix
List of contributors	xi
Series Editors' Foreword	xvii
Acknowledgements	xix
Preface. Ambivalence: practices, patterns and particles of power Alena Ledeneva	xx

1 Introduction   1
   Zoya Kotelnikova and Vadim Radaev

Part I. Interdependency of political power and economic governance: A macro perspective

2 Interrelation between economic freedom and democracy: The case of post-communist countries   14
   Marek Dabrowski

3 The pitfalls of rent-seeking: Alternative mechanisms of resource rent collection in Russia and Venezuela   36
   Alexei Pobedonostsev

4 Contradictions of centralization: Four models of interaction between Russian rural communities and government and agribusiness   58
   Alexander Nikulin and Alexander Kurakin

5 Legitimation of innovation: The case of AI technology for facial recognition   80
   Leonid Kosals

Part II. Power struggles in the economy: An organizational perspective

6 The power of non-compliance: Inter-firm opportunism in Russian consumer markets   102
   Vadim Radaev

7   Abusive supervision in organizations: Power, dependency
    and employee voice in labour relations   122
    Evgeniya Balabanova
8   Beyond the state and digital platforms: (In)formalization
    of freelance contracting in Russia   146
    Andrey Shevchuk and Denis Strebkov
9   Power struggles and quality construction in the market
    for municipal rental housing in Sweden   171
    Elena Bogdanova
10 Private authority in regulating markets: Power dynamics
    around free prior and informed consent (FPIC) in forestry
    and the oil industry in Russia   188
    *Maria S. Tysiachniouk, Sara Teitelbaum, Andrey N. Petrov, and
    Leah S. Horowitz*
11 How brand holders have deprived counterfeiting of legitimacy
    in Russia since the early 2000s   217
    Zoya Kotelnikova
12 Academic excellence through homogenization?
    Gaining legitimacy from the strategic positioning of top-
    ranked universities   237
    Ivan Pavlyutkin and Anastasiia Makareva
13 One man's pill is another man's poison: Ambivalence of
    definitional power – the case of breast cancer drugs in Russia   261
    Elena Berdysheva
14 'Russian Parmesan, even better than the original':
    Exploratory research into organic farmers' valuation strategies   280
    Tamara Kusimova

Part III. Resistance to domination and empowerment in the economy: An individual perspective

15 Everyday politics of consumption: Why cynical consumers
    are disappointed citizens – the case of Moscow during the
    economic crisis of 2014–2017   302
    Regina Resheteeva
16 Childbirth with doulas in Moscow: Between empowerment
    and responsibility   321
    Masha Denisova
17 Empowerment of the disempowered: Assessing the impact
    of young Muscovites through ecological practices   342
    Daria Lebedeva

Index   365

List of figures

2.1	Interrelationship between economic and political freedom in the world, 2019.	18
2.2	Interrelationship between political freedom and GDP per capita level in PPP terms, 2019.	21
2.3	Interrelationship between the FH Nations in Transit Score and EBRD transition indicators, 2001.	23
2.4	Interrelationship between the FHGFS and HFIEF in the former centrally planned economies, 2019.	24
2.5	Slovakia: HFIEF (left axis) vs. FHFIW (right axis) scores, 1994–2007.	28
2.6	Russia: HFIEF (left axis) vs. FHFIW (right axis) scores, 1995–2019.	29
2.7	Georgia: HFIEF (left axis) vs. FHFIW (right axis) scores, 1999–2019.	30
2.8	Hungary: HFIEF (left axis) vs. FHFIW (right axis) scores, 2008–19.	31
8.1	Contracting arrangements between freelancers and their clients (percentages), 2009–19.	154
8.2	Client violations reported in 2019 (percentages).	161
8.3	Solving problem with clients in 2009 and 2019 (percentages from those who had problems in the previous year).	163
10.1	Governance generating network.	192
10.2	Power dynamics in the process of development of the new national FSC standard.	197

10.3	Interactions between members of the SDG in the process of negotiations.	199
10.4	Governance generating network: Sakhalin case study.	204
10.5	Power dynamics in the process of FPIC implementation.	206
11.1	The number of legal cases initiated by Customs against illegal use of trademarks, 2004–19.	231
11.2	The number of arbitration courts trials against administrative violations (illegal use of trademarks), 2004–19.	231
11.3	The number of market dealers sentenced under Article 180, Part 1 of the Criminal Code (illegal use of trademarks), 2004–19.	232

All figures have been drawn by the authors of the chapters they appear in.

List of tables

3.1	The resource revenue of the Russian government and total resource rent.	38
3.2	The resource revenue of the Venezuelan government and total resource rent.	39
4.1	Development models of Russian rural territories.	64
6.1	Basic sample descriptive statistics, per cent.	108
6.2	Descriptive statistics by years and industries, per cent.	113
6.3	Estimated effect of explanatory and control variables on the existence and percentage of partners infringing business contracts as dependent variables.	114
6.4	Estimated effect of explanatory and control variables on the existence of conflict with partners as dependent variable.	115
7.1	Factor analysis results and percentages of respondents faced with AS.	134
7.2	Reliability analysis results and percentage of respondents engaged in voice behaviours.	135
7.3	Means, standard deviations and correlations.	137
7.4	Regression analysis results for abusive supervision.	138
7.5	Regression analysis results for employee voice behaviour.	139
7.6	Results of testing the hypotheses.	139
8.1	Overview of the data collection approach and sample size, by survey wave.	153
8.2	Means or percentages of variables.	156
8.3	Multinomial regression results for the types of agreement formalization.	158

8.4	Logistic regression coefficients for opportunism and problem-solving.	164
10.1	Research on FPIC in the framework of FSC.	195
10.2	Research on FPIC in oil and gas sectors on Sakhalin Island.	195
11.1	Characteristics of the interviews.	222
12.1	Sample list of universities.	245
12.2	Key categories of universities' strategic positioning.	249
12.3	General models of strategic positioning based on the counting of keywords (by groups of universities).	254
17.1	Characteristics of the respondents.	349

List of contributors

Evgeniya Balabanova is Doctor of Sciences in Sociology, and a Professor at the Department of General Sociology at HSE University, Moscow. Her main research areas are economic sociology, organizational research, sociology of management, labour relations, professions, and occupations. She is the author of several books and papers including Organizational Behaviour (2022) (in Russian), 'Employee exit and constructive voice as behavioral responses to psychological contract breach in Finland and Russia' (2022) and 'The job demands and resources as antecedents of work engagement' (2017).

Elena Berdysheva is a senior research fellow in the Laboratory for Studies in Economic Sociology at HSE University. Her main research areas are sociology of markets, sociology of price, sociology of medicine, problems of commodification and marketization in contemporary society. Her works include 'Rethinking prices during an economic crisis: Calculation as a new mode of consumer behaviour in Russia' (2017) and 'Social architectonics of market prices: Basic principles of Russian consumer price perception (a Moscow case study)' (2017).

Elena Bogdanova is a senior lecturer and researcher at the University of Gothenburg, Sweden. Her main research interests are economic sociology and markets for singularities, in particular cultural objects and built environment. Her latest publications include 'Configuring objects and subjects of care in built heritage management: Experimenting with storytelling as a participatory device in Sweden' (2021; co-authored with Linda Soneryd).

Marek Dabrowski is Professor of Economic Sciences at HSE University, Moscow, a non-resident scholar at Bruegel, Brussels and Professor of and

Co-founder and Fellow at the Center for Social and Economic Research (CASE) in Warsaw. He specializes in country-specific and cross-country comparative analysis related to monetary and fiscal policy, macroeconomic trends, financial stability, global economy and global financial architecture, EU and Eurozone economy and economic policy. Having been involved in policy advising and policy research, he has authored multiple academic and policy papers, and he has edited several books including *Fiscal Sustainability Challenges* (2017), *Economic and Social Development of the Southern and Eastern Mediterranean Countries* (2015), *Global versus National Income Inequalities and Their Impact on Global Governance* (2020) and *Factors Determining Russia's Long-Term Growth Rate* (2019).

Masha Denisova is a PhD candidate in the Department of Health, Ethics and Society, Care and Public Health Research Institute at Maastricht University (Netherlands). Her main research interests include science and technology studies, economic sociology, studies of healthcare and human reproduction. She is the co-author of the paper 'A responsible worker and a caring mother: Experiences of Russian commercial surrogates' (2021).

Leah S. Horowitz is an assistant professor at the University of Wisconsin–Madison (United States) with a joint appointment at the Nelson Institute for Environmental Studies and the Department of Civil Society and Community Studies (School of Human Ecology). Her main research interests are grassroots engagements with environmental issues, cultural complexities and power dynamics surrounding the management and exploitation of natural resources, modes of environmental governance and Indigenous communities. She authored the book *Grassroots Environmental Governance: Community engagements with industry* (2017) and multiple articles including 'Globalizing extraction and Indigenous rights in the Russian Arctic: The enduring role of the state in natural resource governance' (2019) and 'Indigenous peoples' relationships to large-scale mining in post/colonial contexts: Toward multidisciplinary comparative perspectives' (2018).

Leonid Kosals is Doctor of Sciences in Economics (Sociology), Professor and Senior Research Fellow of the Laboratory for Studies in Economic Sociology at HSE University and Adjunct Professor in the Centre for Criminology and Sociolegal Studies at the University of Toronto (Canada). His main research interests include shadow economy, organized crime, corruption (including that in law enforcement agencies), clan capitalism in Russia and other countries, social change and transformation of societies in comparative analysis. He is an author of the monographs *Sociology of the Transition into Market Economy in Russia* (1998) and *Why Doesn't Russian Industry Work?* (1994), and of multiple articles in academic journals such as 'From the plan to the market and back: Organizational transformation of the Russian defence industry' (2018).

Zoya Kotelnikova is an associate professor and senior research fellow of the Laboratory for Studies in Economic Sociology at HSE University. Her main research areas are economic sociology, sociology of markets and retail trade. Her recent publications include 'Explaining counterfeit alcohol purchases in Russia' (2017) and 'Recomposition and levelling of consumption expenditures across four economic shocks in Russia, 1994–2014' (2017).

Alexander Kurakin is a senior researcher at the Center for Agrarian Studies of the Russian Presidential Academy of National Economy and Public Administration. He is also a senior researcher at HSE University. His main research areas are economic sociology and agrarian sociology, within which he has published a number of papers, the most recent being 'Framework for sustainable regional development in the Altai Krai' (2020), 'Corporate social responsibility, coexistence and contestation: Large farms' changing responsibilities vis-à-vis rural households in Russia' (2019) and 'Cooperation in rural Russia: Past, present and future' (2018).

Tamara Kusimova is a PhD candidate at the Department of Sociology and Social Anthropology at the Central European University (Vienna) and an analyst at the Centre for Cultural Sociology at HSE University. Her thesis is titled 'The (re-)invention of the new Russian cuisine: Gastropolitics in the new post-embargo Moscow'. Her academic interests include economic and cultural sociology, research on consumption practices and socio-economic inequalities.

Daria Lebedeva is a research assistant at the Laboratory for Studies in Economic Sociology at HSE University. Her academic interests are economic sociology, environmental sociology and ecological practices.

Alena Ledeneva is Professor of Politics and Society at the School of Slavonic and East European Studies of University College London (UK). Her research interests lie in the field of corruption, informal economy, economic crime, informal practices in corporate governance, and the role of networks and patron–client relationships in Russia and around the globe. She is the author of *Can Russia Modernize? Sistema, power networks and informal governance* (2013), *Russia's Economy of Favours: Blat, networking, and informal exchange* (1998) and such later publications as 'Corruption studies for the twenty-first century: Paradigm shifts and innovative approaches' (2017), 'Where does informality stop and corruption begin? Informal governance and the public/private crossover in Mexico, Russia and Tanzania' (2017) and 'Managing business corruption: Targeting non-compliant practices in systemically corrupt environments' (2017).

Anastasiia Makareva is a PhD student at the Institute of Education at HSE University. She is an analyst in the Laboratory for University Development and a research intern at the Centre of Sociology of Higher Education at HSE University. Her main academic interests consider graduate student well-being, the geopolitics of education, global university rankings and academic motivation. Her recent publications include '"And we are so different": Academic heterogeneity of students: Analysis, perceptions, practices' (2019) (co-authored, in Russian) and 'International comparison of the higher education response to global pandemic' (2020) (co-authored, in Russian).

Alexander Nikulin is a Director of the Centre for Agrarian Studies at the Russian Presidential Academy of National Economy and Public Administration. His research interests lie in the field of economic and historical sociology and agrarian sociology. He is the author of numerous articles and scientific studies on agrarian reforms, including 'Russian agriculture during Putin's fourth term: A SWOT analysis' (2019), 'Scenarios for regional development in the Altai Krai and long-term trends' (2020) and 'Corporate social responsibility, coexistence and contestation: Large farms' changing responsibilities vis-à-vis rural households in Russia' (2019).

Ivan Pavlyutkin is a senior research fellow in the Laboratory 'Sociology of Religion' at the Saint-Tikhon's Orthodox University, Moscow (Russia). He is also an associate professor at HSE University. His main academic interests are economic sociology, sociology of religion, family studies, sociology and anthropology of gift, higher education studies and organization studies. His recent publications include 'Stratified university strategies: The shaping of institutional legitimacy in a global perspective'

(2019), 'The revival of tradition, new marriages or network effects: Variability of models of large modern urban families' (2019) and 'When 2 become 1: On the cultural aspect of university mergers' (2018).

Andrey N. Petrov is an associate professor of Geography, a director of the Arctic, Remote and Cold Territories Interdisciplinary Center (ARCTICenter) at the University of Northern Iowa (United States), and an Academic Director in the GeoInformatics Training Research Education and Extension (GeoTREE) Center. In his research he primarily focuses on economic issues in northern communities and policies of regional development in the Canadian and Russian North, human–environment relationships and Arctic socio-ecological systems, postmodern economies and restructuring in the North. He has authored multiple books and monographs such as *Arctic Sustainability Research: Past, present and future* (2017) and *Arctic Social Indicators II: Implementation* (2015), as well as articles and book chapters including 'Towards understanding benefit sharing between extractive industries and indigenous/local communities in the Arctic' (2020) and 'Circumpolar spatio-temporal patterns and contributing climatic factors of wildfire activity in the Arctic Tundra from 2001 to 2015' (2017).

Alexei Pobedonostsev is a PhD researcher in the Department of Political and Social Sciences at the European University Institute in Florence (Italy). He was an invited lecturer in two German universities, the Technical University of Darmstadt and Heinrich Heine University Düsseldorf. His academic interests lie in political economy, comparative politics, international relations and Russian politics. His publications include 'More guns, less crimes? Changes in the legislation on gun control in the United States through the prism of empirical legal studies' (2016) (in Russian), 'More oil, less democracy? The political aspect of the "resource curse" problem' (2018) (in Russian) and 'Nationalization, oil and political regime: A comparative analysis of the experience of the Soviet state and Latin American countries' (2021) (in Russian).

Vadim Radaev is Professor, Doctor Habilitat in Economics and Sociology, Head of the Laboratory for Studies in Economic Sociology of HSE University and Editor-in-Chief of the *Journal of Economic Sociology*. His professional interests lie in the field of economic sociology and sociology of markets. He is the author of ten books, including *Millennials: How Russian society is changing* (2019), *Who Holds the Power in Consumer Markets* (2011) and *Economic Sociology* (2008), and of more than 200 papers both in Russian and in English. The most recent are 'A rise of state activism in a competitive industry: The case of Russian retail trade law of 2009' (2018), 'Crooked mirror: The evolution of illegal alcohol markets in Russia since the late socialist period' (2017) and 'Relational exchange and the degree of embeddedness: An empirical study of supply chains' (2016).

Regina Resheteeva received her PhD in Economic Sociology at HSE University. Her main research interests include new economic sociology, sociology of markets and performativity of economic science. She is the author of the papers 'Rethinking prices during an economic crisis: Calculation as a new mode of consumer behaviour in Russia' (2017), 'What is political about consumption?' (2018) (in Russian) and 'Social architectonics of market prices: Basic principles of Russian consumer price perception (a Moscow case study)' (2017).

Andrey Shevchuk is an associate professor and a senior research fellow in the Laboratory for Studies in Economic Sociology at HSE University. His main research areas are economic sociology, sociology of work, sociology of economic development and comparative political economy. He has been involved in a number of employment research projects and has authored several academic and policy papers, including 'Skill mismatch and work–life conflict: The mediating role of job satisfaction' (2019), 'The autonomy paradox: How night work undermines subjective well-being of internet-based freelancers' (2019) and 'Safeguards against opportunism in freelance contracting on the internet' (2018).

Denis Strebkov is an associate professor and senior research fellow in the Laboratory for Studies in Economic Sociology at HSE University. His research interests lie in the fields of economic sociology, non-standard forms of employment, sociology of cyberspace, sociology of financial behaviour and the stock market. His latest publications are 'Skill mismatch and work–life conflict: The mediating role of job satisfaction' (2019), 'The autonomy paradox: How night work undermines subjective well-being of internet-based freelancers' (2019) and 'Work value orientations and worker well-being in the new economy: Implications of the job demands–resources model among internet freelancers' (2018).

Sara Teitelbaum is an assistant professor in the Sociology Department at the University of Montreal (Canada). Her research interests lie in the field of participatory dimensions of natural resource management, with particular attention to the northern regions, comparative study of boreal forest management, and relations between rural communities and the natural environment. She was an editor of the book *Community Forestry in Canada: Lessons from policy and practice* (2016). She is the author of numerous publications such as 'Indigenous Peoples and collaborative forest governance in northern forests: Examining changes in policies, institutions, and communities' (2019), 'Studying resource-dependent communities through a social-ecological lens? Examining complementarity with existing research traditions in Canada' (2019) and 'Regulatory intersections and Indigenous rights: Lessons from Forest Stewardship Council certification in Quebec, Canada' (2019).

Maria S. Tysiachniouk is a senior researcher in the Department of Geographical and Historical Studies at the University of Eastern Finland. She specializes in environmental movements in Russia, transnational environmental governance, and interactions between oil companies, non-governmental organizations and Indigenous communities. She is the author of the book *Transnational Governance through Private Authority: The case of Forest Stewardship Council certification in Russia* (2012). She has also written more than 210 publications, among the latest 'Global standards, corporate diagrams and indigenous agency: ExxonMobil in Russia and Alaska' (2022), 'Indigenous-led grassroots engagements with oil pipelines in the US and Russia: the NoDAPL and Komi movements' (2021) and 'The politics of scale in global governance: Do more stringent international forest certification standards protect local rights in Russia?' (2021).

Series Editors' Foreword

The Ambivalence of Power in the Twenty-First-Century Economy: Cases from Russia and beyond explores the emerging grey zones between power and economy in modern state-led capitalism from the perspective of ambivalence. Ambivalence here has become embedded in social roles, relations and norms that produce oscillating behaviour; and while ambivalence could be minimized or temporarily resolved, it can never be completely eliminated. The increasing complexity of the contemporary world requires adequate conceptual tools to capture these complex contexts and to shift the focus of enquiry from static social structures to the social processes of their perpetual change. At the same time, ambivalent practices, many of which are informal, fill crucial gaps that enable the reproduction of power regimes and maintain their legitimacy.

This is the first volume in a sequence within the FRINGE series focused predominantly on Russia, but it also complements earlier volumes in the series on Russian literary diaspora, migrants, peripheries and prisons. The volume will be of interest not only to readers interested in Russia but also to those seeking innovative methodologies for working complexity and ambivalence into the analysis of power.

Acknowledgements

This edited volume grew out of the workshop 'Variety of Power in the Economy' organized by HSE University in Moscow in 2020 with the support of the Faculty of Social Sciences and the Basic Research Program at HSE University. We thank all participants, especially Professor Alena Ledeneva and Professor Valeriy Yakubovich, who took part in the HSE University workshop, for their very productive comments and discussions. We would also like to thank Professor Richard C. M. Mole for his invaluable help in preparing this volume.

Preface
Ambivalence: practices, patterns and particles of power

Alena Ledeneva

Ambivalence is a key dimension of complexity. Coined by the Swiss psychiatrist Eugen Bleuler around 1910, the concept of *Ambivalenz* has entered the *Oxford English Dictionary* as 'the coexistence in one person of profoundly opposing emotions, beliefs, attitudes, or urges (such as love and hate, or attraction and repulsion) towards a person or thing'.

In its sociological sense, ambivalence is defined by Robert Merton, and refers to incompatible normative expectations of attitudes, beliefs and behaviour. He gives the example of a doctor who must be both partial and impartial towards a patient. The incompatibility derives from a certain status and the constraints that social structures generate on the holder of that status (Merton 1976, 6–7). Merton's analysis of sociological ambivalence stems from the ethnographic observations of manifest and latent functions by Bronislaw Malinowski and from Pitirim Sorokin's argument that actual social relations are only predominantly of one type or another, rather than comprising pure types, or ideal types in Max Weber's terms. Merton concludes, '[i]t is precisely the matter of not confining our attention to the dominant attributes of a role or social relation that directs us to the function and structure of sociological ambivalence' (1976, 16). The process of looking into the fringes of the power interface between politics and economics in this volume is thus well grounded in sociological thought.

Sociological ambivalence is an outcome of the contradictory demands made of the bearers of a status in a particular social relationship. Since clashing norms cannot be simultaneously expressed in behaviour, they come to be expressed in an oscillation of behaviours: 'of detachment and compassion, of discipline and permissiveness, of personal and impersonal treatment' (Merton 1976, 8). Merton points out that many professions, such as managers and academics, are characterized by the oscillating occurrence of compassion, permissiveness and preferential treatment on the one hand, and of detachment, discipline and impersonal treatment on the other. Merton's principles of ambivalence, operationalized as clashing attitudes or oscillating behaviours, remain essential to the understanding of the working of power and governmentality, or practices through which subjects are governed.

In the context of modernity, ambivalence is associated with fragmentation and failure of manageability, in other words, the blind spots of power. Zygmunt Bauman defines ambivalence as the possibility of assigning an object or an event to more than one category and views it as a language-specific disorder. The main symptom of disorder is the acute discomfort we feel when we are unable to read the situation properly and to choose between alternative actions (Bauman 1990; 1991, 1, 12). The experimental findings of the University of Amsterdam Uncertainty Lab have found that those unable to cope with clashing constraints quite literally 'sweated over their decision' to settle on a view (Leslie 2013).

Bauman lists ambivalence among 'the tropes of the "other" of order: ambiguity, uncertainty, unpredictability, illogicality, irrationality, and ambivalence, brought about by modernity with its desire to organise and to design' (Bauman 1991, 7). In this sense, ambivalence is the opposite of order, thus implying disorder or resistance. In my view, ambivalence can be singled out from Bauman's list for its polarity and oscillating pattern (both order and disorder). In other words, ambivalence defines situations of coexisting theses and antitheses, without certainty of their synthesis, yet without uncertainty as to what the coexisting categories, attitudes and beliefs are. In a physical world, the bipolar pattern of breathing is taken for granted and considered certain, the tripolar state of water (gas, liquid and solid) transforming in particular contexts is predictable and the qualities of semiconductors have been put to use. In social psychology, ambivalence patterns are less predictable and often associated with ambiguity, which might be a step too far if we want to focus on the ambivalence of power.

To distinguish between ambivalence and ambiguity, I would emphasise that the concept of sociological ambivalence is more finite in its polarity, a bi-, tri- or multipolar in contrast to ambiguity. There is little uncertainty as to what the alternatives are (theses and antitheses are clearly defined), and the uncertainty is created by context that highlights one of the possibilities. Despite the analytical clarity of the poles, the complexity of ambivalence rests on the varying degrees of uncertainty in the enacted relationships, norms, behaviours or motives, revealed in a particular context, by a particular practitioner, and an interpretation by the observer.

Ambivalence is not the same as duplicity, a deliberate deceptiveness in behaviour or speech, or intentional double-crossing. The shortest formula for understanding ambivalence is 'theses, antitheses, no synthesis'. The opposites are known, but the outcome of their conflicting tension is non-convergent. The oscillating pattern is not predictable outside a particular context and cannot be assessed probabilistically.

In his book *Einstein's Dice and Schrödinger's Cat*, Paul Halpern explains the work of the two Nobel laureates recognized for their foundational work in the earliest days of quantum mechanics in 1921 and 1933. Each of them had a strong philosophical interest that shaped their worldview. Einstein favoured the work of Spinoza, while Schrödinger had an affinity with Schopenhauer and dabbled in Eastern mysticism. Such influences made them averse to the probabilistic nature of quantum mechanics, despite its stunning experimental success. Einstein famously declared that God 'does not play dice', which prompted Niels Bohr to retort: 'Stop telling God what to do!'

In quantum mechanics, a quantum particle exists in an ambivalent state, but only as long as it is not observed. The moment it is subjected to a measurement, its ambivalence is resolved, and the particle no longer exists in a state of superposition: it takes on a definite modality. The quantum theory cannot predict with certainty which modality the particle will take on upon measurement; it is done based on probability. But the probabilistic nature of quantum mechanics (which Einstein objected to) is a limitation of the theory, not necessarily of the physical world.

Schrödinger invented the cat paradox to support Einstein's criticism of the probabilistic interpretation of quantum mechanics. Schrödinger's cat can be both dead and alive. The idea of the quantum superposition of contrasting states is an interpretation of the solutions of Schrödinger's equation, known as the Copenhagen interpretation, promoted by Niels

Bohr. Although not to Schrödinger's liking, the quantum superposition principle is now generally accepted by physicists. The science of it is complex, but the social world is no less complicated. In social research, objects have a conscious power to resolve the superposition in a fit-to-purpose mode, to reserve a right to remain in two minds or to exercise an (ir)rational choice of being dead.

The ambivalence of power is best grasped by the paradoxes it creates, such as the supporting role of subversive practices in the workings of institutions as in the case of the role of hackers in advancing cybersecurity. In the opening volume of the FRINGE series, *The Global Encyclopaedia of Informality*, the data set of hard-to-categorize social practices, in all their richness and complexity, points to the conflicting constraints and differing similarities in the four modes of human interaction – redistribution, solidarity, market and domination. The analysis reveals four patterns of ambivalence in the workings of doublethink, double standards, double deed and double incentives (Ledeneva et al. 2018). Like quantum particles, informal practices exist in two modalities at once, resolved at the point of observation: informal practices are one thing for insiders and another for outsiders. The 'theses, antitheses, no synthesis' formula can be resolved pragmatically in a particular context (defined as either a thesis or an antithesis) for the observers, but it does not eliminate the state of superposition, or no-synthesis, for the participants, even if/when they pragmatically settle. The switching of the participant–observer perspective in itself opens up numerous dimensions and invites multiple interpretations of power, as illustrated by the volume at hand. The ambivalence of power embraces cases where clear categorizations of 'either/or' and observations of alternative choices are not possible, and the observers of the context have to deal with the superpositions of the 'both' or 'neither/nor' modality.

The typology of social and cultural ambivalence suggested in the first two volumes of the *Encyclopaedia* includes four types of paradoxical superpositions: doublethink (illogical logic), dual utility (the functionality of the dysfunctional and the reverse), double standards (normative relativity for 'us' and 'them') and double motive (resolving the tensions of public and private constraints).

To identify universal patterns and yet preserve the context that helps differentiate the modes of human interaction and modalities of our perception of it has been a paradoxical yet effective tool in dealing with ambivalence. This approach, as well as the types of ambivalence – substantive, normative, functional and motivational – will be useful for readers of the *Ambivalence of Power* volume. The editors and authors of the volume have done their utmost to preserve a focus on the pattern of ambivalence while embracing the key contexts that account for the elusiveness of power and its misrecognized scripts, overlooked in research, education and policy while also constituting know-how and a widely shared open secret in society.

The increasing complexity of the world poses new challenges in the information age with its artificial intelligence algorithms. The volume masters different perspectives, navigates multiple moralities, embraces multiple identities and delves into the grey areas and blurred crossings between politics and economics. Russia has been a great natural laboratory for studying this complexity, of which the cases in this volume provide numerous instances. Comparative perspectives that go beyond Russia, driven by testing the patterns of ambivalence across geographical borders, sectors of the economy and levels of analysis, strengthen the findings further. An understanding of power is especially difficult as it requires expertise across disciplines and area studies.

In his 1948 article 'Science and complexity', Warren Weaver stated that 'an open learning environment would need to be created, where students could be introduced to new and innovative notions of complexity, critical thinking, data visualization and modeling, as well as the challenges of mixed-methods, interdisciplinary teamwork, global complexity, and big data! In short, the social sciences would need to be "opened-up"' (cited in Castellani 2014). The social sciences have yet to develop methodologies that capture the ways ambivalence penetrates, if not determines, our lives to perfect mixed-methods and to institutionalize cross-disciplinary teams, to talk across intellectual boundaries and, ultimately, to accept the limitations of our expertise.

It is possible to overcome the fragmentation of knowledge and compartmentalization of science through a 'network expertise' of scholars: what one can no longer do individually, a cross-disciplinary team can. In the vein of the open social sciences, the Laboratory for Studies in Economic Sociology at the Higher School of Economics, Moscow, has been an island of success – a platform for community outreach, a weekly forum for critical thinking and a hub for wider academic cooperation and research teamwork. By acknowledging that concepts of power in social and political theory are a pluralistic set of relations, the authors explore a range of rich case studies into power struggles around resource curse, agribusiness, counterfeit, artificial intelligence and informal digital labour market, fashion, healthcare, consumption, entrepreneurship and environmental concerns in Russia. The included cases point to a number of significant imbalances, and also responses, that have not yet received sufficient attention in contemporary scholarship. This volume marks the 15th anniversary of the lab.

References

Bauman, Zygmunt. 1990. 'Modernity and ambivalence', *Theory, Culture & Society* 7(2–3): 143–69.

Bauman, Zygmunt. 1991. *Modernity and Ambivalence*. Cambridge: Polity Press.

Bleuler, Eugen. 1914. 'The ambivalence'. Accessed 12 March 2022. https://www.psyalpha.net/de/biografien/eugen-bleuler/eugen-bleuler-1914-ambivalenz.

Castellani, Brian. 2014. 'Focus: Complexity and the failure of quantitative social science', *Focus* 14: 12. Accessed 7 March 2022. https://archive.discoversociety.org/2014/11/04/focus-complexity-and-the-failure-of-quantitative-social-science/.

Halpern, Paul. 2015. *Einstein's Dice and Schrödinger's Cat*. New York: Basic Books.

Ledeneva, Alena (ed.) 2018. *The Global Encyclopaedia of Informality: Understanding social and cultural complexity*. London: UCL Press.

Leslie, Ian. 2013. 'Ambivalence is awesome. Or is it awful? Sometimes it is best to have conflicted feelings', *Slate*, 13 June. Accessed 12 March 2022. https://slate.com/technology/2013/06/ambivalence-conflicted-feelings-cause-discomfort-and-creativity.html.

Merton, Robert K. 1976. *Sociological Ambivalence and Other Essays*. New York: Simon and Schuster.

Oxford English Dictionary. Accessed 12 March 2022. https://www.oed.com/.

Weaver, Warren. 1948. 'Science and complexity', *American Scientist* 36: 536–44.

1
Introduction

Zoya Kotelnikova and Vadim Radaev

How are power and economy interrelated in modern state capitalism, and why does their association contain a great deal of ambivalence? These are the major questions addressed in this book. Let us start with three different cases.

An authoritarian state controls immense resources and exercises its power at different levels of the economy. Such a state imposes effective restrictions over the activity of any counteracting interest groups and is therefore able to implement large-scale centralized reforms in the economy. However, it uses its almost monopolistic power and consolidated resources to maintain an existing order and avoid any serious transformations. Such policy aimed at strengthening the authoritarian power produces controversial results, undermining the economic foundations of the state in the future.

A global producer of consumer goods uses its significant economic power to exercise the rules of the game and promote its exclusive brands in the emerging consumer markets. As these brands grow popular, they become subject to counterfeiting. When the global producer starts protecting its intellectual property rights, the company is confronted with an increasing risk of attracting public attention to the fakes and damaging its original brands even more in the eyes of the disloyal final consumers. Besides, the global producer acknowledges a contradictory impact of counterfeited goods, meaning that sales of these goods reduce its market share but at the same time contribute to the recognition and expansion of original brands in the local markets.

An active young urban resident feels powerless and deprived of opportunities to participate in political life. Instead of engagement in direct political struggles, (s)he turns to the issues of environmental protection which could be perceived as 'non-political'. Joining the ecological movement and taking care of the degrading environment, (s)he becomes empowered and finds a path to civic and political representation.

All three cases occur in diverse areas and at different levels of society. However, they have a lot in common. These cases illustrate the ambivalent nature of power, which represents the main subject of this volume, using the notion of ambivalence as an integrative category for a number of interrelated studies. Ambivalence is defined as a bipolar concept, where the poles are clearly defined as incompatible alternatives and coexist without the possibility of their synthesis (Ledeneva 2014). Ambivalence is categorized as a form of oscillating behaviour, where the actor is unable to make an ultimate choice and is involved in the interplay of opposing options (Merton and Barber 1963; Smelser 1998). Ambivalence reflects competing perspectives oriented towards one and the same object, opposite parts constituting a whole and polarized forces that cannot be fully reconciled (Lüscher 2002; Hillcoat-Nalletamby and Phillips 2011). In this sense, the notion of ambivalence is distinguished from the concept of ambiguity, which presumes multi-polarity and multifaceted phenomena.

The notion of ambivalence originated from psychology and psychoanalysis and was initially connected to the constitution of personal identity. The term was coined by Eugen Bleuler, who looked for the source of ambivalence in the emotional conditions relating to the splitting or even disappearance of strong associations (Bleuler 1911/1950). Bleuler referred to contradictory affective orientations within the same person as one of the symptoms of schizophrenia. He also delineated affective, volitive and intellectual ambivalence. The concept was popularized by Freud (1948, 54–8) as alternating polarities of love and hate and of life and death urges.

Later this concept was borrowed by sociology, emphasizing that ambivalence did not reside within the individual and was not confined to the mixed feelings of a person but was embedded into social relations based upon continuous interactions (Merton 1976). Within this 'relational turn' in the social sciences, firstly, the notion of ambivalence has been transferred from personal identity to social relations. It can be minimized or temporarily resolved, but it can never be completely eliminated. It is both normal and paradoxical (Hajda 1968). Secondly, the category of ambivalence has been extended from the level of interpersonal relations to those of social norms, groups and organizations, which encourages scholars to provide broader socio-structural explanations (Hillcoat-Nalletamby and Phillips 2011). Thirdly, it has been pointed out that ambivalence not only reflects conflicting norms but also presents an ongoing situation based upon continuous transactions and the controversial interplay of agency and structure. Thus, use of the concept of ambivalence leads to the recognition of analysis of social processes rather than social structures as the core of theory and research in social sciences (Hajda 1968; Room 1976). This approach is based upon the assertion that change is perpetual and that any social system is a temporal construction. It implies that ambivalence is generated simultaneously by change and resistance to change (Hajda 1968).

Basically, this kind of oscillating behaviour results from the increasing complexity of the contemporary world. The notion of ambivalence has been defined as a characteristic of modernist and postmodernist societies by Bauman, Giddens and other theorists (Giddens 1990; Bauman 1991).

A great diversity of types of ambivalence is presented in the literature. For example, Ledeneva (2018) suggested a useful taxonomy, including substantive ambivalence (double thinking), normative ambivalence (double standards), functional ambivalence (double deed) and motivational ambivalence (double purpose). The consequences of ambivalence also vary considerably in scale and scope. Ambivalence may provide flexibility, which is necessary for socially accepted human behaviour. Some research perspectives imply that actors are able to do more than just strictly comply with normative prescriptions (Merton and Barber 1963). Other authors emphasize that ambivalence is associated with abusive and deviant behaviour (Room 1976). Overall, ambivalence produces paradoxes that are not easy to resolve. At the same time, ambivalent practices (many of which are informal) fill the gaps produced at different levels of society and maintain the legitimacy of the existing social order.

In previous literature, the sociological concept of ambivalence was applied to a broad variety of areas from family studies (Lüscher 2002; Hillcoat-Nalletamby and Phillips 2011) to scientific knowledge production (Arribas-Ayllon and Bartlett 2014). This volume is focused upon the economic relationships and uses the analytical tools provided by contemporary economic sociology and political economy. Given a great diversity of economic phenomena, ambivalence is also multiple, involving relationships between the state and market actors, inter-firm ties, labour relations within the firm and relations between market sellers and the final consumers.

Particular emphasis in this volume is placed on the use of power as an important source of ambivalence in the economy. Previous studies have shown that ambivalence comes to the fore in 'situations in which actors are *dependent* on one another' (Smelser 1998, 8), varying from so-called half-voluntary emotional dependence to 'total institutions' where participants are 'locked-in'. In this sense, ambivalence is inherent to power relations regardless of what theoretical approach to the concept of power that we adhere to. Nevertheless, it is common to view ambivalence as a characteristic of the behaviour of powerless actors, particularly in formal hierarchical organizations and authoritarian regimes. It implies that the behaviour and attitudes of subordinated actors deprived of essential resources and facing institutional constraints become ambivalent in relation to powerful/incumbent actors (see, e.g., Room 1976, 1056–7; Smelser 1998; Lorenz-Meyer 2001). We would like to highlight that governments and incumbent actors that dominate in organizational fields are also involved in ambivalent practices. Their power never becomes absolute and undisputable. To gain legitimacy and retain their power, even the most powerful actors have to impose self-constraints and set limits to the pursuit of their interests (see, e.g., Haugaard 2012). To avoid pressure from below, they also have to delegate their controlling functions to impersonal structures and new technologies that mediate potential and actual conflicts.

This volume contributes to our understanding of the ambivalent nature of power, oscillating between conflict and cooperation, public and private, global and local, formal and informal, and it does so from an empirical perspective with regard to the economic field. It offers a collection of country-based case studies, representing different political and economic regimes, and it critically assesses the existing conceptions of power from a cross-disciplinary perspective. The diverse analyses of power at the macro, meso and micro levels allow the volume to highlight the complexity of political economy in the twenty-first century. Each chapter addresses key elements of political economy (from the ambivalence of the cases of former communist countries that do not conform with the grand narratives about democracy and markets to the dual utility of new technologies such as facial recognition), thus providing mounting evidence for the centrality of ambivalence in the analysis of power.

Classical mainstream sociologists from Max Weber and Talcott Parsons to Steven Lukes and Anthony Giddens tend to conceptualize power as a multifaceted phenomenon. Recent advances in the theorization of power explore various types of power, identifying additional dimensions (Dobbin and Jung 2015; Granovetter 2017; Haugaard 2020; Tenenbaum 2020; Ledyaev 2021). Dobbin and Jung (2015) drew attention to the capacity of various experts to define social group interests as a new form of power. Haugaard (2020) distinguished a fourth dimension of power, suggesting techniques for creating social subjects. Research focuses on varieties of power, turning power into an all-embracing notion, which makes it harder to compare findings and maintain a meaningful dialogue among researchers (McNamee and Glasser 1987–8; Ledyaev 2021).

Most recent sociological studies focus on varieties of power. Thus, considerable effort is expended into revealing and defining new aspects of power relationships. We suggested switching this focus towards the mechanisms through which power is implemented in the modern economy. We believe that research efforts will be more fruitful if they switch attention from the multifaceted nature of power to its ambivalence.

Our volume sets itself apart from the wealth of previous studies. Firstly, most of the extant literature tends to discuss power in the political field, while the chapters in this volume primarily are about how power is practised in the economy. Secondly, despite recent progress in theorizing power which primarily explores different varieties of power, identifying additional dimensions, this book focuses on the ambivalent nature of the power. Thirdly, instead of analysing the conflict potential of power distributions – the traditional focus of the literature – a bulk of the chapters included in this volume stress the integrative properties of power in the economy. Fourthly, the book discusses power at all levels, combining macro and micro realms of study. Fifthly, contributors suggest that the ambivalence of power can be effectively observed and explained when studied empirically. Finally, the volume focuses mainly on Russia as a vanguard of state power-driven capitalism and an example of emerging markets. In this sense, this intervention differs from the studies mainly focusing on the Western developed democracies and using the approaches of the Eurocentric political economy. Russia presents a case in which an authoritarian state consolidates a large amount of political and economic power used for active intervention at all levels of the economy. This intervention goes far beyond a conventional industrial policy and includes continuous attempts to regulate inter-firm contractual relations (Radaev 2018) and impose restrictions on the retail pricing of basic consumer goods. State intervention is often contradictory in nature and leads to controversial outcomes. This post-communist experience could provide the grounds for valuable lessons that are relevant for the world outside a particular country. A recent book on an ambivalent state exploring the case of Argentina may serve as another illustrative example (Auyero and Sobering 2019). The main argument of this book is that, in the modern economy, power is closely associated with a variety of ambivalent practices at different levels of society. To develop this argument, a number of data sources and research methods are applied by the team of authors including statistical analysis, standardized surveys, in-depth interviews and ethnographic observations.

In Part I of this volume, we discuss how political power and economic governance are intertwined at the macro level. We explain how the concentration or decentralization of power stimulates diverse trajectories of economic development. Depending on the tools used by powerful groups (the state, corporations and communities) to resolve the problem of their legitimacy, some novel and symbiotic models of interaction may evolve to account for the intricate ways in which production and livelihood are intertwined.

Starting from the macro level, the authors of this volume approach ambivalence from very different angles. Marek Dabrowski tries in Chapter 2 to determine whether the market economy and democracy can support or even reinforce each other. Taking the case of post-communist countries, he found that economic governance and the system of political power are interdependent. This interdependence works in both directions due to its having a non-linear character and being implemented with a certain time lag. We would point to the existence of ambivalence emerging in relations between the political regime and economic policy, particularly in the case of more authoritarian states. Formally, authoritarian rule provides more space for centralized reforms compared with democratic rule with its many counteracting interest groups. However, factually, very often authoritarian power is not used for the implementation of serious transformations. The absence of reforms leads to stagnation and decreasing competitiveness.

Following this macro perspective, in Chapter 3 Alexei Pobedonostsev reveals the pitfalls of rent-seeking in Russia and Venezuela. The ambivalence of power in these two oil-producing countries derives from the controversial nature of resource rent, which is both a source of power and a major threat to its retention. In the broader context, Russia and Venezuela face the well-known resource curse, or paradox of plenty, when reliance on the extraction of cheap natural resources strengthens the power of the state in the medium term but tends to undermine it in the long run.

In Chapter 4, Alexander Nikulin and Alexander Kurakin address the controversies of power centralization observed in the interaction of Russian rural communities with the government and large agribusinesses. The expansion of large agribusiness companies is able to increase the effectiveness of rural production. Moreover, local communities and households are often unable to make use of power opportunities and are ready to accept someone else assuming power and responsibility. They often do not resist the power of agribusinesses and are ready to delegate their rights, and therefore to support power centralization. At the same time, the sustainability of rural economic development is often undermined in the medium term. Overall, it demonstrates deficiencies of centralized power.

Leonid Kosals in Chapter 5 examines the influence of new technologies on society and its core values. At the heart of the investigated problem is the ambivalent relationship between pragmatic and moral legitimacies, where pragmatic legitimacy can be achieved without the moral legitimacy associated with the threat of potential or real harm to higher social goals. The ambivalence of power reduces the efficiency of social mechanisms and produces various negative social effects, when powerful actors try to push through technological innovations with contested legitimacy.

Part II of the book focuses on power struggles at the meso level, observed within both historically established and emerging areas of study, including supply chain management, labour relations, the freelance economy, rental housing, natural resource industries, healthcare, higher education and so forth. The contributors explore the relationship between public and private, global and local and formal and informal modes of influence. The chapters in this section highlight conditions that create gaps, overlaps and grey zones between legality and legitimacy. They also discuss alternative mechanisms for establishing control over markets and the role of private authorities in market regulation. The authors identify the empirical conditions under which dominant discourses and hierarchical structures emerge and become habituated or socially contested.

Coming down to the level of inter-firm ties, in Chapter 6 Vadim Radaev explores the 'dark side' of inter-firm cooperation and the ambivalent relations between the bargaining power of market sellers and the practices of contract infringement. Inter-firm opportunistic behaviour is considered a manifestation of the power of non-compliance. Empirical data show that breach of contract more often indicates an abuse of market power by dominant firms rather than resistance to pressures from the firms possessing less bargaining power. This abuse of market power tends to become normalized over time and to reinforce inequality among market actors.

In Chapter 7, Evgeniya Balabanova examines the functional and motivational ambivalence of power in economic organizations. She demonstrates the 'dark side' of managerial power and shows how the abusive power of managers may lead to the rise of voice strategies on the part of dependent employees instead of the expected loyalty, obedience and conformity that are the aim of managerial efforts.

Andrey Shevchuk and Denis Strebkov analyse in Chapter 8 how digital platforms that claim to organize the gig economy subordinate an increasing number of online freelance contractors and even try to substitute the state in regulating the expansion of new labour markets. However, the ambivalent nature of freelance contracting and online work undermines the power of digital platforms and moves an increasing number of transactions outside these platforms.

Studying the market for municipal rental housing in Sweden, in Chapter 9 Elena Bogdanova examines the ambivalence of consultation practices in housing renovations. Empirically, ambivalence reveals itself in two different domains: firstly, in the simultaneous empowerment and disempowerment of tenants in decision-making, and secondly, in the controversial ways 'quality' and 'standards' of housing are defined. The consultation process with tenants presumes that they should have the power to participate in decisions about their future housing. However, dividing the most disputed issues in time and content, the housing companies reduce tenants' power to make judgements about the quality of the interior finishings and exclude them from a whole range of decisions regarding hardware (pipes, electricity and water) and economic sustainability. Tenants are empowered and disempowered at the same time, and therefore decisions are often not taken, whereas the consultation process is dominated by circular arguments.

Maria S. Tysiachniouk and her co-authors in Chapter 10 focus upon governance generating network theory to explain power shifts within global institutions, civil society and company networks, fostering the implementation of sustainability standards in Russia. The presence of strong normative definitions is interpreted by economic actors as a type of *power over*, forcing them to comply, while at the same time representing *power for* Indigenous and local communities, providing a mechanism for the enhancement of their rights.

In Chapter 11, Zoya Kotelnikova shows the ambivalent attitudes of brand holders towards counterfeit products. Firstly, these companies acknowledge that counterfeiters may harm their registered trademarks, but at the same time they make the brands more recognizable and more valuable among consumers (Saviano 2008), even when some people knowingly buy fakes (Crăciun 2012). Secondly, brand holders often have to hide the truth about the presence of counterfeit goods on the market to avoid damaging their brands. Thirdly, the brand holders oscillate between attempts to combat counterfeiting as a private issue regulated by the Civic Code and continuous efforts to bring the state in and use public coercive resources to supress those who infringe on their intellectual property rights by means of the provisions of the Administrative and Criminal Codes.

Turning to the field of global higher education, Ivan Pavlyutkin and Anastasiia Makareva argue in Chapter 12 that the strategic positioning of leading universities also reflects the ambivalence of power. As soon as leading national and regional universities whose activities are embedded in various institutional contexts enter the global academic race, they experience incompatible normative expectations or double standards when managing their legitimacy. Since global academic rankings have become an influential strategic instrument, this has created an 'iron cage' for universities from different cultural localities and forced them to apply standardized governance and educational models, which has led to increasing homogenization in the whole field of higher education.

Addressing the activity of large pharmaceutical companies, Elena Berdysheva in Chapter 13 develops the idea that markets for vital goods contribute to the economization of political life and thus produce both commodities and a political culture of demand for these commodities. Pharmaceutical companies attract significant resources for inventing, testing and manufacturing new medical products. At the same time, they use both productive and restraining definitional power to promote advanced cancer metaphors and cut off viable alternative solutions.

In Chapter 14 Tamara Kusimova uses the case of Russian farmers to explore tension between the global and the local in conditions where international sanctions for some food products were imposed on Russia. Exploiting the idea of authenticity, local farmers produce unique products with their own *terroir* as part of the global industry. Extensive use of patriotic or nationalist rhetoric together with references to the quality of global products by local producers becomes an effective tool for attracting local customers and gaining state support.

In Part III, the book addresses micro-level issues related to the strategies which individuals use to resist and contest the dominant order, work out alternatives and explore opportunities for gaining autonomy.

Regina Resheteeva in Chapter 15 demonstrates how final consumers have reacted to the continuous increase in retail prices by powerful market sellers in the conditions of the economic crises of the 2010s. Consumers identify themselves as clearly disadvantaged parties lacking control over the situation. However, they do not become involved in political protests or economic boycotts. Instead, they express a kind of consumer cynicism and proactively search for ways not to be deceived by the market sellers. Their grassroots practices lead to a partial disavowal of the power of the dominant market actors.

Masha Denisova, in Chapter 16, examines the ambivalent nature of relationships between mothers-to-be and doulas. In contrast to professional doctors establishing their unilateral power over their patients, doulas exercise their professional authority by empowering women and extending their control over childbirth but without forcing them to align with the doulas' professional expertise and opinion. However, mothers' empowerment with doula support looks ambivalent. On the one hand, doulas advocate for women's centricity and empowerment, while on the other, they simultaneously shift the responsibility for decisions made to women. While doulas' assistance is not institutionally recognized, it also raises a question about the stability of the mothers' empowerment.

Finally, Daria Lebedeva (Chapter 17) shows how young people in Russia, being powerless in the dominant political discourse, become involved with ecological policies and calls for environmental protection. By taking care of the degrading environment, young people not only try to keep control over their personal and global futures, but also express and defend their rights as citizens. Engagement in the ambiguous ecological agenda becomes for them a tool of empowerment and political representation.

Overall, scholars in social sciences tend to see power as a 'salient' dimension in economic action (Smelser and Swedberg 2005, 5), making power one of the more difficult notions to be incorporated into theoretical frameworks, especially when explaining how market economy really works. Exercising power through the implementation of control and so-called strategies of governance, to use Foucault's term (Foucault 1980), has grown, but the state and large corporate structures also seem to have outsourced more rights and responsibilities to autonomous entities and technical devices. Anchored in economic sociology and political economy, this book is aimed at making 'visible' the dimensions of power embedded in such novel economic practices.

To conclude, this book is predominantly based on post-communist practices, but we believe that this divergent experience would be relevant to comparative studies of power and economy and contribute to our broader understanding of their changing and ambivalent character.

References

Arribas-Ayllon, Michael and Andrew Bartlett. 2014. 'Sociological ambivalence and the order of scientific knowledge', *Sociology* 48(2): 335–51.
Auyero, Javier and Katie Sobering. 2019. *The Ambivalent State: Police–criminal collusion at the urban margins*. Oxford: Oxford University Press.
Bauman, Zygmunt. 1991. *Modernity and Ambivalence*. Cambridge: Polity Press.
Bleuler, Eugen. 1950. *Dementia Praecox, or the Group of Schizophrenias*, translated by Joseph Zinkin. New York: International Universities Press. Original publication 1911.
Crăciun, Magdalena. 2012. 'Rethinking fakes, authenticating selves', *Journal of the Royal Anthropological Institute* 18(4): 846–63.
Dobbin, Frank and Jiwook Jung. 2015. 'The fourth dimension of power'. In *Re-Imagining Economic Sociology*, edited by Patrik Aspers and Nigel Dodd, 174–94. Oxford: Oxford University Press.
Foucault, Paul-Michel. 1980. *Power/Knowledge*. Brighton: Harvester Press.
Freud, Sigmund. 1948. *Collected Papers*. London: Hogarth Press.
Giddens, Anthony. 1990. *The Consequences of Modernity*. Cambridge: Polity Press.
Granovetter, Mark. 2017. *Society and Economy: Framework and principles*. Cambridge, MA: Harvard University Press.
Hajda, Jan. 1968. 'Ambivalence and social relations', *Sociological Focus* 2(2): 21–8.
Haugaard, Mark. 2012. 'Rethinking the four dimensions of power: Domination and empowerment', *Journal of Political Power* 5(1): 33–54.
Haugaard, Mark. 2020. *The Four Dimensions of Power: Understanding domination, empowerment and democracy (social and political power)*. Manchester: Manchester University Press.
Hillcoat-Nalletamby, Sarah and Judith Phillips. 2011. 'Sociological ambivalence revisited', *Sociology* 45(2): 202–17.
Ledeneva, Alena. 2014. 'The ambivalence of blurred boundaries: Where informality stops and corruption begins', *RFIEA* 12 (Winter): 19–22. Accessed 16 May 2022. https://www.researchgate.net/publication/309573307.
Ledeneva, Alena. 2018. 'Introduction: The informal view of the world – key challenges and main findings of the Global Informality Project'. In *The Global Encyclopaedia of Informality, Vol. 1: Understanding social and cultural complexity*, edited by Alena Ledeneva, 1–27. London: UCL Press.
Ledyaev, Valery G. 2021. 'Conceptual analysis of power: Basic trends', *Journal of Political Power* 14(1): 72–84.
Lorenz-Meyer, Dagmar. 2001. *The Politics of Ambivalence: Towards a conceptualisation of structural ambivalence in intergenerational relations*. LSE Gender Institute New Working Paper Series 2. Accessed 28 April 2021. https://www.lse.ac.uk/gender/assets/documents/research/working-papers/THE-POLITICS-OF-AMBIVALENCE.pdf.
Lüscher, Kurt. 2002. 'Intergenerational ambivalence: Further steps in theory and research', *Journal of Marriage and Family* 64(3): 585–93.
McNamee, Stephen and Michael Glasser. 1987–8. 'The power concept in sociology: A theoretical assessment', *Humboldt Journal of Social Relations* 15(1): 79–104.
Merton, Robert K. 1976. *Sociological Ambivalence and Other Essays*. New York: Free Press.
Merton, Robert K. and Elinor Barber. 1963. 'Sociological ambivalence'. In *Sociological Theory, Values, and Sociocultural Change: Essays in honor of Pitirim A. Sorokin*, edited by Edward Tiryakin, 91–120. New York: Free Press.
Radaev, Vadim. 2018. 'A rise of state activism in a competitive industry: The case of Russian retail trade law of 2009', *Communist and Postcommunist Studies* 51(1): 27–37.
Room, Robin. 1976. 'Ambivalence as a sociological explanation: The case of cultural explanations of alcohol problems', *American Sociological Review* 41(6): 1047–65.
Saviano, Roberto. 2008. *Gomorrah: A personal journey into the violent international empire of Naples' organized crime system*. New York: Picador.
Smelser, Neil J. 1998. 'Presidential address 1997', *American Sociological Review* 63: 1–15.
Smelser, Neil and Richard Swedberg. 2005. 'Introducing economic sociology'. In *The Handbook of Economic Sociology*, edited by Neil Smelser and Richard Swedberg, 3–25. New York: Russell Sage Foundation.
Tenenbaum, Sergio. 2020. *Rational Powers in Action: Instrumental rationality and extended agency*. Oxford: Oxford University Press.

Part I
Interdependency of political power and economic governance: A macro perspective

2
Interrelation between economic freedom and democracy: The case of post-communist countries

Marek Dabrowski

Introduction

The post-communist transition which started in Central and Eastern Europe (CEE) and the former Soviet Union (FSU) in the late 1980s and early 1990s involved changes in both economic and political systems. The necessity of such a dual-track transition came from the spontaneous collapse of the previous political system based on the political monopoly of the Communist Party and its total control over the economy and society. In turn, the collapse of the political system was caused by the deep crisis of a centrally planned economy, which reached its growth limits in the 1980s. The economic crisis undermined the social legitimacy of the communist regime. This made the CEE and FSU transition different from the market-oriented reforms that started in China in 1978 and other communist countries in Asia (Vietnam, Laos and Cambodia) in the mid-1980s, which were initiated and then continued by communist parties, with minor modifications of their political systems and official ideologies (see Roland 2018; Dabrowski 2020).

However, despite the initial hopes and expectations, the dual-track transition did not succeed everywhere, especially in the FSU. After initial progress, its political leg (building a democratic system based on political and citizen liberties and the rule of law) was reversed in Central Asia, the Southern Caucasus and Belarus in the 1990s, and in Russia in the 2000s. In the 2010s, an anti-democratic drift hit part of CEE (Hungary, Poland, North Macedonia and Serbia). The economic leg (building an open market economy) proved more successful and in most of the region the basic foundations of a market system were put in place by the first half of the 2000s. However, further reforms, especially in structural and institutional spheres, have stagnated since then and, in a few cases, they have suffered from partial reversal.

Such unfavourable dynamics in both spheres have raised the question as to the interdependence between economic governance and the system of political power or, more precisely, between economic freedom and democracy. Does a democracy, especially a young and immature one, help an open market economy to operate in an efficient and socially just way or perhaps, as advocates of 'market-friendly' or 'development-friendly' autocracies tend to believe, is it an obstacle?[1] Or to look at it from the opposite direction: can a stable democracy survive in a non-market or only a partly market system?

These questions are not new: they were discussed already at the very beginning of the CEE and FSU transition or even earlier, given that most of the attempts at economic reform undertaken in CEE and the Soviet Union from the mid-1950s onwards failed due to political constraints.[2] Furthermore, their importance is not limited to the CEE and FSU regions. After 1980, the dual-track transition (democratization of political systems and market-oriented economic reforms) also happened in Latin America and in large parts of Asia and Africa. In the early 2010s there was a largely unsuccessful attempt at democratization in the Arab world (the so-called Arab Spring), with a negative impact on its economic and political stability. Finally, the worldwide wave of political populism in the second half of the 2010s has led to both domestic economic distortions and serious trade conflicts.

While the focus of this chapter is the FSU and CEE regions, we will also take a broader view, including long-term historical trends. Our main research objective is to examine the mutual interrelation between economic governance and systems of political power in a dynamic comparative perspective. This interrelation can also be seen from the perspective of the ambivalent character of a political power that should serve the public interest and deliver public goods, but for whom the private interests of those who perform this power often lead to its degeneration. Therefore, building up sufficient checks and balances into a political system can improve both economic and political governance.

The chapter starts with an analysis of historical relations between the market economy and democracy worldwide since the beginning of the nineteenth century. This is followed by a discussion of how the market economy helps democracy and vice versa. Then we move to a regional analysis of the CEE and FSU experience in the context of post-communist transition. Next we offer a continuation of this analysis in the form of a brief presentation of four country case studies on how changes in the system of political power influenced, negatively or positively, economic reforms. Finally, we draw our conclusions.

The analytical narrative, which is supported by a simple statistical and correlation analysis, is the dominant methodological approach in this chapter. However, one must remember that synthetic quantification of numerous qualitative characteristics of both economic and political systems (necessary to conduct cross-country comparison based on statistical analysis or to examine interdependence between economic and political variables) is always associated with the risk of misspecification and mismeasurement.

In this chapter, we use various global cross-country surveys of economic and political freedom, democracy, corruption, business climate and so on, but each of them can be and often are questioned on methodological grounds. Most frequently, they are based on either opinion polls of representatives of the business community or expert assessments, each of them unavoidably containing subjective judgements. Furthermore, most indices have a composite character, that is, they are constructed as a simple or weighted average of several detailed components. This raises an additional methodological question on the composition of synthetic indices and the weightings attached to each individual component, potential autocorrelation between them and so on. Nevertheless, and despite the above-mentioned methodological doubts, we believe that using available numeric surveys, especially if they are conducted systematically over several years by institutions which enjoy a high professional reputation, may enrich our analysis as compared with the hypothetical variant based on a pure narrative.

Global trends

Market economy (often called capitalism) and democracy are relatively new phenomena in human history.[3] The contemporary market economy understood as the system that is based on the private ownership of the means of production and freedom of economic activity (without the privileges and restrictions typical of the feudal era) dates back to the beginning of the first industrial revolution, that is, the end of the eighteenth century. Democracy, in the contemporary sense of this word, that is, a political regime which is based on a government accountable to voters, universal suffrage based on the principle of one person–one vote, individual freedom and the rule of law is an even younger phenomenon built up during the nineteenth and early twentieth centuries. In its complete and mature form, it appeared only at the beginning of the twentieth century.

This time mismatch led to the situation in which the early stages of the system of free-market economy (with a limited role of government) was accompanied by political regimes that, by today's standards, were either non-democratic or only partly democratic. Even if the executive branch of government was democratically elected (the United States) or accountable to a democratically elected parliament (the United Kingdom, France and a couple of other European countries), the franchise was limited, excluding women, people with lower material status, former slaves and so on. Universal franchise became a norm in Europe only after the First World War.[4]

This changed gradually during the twentieth century, with most high-income countries and several middle- and low-income countries having both democracy and a market economy. The fastest growth in the number of democracies was recorded in the two last decades of the twentieth century. This was the period of democratic transition in Latin America, Southeast Asia, CEE and the FSU.

However, in the first two decades of the twenty-first century the progress stopped or, according to some metrics, was even partly reversed. This is clearly demonstrated by the most popular global political surveys: Freedom House's Global Freedom Scores (FHGFS), the Bertelsmann Foundation's Transformation Index (BTI) and the Economist Economic Intelligence Unit's Democracy Index (EEIUDI).

Between 2007 and 2017, the percentage of countries rated by the FHGFS as 'Free' and 'Partly Free' decreased, while the percentage of 'Non-Free' countries increased. Correspondingly, between 2003 and 2017 the population in countries ranked as democracies by the BTI barely increased from 4 billion to 4.2 billion, while in countries ranked as autocracies the number climbed from 2.3 billion to 3.3 billion (Schwarz 2018). The EEIUDI shows a further deterioration of democracy scores worldwide in 2020, due to a large extent to the COVID-19-related restrictions on individual freedoms and civil liberties (EIU 2021).

The list of countries that have recorded a substantial deterioration in political rights and civil liberties since 2007 includes, among others, Azerbaijan, Bahrain, Burundi, Central African Republic, Congo (Brazzaville), Dominican Republic, Ethiopia, Gabon, Honduras, Hungary, Mali, Mauritania, Mexico, Nicaragua, Poland, Russia, Tajikistan, Turkey,

Venezuela and Yemen (Abramowitz 2018; EIU 2021). This negative trend affected not only emerging-market and developing countries with a short historical record of political freedom and democracy, but also some developed countries considered stable democracies that suffered from the wave of political populism. For example, scores for the US deteriorated in all the above-mentioned surveys.

As a result, there are still many non-democratic regimes in the world. Among them, there are examples of both market-oriented autocracies and anti-market and populist dictatorships.

Figure 2.1 plots the 2020 Heritage Foundation Index of Economic Freedom (HFIEF) against the 2020 FHGFS. The HFIEF is the synthetic measure of the degree of economic freedom, macroeconomic stability and property rights protection on a scale from 0 (the least free) to 100 (the freest).[5] In turn, the FHGFS is the sum of political rights (maximum 40) and civil liberty (maximum 60) scores. That is, its scale runs from 0 (the least free) to 100 (the freest), similarly to the HFIEF. Both surveys present 2019 data.

The correlation between degrees of economic and political freedom is not very strong, but it exists. At the same time, there are several outliers.

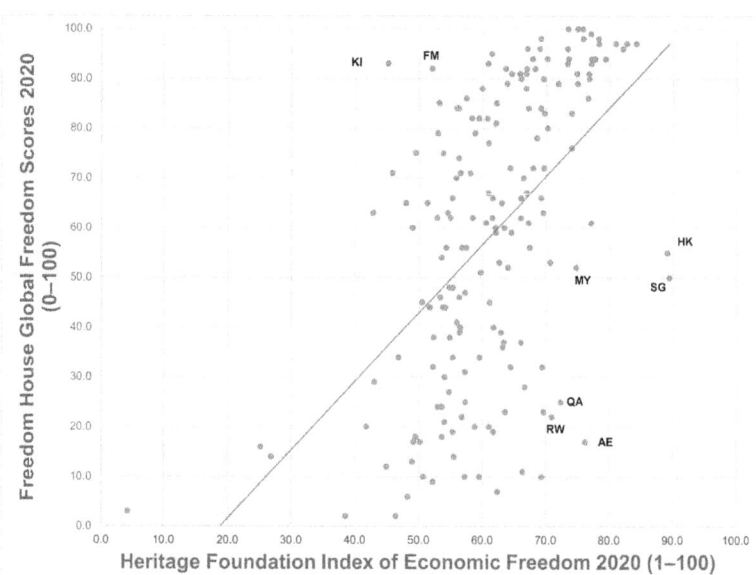

Figure 2.1 Interrelationship between economic and political freedom in the world, 2019. Source: https://www.heritage.org/index/ranking and https://freedomhouse.org/countries/freedom-world/scores.

Hong Kong, Singapore, the United Arab Emirates, Qatar, Rwanda, Bahrain, Malaysia, Azerbaijan and Kazakhstan belong to the group of countries which enjoy more economic than political freedom. One could say they are examples of market-friendly autocracies. Kiribati and Micronesia and a few other countries represent the opposite asymmetry, that is, more political freedom and democracy than economic freedom.

Nevertheless, it is hard to find historical or contemporary examples of a stable and sustainable democracy without a predominantly market economy based on private ownership. The above-mentioned examples of democracies with limited economic freedom relate to cases where all basic institutions of market economy, including private ownership of the means of production, are in place. In the next section we will try to explain why democracy without basic market institutions such as private ownership of the means of production and freedom of market choice is not sustainable.

Market economy and democracy: how they help each other

In this section, we examine in a more detailed manner how a market economy and a democracy can help or even reinforce each other. We start with an analysis of the ways in which a market economy can help build and consolidate a liberal democracy (EBRD 1999, Box 5.3, 113):

1. A market economy makes citizens economically independent of the government, which, unlike in a centrally planned economy, is not the single owner and employer. This is also the reason why one cannot identify examples of democratically managed centrally planned or non-market economies. In such economic systems governments possess too much power and too many instruments for influencing the everyday life of each individual. This also means that individual freedom lacks an economic foundation and that there are no elementary checks and balances in the economic and social spheres provided by a market economy.
2. A market economy also limits the power of government bureaucracy and creates room not only for economic freedom but also for civil liberties. A limited government creates fewer opportunities and, therefore, temptations for power abuse, corruption, state capture by interest groups and so on. Freed from the need to interfere in business activity, the government can concentrate on the delivery of

public goods, and this becomes a key criterion of assessment of the quality of both the government and civil service.
3. A market economy helps support a country's external openness, which not only provides economic and social benefits but also helps in the free flow of information, the application of international human rights standards and additional safeguards against power abuse.
4. It creates demand for the rule of law, which is an indispensable element of an effective liberal democracy (see Fukuyama 2012; 2015).
5. It helps to develop civil society institutions, a broad middle class and a culture of cooperation based on self-interest, which reinforces democracy. In particular, the middle class is often seen as the natural political basis of liberal democracy (Lu 2005; Moyo 2018), although there are also more sceptical opinions about its role (Mei 2019; Motadel 2020).
6. A well-functioning market system helps economic development, which in turn creates demand for political freedom and democracy. Several authors, for example Barro (1999), Lipset (1959), Przeworski and Limongi (1997) and Fukuyama (2004), argue that countries with higher GDP per capita are more likely to be democratic than autocratic, although there are also other determining factors. For example, the availability of large natural resource rent is an obstacle to democratization, even in countries with high GDP per capita (see below). We try to verify this hypothesis by plotting FHGFS against GDP per capita level in purchasing power parity (PPP) terms (Figure 2.2).

Figure 2.2 seems to confirm, at least partly, the hypothesis that higher income per capita is associated with freer political regimes. However, this relation is not very strong. There are several outliers on both sides: quite a large number of low- and lower-middle-income countries have a democratic political system and many high- and upper-middle-income countries are autocracies. Among the latter, one can mention the Gulf and other oil-producing countries (Azerbaijan, Brunei Darussalam, Kazakhstan and Russia), Hong Kong and Singapore. Again, apart from Hong Kong and Singapore, this would be in line with the hypothesis of the anti-democratic impact of a high resource rent.

Such an impact can work via two channels: (1) politicians' preference for private patronage rather than the supply of public goods, and (2) weaker public scrutiny due to lower taxation (which is replaced by a natural resource rent). This is why resource-rich countries require

Figure 2.2 Interrelationship between political freedom and GDP per capita level in PPP terms, 2019. Source: https://www.heritage.org/index/ranking and https://freedomhouse.org/countries/freedom-world/scores.

additional checks and balances in their political systems to resist autocratic tendencies (Collier and Hoeffler 2005).

Looking at the relationship from another angle, one can also identify several channels through which democracy can help build a competitive market economy and ensure that it functions properly (see, for example, de Haan and Sturm 2003):

1. Liberal democracy involves a system of checks and balances, which limits the concentration and abuse of political power (also in the economic sphere) and strengthens the rule of law.
2. Liberal democracy increases the transparency of government actions and constrains opportunities for corruption, rent-seeking and the capture of state institutions by interest groups; therefore, it increases the effectiveness of government operations and regulations (Lundstrom 2005) and creates the long-term guarantee and stability of property rights.
3. The democratic rotation of political elites and their accountability to the electorate also reduce the incidence of power abuse, corruption and state capture, protecting societies from the phenomenon of

'crony capitalism', that is, an economic system which serves the interests of those who are in power and their close associates.
4. Civil liberties support economic freedom.
5. The democratic legitimacy of a government helps it take unpopular but sometimes badly needed economic decisions.
6. Autocratic countries are less open to the external world than democratic ones (Lundstrom 2005), which is of great importance in the era of globalization.

The above findings contradict some opinions (for example, the so-called Lee thesis – see Knutsen 2010) that the system of autocratic power may help carry out market-oriented reforms and take economically rational but unpopular decisions due to the absence of checks and balances and the need in democratic regimes to reach compromises. However, such opinions are based on the myth (or naïve assumption) of the benevolent autocrat who can rule in the best interests of her/his society. In real life, such autocrats do not exist. Their main strategic interest is to hold on to power and maximize personal and group benefits.

More generally, a benevolent political power is a rare phenomenon. The ambivalent nature of political power involves a permanent conflict between public interest, which it is supposed to serve, and the personal or group interests of people who perform this power and often abuse it. This is why the institutions of liberal democracy (in particular, systemic checks and balances) are important to mitigate this conflict. It can be seen very well in the history of post-communist transition in the CEE and FSU regions.

Post-communist transition: a regional analysis

The history of post-communist transition in CEE and the FSU in the 1990s clearly demonstrated the advantages of early democratization. It allowed for the limiting of the influence of the old political elite, consisting of the functionaries of the former communist parties, army, security service, old-style administration, managers of state-owned enterprises ('red' directors), chairmen of state and collective farms and the like, none of them enthusiasts of the market system. Therefore, the fastest and most comprehensive economic transition happened in the Central European and Baltic states, where democratization was the deepest and led to the rapid replacement of the old political elite (Aslund et al. 1996; de Melo et al. 1997; Dethier et al. 1999; Aslund 2002, 359–63). A radical political transformation removed the potential resistance of the old elite, gave economic reformers stronger political legitimacy to take economically needed but often unpopular decisions, and created a window of political opportunity for conducting economic reforms.[6]

At the later stage of transition (late 1990s and early 2000s), a new set of incentives to both economic and political reforms in parts of CEE was created by the process of accession to the European Union (EU) (Roland 2002). In many instances, the EU-related incentives replaced the initial domestic pro-reform consensus, which eroded over time (Dabrowski and Radziwill 2007). In the Western Balkan region this window of opportunity was opened later – after the EU summit in Thessaloniki in June 2003, which offered countries of the former Yugoslavia and Albania the possibility to join the EU. With the exception of the Baltic states, the FSU countries never received this kind of geopolitical offer, which had a negative impact on their economic and political reform process in the new millennium.[7]

While in the first stage of the post-communist transformation the limited attempts at genuine democratization either stopped or significantly delayed market-oriented economic reforms (see above) later

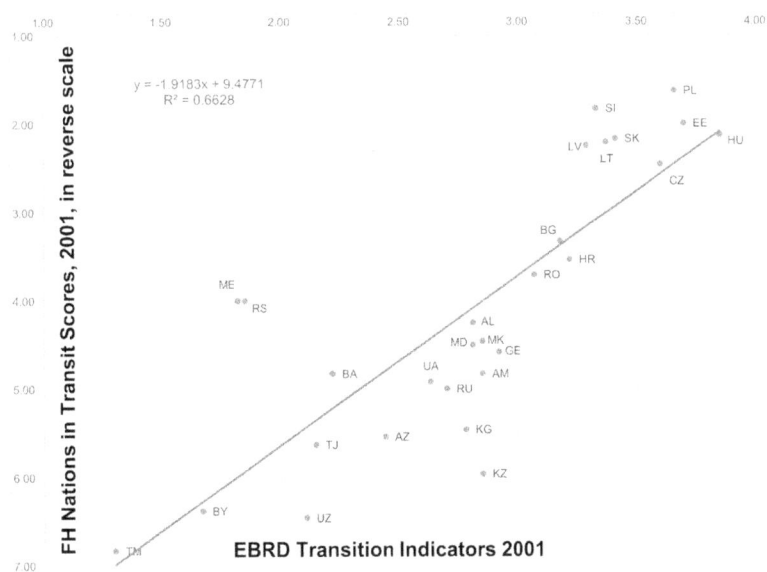

Figure 2.3 Interrelationship between the FH Nations in Transit Score and EBRD transition indicators, 2001. Source: www.ebrd.com/downloads/research/economics/macrodata/tic.xls and https://freedomhouse.org/reports/publication-archives.

on (that is, in the 2000s and 2010s), autocratic tendencies were usually accompanied by widespread corruption, state capture and an increasingly privileged position of oligarchs, who were closely associated with the system of political power and government bureaucracy ('crony capitalism'). This is clearly seen in most FSU countries, and in part of CEE.

At the same time, in countries with unreformed or only partly reformed economic systems there has not been enough space for the emergence of strong groups of entrepreneurs and a market-oriented middle class to fight for political freedom, democratic governance and the rule of law.

The interrelation between progress in economic reforms and political freedom in post-communist countries is illustrated by Figures 2.3 and 2.4. In Figure 2.3, the Freedom House (FH) indices of political and civil liberties are plotted against the transition indicators of the European Bank for Reconstruction and Development (EBRD). Both relate to 2001, that is, the first decade of transition.

At the time of this analysis, EBRD indicators measured progress in economic reforms in nine dimensions – large-scale privatization,

Figure 2.4 Interrelationship between the FHGFS and HFIEF in the former centrally planned economies, 2019. Source: https://www.heritage.org/index/ranking and https://freedomhouse.org/countries/freedom-world/scores.

small-scale privatization, enterprise restructuring, price liberalization, trade and forex system, competition policy, banking reform and interest rate liberalization, securities markets and non-bank financial institutions, and overall infrastructure reform – on a scale from one to four (a higher score meant more advanced reforms).

The FH Nations in Transit (FHNIT) synthetic Democracy Score (on a scale from one to nine; a higher score meant more democracy and political freedom) was an average of its seven subcategories: electoral process, national democratic governance, civil society, local democratic governance, independent media, and judicial framework and independence.

Analysing Figure 2.3, one can draw the conclusion that there existed a rather close correlation between economic and political reforms in the 1990s and the early 2000s. Countries that were leaders in building a democratic political system (Hungary, Czechia, Poland, Slovenia, Slovakia and the Baltic countries) were also the most advanced in market-oriented economic reforms. At the other end of the analysed spectrum, in countries where the system of political power remained unchanged or changed little in comparison with the Soviet past (Turkmenistan, Uzbekistan, Belarus and Tajikistan), progress in building a market mechanism was limited.

Figure 2.4 illustrates a similar interrelation but almost two decades later and using different indicators and expanding the analysed group of countries (by adding the former centrally planned economies in East Asia). The progress in building a market system is measured by the HFIEF while the system of political power is characterized by the FHGFS.[8] Both are measured on a scale from 0 to 100 where higher scores mean more freedom (both economic and political), similarly to Figure 2.1.

Figure 2.4 suggests a certain correlation between economic and political freedom, although not as strong as in Figure 2.3. There are the same leaders of both dimensions as in 2001 – the Baltic countries and Czechia – while Hungary and Poland suffered a substantial downgrade, especially in the second half of the 2010s. Turkmenistan and Tajikistan remained at the bottom of both ratings,[9] while Uzbekistan and Belarus made some improvements on the economic front (their political freedom scores remained largely unchanged).

There are outliers on both sides of the trend line. In Mongolia and Ukraine, the degree of political freedom substantially exceeds the degree of economic freedom. This raises questions about the sustainability of their democratic (or in the case of Ukraine partly democratic) political systems. This question is particularly important in Ukraine where the repeated failures of the economic reform efforts (only partial and incomplete) led to the resurgence of autocratic tendencies, the most spectacular during the presidency of Viktor Yanukovych (see Dabrowski 2017; Havrylyshyn and Kalymon 2020).

There are even more countries on the opposite side of the trend line, that is, countries where the degree of economic freedom is substantially higher than that of political freedom. It applies, in the first instance, to Azerbaijan and Kazakhstan and, to lesser extent, to China, Russia, Belarus, Uzbekistan and Vietnam. However, Figure 2.4 also shows the limits of 'market-friendly autocracies': no country with a low political freedom score (below 30) belongs to the 'mostly free' category in the HFIEF (with a score over 70). Belarus and Russia are at the bottom of the 'moderately free' category (between 60 and 70). China, Vietnam, Cambodia, Laos, Uzbekistan and Tajikistan belong to the economically 'mostly unfree' group (between 50 and 60). Turkmenistan is considered a 'repressed' economy (a score of below 50).

There are also two general conclusions that can be drawn from this part of our analysis. Firstly, a comparison of regression parameters in Figures 2.1 and 2.4 suggests stronger correlation between economic and political freedom in the formerly centrally planned economies of Europe and Asia compared with the global sample. Secondly, CEE countries are more advanced, on average, in building a market economy and liberal democracy compared with the FSU and Asian communist countries.

How do changes in the system of political power impact economic systems and economic policies in CEE and the FSU?

While the graphical correlations in the previous section provide a static picture of the interdependence between economic and political freedom at two points in time (2000 and 2019), this section will be devoted to a dynamic analysis. More precisely, we will try to look at how changes in systems of political power have affected changes in economic governance. Interest in such an analysis comes from the above-mentioned reversal of democratic progress both worldwide and in the FSU and CEE regions observed in the 2000s and 2010s.

According to the FHNIT survey (which covers the FSU and CEE regions), since 2007 one can observe a systematic deterioration in both the synthetic Democracy Score and all its seven subcategories – electoral process, national democratic governance, civil society, local democratic governance, independent media, and judicial framework and independence

– for all the analysed subregions, that is, Central Europe, the Balkans and Eurasia (FSU) (Csaky and Schenkkan 2018; Csaky 2020).

Does the autocratic trend in the FSU and CEE negatively affect economic governance? The cross-country analysis conducted in the previous section suggests a positive answer. The same answer comes from a dynamic analysis of individual countries.

If one looks at developments in countries that experienced an autocratic drift, market-oriented economic reforms were either stopped or partly reversed. This has happened in, among others, Slovakia (1994–8); Belarus after 1996; Russia after 2003; North Macedonia, Turkey and Hungary since the beginning of the 2010s; Ukraine (2010–14); and Poland after 2015. On the contrary, progress in democratization enabled the launch of or return to economic reforms (Slovakia after 1998, Serbia after 2000, Georgia after 2003, Ukraine since 2014 and North Macedonia since 2018).

Below we will briefly analyse four country case studies: Slovakia (1994–2006), Russia (since 1998), Georgia (since 2004) and Hungary (in the 2010s), which offer us a more detailed and sometimes a more nuanced picture. The selection of these particular cases is motivated by (1) the strength of change in the political regime at the given point in time, (2) relative advancement of economic reforms at the moment of political regime change (we are interested in cases of reversal of economic reforms rather than their non-starting) and (3) data availability.

Slovakia

During his third term in office (1994–8), Prime Minister Vladimir Meciar and his People's Party (Movement for a Democratic Slovakia) slowed down or even partly reversed the political and economic reforms of the early 1990s. On the political front, there was substantial deterioration in the civil liberties component of the Freedom House Freedom in the World (FHFIW) survey (the earlier version of the FHGFS),[10] which led to the country being downgraded from 'free' to 'partly free' in 1996–7. Economically, the HFIEF scores deteriorated systematically between 1995 and 2000 (Figure 2.5).

As a result, Slovakia was not invited to start the EU accession negotiation at the EU summit in Luxembourg in December 1997 (unlike Czechia, Estonia, Hungary, Poland and Slovenia), join NATO at the Madrid summit in July 1997 (unlike Czechia, Hungary and Poland) or to join the OECD (unlike Czechia, Hungary and Poland). This series of rejections caused a domestic political shock,[11] which led to the formation

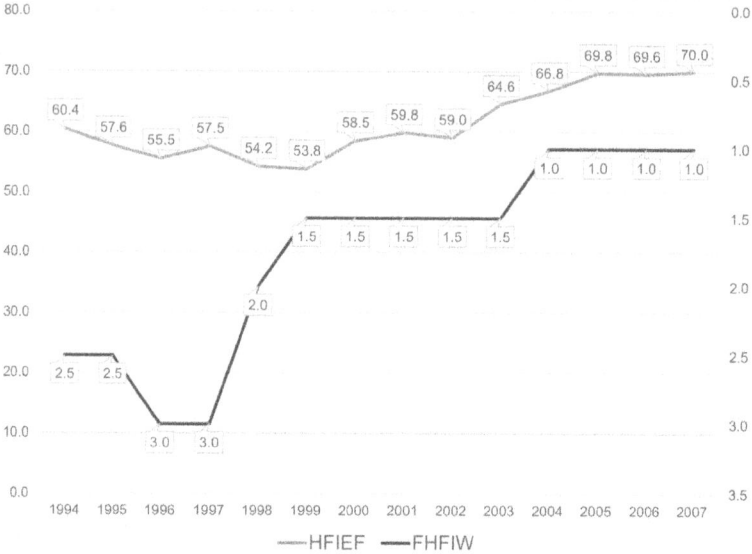

Figure 2.5 Slovakia: HFIEF (left axis) vs. FHFIW (right axis) scores, 1994–2007. Source: https://freedomhouse.org/sites/default/files/2020-02/2020_All_Data_FIW_2013-2020.xlsx and https://www.heritage.org/index/explore?view=by-region-country-year&u=637278786962730727.

of the broad coalition government of Prime Minister Mikulas Dzurinda after the parliamentary election in September 1998. His government returned the country to the path of liberal democratic institution-building and, with some time lag, the continuation of market-oriented economic reforms. Eventually, Slovakia joined the OECD in 2000, and the EU and NATO in 2004. Economic reforms were continued even after the second Dzurinda government was replaced by a left-wing coalition in 2006.

Russia

The deterioration of Russia's FHFIW scores began in 1998 and continued systematically over the two decades that followed (Figure 2.6). In 2004 Russia was downgraded from 'partly free' to 'unfree'. However, its impact on the economic system has not been as clear as one might have expected. Between 1995 and 2015, the HFIEF oscillated around 51 and 52 with some ups and downs. That is, it did not deteriorate as a result of the country's autocratic drift but also did not improve, despite the numerous economic reform programmes adopted by the Russian government. During these 20

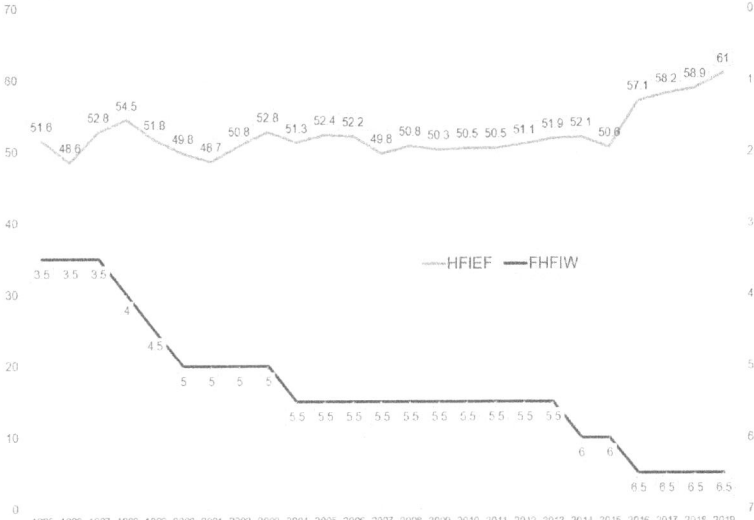

Figure 2.6 Russia: HFIEF (left axis) vs. FHFIW (right axis) scores, 1995–2019. Source: https://freedomhouse.org/sites/default/files/2020-02/2020_All_Data_FIW_2013-2020.xlsx and https://www.heritage.org/index/explore?view=by-region-country-year&u=637278786962730727.

years Russia occupied the bottom of the 'mostly unfree' category, sporadically (1996, 2000–1 and 2007) falling into the group of 'repressed' economies.

The situation has changed, perhaps surprisingly, since 2016, when the further decline in political freedom scores was accompanied by a systematic improvement in the HFIEF. As a result, the Russian economy was upgraded in the HFIEF 2020 (which measures the economic regime in 2019) to 'moderately free'. Even more surprisingly, the highest gains were recorded in the 'property rights' and 'government integrity' categories even if the accompanying narrative paints a rather bleak picture.[12]

Thus, the Russian case does not fully support our hypothesis that autocratic drift has a negative impact on the quality of economic governance, at least according to the metrics used in our analysis.

Georgia

In the 2010s Georgia was systematically rated as the freest FSU economy and one of the freest post-communist economies not only by the HFIEF but also in the World Bank's Doing Business survey (Doing Business

2020). Looking at Figure 2.7, one may find that this position was the result of systematic improvements since 1999 or even earlier. On the political reform front, the country is not such a star performer, although it does not belong to the group of autocracies. It has been systematically rated as a 'partly free' country by the FHFIW survey.

Nevertheless, the dynamic of changes in both spheres (economic and political) looks interesting for our analysis. The periods of acceleration of the economic reforms coincided with periods of political liberalization: in 2004–6, immediately after the so-called Rose Revolution in November 2003; in 2012–13, after the election victory of the Georgian Dream coalition (which renewed the process of democratization); and in 2016–17, as a result of the implementation of the Association Agreement with the EU. On the contrary, the periods in which the political freedom scores deteriorated – 2000–3 (the second term of President Eduard Shevardnadze) and 2007–11 (the end of the first term and second term of President Mikheil Saakashvili) – were associated with the stagnation of economic reforms or even with their partial rollback.

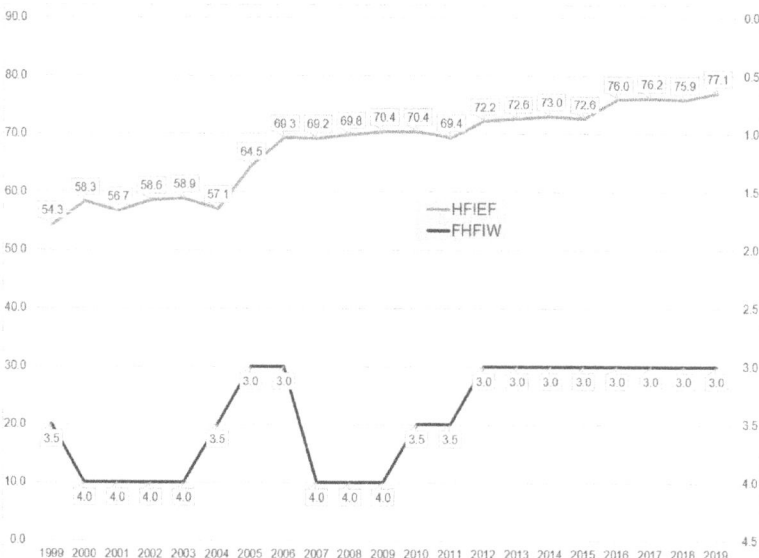

Figure 2.7 Georgia: HFIEF (left axis) vs. FHFIW (right axis) scores, 1999–2019. Source: https://freedomhouse.org/sites/default/files/2020-02/2020_All_Data_FIW_2013-2020.xlsx and https://www.heritage.org/index/explore?view=by-region-country-year&u=637278786962730727.

Hungary

Once a reform leader in the entire CEE–FSU region (see the section 'Post-communist transition: a regional analysis' and Figure 2.3), in the 2010s Hungary started to suffer from autocratic drift. After the overwhelming election victory of the FIDESZ Party in May 2010, which gave it a constitutional majority in the parliament, its leader and Prime Minister Viktor Orbán started to implement, step by step, a model he called an 'illiberal state' (Toth 2014). As a result, the country's scores in the FHFIW survey systematically deteriorated, as illustrated by Figure 2.8. In 2018, Hungary was downgraded to the 'partly free' category, the first such case among the EU member states.

The autocratic drift has negatively affected the economic system. Despite fluctuations, the HFIEF represents a downward trend and Hungary is rated as the only 'moderately free' economy.

Overall, the analysis in this section confirms (perhaps with the exception of Russia) our previous findings on the interrelation between political and economic reforms in the CEE and FSU regions. However, in

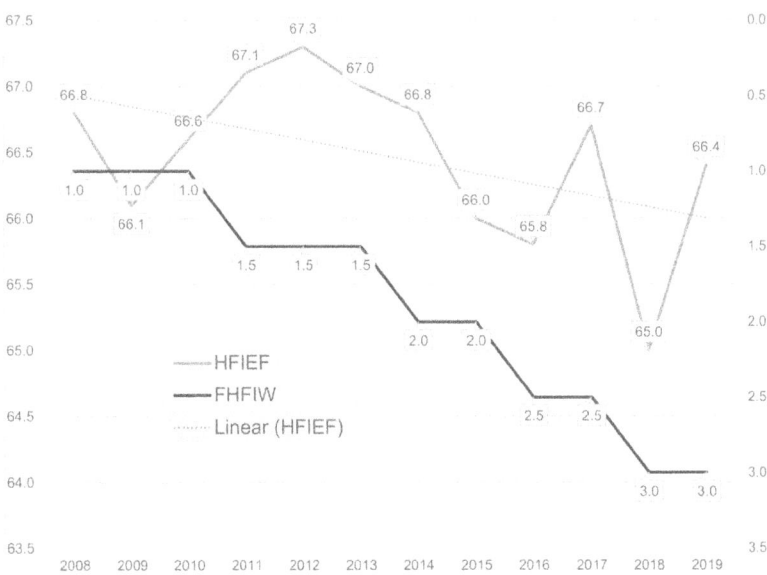

Figure 2.8 Hungary: HFIEF (left axis) vs. FHFIW (right axis) scores, 2008–19. Source: https://freedomhouse.org/sites/default/files/2020-02/2020_All_Data_FIW_2013-2020.xlsx and https://www.heritage.org/index/explore?view=by-region-country-year&u=637278786962730727.

our dynamic analysis changes in political regime have played the role of an exogenous factor, that is, we have focused on a direction of causality going from the system of political power to economic governance. The findings presented in this section should serve as a warning signal that the autocratic drift observed in several FSU and CEE countries may have negative consequences beyond the sphere of civil and political rights, democracy and the rule of law. Most likely, it will undermine economic governance in the region, making it less transparent and more prone to corruption, rent-seeking and oligarchic capture.

Conclusion

With a few exceptions, our analysis confirms the interdependence between economic governance and the system of political power. In the contemporary world this interdependence works in both directions: economic freedom based on a market mechanism helps democracy and political freedom, and vice versa. By contrast, administratively repressed economies with distorted market mechanisms can be found more often in countries with an autocratic system of political power, while the autocratic drift in a political system often leads to more institutional and structural distortions, less competition and imprudent macroeconomic policies.

One explanation of such interdependence may refer to the ambivalent character of political power which, if unconstrained, becomes driven by the private interests (including economic ones) of a ruling elite.

While the discussed interdependence does not have a deterministic character (that is, there are several outliers on both sides of the correlation line), there are clear limits as to how 'market-friendly' autocracies can be and how economically distorted democracy can be. Genuinely free-market economies in autocracies are rare, and non-market democracies, which are politically stable in the longer term, are even rarer.

Furthermore, the examined interdependence has a non-linear character and works with a certain time lag. That is, changes in one sphere do not have an immediate and proportional impact on the other. This has been confirmed, among others, by the country case studies examined in the previous section.

In the former communist economies of CEE and the FSU, the interdependence between a market economy and democratic political system is even stronger than elsewhere in both static and dynamic terms. At the very beginning of the transition period, in the early 1990s, political transition facilitated economic transition. Countries which managed to democratize quickly and remove the old political and economic elite created the space for rapid and comprehensive economic reforms. The economic transition in countries in which the systems of political power did not change or changed only slightly was substantially delayed.

At the later stages of transition or post-transition development, in the 2000s and 2010s, several episodes of autocratic backsliding in both the FSU and CEE stopped further economic reforms and quite often led to their partial rollback. They also ushered in oligarchic systems based on a far-reaching symbiosis between political and economic power ('crony capitalism').

Unlike the situation in CEE and the FSU, the building of a market economy in communist countries in Asia (China, Vietnam, Laos and Cambodia) was initiated and conducted by communist parties, which made little to no changes to the political systems. In the early 2000s, however, Asian economic reforms reached their limits and their economic and political systems do not now differ so much from those of Russia and most of the FSU.

The interdependence between systems of economic governance and systems of political power requires further examination in both empirical and normative terms.

Notes

1. Myrdal (1968, Vol. 2) and Polterovich and Popov (2005) are among those who are sceptical about the helpful role of immature democracy in economic modernization and boosting economic growth.
2. This disappointing experience led many scholars in CEE and the Soviet Union (some of them becoming future reformers) to a conviction that genuine market reforms are impossible without deep changes in the political system, that is, breaking up the political monopoly of a communist party (see, for example, Gaidar 1989).
3. In this chapter we use 'market economy' rather than 'capitalism' because the latter is historically associated with hot ideological debates and, therefore, contains sometimes unnecessary emotional content.
4. See Fukuyama (2015) for a historical analysis of democratic systems.
5. The HFIEF consists of 12 detailed indices related to property rights, judicial effectiveness, government integrity, tax burden, government spending, fiscal health, business freedom, labour freedom, monetary freedom, trade freedom, investment freedom and financial freedom.
6. Balcerowicz (1994) called such a window the 'period of extraordinary politics'.
7. To be fair, not all FSU countries were interested in closer ties with the EU.
8. EBRD transition indicators were discontinued in 2014. FHNIT Democracy Scores do not cover Asian communist (post-communist) countries.
9. Tajikistan has backtracked in both ratings since the early 2000s.
10. In the FHFIW survey higher scores mean less political freedom.
11. The very fact that Slovakia did not receive an invitation to join these three organizations/integration blocs while Czechia did was particularly humiliating for Slovak society.
12. See https://www.heritage.org/index/country/russia.

References

Abramowitz, Michael J. 2018. 'Freedom in the world 2018: Democracy in crisis', Freedom House. Accessed 14 March 2021. https://freedomhouse.org/sites/default/files/2020-02/FH_FIW_Report_2018_Final.pdf.

Aslund, Anders. 2002. *Building Capitalism: The transformation of the former Soviet bloc.* Cambridge: Cambridge University Press.

Aslund, Anders, Peter Boone and Simon Johnson. 1996. 'How to stabilize: Lessons from postcommunist countries', *Brookings Papers on Economic Activity* (1): 217–313. Accessed 14 March 2021. https://www.jstor.org/stable/2534649.

Balcerowicz, Leszek. 1994. 'Understanding post-communist transitions', *Journal of Democracy* 5(4): 75–89.

Barro, Robert J. 1999. 'Determinants of democracy', *Journal of Political Economy* 107(S6): 158–83.

Collier, Paul and Anke Hoeffler. 2005. 'Democracy and resource rents', University of Oxford, Department of Economics, August. Accessed 14 March 2021. http://citeseerx.ist.psu.edu/viewdoc/download?doi=10.1.1.501.5736&rep=rep1&type=pdf.

Csaky, Zselyke. 2020. 'Nations in transit: Dropping the democratic facade in Europe and Eurasia', Freedom House. Accessed 14 March 2021. https://freedomhouse.org/report/nations-transit/2020/dropping-democratic-facade.

Csaky, Zselyke and Nate Schenkkan. 2018. 'Nations in transit 2018: Confronting illiberalism', Freedom House. Accessed 14 March 2021. https://freedomhouse.org/report/nations-transit/nations-transit-2018.

Dabrowski, Marek. 2017. 'Ukraine's unfinished reform agenda', Bruegel Policy Contribution 24/2017, 27 September. Accessed 14 March 2021. https://bruegel.org/wp-content/uploads/2017/09/PC-24-2017-1.pdf.

Dabrowski, Marek. 2020. 'Transition to a market economy: A retrospective comparison of China with countries of the former Soviet bloc', *Acta Oeconomica* 7(S1): 15–45.

Dabrowski, Marek and Artur Radziwill. 2007. 'Regional vs. global public goods: The case of post-communist transition', *CASE Network Studies and Analyses* 336. Accessed 14 March 2021. http://www.case-research.eu/sites/default/files/publications/13493806_sa336_0.pdf.

De Haan, Jakob and Jan-Egbert Sturm. 2003. 'Does more democracy lead to greater economic freedom? New evidence for developing countries', *European Journal of Political Economy* 19(3): 547–63. Accessed 14 March 2021. https://www.sciencedirect.com/science/article/pii/S0176268003000132/pdfft?casa_token=nbgtAkwE52wAAAAA:svGoQWcIJXc2d1IyIAZtC53iI4p3tvo6xzFhxKlRzTmgCMFDYD1-C0S1mkMnyZokIUqZ0b2S6pg&md5=25b89dd2c87e7e0699a6e13d27f78782&pid=1-s2.0-S0176268003000132-main.pdf.

De Melo, Marta, Cevdet Denizer, Alan Gelb and Stoyan Tenev. 1997. 'Circumstances and choice: The role of initial conditions and policies in transition economies', *World Bank Policy Research Working Paper* 1866. Washington, DC: World Bank.

Dethier, Jean-Jacques, Hafez Ghanem and Edda Zoli. 1999. 'Does democracy facilitate the economic transition? An empirical study of Central and Eastern Europe and the former Soviet Union', *World Bank Policy Research Working Paper* WPS 2194. Washington, DC: World Bank. Accessed 14 March 2021. http://documents.worldbank.org/curated/en/918811468776043640/114514322_20041117135529/additional/multi-page.pdf.

Doing Business. 2020. *Doing Business 2020: Comparing business regulation in 190 economies.* Washington, DC: World Bank Group. Accessed 14 March 2021. https://openknowledge.worldbank.org/bitstream/handle/10986/32436/9781464814402.pdf.

EBRD (European Bank for Reconstruction and Development). 1999. *Transition Report 1999: Ten years of transition.* London: European Bank for Reconstruction and Development. Accessed 14 March 2021. https://www.ebrd.com/publications/transition-report-1999-english.pdf.

EIU (Economist Intelligence Unit). 2021. 'Democracy index 2020: In sickness and in health?', The Economist Economic Intelligence Unit. Accessed 14 March 2021. https://www.eiu.com/n/campaigns/democracy-index-2020.

Fukuyama, Francis. 2004. *State Building: Governance and world order in the 21st century.* Ithaca, NY: Cornell University Press.

Fukuyama, Francis. 2012. *The Origins of Political Order: From prehuman times to the French Revolution.* London: Profile Books.

Fukuyama, Francis. 2015. *Political Order and Political Decay: From the industrial revolution to the globalisation of democracy*. London: Profile Books.

Gaidar, Egor. 1989. *Ekonomicheskie reformy i ierarkhicheskie struktury* [Economic reforms and hierarchical structures]. Moscow: Nauka.

Havrylyshyn, Oleh and Basil Kalymon. 2020. 'Ukraine's new government must act fast or face failure', *UkraineAlert*, 5 March. Atlantic Council. Accessed 14 March 2021. https://www.atlanticcouncil.org/blogs/ukrainealert/ukraines-new-government-must-act-fast-or-face-failure/.

Knutsen, Carl H. 2010. 'Investigating the Lee thesis: How bad is democracy for Asian economies?', *European Political Science Review* 2(3): 451–73.

Lipset, Seymour M. 1959. 'Some social requisites of democracy: Economic development and political legitimacy', *American Political Science Review* 53(1): 69–105. Accessed 14 March 2021. https://scholar.harvard.edu/files/levitsky/files/lipset_1959.pdf.

Lu, Chunlong. 2005. 'Middle class and democracy: Structural linkage', *International Review of Modern Sociology* 31(2): 157–78. Accessed 14 March 2021. https://www.jstor.org/stable/41421642.

Lundstrom, Susanna. 2005. 'The effect of democracy on different categories of economic freedom', *European Journal of Political Economy* 21(4): 967–80. Accessed 14 March 2021. https://www.sciencedirect.com/science/article/pii/S017626800500011X?casa_token=9-laTRcgXSwAAAAA:rxoJsL5pjraLoYUdZCdz42SY-ENFPHqj51tP_UYPuvCYPPRCkPxcp-AZAzmZA678cOugb5NrILs.

Mei, Danni. 2019. 'The Growing Middle Class and the Absence of Democracy in China'. MA thesis, City University of New York. Accessed 14 March 2021. https://academicworks.cuny.edu/cgi/viewcontent.cgi?article=4236&context=gc_etds.

Motadel, David. 2020. 'The myth of middle-class liberalism', *New York Times*, 22 January. Accessed 14 March 2021. https://www.nytimes.com/2020/01/22/opinion/middle-class-liberalism-populism.html.

Moyo, Dambisa. 2018. 'Why the survival of democracy depends on a strong middle-class', *The Globe and Mail*, 20 April. Accessed 14 March 2021. https://www.theglobeandmail.com/opinion/article-why-the-survival-of-democracy-depends-on-a-strong-middle-class/.

Myrdal, Gunnar. 1968. *Asian Drama: An inquiry into the poverty of nations*. New York: Pantheon.

Polterovich, Victor and Vladimir Popov. 2005. 'Democracy and growth reconsidered: Why economic performance of new democracies is not encouraging', *New Economic School Working Paper*. Accessed 14 March 2021. https://papers.ssrn.com/sol3/Delivery.cfm/SSRN_ID1755005_code920334.pdf?abstractid=1755005&mirid=1.

Przeworski, Adam and Fernando Limongi. 1997. 'Modernization: Theories and facts', *World Politics* 49(2): 155–83. Accessed 14 March 2021. https://www.jstor.org/stable/25053996.

Roland, Gerard. 2002. 'The political economy of transition', *Journal of Economic Perspectives* 16(1): 29–50. Accessed 14 March 2021. https://www.jstor.org/stable/pdf/2696575.pdf?refreqid=excelsior%3A5279402217648b0535511c00af958a56.

Roland, Gerard. 2018. 'The evolution of post-communist systems: Eastern Europe vs. China', *Economics of Transition* 26(4): 589–614.

Schwarz, Robert. 2018. 'Democracy under pressure: Polarization and repression are increasing worldwide', Bertelsmann Stiftung. Press Release, 22 March. Accessed 14 March 2021. https://www.bertelsmann-stiftung.de/en/press/press-releases/press-release/pid/democracy-under-pressure-polarization-and-repression-are-increasing-worldwide/.

Toth, Csaba. 2014. 'Full text of Viktor Orbán's speech at Băile Tuşnad (Tusnádfürdő) of 26 July 2014', *The Budapest Beacon*, 29 July 2014. Accessed 14 March 2021. https://budapestbeacon.com/full-text-of-viktor-orbans-speech-at-baile-tusnad-tusnadfurdo-of-26-july-2014/.

3
The pitfalls of rent-seeking: Alternative mechanisms of resource rent collection in Russia and Venezuela

Alexei Pobedonostsev

Introduction

In some developing countries, the extraction of natural resources is traditionally a key source of government revenue. In academic literature, such countries are usually referred to as 'rentier states', by which scholars mean 'those countries that receive on a regular basis substantial amounts of external rent' (Mahdavy 1970, 428). In other words, a rentier state is one in which 'the government is the principal recipient of the external rent in the economy' (Beblawi and Luciani 1987, 52). The rentier state concept has become a key element of the so-called resource curse theory (Auty 1993; Menaldo 2016, 43–76). This theory implies that the presence of significant revenues from the export of natural resources (primarily from oil and gas) tends to have various detrimental effects on the political and economic development of resource-rich nations. Analytically, the resource curse is not a unified theory but rather a set of different hypotheses related to the negative consequences of the presence of natural resources. For instance, a number of studies indicate that in resource-rich nations around the world the revenues received from hydrocarbon fuel exports tend to be the fundamental cause of problems such as the deceleration of economic growth (Sachs and Warner 2001; Ross 2012), the weakness of state institutions (Karl 1997; Smith 2007), authoritarian regime stability (Morrison 2015), higher levels of corruption (Bhattacharyya and Hodler 2010), persisting gender inequality (Ross 2008) and unending violent conflicts (Collier and Hoeffler 2004).

The resource curse literature is full of paradoxes and contradictions. For instance, the resource curse literature (including the rentier state conception) says almost nothing about how governments get their hands on oil export revenues. The problem with all existing studies of rentier states (and the resource curse literature as a whole) is that scholars tend to consider the state a priori to be the key beneficiary of oil production. The resource curse theory tends to consider that windfall oil revenues automatically flow into the state's coffers and ignores the fact that in the real world governments need to take fiscal action to collect revenues from oil production (Nakhle 2008). In other words, the process of transforming resource rent into government income is a puzzle for comparative political economy.

However, oil rent does not exist in a vacuum. From a theoretical perspective, the process of resource rent allocation (or resource rent circulation in the economy) includes three stages: resource rent generation, resource rent collection and resource rent redistribution (Vatansever 2021, 5). In all countries, resource rent is generated by companies, collected by the state and redistributed by the government among social groups. In the academic literature, scholars focus on how political leaders spend their windfall revenues from oil production (and use them to strengthen their rule) and ignore how political leaders obtain these revenues. In other words, political science scholars are traditionally interested in the resource redistribution stage and ignore the resource rent collection stage.

In all countries governments are required to take action and use various fiscal instruments to capture resource revenues from the extraction of natural resources. In oil-producing economies, the government usually obtains petrodollars through taxes or dividends paid by oil companies (Nakhle 2008). The resource rent of an oil-producing country is not inevitably transformed into government income because the transformation of resource rent into the resource revenue of the state is a complicated and controversial process.

The contradictory nature of resource rent allocation is especially clear if we look at how differently the process of resource rent collection is organized in petrostates as similar as Russia and Venezuela, the two paradigmatic oil-producing countries of the twenty-first century.

The development of Russia and that of Venezuela have demonstrated several common features for the last few decades. In both countries, the economic crisis of the 1990s undermined the stability of democratic institutions and caused the formation of personalist authoritarian regimes at the beginning of the twenty-first century. In both countries, the oil boom of the 2000s stimulated economic growth and the consolidation of authoritarian rule. Given the high oil prices, the governments of both countries decided to carry out partial nationalizations of the assets of private oil companies for the benefit of state-owned oil companies in the early 2000s. At first glance, the impression could arise that Russia and Venezuela were political and economic twins during the first decade of the twenty-first century. The similarity between the two countries was especially strong before Hugo Chavez's death in 2013 and the beginning of the catastrophic economic and political crisis in Venezuela. After 2013 the similarities between Russia and Venezuela gradually waned.

Table 3.1 The resource revenue of the Russian government and total resource rent

Year	Government's resource revenue (% GDP)	Total resource rent (% GDP)	State's capture of resource rent
2000	5.12	21.69	0.24
2001	5.31	19.92	0.27
2002	5.3	17.45	0.3
2003	5.88	17.61	0.33
2004	7.27	17.11	0.42
2005	11.83	18.25	0.65
2006	11.99	19.41	0.62
2007	9.87	17	0.58
2008	11.77	19.27	0.61
2009	8.28	15.4	0.54
2010	8.94	15.97	0.56
2011	10.68	17.99	0.59
2012	10.31	15.92	0.65
2013	9.61	14	0.69
2014	10.3	13.27	0.78
2015	8	10.33	0.77
2016	6.1	8.84	0.69

Source: The statistical data about governmental resource revenue is taken from the Government Revenue Dataset provided by the International Center for Taxation and Development. The statistical data about total resource rent is taken from the World Bank website. The variable 'state's capture of resource rent' is calculated as a ratio between governmental resource revenue and total resource rent. This variable refers to a percentage of total resource rent, which the government transforms into revenue.

However, despite some common features, Vladimir Putin's Russia and Hugo Chavez's Venezuela demonstrate different patterns of resource rent allocation. State leaders of both countries implemented two different strategies of resource rent collection in the early 2000s. The key difference between these strategies lies in the percentage of total oil rent that each government captures and transforms into its income. While in Russia almost all petrodollars collected by the federal government flow into the state budget, with 60–70 per cent of the total resource rent transformed into budgetary revenue (Table 3.1), in Venezuela only 10–15 per cent of the oil rent collected by the central government ends up in the state budget (Table 3.2). This difference between Russia and Venezuela is puzzling because both countries have nationalized petroleum industries with powerful national oil companies (NOCs). As, in theory, the nationalized model of the petroleum industry enables the state to capture almost all revenues from oil production (Mahdavi 2020, 159–60), Russia and Venezuela should have similar patterns of resource rent collection. However, economic statistics show that the government of Venezuela transforms a less significant percentage of the total resource rent into government income than would be expected given that this Latin American country has a nationalized petroleum industry and a great amount of oil rents.

Table 3.2 The resource revenue of the Venezuelan government and total resource rent

Year	Government's resource revenue (% GDP)	Total resource rent (% GDP)	State's capture of resource rent
1980	14.92	34.89	0.43
1981	20.97	25.48	0.82
1982	14.23	14.25	1
1983	11.74	17.78	0.66
1984	14.8	19.41	0.76
1985	13.72	16.89	0.81
1986	8.56	8.54	1
1987	9.76	16.79	0.58
1988	10.47	10.55	0.99
1989	14.94	21.6	0.69
1990	13.81	29.77	0.46

Year	Government's resource revenue (% GDP)	Total resource rent (% GDP)	State's capture of resource rent
1991	13.67	17.7	0.77
1992	8.23	16.69	0.49
1993	6.7	16.89	0.4
1994	5.25	16.29	0.32
1995	4.24	14.58	0.29
1996	5.8	23.93	0.24
1997	7.54	18.02	0.42
1998	1.32	8.88	0.15
1999	2.21	12.67	0.17
2000	4.23	20.02	0.21
2001	2.54	13.96	0.18
2002	0.92	18.23	0.05
2003	1.47	21.12	0.07
2004	1.79	26.49	0.07
2005	3.68	31.58	0.12
2006	4	30.39	0.13
2007	4.04	22.04	0.18
2008	2.63	22.01	0.12
2009	1.83	10.68	0.17
2010	0.86	12.71	0.07
2011	1.22	24.19	0.05
2012	1.4	18.72	0.07
2013	1.13	17.97	0.06
2014	2.23	11.82	0.19

Source: The statistical data about governmental resource revenue is taken from the Government Revenue Dataset provided by the International Center for Taxation and Development. The statistical data about total resource rent is taken from the World Bank website. The variable 'state's capture of resource rent' is calculated as a ratio between governmental resource revenue and total resource rent. This variable refers to a percentage of total resource rent, which the government transforms into revenue.

Resource rent is a source of political and economic power in oil-producing countries. Those leaders who control the circulation of oil rents across social groups control the distribution of power in these countries. The ability of the state to collect and redistribute resource revenues is crucial for the power of political leaders in oil-exporting nations. Without this ability leaders cannot exercise their power properly. Therefore, the analysis of resource rent collection in Russia and Venezuela should shed light on the machinery of power in resource-rich societies.

In this chapter, I explain the different patterns of oil rent collection in Venezuela and Russia. I wonder why these oil-producing countries are not alike. Why do governments of some nations successfully collect oil revenue, while governments of other countries fail to do so? What political and economic factors determine the success of resource rent collection in Russia and the failure of resource revenue collection in Venezuela?

This chapter has the following structure. Firstly, in the literature review, I theoretically summarize what factors can affect the process of resource rent allocation in oil-producing economies. Secondly, in the analysis of the Russian case, I show how this country in the 2000s became an excellent example of a petrostate, the NOCs of which allow the state to capture the best part of the oil export revenue. Thirdly, in the analysis of the Venezuelan case, I explain why the government of this Latin American country collects such an insignificant amount of oil revenue for the state budget. Fourthly, in conclusion, I bring a theoretical perspective to my comparative study of Russia and Venezuela. In this part of the chapter, I wonder how the ambivalence of power manifests itself in the process of resource rent collection in the cases of Venezuela and Russia.

Literature review

The classical theory of rational choice claims that all state leaders seek to maximize their power (Wintrobe 1998; Mueller 2003) and the key goal of every political leader (authoritarian as well as democratically elected) is to stay in office as long as possible (Bueno de Mesquita et al. 2003). There is no reason to believe that the state leaders of oil-producing countries are the exception to the rule.

For the political leaders of petrostates, oil export revenue is the most obvious instrument they can use to maximize power. Thus, political leaders have powerful incentives to maximize their revenues from oil production because in petrostates oil revenue maximization inevitably leads to power maximization. Control over oil revenue flows allows state leaders to strengthen their political positions. For instance, in authoritarian countries, political leaders can invest petrodollars in strengthening the repressive apparatus and buying the loyalty of the masses (Ross 2001, 333–6), while in democratic countries state leaders can seek to increase their popularity by using oil revenues to expand social programmes (Karl 1997, 116–37; Dunning 2008). In other words, the accumulation of oil export revenues in the hands of state leaders gives them the financial resources to strengthen their rule in the long term, so they have a strong interest in maximizing oil export revenue.

The maximization of oil revenues can be achieved by nationalizing the petroleum industry to the benefit of state leaders. Some scholars point out that the nationalization of petroleum industries, which occurs from time to time in oil-exporting countries, is determined by the wish of political leaders to maximize their windfall revenues from oil production (Guriev et al. 2011; Warshaw 2012; Mahdavi 2014). There is some evidence in the academic literature that the ownership structure of the petroleum industry seriously affects the ability of the state to raise revenue from oil exports and to collect resource rent (Jones Luong and Weinthal 2010; Mahdavi 2020). The nationalized petroleum sector potentially gives the government more instruments to obtain revenues from oil production than the privatized model of petroleum ownership. For instance, the nationalized petroleum industry allows the government to effectively control the sector and strengthen the financial power of the state.

Historically, the wave of mass nationalizations of petroleum industries spread across the developing countries in the 1970s after the dramatic increase in the price of oil (Korbin 1985; Yergin 1991). In the early 1970s, the governments of many oil-producing nations decided to expropriate the assets of international oil companies and establish giant NOCs for the efficient control of the nationalized petroleum industries. The key driver of these actions was the wish of many state leaders to gain all the benefits from the increase in oil prices, which took place in the 1970s. In other words, their behaviour was stimulated by the logic of oil revenue maximization.

In his book *Power Grab: Political survival through extractive resource nationalization*, Paasha Mahdavi argues that in oil-exporting countries, the nationalization of the petroleum industry is driven by the wish of authoritarian leaders to maximize the likelihood of their future political survival (Mahdavi 2020). He demonstrates the results of a statistical study according to which the nationalization of the resource extractive industry of a country tends to increase the probability of the future political survival of the leader of the country in question (Mahdavi 2020, 161–7). So, in countries with nationalized petroleum industries, political leaders stay in power longer than political leaders of oil-producing countries in which the oil industry has not been expropriated. In other words, the nationalization of oil sectors stabilizes authoritarian regimes in the long term because regime leaders gain access to greater financial resources, which they can use for the purpose of repression and public spending. Mahdavi also points out that the nationalization of oil industries usually leads to a significant increase in the size of the government's oil revenue (Mahdavi 2020, 159, 173).

However, nationalizing petroleum industries is not always as beneficial as it seems at first glance. Christian Wolf demonstrates that NOCs 'significantly underperform the private sector in terms of output efficiency and profitability' (Wolf 2009, 2642). He also points out that NOCs tend to be less efficient than private companies in terms of oil production (Wolf 2009, 2649–50). The low efficiency of the nationalized petroleum industry could undermine the ability of the government to raise significant revenue from oil production in the long term because the state will have to provide subsidies to the sector to compensate for its inefficiency.

Since the 1970s the leaders of many oil-producing countries have nationalized their petroleum industries. These actions boosted the budgets of many petrostates and the financial resources of their leaders (Yergin 1991). Some scholars point out that in oil-producing countries authoritarian regimes exist longer on average than authoritarian regimes in oil-poor countries (Wright et al. 2015). In part, the longevity of political regimes in many oil-producing countries can be explained by the fact that nationalized petroleum industries in these countries successfully generate significant amounts of petrodollars for state leaders.

In *Nontaxation and Representation: The fiscal foundations of political stability*, Kevin Morrison points out two possible mechanisms whereby state leaders can use oil export revenues to stabilize the regime and maximize their power (Morrison 2015). On the one hand, political leaders can boost social spending to buy the loyalty of the population. On the other hand, oil export revenue can be used by leaders to reduce the tax burden on the masses. These measures allow state leaders to block potential popular demands for democratization and accountability following the logic of 'no taxation without representation' (Ross 2004, 230–2). In other words, the ability of state leaders to transform oil export revenue into social benefits for the population is quite important for regimes' survival.

In the comparative political economy of welfare capitalism, it is the state that is traditionally considered to be the key operator of social programmes and the driver of the politics of redistribution in advanced economies (Esping-Andersen 1990). However, in some developing countries, the role the state plays in the operation of social programmes can be less significant than in developed nations. While in advanced economies welfare policy is based on the principles of universalistic social protection, in some poor developing countries social programmes are often used by political leaders for clientelism and patronage (Stokes et al. 2013; Diaz-Cayeros et al. 2016). The key difference between universalistic and clientelistic social protections is that while universalistic social programmes are guaranteed and funded by the state, clientelistic social protection is guaranteed by political leaders rather than the state and can be operated by informal funds (Diaz-Cayeros et al. 2016, 26).

The weakness of the state is potentially one of the most dramatic consequences of the resource curse. The academic literature claims that oil export revenues can generate very damaging effects on the quality of state institutions in developing countries (Karl 1997; Smith 2007). These effects can be so detrimental to the state that political leaders could lose their control over state institutions. Some scholars even propose to rename the 'resource curse' as the 'institutions curse' (Corrales and Penfold 2015; Menaldo 2016) because the weakness of state institutions is a fundamental characteristic of many resource-rich nations. The weakness of the state (and its capacities) affects the ability of the government to provide social benefits and public goods to the population. In petrostates, the weakness of state institutions challenges the ability of political leadership to collect and redistribute windfall revenues. In countries with extremely weak state institutions, leaders have no choice but to establish alternative (non-state) mechanisms for the collection and redistribution of oil rents. The use of these mechanisms can lead to the formation of clientelistic networks and further erosion of the state and its infrastructural power (Mann 1984).

Summing up, the academic literature shows that control over oil revenues is a very important factor for the political survival of state leaders in petrostates (Morrison 2015; Mahdavi 2020). Political leaders strive for oil revenue maximization because it maximizes their power. However, in the academic literature, some scholars assume implicitly that the desire of state leaders to control oil revenues leads to the transformation of all petrodollars into the budgetary revenues of the state. However, it is not always the case. Political control over petrodollars can also be exercised informally using non-public funds rather than collecting all petrodollars in the state budget. State leaders can accumulate oil export revenues in informal funds and use them for their own political needs without any public scrutiny. In theory, the use of informal mechanisms of resource rent allocation makes some sense for the political leaders of countries whose state capacities are very weak. On the contrary, in countries with relatively strong state capacities, political leaders should have powerful incentives to use the state rather than informal practices to control the process of resource rent allocation.

Russia as a perfect petrostate

After the dissolution of the Soviet Union in 1991, the problem of the radical transformation of all sectors of the economy (including the oil and gas industries) became a big issue in Russian politics (Gaidar 2007). The post-communist economic transition and market reforms included the mass privatization of oil fields and state-owned petroleum assets. The old bureaucratic model of industrial management was replaced by a market-based corporate system in the oil and gas sectors (Gaddy and Ickes 2005). However, in the 1990s the privatizations of the oil and gas industries in Russia were dissimilar because the federal government implemented different strategies for the sale of these two sectors. While the oil industry was bought up almost exclusively by private companies, the assets of the gas industry were accumulated in the hands of the newly established state-run company Gazprom.

In the 1990s, the post-communist privatization of the petroleum industry resulted in the division of the state-owned oil assets among recently established private oil companies. Pauline Jones Luong and Erika Weinthal point out that Russia's privatization of the petroleum industries was atypical for post-Soviet countries (Jones Luong and Weinthal 2010). While in other post-Soviet republics foreign companies actively participated in the privatization of oil industries, in Russia it was domestic private companies that were the key winners of the privatization process in that they gained exclusive control over the petroleum industry. Some of the businessmen who privatized the oil sector in the 1990s subsequently became well-known as Russian 'oligarchs' (Hoffman 2002).

Unlike the oil industry, ownership of the gas sector did not pass to private companies. The ministry of the gas industry of the Soviet Union was transformed into Gazprom, the national gas company of Russia, which became the monopoly gas producer in Russia and one of the leading gas companies in the world (Gustafson 2012). However, despite the status of the national gas company, Gazprom initially had a mixed ownership structure in which the federal government did not have a majority shareholding. The state did not have full control over Gazprom until the mid-2000s, when the federal government returned the company to state control.

The privatization of the oil sector occurred under conditions of an economic crisis and the deep transformation of Russian society (Gaidar 2007). Economic reforms and the dissolution of the Soviet Union resulted in a deep crisis of state capacity in Russia and other transitional nations (Volkov 2002). In the 1990s and early 2000s, the Russian federal government proved itself to be very poor at capturing revenue from oil and gas production. The state did not have efficient fiscal instruments to force private oil companies to pay taxes to the state budget (Jones Luong and Weinthal 2010). While in the 1990s oil companies and oligarchs were very strong and powerful, the Russian state was very weak and chaotic and thus struggled to bring order to the regulation of the economy.

The privatization of the petroleum industry had positive as well as negative effects on the Russian economy. On the one hand, privatization radically improved the efficiency of the oil sector in the post-Soviet period, which was a fundamental cause of the economic boom of the 2000s (Aleksashenko 2018). Gustafson thinks that the transformation of the petroleum industry in the early 1990s produced the 'economic miracle' of the Russian oil sector one decade later (Gustafson 2012). This 'miracle' was characterized by the relatively high efficiency of the oil sector and the increase of oil production in Russia in the late 1990s and the early 2000s. In other words, private oil companies radically improved the productivity and efficiency of the oil sector compared with the Soviet era. However, in the 1990s the privatized model of the oil sector and the low level of state capacity undermined the ability of the federal government to transform resource rent into government income.

There were two problems for the Russian government in the 1990s in the context of resource rent collection. Firstly, the general level of state capacity was quite low, which meant that the government did not have efficient instruments of resource rent collection. Secondly, in the 1990s the international oil price was very low, so the state was afraid to impose heavy taxes on the petroleum industry as it would make oil production unprofitable. Moreover, under conditions of low oil prices, increasing the fiscal burden on oil companies could have a harmful effect on the ongoing modernization of the petroleum sector.

Everything changed after Vladimir Putin took power in 2000. His rise to power coincided with the increase in international oil prices and the improvement of Russian state capacity. The oil price recovery created good conditions for the state to increase the tax burden on the petroleum sector and oil companies. In the early 2000s, some political and administrative reforms were carried out by Putin's team, which allowed the government to strengthen its control over the bureaucratic apparatus at all levels. These reforms improved Russian state capacity but also eventually resulted in the consolidation of power in Russia and the rise of Putin's regime (Gel'man 2015).

In the 2000s the successful development of the privatized oil sector was a key driver of economic growth in Russia and the rise of Putin's popularity (Treisman 2014). However, Putin decided to carry out the nationalization (or renationalization to be precise) of the oil sector and kill the goose that had laid the golden eggs. Putin's politics of renationalization meant the return of some strategic economic assets to the state (Aleksashenko 2018; Aslund 2019, 97–131). The existence of prosperous private oil companies (owned by powerful oligarchs) conflicted with the interests of Putin's regime in the long term. The logic of political survival pushed Putin to concentrate all resources and economic assets in the hands of the state or the hands of the companies affiliated with the Kremlin.

The so-called Yukos affair was the first episode of the transformation of the Russian petroleum industry (as well as of the basic principles of Russian politics) in the early 2000s (Volkov 2008). Yukos was a leading oil company in Russia, which was expropriated by the state in 2003. As a result of the Yukos affair, the assets of the oil company were expropriated by the state-owned company Rosneft, while the Yukos CEO, Mikhail Khodorkovsky, was sent to prison for 10 years. From a theoretical perspective, the nationalization of the leading oil company could be explained by the desire of Putin to maximize his power through the maximization of state revenues from oil production (Mahdavi 2020).

The Yukos affair was the most important but not the only episode of the renationalization of the petroleum industry in Putin's Russia. In the 2000s Gazprom also started collecting the assets of private oil companies. For instance, in 2005 Gazprom bought the major shares of Sibneft, the private oil company owned by Roman Abramovich, for 13 billion dollars. As a result of this deal, Gazprom expanded its business specialization from gas production to include the production of oil (Gustafson 2012). Moreover, in the 2000s the federal government increased its participation in the shares of Gazprom, as a result of which the state gained control over the gas company. It was an important moment in the renationalization of the Russian oil and gas sectors because in the previous decade the federal government did not have full control over Gazprom, despite the company's formal status as the national gas company.

The renationalization of the petroleum industry in the early 2000s allowed the federal government to improve the process of resource rent collection. The state obtained efficient instruments for the capture of resource revenue. In the early 2000s, Putin's administration carried out some important changes in the administration of petroleum taxation (Vatansever 2021). The lion's share of all government resource revenue came from two taxes: export duty and severance tax (or NDPI in the Russian language). The introduction of these two taxes optimized petroleum taxation, as the result of which the process of resource rent collection and the administration of tax collection became more efficient in comparison with the 1990s (Jones Luong and Weinthal 2010).

The renationalization of the petroleum industry had a negative impact on the efficiency of oil production in Russia over the long term. There is some evidence that the quality of the management of the petroleum industry decreased dramatically after its renationalization in comparison with the late 1990s and early 2000s. In other words, the nationalization of the industry did not result in the flourishing of oil production in Russia. Moreover, eventually, in the 2010s the petroleum industry started suffering from deep inefficiency and corruption.

The radical improvement in petroleum tax collection allowed the state to accumulate a significant amount of oil revenue in the state budget, with the result that the federal government became rich enough to increase public spending in the 2000s. Between 2000 and 2008 the total amount of government spending (including social spending) increased several fold. However, despite the significant rise in government income during the oil boom of the 2000s, the budgetary and financial policies of the Kremlin were quite conservative and cautious. Putin's Minister of Finance, Alexei Kudrin, 'utilized' part of the windfall revenues, which were concentrated in newly established sovereign wealth funds (SWFs).

As was the case with other petrostates which had established similar funds, in Russia the SWFs were created with the aim of (1) controlling economic overheating, (2) containing inflation and (3) saving money for the future. The collection of revenue from oil production was conducted by the state so successfully that the Kremlin decided to save money for a rainy day in the event that the international oil price were to fall (Vatansever 2021). So, the basic economic function of SWFs was to remove petrodollars from circulation in the Russian economy during the oil boom of the 2000s. The creation of such funds allowed the Russian government to survive the financial crisis of 2008–9, which hit the

Russian economy hard due to the sharp drop in the oil price. Moreover, financial reserves from the SWFs helped Russia to maintain macroeconomic stability during the economic crisis of 2014–16.

Putin's economic policy can be characterized as neoliberal etatism, the basic principles of which are state control over all strategic economy sectors (including the petroleum industry), monetary conservatism and moderate social spending. Even in the years of high oil prices (such as 2007–8 and 2012–13), the Russian state did not carry out a massive redistribution of petrodollars through ambitious social programmes because the financial authorities feared an increase in inflation and other macroeconomic effects. However, even though the Russian financial authorities were converts to the neoliberal faith, the Russian neoliberal paradigm differs from classical archetypes (Harvey 2005; Appel 2011). The basic difference between Putin's neoliberalism and the neoliberal practices of advanced capitalist economies is that in Russia all revenue flows into the state's coffers, while in the other neoliberal economies, at least in theory, wealth concentrates in the hands of banks and corporations. The key goal of Putin's economic policy, or Putinomics (Miller 2018), is to maintain macroeconomic stability and to ensure the continued existence of Putin's regime.

Venezuela as a paradoxical petrostate

Venezuela is a country with a nationalized petroleum industry. The oil sector was nationalized in 1975 and, as a result, the expropriated oil assets were concentrated in the hands of the newly established state-owned oil company PDVSA (Petróleos de Venezuela). During the oil boom of the 1970s and 1980s, PDVSA was a 'cash cow' for the government of Venezuela (Karl 1997). Even after the decrease in oil prices in 1986 PDVSA was a relatively efficient NOC, but at that time the efficiency of the petroleum sector did not translate into additional resource revenue for the state because the international oil price was low. David R. Hults points out the paradoxical situation that 'while PDVSA continued growing during the 1980s, the Venezuelan economy faltered' (Hults 2012, 428). In the 1990s the oil price remained very low, so these years can be characterized as the 'lost decade' of the Venezuelan economy.

Everything changed in 1998 when Hugo Chavez, a populist outsider, won the presidential election. During the electoral campaign, Chavez exploited the rhetoric of resource nationalism, according to which all profits from oil production should be owned by the people rather than international investors and corrupt elites (Hellinger 2016; Rosales 2018). After the electoral victory of 1998, the Chavez administration faced a deep political crisis in Venezuela. The old elites openly demonstrated their disloyalty to the new president and his reform agenda. Chavez launched a series of political and economic reforms aimed at dismantling the whole system of government, which had existed in Venezuela since 1958. Chavez carried out the constitutional reform and won the referendum of 1999, which polarized and politicized the divided Venezuelan society. While what Chavez wanted was to create a new political system through the destruction of the old regime (Brewer-Carías 2010), what ensued in the late 1990s and the early 2000s was the disorganization of the administrative capacity of the Venezuelan state.

The constitutional reform and the political conflict with the old elites in 1999 set the trajectory of the political development of Venezuela in the decades that followed. The weakening of formal political institutions in a bid to strengthen the political power of the authoritarian leader resulted eventually in the collapse of statehood in Venezuela. In the 2010s under Chavez's successor Nicolas Maduro, Venezuela looks more like a failed state than a prosperous petrostate.

In the first years of his presidency, Chavez launched the serious reform of the petroleum industry and the state-owned oil company PDVSA. The 2001 Hydrocarbons Law imposed very strict restrictions on the participation of international capital in the process of oil production in Venezuela. The implementation of this law resulted in the escalation of political conflict between the Chavez administration and PDVSA. The struggle for the autonomy of the company led to a series of strikes in PDVSA in 2002 and 2003. These strikes had very detrimental effects on the petroleum industry of Venezuela and the catastrophic decrease of oil production in the short term. For instance, in November 2002 the level of oil production was 3.3 million barrels per day, while in January 2003 the level of oil production was only 700,000 barrels per day (Hults 2012, 433). However, Chavez quickly took control of the situation in that '[d]uring early 2003, the government shed more than 18,000 of the company's 33,000 employees' (Hults 2012, 434). This decision by the Chavez administration was a catastrophe for the efficiency of the Venezuelan oil sector because many qualified workers lost their jobs.

All these actions by the Chavez administrations led to a decline in PDVSA's efficiency and the state's ability to collect revenues from oil production. However, the efficiency of the petroleum sector itself deteriorated as a result of the non-market regulation of petroleum prices in the years of Chavez's presidency. For instance, PDVSA was obligated to sell gasoline (petrol) at very low prices. Still today Venezuela has the cheapest gasoline prices in the world for domestic consumers. Low gasoline prices were an important instrument used by the Chavez regime to 'buy' the loyalty of the population. However, the production of cheap gasoline was money-losing for PDVSA and cost 15–20 billion dollars annually (Rodriguez et al. 2012). The production of cheap gasoline goes against the logic of the market economy, so the government of Venezuela had to subsidize PDVSA through various tax cuts. Hence, the production of cheap gasoline was very beneficial politically for Chavez but very expensive economically. In the long term, the production of cheap gasoline undermines the efficiency of the Venezuelan petroleum industry.

PDVSA was also required to assume other functions that are not typical for state-owned oil companies. Chavez's decision to take control of PDVSA and its management in 2002–3 resulted in the transformation of the role the company played in the economy and Chavez's state. The national oil company was obliged to provide some public goods to the population, while real formal institutions were partially destroyed and unable to function well. Under Chavez, PDVSA became a parallel state ('*estado paralelo*'), which assumed many of the functions of the central government. In addition to formal tax pressure on the company, the government of Venezuela imposed heavy non-budgetary obligations on PDVSA. David R. Hults points out that 'PDVSA has actually taken over more administrative functions than its pre-Chavez incarnation' (Hults 2012, 443). The expansion of PDVSA's role in regulating the economy allowed the Chavez administration to make up for its inability to run the bureaucratic apparatus due to the attempts of the old elites to block and sabotage all of Chavez's actions. While Venezuela's political system was fragmented and the state capacity of the country was low in the early 2000s, it was less risky for Chavez to spend petrodollars through the funds of PDVSA than to spend resource revenues through formal mechanisms and public institutions (such as the state budget).

Chavez implemented a very unusual model of resource rent allocation, which is atypical for petrostates with nationalized petroleum industries. In this model, a significant amount of the resource revenue is redistributed through non-budgetary mechanisms rather than through public spending of the state budget. The non-budgetary mechanisms of redistributing the oil revenue took the form of the Bolivarian missions targeted at solving social problems. These missions were a key instrument of social policy in the years of Chavez's presidency. All missions were funded primarily by PDVSA through informal funds, while the government did not participate actively in financially supporting these programmes.

The non-budgetary obligations of PDVSA, most of which were affiliated with missions, increased 30-fold between 2003 and 2008 (Hults 2012, 449). Kirk A. Hawkins points out that missions are funded primarily by direct transfers from PDVSA and estimates that 'only 8% to 24% of the funds came from the regular national budget, depending on the year' (Hawkins 2010, 199). In addition to the Bolivarian missions, PDVSA was obligated to fund the FONDEN (the National Development Fund), which was created in 2005 to implement infrastructure projects (schools, roads, hospitals, etc.). The principles of the work of FONDEN were equivalent to the Bolivarian missions. In total PDVSA sent 27 billion dollars to the fund between 2005 and 2008 (Hults 2012, 449).

The nature of the Bolivarian missions is very similar to the clientelistic practices of other Latin American countries, in which political leaders redistribute state revenue to targeted social groups through private goods rather than generating universalistic public goods to everyone (Stokes et al. 2013; Diaz-Cayeros et al. 2016). However, in Chavez's Venezuela, the budgets of the missions were so generous and ambitious that Hawkins is not sure that these social programmes can be classified as a classical example of clientelistic practices (Hawkins 2010). Matthew Rhodes-Purdy characterizes the clientelistic practices of the Chavez regime as 'participatory populism' (Rhodes-Purdy 2017) because ordinary citizens were allowed to participate in the operation of social programmes. Under Chavez the organizations of workers' councils, the so-called Bolivarian circles or *círculos bolivarianos*, were actively involved in the operation of Bolivarian missions. In other words, the political regime delegated the distribution of petrodollars (at least, a certain part of oil rents) to its core supporters at the local level. The Bolivarian circles formally were the institutes of civil society rather than the state, so this institutional architecture of the Venezuelan 'welfare state' could explain why the central government did not concentrate all its windfall oil revenues in the state budget.

Following the logic of the parallel state, PDVSA assumed some basic government functions, such as the provision of public goods (or private goods to be precise). The general level of public administration in Venezuela under Chavez was quite low, so it may have been more efficient to spend resource revenue through PDVSA and non-budgetary funds rather than spending petrodollars through formal institutions (such as the state budget). Chavez faced political resistance from the old elite and the bureaucracy in the first years of his presidency, so he had good reason to believe that the state apparatus was not loyal to him. The Venezuelan political elite was very fragmented, so Chavez did not have total control over the bureaucracy at all levels. Thus, he had to invent new, alternative mechanisms for the collection and redistribution of oil revenues as a way of risk-hedging for his regime under conditions of a fragmented political system and weak state capacity. For political reasons, the executive branch did not want to face the scrutiny of public spending by the parliamentary opposition (as well as opposition in regional governments), which was very active and powerful in the early 2000s.

In the years of Chavez's presidency, Venezuela faced classical manifestations of the resource curse such as economic troubles and the erosion of the state (including the radical weakening of state capacity and state institutions). Terry Karl points out that Venezuelan statehood has never been particularly strong (Karl 1997). Even in the 1970s and 1980s, during the 'golden age' of the Venezuelan economy, the political institutions of this Latin American country (and its state institutions) were far from being strong and effective. However, under Chavez, the quality of Venezuela's state capacity deteriorated so much that the state could not be an effective operator of social programmes anymore. In other words, the Venezuelan state could not guarantee Chavez full control over the collection and distribution of oil rents. The weakness of state capacity pushed Chavez to delegate the functions of the operator of social programmes to non-state actors such as the Bolivarian circles and PDVSA.

Conclusion

The abundance of natural resources carries both opportunities and risks for political leaders of oil-producing countries. On the one hand, resource rents are sources of political power since in resource-rich nations those who control the distribution of petrodollars control the distribution of power. On the other hand, power based on the extraction of natural resources eventually tends to destroy itself because the flow of oil rents tends to gradually erode state institutions, which leaders need to exercise their power. This erosion of the state (and its capacity) is one of the well-known manifestations of the resource curse in the academic literature (Karl 1997; Smith 2007).

The state is a core element of any political system, which legitimizes the existing political and economic order. However, the role of the state is especially strong in oil-producing countries because a rentier state takes the functions of the collection and redistribution of oil rents across social groups. In oil-producing countries, the state is usually a key instrument of resource rent allocation, without which political leaders cannot control the redistribution of petrodollars and exercise their power. The academic literature claims that in oil-exporting economies, the state often falls victim to the resource curse, which leads to weakening of its institutions. Under the conditions of weak state capacities, political leaders eventually lose the ability to use the state for successful collection and efficient redistribution of petrodollars for their political purposes. The fall of state capacity (caused by the resource curse) potentially undermines the foundations of political power in resource-rich countries as well as the ability of political leaders to use oil export revenues to hold on to power in the long term.

The ambivalence of power in oil-exporting economies manifests itself in the fact that oil rents are both a source of power and a major threat to its retention. The comparative analysis of Russia and Venezuela illustrates this power ambivalence of resource rent for Putin and Chavez. What unites both leaders is that they took almost all political advantages from the high oil prices of the 2000s and actively used windfall revenues for the maximization of their rule. At the same time, in the 2000s, both regimes faced serious economic and political risks, which could lead to the erosion of the state institutions of both countries and overheating of their economies. For Putin and Chavez, the boom of oil prices was not only 'the manna from heaven' but also a serious political risk, which they had to minimize to survive politically.

In both countries, political leaders had to implement various practices to minimize the potential political risks from the resource curse. However, Putin and Chavez dealt differently with side effects of the resource curse, including the risks of state capacity erosion. While Putin's regime managed to avoid the radical weakening of the state and even strengthened its capacity during the oil boom of the 2000s, Venezuela's state capacity in the 2000s deteriorated so much that Chavez had to establish alternative (non-state) mechanisms for the collection and redistribution of resource rent. The radical deterioration of Venezuela's state capacity pushed Chavez to transfer a few traditional state functions such as the operation of social programmes to PDVSA and the Bolivarian circles. The difference between Russia and Venezuela in resource rent collection (Tables 3.1 and 3.2) can be considered as the statistical illustration of the fact that during the oil boom of the 2000s the state capacities of these countries were not similar. Whereas Russia managed to minimize the political and economic threats of the resource curse (such as the weakening of the state), in Venezuela the political leadership failed to escape from the resource curse problems, including the collapse of state capacity.

The erosion of the Venezuelan state challenged Chavez's regime and pushed the political leadership to deprive the state of its traditional monopoly on the collection and redistribution of resource rent. The rise of the dysfunctionality of the state undermined the political power of Chavez because his administration faced the administrative inability of the Venezuelan state to redistribute petrodollars for the clientelistic needs of the regime. In the years of Maduro's presidency (after 2013), this problem was exacerbated by the general crisis of the regime's legitimacy, which led to the transformation of Venezuela into a failed state in the late 2010s (Corrales and Penfold 2015).

In contrast, in the 2000s Putin strengthened his power through the strengthening of the state and its ability to collect and redistribute oil export revenues. The neoliberal financial policy, for instance, was an important factor of Putin's success in the minimization of the risks of the resource curse in the 2000s. The increase of Russia's state capacity allowed Putin to maximize his personal power and stabilize his regime. However, the success of Putin's economic policy was not everlasting. In the 2010s the problems of Russian economic development – caused by geopolitical contestations as well as the resource curse – started to undermine Putin's power through the gradual erosion of state institutions and the stagnation of the economy. Triggering the growth of the Russian economy (and being the cause of Putin's power) in the 2000s, the abundance of natural recourses eventually turned out to be the fundamental obstacle to Russian economic development and a threat to Putin's power in the late 2010s and early 2020s. Therefore, every petrostate is a 'colossus with feet of clay', whose reliance on the extraction of natural resources strengthens the power of the state (and its leader) in the medium term but tends to undermine it in the long run.

References

Aleksashenko, Sergei. 2018. *Putin's Counterrevolution*. Washington, DC: Brookings Institution Press.

Appel, Hillary. 2011. *Tax Politics in Eastern Europe: Globalization, regional integration and the democratic compromise*. Ann Arbor: University of Michigan Press.

Aslund, Anders. 2019. *Russia's Crony Capitalism: The path from market economy to kleptocracy*. New Haven, CT: Yale University Press.

Auty, Richard. 1993. *Sustaining Development in Mineral Economies: The resource curse thesis*. London: Routledge.

Beblawi, Hazem and Giacom Luciani. 1987. *The Rentier State*. London: Croom Helm.

Bhattacharyya, Sambit and Roland Hodler. 2010. 'Natural resources, democracy and corruption', *European Economic Review* 54: 608–62.

Brewer-Carías, Allan. 2010. *Dismantling Democracy in Venezuela: The Chávez authoritarian experiment*. New York: Cambridge University Press.

Bueno de Mesquita, Bruce, Alastair Smith, Randolph Siverson and James Morrow. 2003. *The Logic of Political Survival*. Cambridge, MA: MIT Press.
Collier, Paul and Anke Hoeffler. 2004. 'Greed and grievance in civil war', *Oxford Economic Papers*, 56: 563–95.
Corrales, Javier and Michael Penfold. 2015. *Dragon in the Tropics: The legacy of Hugo Chávez*. Washington, DC: Brookings Institution Press.
Diaz-Cayeros, Alberto, Federico Estévez and Beatriz Magaloni. 2016. *The Political Logic of Poverty Relief: Electoral strategies and social policy in Mexico*. Cambridge: Cambridge University Press.
Dunning, Thad. 2008. *Crude Democracy: Natural resource wealth and political regimes*. Cambridge: Cambridge University Press.
Esping-Andersen, Gosta. 1990. *The Three Worlds of Welfare Capitalism*. Princeton: Princeton University Press.
Gaddy, Clifford and Barry Ickes. 2005. 'Resource rents and the Russian economy', *Eurasian Geography and Economics* 46: 559–83.
Gaidar, Ygor. 2007. *Collapse of an Empire: Lessons for modern Russia*. Washington, DC: Brookings Institution Press.
Gel'man, Vladimir. 2015. *Authoritarian Russia: Analyzing post-Soviet regime changes*. Pittsburgh, PA: University of Pittsburgh Press.
Guriev, Sergei, Anton Kolotilin and Konstantin Sonin. 2011. 'Determinants of expropriation in the oil sector: A theory and evidence from panel data', *Journal of Law, Economics, and Organization* 27: 301–23.
Gustafson, Thane. 2012. *Wheel of Fortune: The battle for oil and power in Russia*. Cambridge, MA: The Belknap Press of Harvard University Press.
Harvey, David. 2005. *A Brief History of Neoliberalism*. Oxford: Oxford University Press.
Hawkins, Kirk A. 2010. *Venezuela's Chavismo and Populism in Comparative Perspective*. Cambridge: Cambridge University Press.
Hellinger, Daniel. 2016. 'Resource nationalism and the Bolivarian revolution in Venezuela'. In *The Political Economy of Natural Resources and Development: From neoliberalism to resource nationalism*, edited by Paul Haslam and Pablo Heidrich, 204–20. New York: Routledge.
Hoffman, David. 2002. *The Oligarchs: Wealth and power in the new Russia*. New York: Public Affairs.
Hults, David R. 2012. 'Petroleous de Venezuela, S.A. (PDVSA): From independence to subservience'. In *Oil and Governance: State-owned enterprises and the world energy supply*, edited by David R. Hults, Mark C. Thurber and David G. Victor, 418–77. Cambridge: Cambridge University Press.
Jones Luong, Pauline and Erika Weinthal. 2010. *Oil is Not a Curse: Ownership structure and institutions in Soviet successor states*. Cambridge: Cambridge University Press.
Karl, Terry. 1997. *The Paradox of Plenty: Oil booms and petro-states*. Berkeley: University of California Press.
Kobrin, Stephen. 1985. 'Diffusion as an explanation of oil nationalization: Or the domino effect rides again', *Journal of Conflict Resolution* 29: 63–88.
Mahdavi, Paasha. 2014. 'Why do leaders nationalize the oil industry? The politics of resource expropriation', *Energy Policy* 75: 228–43.
Mahdavi, Paasha. 2020. *Power Grab: Political survival through extractive resource nationalization*. Cambridge: Cambridge University Press.
Mahdavy, Hossein. 1970. 'The patterns and problems of economic development in rentier states: The case of Iran'. In *Studies in Economic History of the Middle East: From the rise of Islam to the present day*, edited by M. A. Cook, 59–75. London: Oxford University Press.
Mann, Michael. 1984. 'The autonomous power of the state: Its origins, mechanisms and results', *European Journal of Sociology / Archives Européennes de Sociologie / Europäisches Archiv für Soziologie* 25: 185–213.
Menaldo, Victor. 2016. *The Institutions Curse: Natural resources, politics, and development*. Cambridge: Cambridge University Press.
Miller, Chris. 2018. *Putinomics: Power and money in resurgent Russia*. Chapel Hill: University of North Carolina Press.
Morrison, Kevin. 2015. *Nontaxation and Representation: The fiscal foundations of political stability*. Cambridge: Cambridge University Press.
Mueller, Dennis. 2003. *Public Choice III* (3rd edn). Cambridge: Cambridge University Press.

Nakhle, Carole. 2008. *Petroleum Taxation: Sharing the oil wealth: A study of petroleum taxation yesterday, today and tomorrow*. London: Routledge.

Rhodes-Purdy, Matthew. 2017. *Regime Support Beyond the Balance Sheet: Participation and policy performance in Latin America*. Cambridge: Cambridge University Press.

Rodriguez, Pedro L., José R. Morales and Francisco J. Monaldi. 2012. 'Direct distribution of oil revenues in Venezuela: A viable alternative?', *Center for Global Development Working Paper* 306, 1–34.

Rosales, Antulio. 2018. 'Pursuing foreign investment for nationalist goals: Venezuela's hybrid resource nationalism', *Business and Politics* 20: 438–64.

Ross, Michael. 2001. 'Does oil hinder democracy?', *World Politics* 53: 325–61.

Ross, Michael. 2004. 'Does taxation lead to representation?', *British Journal of Political Science* 34: 229–49.

Ross, Michael. 2008. 'Oil, Islam, and women', *American Political Science Review* 102: 107–23.

Ross, Michael. 2012. *The Oil Curse: How petroleum wealth shapes the development of nations*. Princeton: Princeton University Press.

Sachs, Jeffrey and Andrew Warner. 2001. 'Natural resources and economic development: The curse of natural resources', *European Economic Review* 45: 827–38.

Smith, Benjamin. 2007. *Hard Times in the Lands of Plenty: Oil politics in Iran and Indonesia*. Ithaca, NY: Cornell University Press.

Stokes, Susan, Thad Dunning, Marcelo Nazareno and Valeria Brusco. 2013. *Brokers, Voters, and Clientelism: The puzzle of distributive politics*. Cambridge: Cambridge University Press.

Treisman, Daniel. 2014. 'Putin's popularity since 2010: Why did support for the Kremlin plunge, then stabilize?', *Post-Soviet Affairs* 30: 370–88.

Vatansever, Adnan. 2021. *Oil in Putin's Russia: The contests over rents and economic policy*. Toronto: University of Toronto Press.

Volkov, Vadim. 2002. *Violent Entrepreneurs: The use of force in the making of Russian capitalism*. Ithaca, NY: Cornell University Press.

Volkov, Vadim. 2008. 'Standard Oil and Yukos in the context of early capitalism in the United States and Russia', *Demokratizatsiya* 16: 240–64.

Warshaw, Christopher. 2012. 'The political economy of expropriation and privatization in the oil sector'. In *Oil and Governance: State-owned enterprises and the world energy supply*, edited by David Hults, Mark C. Thurber and David G. Victor, 35–61. Cambridge: Cambridge University Press.

Wintrobe, Ronald. 1998. *The Political Economy of Dictatorship*. Cambridge: Cambridge University Press.

Wolf, Christian. 2009. 'Does ownership matter? The performance and efficiency of state oil vs. private oil (1987–2006)', *Energy Policy* 37: 2642–52.

Wright, Joseph, Erica Frantz and Barbara Geddes. 2015. 'Oil and autocratic regime survival', *British Journal of Political Science* 45: 287–306.

Yergin, Daniel. 1991. *The Prize: The epic quest for oil, money, and power*. New York: Simon & Schuster.

4
Contradictions of centralization: Four models of interaction between Russian rural communities and government and agribusiness

Alexander Nikulin and Alexander Kurakin

Introduction

The market reforms of the early 1990s triggered dramatic changes in rural Russia (for an overview, see Uzun and Shagaida 2015; Wegren et al. 2018). Unlike the Global South, Russia had a different starting position in the capitalist transition, as it shifted not from traditional agriculture to capitalist agriculture, but from already industrialized agriculture to capitalist institutions. However, that institutional shift came with a profound rearrangement of power relations in rural areas. In this chapter we analyse the ambivalent effect of power relations on sustainable rural development by providing the models of interaction of Russian rural communities with the government and large agribusinesses.

Recently, Russia has emerged as an important actor on the international food markets but is still struggling with many social problems in rural areas. Despite the rise of Russian agribusiness (state–corporate coalitions), statistical surveys indicate that many rural households have been abandoned and rural settlements have disappeared (Rosstat 2018), and that process is still under way. This contradiction of Russian agrarian capitalism is quite apparent, as it represents the ambivalence of capital per se, which produces both prosperity and poverty. However, other contradictions are less obvious. Russian rural territories (even neighbouring ones) evolve in different directions and at different speeds.

This chapter seeks to explain the uneven development of rural territories in Russia through the lens of ambivalent power relations. The capitalist transformation of Russian agriculture has led to well-documented differences between regions, such as fast growth in the south and equally fast decline in the north. The explanation of this difference is quite apparent: agrarian capital goes to fertile zones with favourable climate, while territories which previously received subsidies from the planned economic system now suffer from a lack of investments, although there are cases that contradict this trend.

Firstly, if we make a distinction between agriculture and rural territories, we have to admit that agricultural growth does not necessarily lead to rural development and vice versa. Numerous international studies show that the transition to capitalism in agriculture often comes with a lot of drawbacks, negatively affecting the lives of rural populations. Secondly, we can find examples of relatively sustainable areas against the background of desperate decline in rural life as well as contrasting examples of stagnation of rural life against the background of economic growth. Our chapter provides a set of case studies which aim to show the reasons for these counter-intuitive outcomes.

Of course, one can analyse various factors influencing the rural development of particular cases. This chapter considers just one, namely, the power relations in play in rural territories. This chapter shows the ambivalent results of that power. It argues that if we only consider the type of winners in a rural territory (for instance, agribusinesses versus smallholders), we will not be able to explain the contradictory outcomes for rural sustainability. The question is not just about who wins. Thus, we suggest that the degree of power concentration or decentralisation is an additional dimension of power relations, which helps to explain the contradictions of rural development.

Power in rural areas: rural communities, agribusiness and the state

From an economic perspective, we consider a rural territory to be a place with a combination of production factors: labour, land and capital. Historically, rural territories were synonymous with agricultural production. Later those concepts became disconnected not only logically, but also practically. However, despite there no longer being an a priori relationship with agriculture, our chapter focuses on rural areas which are used for agricultural production and depend on it.

From a social perspective, a rural territory is a place for people to live. Firstly, it includes the social infrastructure demanded by the local population: roads, gas, water, electricity, schools, hospitals, shops, entertainment and so forth. Secondly, it is related to the opportunities for people to earn a living. Vorbrugg (2019) called the erosion of the social dimension of Russian rural territories, which followed the market reforms, a 'dispersed dispossession'. He used that term to distinguish between popular land-grabbing discourse, which implies 'quick', visible and overt violence and is applied mostly to the Global South, and rural transformations in many Russian regions, where the struggle for land is not an acute problem at all. We consider the social dimension to be a source of legitimation for a given combination of labour, land and capital on a rural territory. It implies that local communities do not always fight for independence and self-government. Instead, they tend to support any combination of labour, land and capital, including a monopoly of state ownership or agribusiness, if it can provide decent social development. This may partly explain why, unlike in the Global South with its numerous rural resistance movements, the Russian rural population remains silent (Mamonova and Visser 2014).

We consider the combination of labour, land and capital through the lens of power relations in the economy. We use a simple interpretation of power as the capability to control labour, land and capital. By control we mean the ability to acquire those resources (from a rural territory itself or outside) and to manage their flows. On the one hand, access to production factors is necessary to start efficient production. On the other, the concentration of these factors in the hands of a single actor can also have negative social consequences.

The central argument of this chapter is that the concentration of power in economic relations leads to the concentration of labour, land and capital in the hands of a single actor (or homogeneous group of actors) and, in turn, results in the degradation of a rural territory.

This argument highlights the ambivalent role of power relations in sustainable rural development. It shows that positive or negative outcomes for sustainable development are not determined by who has the upper hand in a power struggle. It is not enough to identify the winner; it is equally important to figure out how the power is structured. Therefore, any winner (agribusiness, the state or smallholders) can produce contradictory results for a rural territory.

Critical agrarian studies used to blame the global corporate food system for its negative impact on sustainability. At the core of this critique lies the statement of monopolized power in the hands of transnational food corporations. Moreover, monopoly of economic power is criticized both from neoclassical economics and lefties, though each side suggests different remedies. While economists seek the solution in competitive markets and free trade, critical agrarian scholars suggest alternatives, which mostly rely on small-scale local producers and special market networks, which directly link producers with consumers, thus avoiding the global food system.

While supporting the general claim that monopolies tend to produce unsustainability, we argue that monopolization of economic power reveals its ambivalent effect. Firstly, at the level of organizational populations, monopoly takes the form of prevalence. For instance, while a single small-scale producer does not have substantial economic power, a whole sector can be dominated (prevailed) by small-scale producers. Below we show that this unification of the rural economic landscape can also have negative consequences in terms of sustainability.

Secondly, discussions on economic power often imply that power is always a desirable prize. However, if power is not taken but simply given, this statement becomes questionable. Power is complemented with capability, willingness and responsibility/risk. As a rule, large capital has all that and therefore seeks power, while the rural population often does not know what to do with power. Post-Soviet agrarian reforms in Russia serve as a good example of the ambivalent relations between the de-monopolization of centralized planned agriculture and sustainable rural development, when the rural population mostly ignored the opportunity to become a 'master' on their own land.

The Russian case shows that the concentration of power in the hands of any type of actor has a negative impact on rural sustainability. In this section we briefly illustrate our argument with reference to the extreme cases of agribusiness and household domination.

The domination of agribusiness turns a rural territory as a place to live into an agricultural territory as a space for food production. In extreme cases, the latter means that there is no need for people anymore, as the development of agricultural machinery leads to the further substitution of human labour in agriculture. The second option exemplifies to some degree the 'art of not being governed' (Scott 2009), which in Russia is not a happy tale either. Like Scott's stateless Zomia highlands of Southeast Asia, some remote Russian regions and settlements found themselves outside state control and regulation. Russian geography always helps people to avoid or reduce state control. Moreover, after the collapse of the centralized Soviet state, the capacity and willingness of the Russian government to control everything weakened substantially. Those communities can be labelled as autonomous, isolated or even autarkic (see Pozanenko 2018). However, in contrast to deliberate avoidance of state control in the case of Zomia, many Russian communities are not happy with the disappearance of the state. Here households obtain the power to control resources but are not able to attract investments. As a result, in extremely remote areas these communities turn to hunting and gathering, while in less extreme cases they abandon previously cultivated land, switch to non-agricultural activities or migrate. However, even in remote areas rural people can overcome the atomization of households and act as a community, which gives them opportunities for sustainable development.

The decentralization of power gives rural communities opportunities for development, as it provides a balance between these extreme situations. Decentralization means competition for production factors and, at the same time, the ability to obtain a sufficient amount of these factors for effective economic activity. Therefore, decentralization could mitigate the consequences of negative economic trends, while concentration could spoil the effects of economic growth.

We argue that the distribution of power (concentration or decentralization) serves as one of the factors explaining contradictions of rural development in Russia. The latter has been studied by many agrarian scholars, who provide considerable evidence for different models of evolution of rural territories.

During perestroika, in the final period of the Soviet Union, Shanin (1989) framed four models of Soviet agricultural development. The first model is based on the principle which prioritizes large and technically advanced agricultural enterprises (the period of Stalin's five-year plans). The second model represents the further enlargement of agricultural enterprises and intensive capital investments in agriculture and rural social infrastructure (the Khrushchev and Brezhnev periods). The third model questions the priority given to large farms and underlines the importance of personal interest on the part of rural labour in hard and responsible work (the importance of market stimulation in the perestroika period). The fourth model, while acknowledging the importance of economic interest, argues that the emergence of strong and independent rural communities is the key factor in sustainable rural development. In other words, successful agriculture is based on a socio-cultural foundation.

Neoliberal market reforms gave life not only to capitalist institutions and practices, but also to archaic social relations, complemented with residual Soviet practices. Nikulin (1999; 2002; 2003) studied those paradoxical hybrids and suggested models of patrimonial government, symbiotic appropriation and redistribution in post-Soviet large farm enterprises. These descendants of collective farms inherited the latter's dual internal structure, which consists of industrialized farms and a number of household economies of farm workers. These different parts, while having diverse interests, have to compromise with each other under the patrimonial management of the head of a farm (former kolkhoz or sovkhoz),[A] who has to find a balance between profit-seeking and social responsibility. That symbiotic model is slowly but surely transforming into the model of a capitalist farm, albeit preserving local differences (Nikulin 2002; 2010). Lindner (2002) suggested the model of reproductive cycles of wealth and poverty, which explains local differences in rural development.

Nefedova (2003) suggested a typology of rural regions in post-Soviet Russia, in which she sets out the continued differences between centres and peripheries as well as between fertile and non-fertile zones. Later, Pallot and Nefedova (2007) demonstrated the diversity of household agriculture in various regions. Nefedova (2013) suggested a number of models of rural development in non-fertile regions in central Russia and the Russian North. She underscores that it is impossible to preserve the Soviet model of intensive agriculture in these areas, so further depopulation and the abandonment of lands are inevitable. However, some local forms of activity and development seem possible. Those activities vary from farming, inherited from kolkhozes but reduced in scale, to the use of local natural resources (e.g., forests and rivers), tourism, as well as cultural, historical and ecological services. Pokrovskij (2008) also sees a way to transform the Russian northern rural territories by engaging in non-agricultural activities.

Pozanenko (2018) studied a number of remote or isolated rural settlements and suggested that autarky (autonomy, self-sufficiency) can sometimes strengthen the sustainability of a rural settlement. He also studied the exotic phenomenon of eco-villages (Pozanenko 2016), where inhabitants try to create autonomous communities based on various religious, philosophic or mystical ideas (see also Karpov 2017).

A Both are abbreviations. Kolkhoz is a collective farm (formally, artel or cooperative) while sovkhoz is a soviet farm, i.e. state-owned enterprise.

Averkieva (2017) proposed a symbiotic model for the Tarnog district in the Vologda region. Applying this model, she tries to explain the relatively successful development of the district despite its unfavourable geographic and economic location. Below we will use Averkieva's case study for our own classification.

Fadeeva (2015) distinguishes four institutional models of rural communities: corporate-paternalistic, corporate-entrepreneurial, family-consuming and family-entrepreneurial. Those models reflect the relative power and goals of corporate and family farming. One of her book's main ideas is that the prevalence of a single model leads to negative consequences for rural communities. We borrowed this idea for our analysis of power distribution in rural territories. However, our final classification differs notably from Fadeeva's.

We conclude that the majority of scholars identify four fundamental characteristics in the evolution of post-Soviet Russian rural communities: autarky (autonomy, self-sufficiency), symbiosis, plurality and monopoly. Considering previous findings, we suggest our own classification of diverse trends in Russian rural development: namely, roadside economy,[1] symbiotic economy, mixed economy and unipolar economy, each of which, in turn, has micro and macro versions (see Table 4.1). Our empirical research over the last decade also confirms that the evolution trajectory of rural communities dissolves into those four major directions.

We compiled the table using Shanin's (1988) concept of expoliary economies and Chayanov's (1966) approach to the theory of non-capitalist economic systems. However, the table serves illustrative purposes only. According to Shanin, the modern worldview identifies two poles of power, state and markets, while in-between those poles lie various forms of social institutions and relations, which are often

Table 4.1 Development models of Russian rural territories

	Roadside economy	Symbiotic economy	Mixed economy	Unipolar economy	
				Micro	Macro
State	−	+	+	−	+
Households	+	+	+	+	−
Small Business	+	+	+	−	−
Community	+	+	−	−	−
Markets	−	+	+	−	+

neglected by theoretical and political orthodoxy. The most important of those ex-polar structures are households, self-subsistent, self-employed economies, and local communities, which often represent the informal economy (households, small business and community in Table 4.1). Each model, therefore, is characterized by the visible presence or absence of those five types of actors/structures. Their interplay produces the distinct form of power distribution in a given rural community. Table 4.1 illustrates our case studies rather than providing a generalized argument.

The four models of rural development presented above are based on five case studies of rural settlements and districts in different Russian regions as well as on one generalized example of agribusiness dominance. The data on four case studies come from previous projects (based on a qualitative approach) and fieldwork by the authors in 2016–19. The relevant information is, therefore, drawn from various interviews.

The roadside economy model is exemplified by the cases of Stupnaya (10 interviews, 2017–18) and Malorossiyka (10 interviews, 2016). The mixed model is presented by Razdolnaya (55 interviews, 2017–18). The micro version of the unipolar economy model is reflected in the case of the Chernyshevsky district (10 interviews, 2019). We changed the real names of the settlements and the districts as well as the people's names. The example of a symbiotic economy model was borrowed from the article by Averkieva (2017). Finally, we showed the macro version of the unipolar model via a generalized example of agribusiness strategy in agriculturally attractive regions (near large cities and in fertile regions). Here we base our claims on 22 interviews from the Belgorod, Altai, Voronezh and Krasnodar regions as well as on publications by our colleagues.

Our set of interviews includes managers of corporate farms, farm wage labourers, local (regional or district) experts, family farmers, smallholders, local activists, local non-agricultural entrepreneurs and rural dwellers. That variety allows us to examine local events from different angles.

Case study of regional models of rural territories

The four models suggested above form a continuum from a situation in which power is concentrated in the hands of rural communities (roadside model) to a situation in which power is concentrated exclusively in the hands of either agribusiness or dispersed households (unipolar model). Between those extreme poles we place symbiotic and mixed models. A symbiotic model represents an equilibrium in power relations between communities, the state and business, with communities dominating. A mixed model represents the coexistence of diverse forms of agriculture, such as family, small, medium and large farms, with large agribusiness dominating.

Roadside economy

The roadside model of resource control is typical for peripheral, remote rural territories, which are unattractive for business and hard to reach for state control. Rural communities there tend to construct a locally specific and largely autonomous way of living, relying mostly on their own resources and capabilities and trying to preserve and develop local economic self-sufficiency. We provide two examples of roadside economies.

Stupnaya is a village located in the midst of taiga forests in the southern part of the Archangelsk region and has historically always been one of the most peripheral agricultural regions in the Russian North, where almost 120 rural settlements have vanished in the last half-century. However, Stupnaya exemplifies resistance to the steady depopulation of the rural Russian North. One of the most remote villages in the district, Stupnaya is connected with other settlements by unsurfaced roads, which are almost impassable in autumn and spring.

Stupnaya was established in the eighteenth century as the centre of a cluster of small villages (10–15 households each). After collectivization, Stupnaya became the central settlement for a local kolkhoz. In the 1960s, according to a typical architectural plan, the kolkhoz constructed a square in the centre of Stupnaya with three wooden buildings in the local style – a kolkhoz office, a club and a school combined with a kindergarten. At the end of the Soviet period over 400 people lived in Stupnaya, while today only 200 remain. Moreover, the Stupnaya settlement cluster shrank to its centre, and tiny villages of the cluster became completely depopulated. Only a few houses there still serve as summer cottages for the descendants of the original owners, who now live elsewhere.

According to late Soviet as well as post-Soviet agricultural criteria, Stupnaya has a very disadvantageous location in economic and geographical terms. However, it survived and is even developing relatively well in comparison with the majority of the rural settlements in Kargopol, which have either already vanished or are quickly shrinking. We now discuss the reasons for its viability.

When considering the disappearance of rural settlements in Russia today, we have so far only mentioned external economic–geographical factors. However, internal factors relating to the socio-cultural organization of local communities are no less important. For instance, in recent decades rural settlements in a number of Russian regions which preserved their traditional rural ethnic, religious and communal values have demonstrated a higher degree of viability.

At first glance, Stupnaya does not possess any specific traditional rural virtues. It is not a settlement of Old Believer Christians with strict religious discipline, nor is it either a Tatar or Bashkirian ethnic community with dominant values associated with a traditional rural lifestyle. Indeed, Stupnaya is still populated almost exclusively by local people, but that does not explain its viability in the globalizing market economy despite the rough northern climate.

First of all, we underline the personal factors such as the management skills of local leaders (e.g., directors and entrepreneurs). Already in the late Soviet period, the well-being of a kolkhoz community strongly depended on the chairman's decision-making and motivation. Stupnaya was lucky with its chairman, a native man, who managed the local kolkhoz from the mid-1960s until the end of the 1980s. In that period, Stupnaya obtained its social infrastructure, relatively advanced milk production in the kolkhoz, which was symbiotically combined with household agriculture and logging. Stupnaya inherited a solid Soviet legacy that helped it to survive in the later years of the market reforms of the 1990s. For almost a decade the former kolkhoz struggled for survival but was unable to adjust to the new economic environment and deal with the problems of marketing and re-equipment. Finally, the farm collapsed in the late 1990s and local households took the residual cows from the farm's herd. However, households were not able to find sales channels for their milk, as it was hard for them to transport milk such a long distance. Thus, the remote location of Stupnaya hindered its economic integration into wider market networks. The economy of Stupnaya shrank to subsistence household agricultural production and precarious jobs in logging nearby. It led to intensified out-migration, alcoholism and offensive behaviour.

A new crisis manager, Morozov, revived milk production in Stupnaya. He managed to obtain loans for new equipment and a milk herd, combining milk farming and timber processing. In a short period, Stupnaya milk farms became some of most productive not only in the district but in the Archangelsk region as a whole. Moreover, Morozov spends the farm's resources to support the social infrastructure of the village. He converted economic success into political capital by winning the district election to the Archangelsk parliament. In turn, this position helps business, increasing the possibilities of obtaining loans and subsidies.

As is the case with many agricultural post-Soviet farmers, Morozov combines the elements of a capitalist entrepreneur with a Soviet executive. On the one hand, Morozov acquired over half of the farm's shares and has now become its de facto majority owner. On the other, he carefully maintains the image of continuity between his current management and the previous kolkhoz practices. He put together old and new photos, documents and graphs on the walls of the farm office in a bid to convey the historical continuity of milk farms in Stupnaya. During conversations and meetings with the workers and local dwellers, he demonstrates his respect for Soviet traditions.

The second factor supporting Stupnaya's viability is the activism of the local community. For example, an active religious community emerged in Stupnaya, headed by an active priest and churchwarden. As a result, one of the first churches in a rural settlement in the district was built in Stupnaya. Moreover, Stupnaya has an active territorial self-government organization (TSO), which has accomplished several infrastructure projects (for instance, improvements to the children's playground). The TSO and religious community together supported the construction of a small wooden hostel near the church. Those examples show that, despite Stupnaya's community not being the driving force behind local activism, it still provides a favourable environment for it. Although local people do not initiate activities, they are ready to support them.

Another important feature of Stupnaya's community is that people are capable of conscious collective action in the public interest. They became, at least partly, a community for themselves. People engaged in collective action in response to an attempt at a hostile takeover of the milk farm by Archangelsk businessmen from the timber industry. Seven years ago, the businessmen surprised everyone when they suddenly turned up at a general meeting at the milk farm. They criticized Morozov and offered shareholders a good price for the farm's shares. Back then, the prospects for the milk farm were uncertain and, therefore, their offer had a good chance of being accepted. It was an emotional meeting. The 'invaders' promised fantastic prospects for everyone. However, the working collective decided that the unexpected visitors were interested only in predatory logging in the surrounding forests and would simply sell off their newly created milk farms. As a result, the vast majority of the shareholders decided to decline the offer and demonstratively sold their shares to Morozov during the meeting, thus making him the controlling shareholder.

Today, the remote village of Stupnaya represents a site of economic and social stability, surrounded by declining rural areas in the Russian North. The milk farm is steadily modernizing; Morozov provides a sufficient number of jobs for the villagers on the farm and in logging. He also uses his administrative position as a deputy in the local parliament to win additional subsidies for the farm and for the social sphere of Stupnaya. The local religious community and TSO also contribute to rural development. In sum, the combination of talented leaders and local activism provided viability even to such a disadvantageously located village as Stupnaya.

The second example of a roadside model is the case of the village of Malorossiyka in Altai Krai (see Kulunda 2020). Malorossiyka stands in the middle of a windy Kulunda steppe near the border with Kazakhstan. It was established in 1908 by peasant migrants who participated in the peasant migration campaign initiated by Stolypin's agrarian reforms. Some 135 people lived in Malorossiyka in 1991 but today only 38 inhabitants remain. In Soviet times, a branch of a larger sovkhoz was located in Malorossiyka and specialized in crop production (wheat and sunflowers). As elsewhere, local kolkhozes and sovkhozes were in a severe crisis after the collapse of the Soviet Union. The sovkhoz went bankrupt in the mid-1990s. Therefore, the Malorossiyka branch was reorganized into a partnership of peasant farms, which also had no success in farming, as the traditional specialization in grains did not suit that relatively small, family-based mode of production. One of the leaders of the partnership, Kashira, a native of Malorossiyka, decided to radically change the specialization of the enterprise. He switched to the exotic (for the steppe region) practice of goose breeding, as Malorossiyka has access to water resources from the nearby lake and artesian wells. Crop production was reduced to forage grain, while from 1997 to 2018 the geese headcount increased from 3,000 to 25,000. Kashira and the workers of the goose farm had to acquire new knowledge, purchase special equipment and construct new buildings without sufficient money for investments. Therefore, they did it slowly, step by step, repurposing old equipment when they could.

Today, the goose farm in Malorossiyka is a stable, profitable enterprise with well-thought-out logistics. Its produce goes not only to consumers in Altai Krai, but also to Khakassia, Kazakhstan, Novosibirsk, Novokuznetsk and Kemerovo. Paradoxically, these trade linkages only strengthened the peripheral mode of living in the tiny Malorossiyka community. As Kashira explains, 'today it is better to live and work on one's own, trying to reduce any sort of dependence on anyone and anything'. Unlike Altai producers of grain, milk and meat, who have to intensively compete with each other, the goose farm in Malorossiyka has not yet faced any worthy competitors. There is stable demand for goose meat for thousands of kilometres, the prices are lower and the product is more marketable in comparison with alternatives. Several farmers tried to copy Kashira's project but did not succeed. Kashira and his staff acquired the elements of local knowledge in goose breeding. That local knowledge may seem somewhat mystical. For example, Kashira argues, 'geese fertility and weight increment depend even on the strength and direction of winds in this area'.

Other branches of local agriculture (grain, meat, milk, vegetables and fruits in households) provide production for internal consumption, and together they significantly limit the Malorossiyka subsistence economy's dependence on the outside world. Moreover, Kashira even supports this autonomy. For instance, he delayed for as long as he could establishing an internet connection, as he expected that this would result in the intensification of bureaucratic control and requests for accounting and reporting. Furthermore, like in other agricultural regions in Russia, cases of land grabbing and redistribution happen in Altai Krai, although Kashira's farm has not yet been the target of a hostile takeover. However, a major businessman offered Kashira a good price to sell his farm but Kashira refused. Kashira identifies himself not as an entrepreneur but as the leader and protector of the local community and his native land. He commented on his refusal to sell the farm:

> He does not care; he snatches what he wants and goes away. He does not need the village; he does not need the pensioners. To sell the farm to a man like him means to betray … everything you live for and everyone you are proud of. No way. It seems that I have to prolong my duty of a watchman of the village and memory.

The district administration does not intensively interfere in local life, as there are plenty of other depressed rural settlements with high unemployment rates. Therefore, economically stable Malorossiyka serves as a successful example which does not require help and subsidies.

Both examples of relatively successful roadside economies show the significant role of local leadership that seeks a balance between local economic self-sufficiency and carefully selected connections with the outside world of markets and municipal and state administrations. Large capital rarely wants to capture local resources in those remote areas simply because the latter are not economically attractive. But even when outsiders try to do it, local leaders and communities resist and fight for their autonomy. Local administrations also like autonomous, self-sufficient settlements because they do not claim support and do not create trouble. The major weakness of communities such as these is their dependence on their leaders, who cannot survive forever. Respondents from those communities clearly understand that and feel concerned about it. This problem is especially acute when the leadership is not backed up by local institutions and solidarity.

Symbiotic model

The symbiotic model of control and redistribution of local resources is based primarily on the coexistence and interpenetration of various branches of the local economy as well as on the fusion of formal and informal institutions and practices. Like roadside economies, symbiotic models are also typical for non-fertile Russian regions and peripheral settlements, although not for remote, almost isolated places, which are favourable for the emergence of roadside economies. Furthermore, symbiotic systems require larger communities than roadside economies and they can emerge in the centres of rural settlement clusters or even in the centres of districts.

An example of a symbiotic model is the Tarnog settlement (and Tarnogsky district more broadly) in the Vologda region, which was investigated by Averkieva (2017). Tarnog is the centre of the district on the north-eastern periphery of the Vologda region with a population of slightly over 3,000. It is located far from Vologda city and from railroads and federal highways. However, it demonstrates one of the most stable and successful economic developments in the region. We argue that the reason for this success, despite the unfavourable economic location, is the well-designed symbiotic combination of local economic activities and social institutions.

Tarnog has the advantage of being a long-inhabited territory with local traditions, lifestyle and community. Furthermore, unlike many other long inhabited regions in Russia's non-fertile zone, Tarnog managed to preserve its community, trust and social capital, which was strengthened by protective local policies. As a result, economic power is decentralized and dispersed between communities, local business and administration. This system provides not only economic flexibility but also the ability to resist the external invasion of large capital.

For several post-Soviet decades, Tarnog has demonstrated the benefits of the coexistence between timber processing and family farming dispersed throughout surrounding clusters of tiny rural settlements (10–15 households each). In 2016, 95 small timber processing firms were active in the Tarnogsky district. They process wood for the local market and contract with a wide network of traders. They produce a wide range of intermediate wooden products as well as process logging waste (e.g., fuel briquettes, bedding for cattle, toilet filler).

Agriculture and forestry have always been intertwined in the northern non-fertile territories. The Tarnog district has 11 small milk farms, which were established on the ruins of former kolkhozes. The majority of those farms are affiliated with timber-processing firms. As timber production is on average more profitable than milk farming, the local administration sometimes enforces and encourages symbiosis between timber and milk production. A dairy factory, which was constructed in the Soviet period, still plays the central role in local milk farming. It creates sufficient demand for milk from local milk farms and sells packaged milk and butter to other districts in the Vologda region and even to the Archangelsk region. This flexible symbiotic system creates the basis for the sustainable development of Tarnog.

Nonetheless, Tarnog's enterprises and community more broadly are not autarkic at all. Tarnog's timber processing firms are well-known suppliers to Moscow markets. They are able to redistribute their labour and financial resources between timber and milk production, thus adjusting to market fluctuations. According to Averkieva, the local population is also ready and able to engage in flexible labour, switching between timber processing, milk production and gathering forest fruits and vegetables (mushrooms, berries, herbs, etc.). As a result, the population of Tarnog has remained stable for the last 30 years of the post-Soviet period, which stands out against the tendency towards depopulation in the northern non-fertile zone at large.

Large timber enterprises as well as agribusiness have not yet tried to acquire local producers. Firstly, local wood resources would be insufficient for large capital. Secondly, large investors seek out large enterprises. Indeed, it is much easier to take control of a single large producer and invest in re-equipment with technologies suitable for large-scale production than to deal with more than 90 small firms as in Tarnog. Although large timber holding is a more productive enterprise with modern and effective machines than small firms, the latter provide more jobs. Moreover, a network of small timber firms produces a more diversified range of goods, while a huge holding tends to specialize in mass standardized products. Finally, small timber firms are registered in Tarnog and pay taxes directly to the local budget. Those reasons prevent the local administration from attracting large investors. The director of the milk plant underlined in an interview that, on the one hand, the milk plant seeks to promote its products to various regions, but, on the other, he eschews publicity in a bid to avoid unnecessary attention to his enterprise from outsiders.

Thus, symbiotic, as well as roadside, organizational models of rural communities demonstrate some sort of distrust towards outsiders, especially if they are large and powerful and, therefore, can destroy the local equilibrium of interests and power relations.

Mixed model

The mixed model is more relevant for rural communities of Russia's central and southern fertile regions. The rural areas here are more attractive for commercial agriculture and are densely populated. As a result, these regions demonstrate greater variety in the composition of agricultural producers. While in the Russian North and the remote Siberian areas only household production, occasional individual smallholdings and sporadic agricultural and timber enterprises prevail, fertile regions demonstrate highly diversified mixed economies of households, small and large family farms, independent agricultural enterprises and huge agribusinesses.

Rural communities in these attractive, well-developed and market-oriented regions have about 3,000–7,000 inhabitants. It is impossible to find isolated communities or symbiotic economic systems here because intensive competition and the struggle for resources destroy local communities of economic actors based on trust and mutual support.

The village of Razdolnaya in the Krasnodar region is an example of a mixed-model rural community. Razdolnaya was founded by Cossacks 150 years ago. In the late Soviet era economic life in Razdolnaya was organized around a prosperous kolkhoz, which cultivated a land area of about 14,000 hectares. In the 2000s, the chairman and the chief managerial staff (accountant, agronomist, livestock specialist, economist and engineer) privatized the kolkhoz land and equity and established six agricultural enterprises based on six former kolkhoz production teams (brigades). Each enterprise has 2,000–3,000 hectares and is well equipped with agricultural machines. Razdolnaya also has several small family farms, which were organized during the agricultural reforms at the beginning of the 1990s.

In contrast to Razdolnaya, the neighbouring agricultural enterprises (former kolkhozes) were bought out by agribusinesses from Kransodar, Rostov and Moscow. Razdolnaya only managed to avoid a takeover because the former kolkhoz was divided into several relatively small farms. Therefore, they became less attractive for agribusinesses, as the latter prefer to acquire an entire kolkhoz with all its land. The takeover of six medium-sized farms in Razdolnaya one by one would have been a long and costly process, so agribusinesses did not make any serious attempts to acquire the land of the former kolkhoz.

However, when, after several bad managerial decisions, one of the six farms was on the brink of bankruptcy, one of the corporate farms immediately bought it. The other corporate farm acquired 230 hectares of the former kolkhoz land, recultivated it and started to produce apple saplings for sale.

This mixture of several family farms, medium-sized agricultural enterprises, a couple of representatives of agribusiness and household agricultural production favours intensive competition, which boosts labour productivity that, in turn, causes local unemployment. Although family farmers, independent farms and agribusinesses seek to buy out shares in the land from the former kolkhoz members, more than a half of Razdolnaya's inhabitants still own the shares. Therefore, agricultural producers compete fiercely for the right to rent the land, which leads to steadily increasing land prices and rent.

The relatively advantageous economic position of the community shareholders is not reinforced by the local self-government, which is not able to influence social and economic processes on the territory. As a result, Razdolnaya represents a rural territory of relatively prosperous and successful households, farms and agribusinesses, but it does not constitute a rural community with its own interests.

Unipolar economy

Unipolar models emerge as a result of either government policy or economic expansion by powerful market actors, leading to a decrease in the variability of organizational forms. It represents a single economic mode of production, which survived after a transformational shock or came to power and dominates alternative organizational forms. Generally, it decreases the possibility of the sustainable development of local communities, as they have to rely on a single alternative.

Soviet collective agriculture, dominated by large, industrialized state-governed farms, fuelled the tendency for the unipolar model. Alternative forms of peasant farming and capitalist farms were forbidden, while agricultural cooperatives were also under state control. However, collective farms evolved into a kind of symbiotic system between large farms and household economies of their members/workers. Moreover, Soviet collective farming favoured diversified production and avoided monocropping. Thus, organizational monopolization was compensated for by production diversification. Paradoxically, it was the post-Soviet reforms which sought to diversify the agricultural landscape that led to the increasing unification of rural areas.

Today, the above-mentioned unipolar model takes two opposite forms. The first, micro form constitutes self-subsistence households of a local ageing population. The reorganization of collective farms led to their collapse but no alternative organizational forms emerged in their place, including efficient peasant farms united in a broad cooperative network, as the reformers had planned. The dominance of household production leads to poverty and out-migration. Rural municipalities have no resources to maintain the local social infrastructure.

The second, macro form results from the invasion of huge capitalist investors, who use rural territories to organize high-technology agricultural production. This expansion of large capitalist farms takes place mostly in the fertile central and southern parts of rural Russia and often leads to the oppression of alternatives in the form of small and medium-sized agricultural enterprises and family farms via land grabbing. Large capital usually orients itself towards monocultures that bring maximum profits, thus erasing the local variability of crops, organizational forms and occupations. Moreover, their declarations of social responsibility very often stay only on paper. Paradoxically, such high-technological agriculture often comes with unemployment, poverty and the deterioration of the local social infrastructure.

Below we give examples of both sides of the unipolar model. The Chernyshevsky district in the Moscow region exemplifies the dominance of the household economy. It is still one of the most backward districts in the Moscow region. Therefore, the wave of dacha (second or summer house for Russian urban population) building has not yet affected it. From 1991 to 1996, the district was headed by a local native, a well-known 'foreman of perestroika'. Being an advocate of market reforms, Muravkin consistently implemented them in his territory. First, instead of the formal reorganization of kolkhozes and sovkhozes, he decisively dissolved them. Second, he managed not only to redistribute land shares on paper but to register real pieces of land (five hectares each) to former members of the kolkhozes and sovkhozes.

The results were discouraging. The vast majority of the newly emerged owners of five hectares of agricultural land could not become efficient market-oriented farmers. The reasons were quite obvious. The land size was insufficient for profitable agriculture. People were not ready for entrepreneurial activities; they lacked knowledge of modern agricultural production. Individual farming did not receive enough support from the state and cooperative organizations. They faced unfavourable pricing for agricultural produce and so forth. As a result, the inhabitants of the villages in Chernyshevsky had neither the capability nor the desire to cultivate the entire five-hectare piece of land. Instead, they proceeded to cultivate only their household plots, just to provide for themselves. Moreover, the district could not attract any large-scale agricultural producers to substitute for the dissolved kolkhozes and sovkhozes. As a minimum, investors need hundreds (or better several thousands) of hectares to start profitable agriculture, while the transaction costs of collecting that amount out of five-hectare parcels are very high. Agricultural land, uncultivated for many years, needs additional investment. In addition, the production infrastructure of former kolkhozes and sovkhozes almost disappeared. That is why investors prefer neighbouring districts, where local administrations kept the land undistributed and preserved the infrastructure of large Soviet enterprises.

Only over the past decade has the dominance of parcel agriculture in the Chernyshevsky district slowly begun to develop towards a mixed model. First, the number of small family farms increased. While in 2010 there were only five active smallholdings, in 2020 the number increased to 50, including five relatively large farms cultivating hundreds of hectares. Many of the newly created farms try to specialize in eco-food and recreation services. The five-hectare parcels are gradually being re-registered as land for country housing. In sum, the Chernyshevsky district is slowly transforming its unipolar model into a mixed model of eco-food production, recreation and country housing.

The second generalized example of the opposite form of a unipolar model comes from the suburban regions of Moscow and St Petersburg (Nefedova 2013) as well as from some black-earth regions. Here we refer to the studies by Fadeeva (2015) in the Belgorod and Novosibirsk regions as well as our own fieldwork in the Belgorod, Altai, Voronezh and Krasnodar regions (see, for instance, Visser et al. 2019). Large agribusinesses radically transform the lives of local communities. Firstly, agribusinesses construct huge buildings for poultry and/or pork production near villages. Those agricultural factories emerge as closed territories for reasons of veterinary and economic safety. Secondly, large enterprises tend to hire workers from neighbouring administrative centres and provide corporate buses to transport them to the farm in the morning and from the farm back home in the evening. Sometimes, they even build special cottage settlements for their staff. Thirdly, agribusinesses tend to eliminate any competitors in the territory, including households which have chickens or pigs. Fourthly, unlike kolkhozes and sovkhozes, which usually maintained the social infrastructure in the villages, agribusinesses rarely display socially responsible behaviour, except for situations in which the regional administration forces them to do so (as in the Belgorod region, for example).

Conclusion

The case studies presented here show that sustainable rural development depends on power relations and power distribution in rural territories. It is the ambivalence of that power which produces the variety of outcomes shown above. We argue that any sort of concentration of economic power can lead to negative social outcomes. Of course, this is only one of many factors which contribute to sustainable rural development.

In conclusion we discuss the issue of power legitimacy, which serves as an additional source of the ambivalent effect of power on sustainable development. Case studies of power concentration show that the problem of legitimacy is unsolved here. Agribusinesses try to avoid it by minimizing any dependence on local communities. Large companies tend to buy or grab the local land and use capital and labour from outside. The reverse case of the Chernyshevsky district (the dominance of smallholders) shows that land reform did not comply with what local people needed and wanted.

On the contrary, the roadside economies which we observed managed to solve the legitimacy problem. We can say that it is the only reason why those communities survived. The communities of both Stupnaya and Malorossiyka are largely dependent on their local farms, which people profoundly support.

Successfully solving the legitimacy issue is the precondition for the evolution of the mixed and symbiotic models described above. Legitimacy in the mixed, symbiotic and roadside models stems from the ability to contribute to the development of the social dimension of rural territories. It does not mean that they produce prosperity, especially in roadside economies with poor populations. It means that local inhabitants see them as a valuable source for their livelihoods.

However, we do not argue that the prevalence of either agribusinesses or smallholders always fails to legitimate local power. We purposively chose cases which contradict the arguments of proponents of both large-scale and small-scale agrarian capitalism to highlight the ambivalence of power relations.

The chapter goes beyond the widespread critique of the predatory and exploitative nature of agrarian capitalism. Instead of claiming that small is beautiful, we argue that variety is beautiful. The case of rural Russia shows that beyond exploitation and dispossession, agrarian capitalism produces diverse outcomes. Every case which we examined indicates a distinctive form of capitalist relations, produced by the ambivalence of power.

Acknowledgements

Support from the Program for Basic Research of the National Research University Higher School of Economics (HSE University) is gratefully acknowledged.

Notes

1   We prefer to use the term 'roadside economy' instead of autarky or isolation because it is less strong and restrictive. Our cases are less extreme, and therefore more widespread, than those described by Pozanenko (2018), where regular transport links are either almost or literally absent.

References

Averkieva, Ksenia. 2017. 'Simbioz sel'skogo i lesnogo hozyajstva na staroosvoennoj periferii Nechernozem'ya: opyt Tarnogskogo rajona Vologodskoj oblasti' [Symbiosis of agriculture and forestry on the early-developed periphery of the non-black earth region: the case of the Tarnogsky district of the Vologda region], *Russian Peasant Studies* 2: 86–106.
Chayanov, Aleksandr. 1966. *The Theory of Peasant Economy*, edited by Daniel Thorner, Basile Kerblay and R. E. F. Smith. Homewood, IL: Richard D. Irwin.
Fadeeva, Olga. 2015. *Sel'skie soobshchestva i hozyajstvennye uklady: ot vyzhivaniya k razvitiyu* [Rural communities and economic structures: from survival to development]. Novosibirsk: IEIE SB RAS.
Frühauf, Manfred, Georg Guggenberger, Tobias Meinel, Insa Theesfeld, and Sebastian Lentz (eds.). 2020. *KULUNDA: Climate Smart Agriculture: South Siberian agro-steppe as pioneering region for sustainable land use*. Cham: Springer.
Karpov, Anatoly. (2017). 'Forum "Ustojchivoe razvitie poselenij" na Dobroj zemle' [Forum 'Sustainable Development of Settlements' in the Dobraya Zemlya (Kind land in the Vladimir region)], *Russian Peasant Studies* 2: 191–4.
Lindner, Peter. 2002. 'Differenciaciya prodolzhaetsya: reprodukcionnye krugi bogatstva i bednosti v sel'skih soobshchestvah Rossii' [The differentiation continues: reproductive circles of wealth and poverty in Russia's rural communities]. In *Refleksivnoe krest'yanovedenie: desyatiletie issledovanij sel'skoj Rossii* [Reflexive peasant studies: a decade of studies of rural Russia], edited by Teodor Shanin, Alexander Nikulin, and Viktor Danilov, 386–406. Moscow: Rosspen.
Mamonova, Natalya and Oane Visser. 2014. 'State marionettes, phantom organisations or genuine movements? The paradoxical emergence of rural social movements in post-socialist Russia', *Journal of Peasant Studies* 41: 491–516.
Nefedova, Tatyana. 2003. *Sel'skaya Rossiya na pereput'e: Geograficheskie ocherki* [Rural Russia at the crossroads: geographical essays]. Moscow: Novoe izdatel'stvo.

Nefedova, Tatyana. 2013. *Desyat' aktual'nyh voprosov o sel'skoj Rossii: otvety geografa* [Ten relevant questions about rural Russia: the answers by a geographer]. Moscow: Lenand.

Nikulin, Aleksandr. 1999. 'Konglomeraty i simbiozy v Rossii: selo i gorod, sem'i i predpriyatiya' [Conglomerates and symbioses in Russia: rural and urban, families and enterprises]. In *Neformal'naya ekonomika: Rossiya i mir* [Informal economy: Russia and the world], edited by Teodor Shanin, 240–69. Moscow: Logos.

Nikulin, Aleksandr. 2002. 'Kruphozy sovremennoj Rossii: varianty razvitiya' [The 'krupkhozy' – the large farms of present-day Russia and the different ways of rural development]. In *Refleksivnoe krest'yanovedenie: desyatiletie issledovanij sel'skoj Rossii* [Reflexive peasant studies: a decade of studies of rural Russia], edited by Teodor Shanin, Alexander Nikulin, and Viktor Danilov, 407–19. Moscow: Rosspen.

Nikulin, Aleksandr. 2003. 'The Kuban kolkhoz between a holding and a hacienda: Contradictions of post-Soviet development', *Focaal* 41: 137–52.

Nikulin, Aleksandr. 2010. 'Oligarhoz kak preemnik postkolhoza' [Oligarchoz as the successor of a post-kolkhoz], *Journal of Economic Sociology = Ekonomicheskaya sotsiologiya* 11: 17–33.

Pallot, Judith and Tatyana Nefedova. 2007. *Russia's Unknown Agriculture: Household production in postsocialist rural Russia*. Oxford: Oxford University Press.

Pokrovskij, Nikita. 2008. 'Perspektivy rossijskogo Severa: sel'skie soobshchestva' [The prospects of Russian north: rural communities], *Mir Rossii* 17: 111–34.

Pozanenko, Artemy. 2016. 'Samoizoliruyushchiesya soobshchestva: Social'naya struktura poselenij rodovyh pomestij' [Self-isolated communities: the social structure of kin's domain settlements], *Mir Rossii* 25: 129–53.

Pozanenko, Artemy. 2018. '"Otdel'naya tipa respublichka": strukturnye osobennosti prostranstvenno izolirovannyh lokal'nyh sel'skih soobshchestv' ['A separate little republic': structural specifics of spatially isolated local rural communities], *Mir Rossii* 27: 31–55.

Rosstat. 2018. *Itogi Vserossijskoj sel'skohozyajstvennoj perepisi 2016 goda. T.8. Atlas perepisi* [Results of the Russian agricultural census in 2016. Vol. 8. Census atlas]. Moscow: Statistika Rossii.

Scott, James. 2009. *The Art of Not Being Governed: An anarchist history of upland Southeast Asia*. New Haven, CT and London: Yale University Press.

Shanin, Teodor. 1988. 'Expoliary economies: A political economy of margins: Agenda for the study of modes of non-incorporation as parallel forms of social economy', *Journal of Historical Sociology* 1: 107–15.

Shanin, Teodor. 1989. 'Soviet agriculture and perestroika: Four models: The most urgent task and the furthest shore', *Sociologia Ruralis* 29: 7–22.

Visser, Oane, Aleksandr Kurakin and Aleksandr Nikulin. 2019. 'Corporate social responsibility, coexistence and contestation: Large farms' changing responsibilities vis-à-vis rural households in Russia', *Canadian Journal of Development Studies* 40: 580–99.

Vorbrugg, Aleksandr. 2019. 'Not about land, not quite a grab: Dispersed dispossession in rural Russia', *Antipode* 51: 1011–31.

Wegren, Stephen, Aleksandr Nikulin and Irina Trotsuk. 2018. *Food Policy and Food Security: Putting food on the Russian table*. Lanham, MD: Lexington Books.

5
Legitimation of innovation: The case of AI technology for facial recognition

Leonid Kosals

Introduction

Social ambivalence is closely tied to both social change and resistance to social change (Hajda 1968, 25). As such, social ambivalence is an essential part and by-product of innovation. Innovation includes so-called creative destruction (Schumpeter 2010) – the emergence of some new products, technologies, organizational forms, institutions and so forth and, at the same time, removal of outdated elements of technological and social systems. This 'embedded ambivalence' is ramified in various parts of an organization and society, including social realms such as markets, enterprises, non-governmental organizations (NGOs), families, values and power relations.[1] Alongside positive technological change, this ramification produces uncertainty, social tensions and disorganization within these realms, in particular damaging the system of social values.

The focus of this chapter is the societal response to ambivalence in innovation. Apparently, the purpose of this response in all times and circumstances is to make favourable conditions for acceleration of the benefits of innovation and to neutralize its destructive aspects. However, in various countries with different socio-economic and socio-cultural settings, understanding of the positive outcomes and destructive effects may vary. What is perceived as unacceptable in some settings is considered quite normal in others, and vice versa. And these variations significantly depend on the system of values.

In his seminal book *Active Society*, Amitai Etzione (1968) argued that if society is going to protect its core values from the destructive aspects of technological change, it should actively change itself by undergoing societal restructuring. The focus of the book was on societal change as a response to the dark side of innovation, which can harm society, even if it is inactive. However, the book did not consider societal 'activeness' in the realm of innovation: the active societal response to the social selection and restructuring of the realm of innovation, which also serves to protect the core values of society, was not analysed properly. Meanwhile, if we look at the diffusion of various innovations in different socio-political and socio-cultural contexts, we can see that the same innovation can be accepted in some countries and rejected in others due to active changes being made to specific innovations in order to protect core values. Despite the fact that there have been many studies on the social aspects of innovation since the publication of *Active Society* (see the updated look on *Active Society* in McWilliams 2006), the link between core values and the social selection of innovation remains understudied.

Active Society came out at the beginning of the third industrial revolution, when information technologies started changing industry and society. The ongoing fourth industrial revolution has now renewed the research agenda for studies into the link between core values and technologies. At the core of the fourth industrial revolution is the transformation of the production process at industrial enterprises, the emergence of the so-called smart factory that will operate as a 'cyber-physical system'. This system is a set of computer-controlled processes and objects, including robots, which interact with the external environment, where software and physical elements closely intertwine and interact with each other in many ways automatically and without human intervention (Mousterman and Zander 2016). Such enterprises will be very flexible, paying much greater attention to individual customer requirements than traditional management. At the same time, due to its greater flexibility and customization, it can serve a much broader, global market than traditional industrial companies. These will be highly automated firms in which cloud technologies, big data, the Internet of Things, 3D printing and so forth will be widely used, with decentralized decision-making (Shrouf et al. 2014; Wang et al. 2016). Artificial intelligence (hereinafter referred to as AI) is a kind of electronic brain of such enterprises, which is necessary to coordinate the functioning of various elements of a smart enterprise, as well as to provide a flexible interface when a person interacts with its various subsystems. In this capacity, it is an essential element of the fourth industrial revolution (Skilton and Hovsepian 2018; Benotsmane et al. 2019). Therefore, for this research I have chosen AI technology as one of the key elements of the fourth industrial revolution, often representing the bright side of the innovation.[2]

Meanwhile, AI technologies have their dark side, which is reflected in public opinion. On the one hand, there are acute, traditional (anti-) technological fears about the jobless economy, technological unemployment, inequality and so forth (Aronowitz and DiFazio 2010; Frey and Osborne 2013; Mokyr et al. 2015). The global COVID-19 pandemic, alongside the many widespread conspiracy theories, exacerbated these fears.

On the other hand, the empirical evidence does not support many of these fears, although some of them turn out to be well founded. For example, a recently published extensive study of the influence of robots on the labour market in 74 developed and developing countries in 2004–16 showed that robotization positively affects labour productivity and employment and negatively influences inequality in the sample as a whole: 'It further appears that increased robot adoption makes the rich become richer, although no evidence of so-called technological unemployment is witnessed' (Fu et al. 2021, 678). Additionally, robotization influences developed and developing countries heterogeneously: there is a positive effect on labour productivity and employment in developed countries but no significant evidence for such in developing states (Fu et al. 2021). This is evidence of embedded ambivalence in the influence of new technologies on society and its core values during intense processes of change, while the diffusion of innovation is at an initial and therefore fragile and contested stage. Therefore, it is still unclear what the balance sheet of pros and cons of innovation is and to what extent innovation harms the core values of society.

In this chapter, I offer several methodological lenses for the study of the legitimation of innovation as a useful tool for understanding why in some socio-economic contexts innovation is thriving, whereas in others it has been inhibited or even stopped. I argue that there are opposite responses to the embedded ambivalence in innovation from countries with various core values: democratic with high value of human rights versus non-democratic states where human rights are undervalued. The first group is represented by the United States and Canada, whereas China represents the opposite side. Russia is in-between these two opposite entities. Being 'between East and West',[3] Russia has ambivalent core values, which makes it an especially interesting case for analysing innovation, as a study of 'double ambivalence', since innovation itself has a dual nature.

The chapter includes a literature review where the classic and modern views on legitimacy are considered. Then I describe the methodology of the case study to apply to AI facial recognition technology in comparative socio-economic and cultural contexts. This piece includes the analysis of variations in the societal response to ambivalence in innovation in four countries: Canada, the US, Russia and China. The chapter ends with a discussion of the proposed case and my conclusions.

The literature review

The classic view on legitimacy, developed by Emile Durkheim and Max Weber, focused on the legitimacy of authority and the state. They researched the moral grounds of political authority, the state and state building to analyse the social roots of sustainable political order beyond force and violence to explain why individuals do or do not support law and order and political authority. As Weber argued, 'the basis of every system of authority, and correspondingly of every kind of willingness to obey, is a belief, a belief by virtue of which persons exercising authority are lent prestige' (Weber 1964, 382). As is well known, he identified three major sources of legitimacy: tradition, charisma and the legality of authority.

Emile Durkheim, who considered the state an 'organ of social thought',[4] argued that to establish a social order, two-way relations should be in place whereby the people obey social order and the state 'tells them what is right'.[5] At the same time, it is worth noting that he outlined the difference between the West and Russia in these two-way relations:

> In the West, the state has succeeded in superimposing itself on political orders already in existence and divided among themselves by all sorts of conflicts of interest, and it has made it its business and *raison d'être* to merge them and unify them. In Russia, by way of contrast, it is unity that is more of a primary factor, and it is the state that has dispersed the population into distinct political orders; it is the former which has divided the inhabitants into categories and classes in order to give society a more solid base. (Durkheim 1998, 345)

In other words, according to Durkheim, in the West society is relatively autonomous from the state and they interact as equal entities at least, while in Russia the state plays the prime and leading role in shaping the social order. Potentially, this approach assumes that there can be various problems with legitimizing authority in Russia and that the role of moral grounds and citizens' obedience can be different from the West too.

In the twentieth century, Carl Schmitt played a prominent role in the study of legitimacy. He revealed and analysed the conflicted relationship between legitimacy and legality in the 1930s (Schmitt 2004), which is of special importance for this research. Schmitt demonstrated the controversial relationship between the two concepts in that any social phenomenon can be simultaneously legal but illegitimate or illegal but legitimate. In turn, this conflict can generate social controversies in various political and economic structures, which can harm the core values of society and often may only be resolved after much social upheaval and loss of life. For example, the conflict between legality and legitimacy in the Weimar Republic that was the focus of Schmitt's study was only resolved by Germany's defeat in the Second World War.

Considerable research on legitimacy in disciplines such as political science, economics and management, law and criminology, public administration, anthropology and sociology has been carried out over the last few decades.

Sociological research on the legitimacy of innovation began relatively recently, mainly in the past two decades. In these studies, legitimacy is treated as a social process, where legitimacy can be acquired through social interactions by participants in the development, diffusion and use of a new product (technology, organizational form or services) among themselves and with the state and society, including local communities, city residents, NGOs and others (Johnson et al. 2006). In this chapter, this very process of acquiring (or not acquiring) legitimacy will be called legitimation. I categorize these studies into two groups. The first includes the legitimacy of innovation when a new market for a new product emerges (Navis and Glynn 2010; Markarda et al. 2016; Wang et al. 2019). The second focuses on the legitimacy of innovation in particular companies or any other agents (Blanco et al. 2013; Petkova 2018; Schoon and DeRoche 2019).

A good example of research in the first group is Navis and Glynn's study of the legitimacy of satellite radio technology in 1990–2005 (Navis and Glynn 2010). In order to understand how new markets emerged, the authors analysed the diffusion of the technology by means of qualitative and quantitate data. They revealed that the technology was legitimized in 2002 when it became widely available in the retail sector and its subscribership grew significantly. Overcoming the legitimacy threshold in 2002 led to the institutionalization of the technology. The self-presentation of the companies and the attention of the consumer then shifted from the shared, collective identity (as 'satellite radio' providers) to the individual firms. This helped some companies achieve a competitive advantage and, in particular, to occupy a more exclusive satellite radio category (for example, as a premier sports channel).

A good example of research in the second group is Petkova's study of the legitimation of digital technologies in the recently established e-commerce fashion industry (Petkova 2018). She showed how one of the newly established players in this industry struggled to achieve legitimacy in the eyes of traditional fashion companies as well as their peers in digital fashion. The author revealed that traditional fashion media companies that mimicked online their traditional offline practices but did not closely interact with their online peers failed. They relied on the pragmatic legitimacy of their offline parental companies and failed because of the lack of moral legitimacy in the realm of digital fashion. Interestingly, some major internet companies, possessing moral and pragmatic legitimacy in the digital space, failed in the digital fashion industry due to their lack of pragmatic legitimacy in traditional fashion. Meanwhile, the company in question, while achieving pragmatic legitimacy in the traditional fashion industry, established alliances with their peers in digital fashion that helped them achieve moral legitimacy in both worlds, traditional and digital fashion. As a result, being an outsider at the very beginning, the company later became one of the largest global e-commerce fashion retailers.

Sociological studies of the legitimacy of innovation have identified four stages of legitimation (Johnson et al. 2006). In the first stage, the innovation emerges in response to an existing unmet need, often at the local level. In the second stage, the innovation is adopted locally. It acquires support and a social licence to operate in a limited space, including a separate small group, organization or territory. In the third stage, the innovation starts to be diffused when it begins to be accepted by other local communities. Finally, in the fourth stage, the innovation is widely diffused when it becomes familiar to large social groups, jurisdictions, territories and states. At the same time, the legitimation of one or another innovation may not go beyond any of these stages. For example, it may stop at the second stage, that is, not go beyond the local community.

However, these studies failed to address the social mechanisms underpinning the legitimation of innovation having an ambivalent nature, in particular the role of the core societal values. What are the factors that influence legitimation in various political, socio-economic and socio-cultural contexts? Do core values play any role? These are the main research questions for the research presented in this chapter.

Research methodology

Depending on the focus of analysis, the literature distinguishes between different types of legitimacy, such as international legitimacy (Neuman 2018) or political legitimacy (Giannini 2018). Given the focus of our research, we will consider the legitimacy of innovation in three social contexts: the state, business and the population. While it is, of course, possible for legitimacy to be recognized in only one or two contexts, such as business and the state, the particular form of innovation must be recognized in all three contexts for it to acquire 'full' legitimacy. In some cases, 'partial' legitimacy may be enough for the successful diffusion of the innovation; for example, business legitimacy may be sufficient for a business-to-business niche innovation. In other situations, for example, if an innovative product is offered to the population and the population 'does not recognise' it, partial legitimacy can quite significantly slow down the diffusion of innovation.

With regard to the essence of the innovation process, I distinguish three types of legitimacy: cognitive, pragmatic and moral. The cognitive includes more or less complete and realistic information and knowledge about the content of the innovation. Pragmatic legitimacy is expressed in the belief that the innovation brings practical benefits (financial profits, improved satisfaction of a particular need, achievement of political goals, etc.). Moral legitimacy means that the innovation has a moral justification, helps to achieve higher social goals and does not violate moral norms but rather promotes social justice and the integration of communities and society as a whole, contributes to the improvement of people's lives, helps vulnerable social groups and so forth (Kumar and Das 2007; Bunduchi 2016; Petkova 2018). In other words, these three types of legitimacy reflect the extent to which different social groups have knowledge about new technologies, whether they believe that these technologies bring practical benefits and in what form, and also whether they harm society and its highest social goals. In this chapter, I plan to focus on both pragmatic and moral legitimacies.

At the same time, the acquisition of legitimacy or legitimation is a social process, that is, it unfolds over time, embracing the four aforementioned stages. All these stages are accompanied by social interactions between the actors in the development and implementation of the innovation between themselves and the external environment.

In this study I proceed from the assumption that the diffusion of the innovation (AI technologies) depends on its legitimation: if these technologies are legitimate, then the social interactions of the agents contribute to the acceleration of the development and diffusion of AI technologies; if they are not, then social barriers arise in AI's path, which complicate or even halt its development and diffusion.

At the core of the problem under examination is *the ambivalent relationship between pragmatic and moral legitimacies*: pragmatic legitimacy can be achieved without the moral legitimacy associated with the threat of potential or real harm to higher social goals (morality, social integration, etc.), first of all, because of creative destruction. The speed and success of the diffusion of AI technologies as well as their real socio-economic effect and the trade-off between benefit and harm depend on how this conflict is resolved in a particular state, jurisdiction or territory.[6]

Nevertheless, the diffusion of illegitimate innovations (or innovations with contested/partial legitimacy) is possible if there is pressure from the state or influential non-state actors, which, in turn, can lead to various negative formal and informal social and economic effects and forms of dysfunction for individuals, organizations and society in general.

These cases are of particular interest for our research and therefore we are intentionally considering a case of diffusion of innovation with 'contested' legitimacy. Such cases explicitly highlight the role of core societal values in contrast to cases where legitimacy was achieved without significant controversy because in the former case the involved actors are certainly in the position of having made an actual choice. Concisely, it is the case when values matter.

To study the legitimation of innovation we chose the case study methodology. As John Gerring argued, comparing this methodology to the conventional quantitative approach, its strength lies in the opportunities for the analysis of the causal mechanisms: 'the opportunities for investigating causal pathways are generally more apparent in a case study format' (Gerring 2007, 48) and '[c]ase studies are thus rightly identified with "holistic" analysis and with the "thick" description of events' (Gerring 2007, 49).

Looking for a case of AI technology with 'contested legitimacy', I selected facial recognition technology, where the legitimacy of AI technology is challenged and its diffusion is controversial and faces opposition in society, especially its use by the police. I describe the legitimacy of this technology in North America, China and Russia, cases where there are acutely salient differences in the outcomes of the social mechanism for legitimation.

The case of facial recognition technology

Canada

The Office of the Privacy Commissioner of Canada (OPC) released the Joint investigation of Clearview AI report (Joint Investigation of Clearview AI, Inc. 2021) on its investigation of the activities of the US-based firm Clearview AI on 2 February 2021.[7]

Clearview AI offers police departments and other law enforcement agencies a computer-based AI facial recognition system. The data set for this software includes almost 4 billion computer images and related personal data, which were collected from social media and other open internet sources. Hundreds of law enforcement agencies throughout North America use this technology, although Clearview AI has suspended sales of the technology to private firms since mid-2020. This technology showed very high efficiency and some police officers who use it say it is helping to solve crimes:

> In February (2019), the Indiana State Police started experimenting with Clearview. They solved a case within 20 minutes of using the app. Two men had gotten into a fight in a park, and it ended when one shot the other in the stomach. A bystander recorded the crime on a phone, so the police had a still of the gunman's face to run through Clearview's app. They immediately got a match: the man appeared in a video that someone had posted on social media, and his name was included in a caption on the video. 'He did not have a driver's license and hadn't been arrested as an adult, so he wasn't in government databases,' said Chuck Cohen, an Indiana State Police captain at the time. (Hill 2020)

Although police in North America have used facial recognition technologies for almost two decades, they are restricted to government-generated data sets and, as a result, their capacity is much less than that of Clearview AI; even the FBI's database is ten times smaller (Hill 2020).

The aforementioned report argued that this technology violates the Privacy Act and cannot be used in Canada because the personal data included in the database were collected without the consent of citizens. Moreover, there was a requirement for Clearview AI to remove all information about residents of Canada and not to use it in Clearview AI products in other countries. Previously, about 50 organizations in Canada had used Clearview AI technology, but most of them suspended its use after the OPC announced the launch of an investigation in mid-2020. The release of the report means a de facto ban on its use in Canada.

This is not the first time in Canada that the OPC has called for a ban on facial recognition technologies. The OPC released a report on their investigation of the Cadillac Fairview Corporation Limited (Joint Investigation of the Cadillac Fairview Corporation Limited 2020) at the end of 2020. The report concluded that Toronto-based Cadillac Fairview, one of North America's largest office owners, had built software in its information kiosks in 12 large malls that collects images of visitors without their knowledge and estimates their approximate age and sex, as well as other information. In total, they collected more than 5 million images of buyers. The report argued that this practice was contrary to the Privacy Act. The day after the report was released, Cadillac Fairview announced that it was removing the software in question from its information kiosks.

In Canada a considerable number of academic articles and reports as well as reports from human rights organizations have analysed algorithms and AI technologies, including facial recognition. Many of them included critical assessments of the dangers of these algorithms in terms of human rights violations,[8] which also played a role in shaping public attitudes towards these technologies.

This, of course, does not mean that facial recognition technologies, and AI technologies in general, are prohibited in Canada. However, this suggests that they face a rather tough social filter, embedded in the public's fears that these technologies may cause them some significant harm. This filter prevents facial recognition technologies from being diffused as quickly as they would otherwise be if only economic and technological factors were at play.

The United States

The United States is characterized by a much wider variety of legal and enforcement practices. In particular, there is no federal privacy law that could limit the diffusion of AI facial recognition technologies to the same extent as in Canada. Facial recognition technologies such as Clearview AI are used in many US regions and cities but in some they are also restricted or prohibited. The social response to these technologies is strong and varied. In particular, the authorities of a number of states, individuals and companies, including Facebook, YouTube and others, filed lawsuits against Clearview AI. However, not all claims have been resolved in the courts. In some police departments, commercial facial recognition technologies, including Clearview AI, are forbidden, for example, in the Los Angeles police department, one of the largest in the United States. Thus, the legitimation of facial recognition technologies in the United States is still in process and, while it is unclear what restrictions society wishes to place on them and what requirements society has of them, they are now in the process of being formed as a result of the discussion of lawsuits and public debates. At the same time, there is also a significant corpus of academic articles and reports from human rights organizations with critical assessments of these technologies.

The situation in North America by no means exhausts the diversity of the process of legitimation of AI technologies.

China

Unlike North America, China has almost no barriers to the diffusion of facial recognition technologies or any other AI technologies. There have been no human rights lawsuits, public criticism or opposition to these technologies, which, of course, does not mean that everyone in China supports them. It is known that in China they diffuse at a very high rate. For example, there were more than 100 million people using facial recognition technology for mobile payments in 2019, which, of course, facilitates and speeds up the payment process but comes with a loss of privacy (Kawakami and Hinata 2019). There are many uses for this technology in China, including its extensive use by the police and other law enforcement agencies, one example being the total surveillance and control system established in the Xinjiang Uygur Autonomous Region (Leibold 2020). It includes a whole range of modern technologies (voice and facial recognition, GPS tracking and other machine learning technologies) aimed at achieving the socio-political and ethno-cultural goals of total control and changing the behaviour and consciousness of an entire ethnic group.

Moreover, China actively exports electronic surveillance technologies to many countries: these Chinese technologies are now used by consumers in more than 80 countries (Greitens 2020). Of course, many of them, including Russia, are trying to diversify their supply and not depend solely on China (Kovachich 2020). It is unclear, however, to what extent is it not only the technologies that are exported, but also the accompanying socio-cultural norms and standards for their application.

PwC has predicted that AI technologies will make a 14 per cent contribution to the growth of the world economy in the period 2017–30, which is approximately 15.7 trillion dollars, of which China will be the main beneficiary, gaining a 26 per cent share, while North America will achieve an average of just 14 per cent (Rao and Verweij 2017).

Russia

Facial recognition technologies are actively developed and used in Russia. For example, one of the world's largest urban video surveillance systems has been set up in Moscow (Kovachich 2020). In explaining their extensive investment in the system, the Moscow authorities argued that it would do a lot to fight crime in the city. However, no solid evidence has been provided about how successful and effective this system has been in fighting crime. People have reasonable doubts about establishing facial recognition in Moscow, which could be derived from the existence of the so-called *palochnaya systema*, the quasi-centralized system of planning in operation in Russian law enforcement (Paneyakh 2014). This system incentivizes police officers who select which cases to pursue to reject those that are hard to solve. Very often, police officers refuse to register such 'hard cases' and address only offences that are easy to investigate and where it is easy to convict a perpetrator. As a result, people have a lack of confidence in the police and often do not report crimes at all. Therefore, the Russian criminal justice system is overwhelmed with latent crime, including offences that the police refused to register or that were not reported by the victims. And facial recognition technology cannot eliminate this institutional feature of the criminal justice system rooted in the peculiarities of Russian politics.

However, there is considerable evidence that this system is being used beyond regular crime fighting, firstly by targeting activists engaged in political protest.[9] Secondly, the system was extensively used during the COVID-19 pandemic. The Moscow authorities as well as those of some other cities established a system of so-called social monitoring to trace people who had contracted the coronavirus based on facial recognition and then punish those who violated the rules. For example, in Moscow up to July 2020, more than 447,000 people were registered on the system, and nearly 94,000 penalties were imposed, mostly for leaving home,[10] despite the technology's 20–25 per cent error rate; even in cases of technological errors, penalties have sometimes still been upheld by the courts.[11] In other words, the system was used not to fight crime but to control people's behaviour.

Moreover, a black market for offers to access the facial recognition system has emerged in Moscow (Kaganskikh 2019). Anyone willing to pay a small amount of money (200–300 US dollars) online can be granted limited access to the facial recognition system in Moscow to trace her/his business competitor, wife or husband and so forth.

This causes, among other things, public criticism, similar to that which exists in many Western countries from the standpoint of human rights violations. In Russia, lawsuits were also filed against these technologies on grounds of human rights violations based on the Federal Law of 27 June 2006 No. 152-FZ On Personal Data. However, all the decisions of the courts went against the plaintiffs.[12]

Thus, in Russia, the social filter, although it has some effect, is obviously weaker than in North America and, as a result, the video surveillance system continues to expand, without encountering salient obstacles that such technologies face in some other countries. For example, quite recently, at the height of the coronavirus pandemic, in December 2020, the Moscow authorities announced an auction to develop technology for the recognition of human silhouettes.[13]

Discussion: power with and without ambivalence

The case study of AI facial recognition technology shows that the acceptance and diffusion of innovations are not only dependent on technological, economic and legal factors. While it is, of course, important how well a particular technology works, how much profit it generates for a business and whether its application violates the law, it is also very important to understand the diffusion of innovations as a social process. It involves many actors with their own systems of values and motives, and it depends on the attitude of both society as a whole and various influential social groups, organizations and institutions, including human rights organizations, political parties, government agencies and others. Their position, assistance or opposition can have multiple consequences for the diffusion of a particular innovation. Possible consequences could be that the innovative products will turn out to be too expensive due to the introduction of additional regulatory standards (taxes, labour safety standards, etc.), may be slowed down due to the requirements of additional expertise and the provision of information on safety, for example, or stopped altogether.

Thus, it may turn out that the same technology can diffuse quickly and smoothly in one socio-political and cultural context (country or region), more slowly and with difficulty in a second, and be generally prohibited in a third.

Power is well embedded in the social interactions about the diffusion of innovation in a 'Foucauldian' way: it is everywhere (Foucault 1998). And every step the innovation takes along the path towards legitimation is the result of many encounters by the 'micro-powers', where sometimes those interested in pushing innovation through and those interested in blocking it interact with each other. Of course, often the trajectory of their efforts can finally coincide, and then legitimacy is successfully achieved or happily blocked. There is no explicit ambivalence of power in such a case.

However, power is well embedded in creative destruction too. As such, power is an element of the embedded ambivalence of innovation since creative destruction is an essential side of the innovation process and some parts of the technological and social systems should be removed to provide legitimacy and diffusion of innovation. During power conflicts at legitimation, both agents of innovation and potential victims use their own powers. The former try to innovate, while the latter strive to protect their status. In the case of AI facial recognition technologies, the victims of creative destruction are large social groups who can lose their individual privacy and human rights.

After all, the outcomes of this struggle depend on core values.[14] One of their dimensions is the role of human rights, support for which is high in democratic and low in non-democratic societies. In Canada, which, among our case studies, has the most stringent human rights laws including the Privacy Act, the social filter is the toughest, with many AI facial recognition technologies banned despite their potential economic benefits. In other words, although pragmatic legitimacy was achieved, the moral legitimacy of some facial recognition technologies failed. In the United States, where human rights are not so consolidated as in Canada, the moral legitimacy of the same technologies is contested, and their legitimation is still in process.

In China, with its socialist system of appropriate collectivist values without a pronounced idea of human rights for individuals, both pragmatic and moral legitimacies are achieved. As a result, the diffusion of facial recognition technologies is the fastest.

In the cases of Canada and China, there is no explicit evidence of the ambivalence of power, whereas the cases of Russia and the United States are more complicated.

Russia is an interesting case of a society with pronounced ambivalence in its core values. On the one hand, Russia has laws for the protection of human rights including the Federal Law on Personal Data. The contents of the Russian laws on human rights are not much different from those in the West, including North America. On the other hand, the authorities and courts in Russia often do not use these laws in the same way as in the West. This is because the gap between 'law in action' and 'law on the books' (Gould and Barclay 2012) is significantly larger in Russia than in the West. This gap is so big that one can talk of selectivity in Russian law enforcement.[15]

This is in line with the Russian legal tradition with its legal dualism, formalism, technicality and instrumentalism of the law (Hendley 2011; Borisova and Burbank 2018; Kurkchiyan 2018; Bækken 2019). This legal setting shapes the preconditions for the ambivalence of power while legitimizing facial recognition technologies: the Russian authorities maintain the Law on Personal Data and simultaneously push through the innovation with contested legitimacy, which may violate this law. The Russian authorities not only fail to initiate investigations, as in Canada, or conduct due process, as in the United States, but also, when citizens go to court, the authorities usually dismiss their claims or informally influence the judges to refuse a plaintiff's case. We could call this the Russian-style relationship between state and society, as Durkheim argued. However, in contrast to the late nineteenth and early twentieth centuries, this relationship has become saliently ambivalent because the society in Russia today has become more active than at that time. This understanding is rather in line with the critiques and further developments of Durkheim's analysis of Russia, as M. Gane argued, considering Durkheim's thesis that Russian society is rather the product of the state, and not vice versa.

This is not I think to be interpreted, as Horowitz has recently suggested, to mean that this inversion of state and society was 'the source of autocracy, an order based on coercion rather than on consent' (Horowitz 1982, 371) but to suggest 'the limits, the superficiality of the society thus created' (Gane 1984, 327). Moreover, Russian society, being in some sense relatively 'superficial', appeared as active, trying to protect its core values in its interactions with an authoritarian state in the case of the legitimation of facial recognition technologies.

As a result, the decision of the authorities to push the diffusion of facial recognition technology without full legitimacy has produced some negative effects. This means that, although pragmatic legitimacy is achieved in terms of political gain for the authorities, there is no full moral legitimacy and therefore there is no clear path for the diffusion of facial recognition technologies in Russia, as there is in China.

In the US case, where there is no ambivalence in society's core values, the source of the ambivalence in power, with regard to the legitimation of innovation, is the highly decentralized legal system and mechanism of law enforcement, with the lack of a federal law regulating personal data usage. As a result, the conflict between pragmatic and moral legitimacy is played out in protracted disputes between citizens (human rights advocates, NGOs) and the companies making facial recognition technologies. Both parties possess some 'micro powers'. The mosaic of clashes between such 'micro powers' in the United States constitutes the ambivalence of power in the legitimation of facial recognition technology.

There is a kind of trade-off between pragmatic and moral legitimation, and one can be achieved at the expense of the other. Finally, this trade-off depends on the core values that define the criteria for pragmatic and moral legitimation. For example, human rights are among the criteria for moral legitimation in North America, in contrast to China. Hence, China will benefit from economic growth, although this is fraught with the risk of stoking social tensions if the values of Chinese society begin to change in the long run. In the other scenarios, if North America lags in terms of economic growth, it can accelerate new AI technologies without violating human rights, or perhaps they will be forced to downgrade human rights as a criterion of legitimacy. In Russia, for pragmatic legitimation, political gains for the authorities are a top priority, in contrast to economic gains and human rights in North America.

Conclusion

The legitimation of innovation has many dimensions. For example, it can include a legal component, the mobilization of existing laws (Black 1973), and in principle, the development of new legal norms can be initiated too. It can include certain actions by civil society, for example, criticism in the press or protests against a particular innovation, economic policy measures, including the direct stimulation by the state of some innovations, and so forth. However, it should be borne in mind that all these actions to one degree or another reflect the core values of society. So, a legal ban on the diffusion of a particular innovation on the grounds of human rights law reflects the value of human rights in society: if they are highly valued, the law is used; if not, then the corresponding legal norms either do not exist or are not applied. In other words, values act as a kind of 'trigger' that 'turns on' (or 'does not turn on') the action of various social institutions.

As a matter of fact, the legitimation of innovation works as a particular system of social immunity, which includes social filters that slow down the diffusion of innovation, adjust them or change them in line with societal values as well as, in certain cases, stopping their diffusion if society believes that they could cause significant social harm. At the same time, the structure of this social immune system can differ from society to society, depending on political, cultural and other institutions. The system of social immunity includes a set of criteria by which society is guided, including values, when it 'filters out' some innovations and gives the green light to others. The ambivalence of power reduces the efficiency of social immunity and produces various negative social effects when powerful actors push through innovation with contested legitimacy. Although in principle it is known that the legitimation of innovation can have a positive economic effect, a deeper knowledge of these criteria and an understanding of how they 'work' will make it possible to better predict the successes and failures of the diffusion of various innovations in different socio-economic, political and cultural contexts.

Acknowledgements

The author appreciates the support from the Program for Basic Research of the National Research University Higher School of Economics (HSE University, Moscow).

Notes

1. I borrowed the term 'embedded ambivalence' from the paper written by Miller (2020), where ambivalence was analysed as an essential element of the problem under study.
2. The initial stage of the study was carried out with M. M. Yachnik and published in Kosals and Yachnik (2020a) and Kosals and Yachnik (2020b).
3. According to many scholars, although still debatable, the vision of Russia as a country 'between East and West' remains relevant in the Russian context and generates discussions to date: see, for example, Shlapentokh (2007), Ivanov (2008) and Korosteleva and Paikin (2021).
4. 'Strictly speaking, the state is the very organ of social thought' (Durkheim 1957, 51).
5. 'What is needed if social order is to reign is that the mass of men be content with their lot. But what is needed for them to be content is not that they have more or less, but that they be convinced they have no right to more. And for this, it is absolutely essential that there be an authority whose superiority they acknowledge and which tells them what is right' (Durkheim 1962, 242).
6. In the academic literature, there are a number of studies focused on the controversy between pragmatic and moral legitimacy, but not in the realm of innovation (Bowen 2019; Melé and Armengou 2016).
7. It is an independent agent of the Canadian Parliament (https://www.priv.gc.ca/en/about-the-opc/) that monitors compliance with the Privacy Act (1985, https://laws-lois.justice.gc.ca/PDF/P-21.pdf). The act regulates the rules for the collection and use of personal data in Canada.
8. See, for example, Citizen Lab (Munk School of Global Affairs and Public Policy, University of Toronto) report by Robertson et al. (2020) or Chiao (2019).
9. See, for example: Медуза. 6 ноября 2019 'Суд отказался запрещать систему распознавания лиц на улицах Москвы' (Meduza, 6 November 2019 (интернет-издание, внесённое в список иностранных агентов в России), 'The court refused to prohibit the facial recognition system on the streets of Moscow'). https://meduza.io/news/2019/11/06/sud-otkazalsya-zapreschat-sistemu-raspoznavaniya-lits-na-ulitsah-moskvy.
10. See РБК. 22 июля 2020 'Власти Москвы назвали число штрафов за нарушение самоизоляции' (RBC, 22 July 2020, 'Moscow authorities called the number of fines for violation of self-isolation'). Accessed 26 January 2021. https://www.rbc.ru/rbcfreenews/5f18216a9a7947cc5b5f8423.

11 See Открытые медиа. 21 июля 2020 'У системы слежки за москвичами погрешность — более 20%: штрафуют при неполном сходстве фото с оригиналом' (сайт издания заблокирован в России) (Open Media, 21 July 2020, 'The tracking system for Muscovites has an error of more than 20%: they fined if the photo is not entirely similar to the original'). Accessed 2 February 2021. https://openmedia.io/news/n3/u-sistemy-slezhki-za-moskvichami-pogreshnost-bolee-20-shtrafuyut-pri-nepolnom-sxodstve-foto-s-originalom/.

12 See, for example, Медиазона. 3 марта 2020 'Суд в Москве отклонил второй иск о запрете системы распознавания лиц' (интернет-издание, внесенное в список иностранных агентов в России) (Mediazona, 3 March 2020, 'Moscow court rejects second lawsuit to ban the facial recognition system'). Accessed 10 February 2021. https://zona.media/news/2020/03/03/popova-isk.

13 See Единая информационная система в сфере закупок. 7 декабря 2020 'Поставка программного обеспечения Видеодетектор для поиска силуэтов людей в кадре' (Unified information system in the field of procurement, 7 December 2020, 'Supply of Video Detector Software for Searching People Silhouettes in the Frame'). Accessed 15 February 2021. https://zakupki.gov.ru/223/purchase/public/purchase/info/common-info.html?regNumber=32009771514.

14 'Общественные ценности влияют на отношение к искусственному интеллекту и его юридическому оформлению' ('Social values influence attitudes towards artificial intelligence and its legal design') Симачев – Simachev 2019, 62.

15 See chapter 5, 'Selective law enforcement as a mechanism enforcing informal rules', in Bækken (2019, 107–26).

References

Aronowitz, Stanley and William DiFazio. 2010. *The Jobless Future*. Minneapolis: University of Minnesota Press.

Bækken, Håvard. 2019. *Law and Power in Russia: Making sense of quasi-legal practices*. London: Routledge.

Benotsmane, Rabab, György Kovács and László Dudás. 2019. 'Economic, social impacts and operation of smart factories in Industry 4.0 focusing on simulation and artificial intelligence of collaborating robots', *Social Sciences* 8(5): 143. Accessed 5 January 2020. https://doi.org/10.3390/socsci8050143.

Black, Donald J. 1973. 'The mobilization of law', *Journal of Legal Studies* 2: 125–49.

Blanco, Belen, Encarna Guillamón-Saorín and Andrés Guiral. 2013. 'Do non-socially responsible companies achieve legitimacy through socially responsible actions? The mediating effect of innovation', *Journal of Business Ethics* 117: 67–83.

Borisova, Tatiana and Jane Burbank. 2018. 'Russia's legal trajectories', *Kritika: Explorations in Russian and Eurasian History* 19: 469–508.

Bowen, Frances. 2019. 'Marking their own homework: The pragmatic and moral legitimacy of industry self-regulation', *Journal of Business Ethics* 156: 257–72.

Bunduchi, Raluca. 2016. 'Legitimacy-seeking mechanisms in product innovation: A qualitative study', *Journal of Product Innovation Management* 34: 315–42.

Durkheim, Emile. 1957. *Professional Ethics and Civic Morals*. London: Free Press.

Durkheim, Emile. 1962. *Socialism*. New York: Collier.

Durkheim, Emile. 1998. *Contributions to l'Année Sociologique*. New York: Free Press.

Etzione, Amitai. 1968. *Active Society: A theory of societal and political processes*. New York: Free Press.

Foucault, Michel. 1998. *The History of Sexuality: The will to knowledge*. London: Penguin.

Frey, Carl Benedikt and Michael A. Osborne. 2013. 'The Future of Employment: How susceptible are jobs to computerisation?' Paper given at the *Machines and Employment* workshop, Oxford University, 17 September 2013. Accessed 3 February 2021. https://www.oxfordmartin.ox.ac.uk/downloads/academic/The_Future_of_Employment.pdf?link=mktw.

Fu, Xiaoqing (Maggie), Qun Bao, Hongjun Xie and Xiaolan Fu. 2021. 'Diffusion of industrial robotics and inclusive growth: Labour market evidence from cross country data', *Journal of Business Research* 122: 670–84.

Gane, Mike. 1984. 'Institutional socialism and the sociological critique of communism (introduction to Durkheim and Mauss)', *International Journal of Human Resource Management* 13: 304–30.

Gerring, John. 2007. *Case Study Research: Principles and practices.* New York: Cambridge University Press.

Giannini, Tyler R. 2018. 'Political legitimacy and private governance of human rights: Community–business social contracts and constitutional moments'. In *Human Rights, Democracy, and Legitimacy in a World of Disorder,* edited by Gerald L. Neuman and Silja Voeneky, 209–33. Cambridge: Cambridge University Press.

Gould, Jon B. and Scott Barclay. 2012. 'Mind the gap: The place of gap studies in sociolegal scholarship', *Annual Review of Law and Social Science* 8: 323–35.

Greitens, Sheena Chestnut. 2020. *Dealing with Demand for China's Global Surveillance Exports.* Washington, DC: Brookings Institution. Accessed 10 February 2021. https://www.brookings.edu/research/dealing-with-demand-for-chinas-global-surveillance-exports/.

Hajda, Jan. 1968. 'Ambivalence and social relations', *Sociological Focus* 2: 21–8.

Hendley, Kathryn. 2011. 'Varieties of legal dualism: Making sense of the role of law in contemporary Russia', *Wisconsin International Law Journal* 29: 233–62.

Hill, Kashmir. 2020. 'The secretive company that might end privacy as we know it', *New York Times,* 18 January. Accessed 20 January 2021. https://www.nytimes.com/2020/01/18/technology/clearview-privacy-facial-recognition.html.

Horowitz, Irving L. 1982. 'Socialization without politicization: Emile Durkheim's theory of the modern state', *Political Theory* 10: 353–77.

Ivanov, Vyacheslav V. 2008. 'Russia between East and West? Remarks on comparison of cultures', *Russian Journal of Communication* 1: 113–26.

Johnson, Cathryn, Timothy J. Dowd and Cecilia Ridgeway. 2006. 'Legitimacy as a social process', *Annual Review of Sociology* 32: 53–78.

Kawakami, Takashi and Yusuke Hinata. 2019. 'Pay with your face: 100m Chinese switch from smartphones: Facial recognition technology spreads rapidly at the expense of privacy', *Nikkei Asian Review,* 16 October. Accessed 2 February 2021. https://asia.nikkei.com/Business/China-tech/Pay-with-your-face-100m-Chinese-switch-from-smartphones.

Kollektiv avtorov (team of authors) (ruk. (headed by) Yuriy. V. Simachev). 2019. *Razvitie regulirovaniya: novye vyzovy v usloviyah radikal'nyh tekhnologicheskih izmenenij.* Doklad. Moskva. [Regulation of the development: new challenges in the face of radical technological change]. Moscow: HSE University Press, 2019.

Korosteleva, Elena and Zachary Paikin. 2021. 'Russia between East and West, and the future of Eurasian order', *International Politics* 58: 321–33.

Kosals, Leonid and Maria Yachnik. 2020a. 'Rynok tekhnologij iskusstvennogo intellekta v Rossii: social'nye usloviya zarozhdeniya Stat'ya 1. Podhody k issledovaniyu i vydelenie granic rynka' [The market for technologies of artificial intelligence in Russia: social conditions of emergence. Article 1. The methodology of research and identifying the market agents], *Obshchestvennye nauki i sovremennost'* 2: 5–24.

Kosals, Leonid and Maria Yachnik. 2020b. 'Rynok tekhnologij iskusstvennogo intellekta v Rossii: social'nye usloviya zarozhdeniya. Stat'ya 2. Razrabotchiki, potrebiteli i gosudarstvo: vzaimootnosheniya i perspektivy' [The market of artificial intelligence technologies in Russia: social conditions of origin. Article 2. Developers, consumers and the state: relationships and prospects], *Obshchestvennye nauki i sovremennost'* 3: 5–17.

Kovachich, Leonid. 2020. 'Sdelano ne v Kitae: kak ustroena sistema videonablyudeniya Moskvy' [Made not in China: how the video surveillance system of Moscow works], Moscow: Moskovskij Centr Karnegi. Accessed 5 February 2021. https://carnegie.ru/2020/08/05/ru-pub-82419

Kumar, Rajesh and T. K. Das. 2007. 'Interpartner legitimacy in the alliance development process', *Journal of Management Studies* 44: 1425–53.

Kurkchiyan, M. 2018. 'The distinctive features of Russian legal culture'. In *Constructing Legal Culture through Institutional Reforms: The Russian experience.* Report and Analysis of a Workshop Held at Wolfson College, Oxford, edited by M. Kurkchiyan. Oxford: Foundation for Law, Justice and Society.

Leibold, James. 2020. 'Surveillance in China's Xinjiang region: Ethnic sorting, coercion, and inducement', *Journal of Contemporary China* 29: 46–60.

Markarda, Jochen, Steffen Wirth and Bernhard Truffer. 2016. 'Institutional dynamics and technology legitimacy: A framework and a case study on biogas technology', *Research Policy* 45: 330–44.

McWilliams, Wilson Carey (ed.). 2006. *The Active Society Revisited*. Lanham, MD: Rowman & Littlefield.

Melé, Domènec and Jaume Armengou. 2016. 'Moral legitimacy in controversial projects and its relationship with social license to operate: A case study', *Journal of Business Ethics* 136: 729–74.

Miller, Zinaida. 2020. 'Embedded ambivalence: Ungoverning global justice', *Transnational Legal Theory* 11: 353–81.

Mokyr, Joel, Chris Vickers and Nicolas L. Ziebarth. 2015. 'The history of technological anxiety and the future of economic growth: Is this time different?', *Journal of Economic Perspectives* 29: 31–50.

Mousterman, Pieter and Justyna Zander. 2016. 'Industry 4.0 as a cyber-physical system study', *Software and Systems Modeling* 15: 17–29.

Neuman, Gerald L. 2018. 'Human rights, treaties, and international legitimacy'. In *Human Rights, Democracy, and Legitimacy in a World of Disorder*, edited by Gerald L. Neuman and Silja Voeneky, 51–72. Cambridge: Cambridge University Press.

Office of the Privacy Commissioner of Canada. 2020. 'Joint Investigation of the Cadillac Fairview Corporation Limited', 28 October. Accessed 10 January 2021. https://www.priv.gc.ca/en/opc-actions-and-decisions/investigations/investigations-into-businesses/2020/pipeda-2020-004/.

Office of the Privacy Commissioner of Canada. 2021. 'Joint Investigation of Clearview AI, Inc.', 2 February. Accessed 5 February 2021. https://www.priv.gc.ca/en/opc-actions-and-decisions/investigations/investigations-into-businesses/2021/pipeda-2021-001/.

Paneyakh, Ella L. 2014. 'Faking performance together: Systems of performance evaluation in Russian enforcement agencies and production of bias and privilege', *Post-Soviet Affairs* 30: 115–36.

Petkova, Iva. 2018. '*Digital Moda*: Institutionalizing legitimacy in the fashion industry'. In *Engineering Legitimacy: How institutional entrepreneurs in e-commerce bring fashion companies into the digital age*, by Iva Petkova, 103–36. Cham: Palgrave Macmillan.

Rao, Anand S. and Gerard Verweij. 2017. 'Sizing the prize: What's the real value of AI for your business and how can you capitalise?' PWC. Accessed 9 February 2021. https://www.pwc.com/gx/en/issues/analytics/assets/pwc-ai-analysis-sizing-the-prize-report.pdf.

Robertson, Kate, Cynthia Khoo and Yolanda Song. 2020. *To Surveil and Predict: A human rights analysis of algorithmic policing in Canada*. University of Toronto. Accessed 5 February 2021. https://citizenlab.ca/wp-content/uploads/2020/09/To-Surveil-and-Predict.pdf.

Schoon, Eric W. and Courtney DeRoche. 2019. 'Legitimacy building in policy and practice: The case of US private military and security contractors (PMSCs) in Afghanistan'. In *The Sociology of Privatized Security*, edited by Ori Swed and Thomas Crosbie, 67–83. Cham: Palgrave Macmillan.

Schumpeter, Joseph A. 2010. *Capitalism, Socialism and Democracy*. London: Routledge.

Shlapentokh, Dmitry. 2007. *Russia between East and West: Scholarly debates on Eurasianism*. Leiden: Brill.

Shrouf, Fadi, Joaquín Ordieres and Giovanni Miragliotta. 2014. 'Smart factories in Industry 4.0: A review of the concept and of energy management approached in production based on the internet of things paradigm', *2014 IEEE International Conference on Industrial Engineering and Engineering Management*, IEEE. Accessed 10 January 2021. https://ieeexplore.ieee.org/abstract/document/7058728.

Skilton, Mark and Felix Hovsepian. 2018. *The 4th Industrial Revolution: Responding to the impact of artificial intelligence on business*. Basingstoke: Palgrave Macmillan.

Wang, Shiyong, Jiafu Wan, Di Li and Chunhua Zhang. 2016. 'Implementing smart factory of Industry 4.0: An outlook', *International Journal of Distributed Sensor Networks* 12. Accessed 20 January 2020. http://dx.doi.org/10.1155/2016/3159805.

Wang, Tao, Ting Zhang and Zhigang Shou. 2019. 'The double-edged sword effect of political ties on performance in emerging markets: The mediation of innovation capability and legitimacy', *Asia Pacific Journal of Management* 38: 1003–30. Accessed 4 February 2021. https://doi.org/10.1007/s10490-019-09686-w.

Weber, Max. 1964. *The Theory of Social and Economic Organization*. New York: Free Press.

Part II
Power struggles in the economy: An organizational perspective

6
The power of non-compliance: Inter-firm opportunism in Russian consumer markets

Vadim Radaev

Introduction

Let us start with the notion of ambivalence, which is defined as a simultaneous presence of contradictory tendencies in behaviour (Hajda 1968). Following the 'relational turn' in the social sciences (Hillcoat-Nalletamby and Phillips 2011), we assume that ambivalence is not confined to interpersonal relations but is also an inherent feature of inter-firm ties in the sense that they combine polarized forces that cannot be fully reconciled. Understanding ambivalence is particularly important for channel relationships between retailers and suppliers that simultaneously involve opposite elements including cooperation and competition, autonomy and interdependence, striving for continuity and change, loyalty to old partners and the search for new ties, and compliance with the rules and deviance from these rules. Ambivalence can be reduced by negotiation and compliance with the existing rules but cannot be entirely eliminated. Inter-firm relations always contain some tensions backed by the existence of alternatives, for example, possibilities to change the partner.

  All channel relationships contain strong elements of power that are also ambivalent in nature, combining intentions to follow one's own interests by subordinating one's partners and the need to maintain stable relationships and avoid conflicts that may destroy these relationships. Ongoing power relationships cannot be confined to unconditional domination or subordination but are largely based upon mutual interdependence. Thus, power in exchange relations always presents an ambivalent and changeable combination of domination and obedience.

Ambivalence of inter-firm ties may result in relational conflicts, particularly when exchange parties fail to comply with the rules (Radaev 2013). Non-compliance constitutes a specific form of abuse of power in channel relationships involving inter-firm opportunism, that is, 'self-interest seeking with guile' (Williamson 1975, 6). Opportunistic behaviour remains a common issue in channel relationship management, encompassing a range of behaviours that include stealing and cheating, withholding and distorting information, breach of contract and relational norms, and many other types of confusing behaviour that are contrary to channel partners' expectations (Wathne and Heide 2000; Luo 2006). Opportunism presents a serious threat to channel performance and the quality of relationships. It can increase transaction costs, undermine trust and commitment, and lead to the deterioration and even termination of relationships (Hawkins et al. 2013).

Inter-firm opportunism has received a great deal of attention from researchers (for meta-analyses, see Crosno and Dahlstrom 2008; Hawkins et al. 2008; Wang and Yang 2013). However, despite the extant literature, this 'dark side' of such cooperative relationships still calls for further exploration (Kang and Jindal 2015; Abosag et al. 2016). Our understanding of inter-firm conflicts associated with opportunistic behaviour remains limited (Lumineau et al. 2015). Besides, empirical studies of opportunism have mostly drawn on surveys conducted in the US and West European contexts (Lumineau and Oliveira 2020).

In this study, we focus on a specific type of inter-firm opportunism dealing with the explicit violation of contractual obligations. Breach of contract has been widely recognized as one of the main forms of opportunistic behaviour (Paswan et al. 2017). Our previous studies showed that this practice was widespread in Russian business (Radaev 2013). According to existing classifications, the infringement of business contracts constitutes an *ex post* form of opportunism, occurring after a business contract has been drawn up, rather than *ex ante* opportunism, which takes place before a business relationship has been established (Brown et al. 2000; Ting et al. 2007). It is a strong form of opportunism in that it violates the terms of a contract in contrast to weak forms, such as violating the norms of the relationship (Luo 2006; Hawkins et al. 2013; Abosag et al. 2016). This type of behaviour is also classified as objective rather than being perceived as opportunism (Smith et al. 1995; Wang and Yang 2013).

There is an ambivalent relationship between contract infringement and market power. On the one hand, breach of contract could be a form of abuse of market power by the incumbent. On the other, breach of contract might be a manifestation of resistance to pressures imposed by a more powerful channel partner. In the latter case, non-compliance with contractual terms could be interpreted as the exercise of power by the weak. Whether we have an abuse of power or resistance to power is largely an empirical question that will be treated in this study. But in any case, contract infringement could be treated as a manifestation of the inability of channel partners to cope with the ambivalence of their exchange relationships.

The literature still lacks a fully synthesized analysis of the antecedents and consequences of inter-firm opportunism (Ting et al. 2007; Hawkins et al. 2008). Our research combines analyses of the antecedents and consequences of opportunism as explained and explanatory variables, respectively. In previous studies, antecedents have included environmental and dyadic processes and organizational factors, whereas consequences have included organizational performance, overall satisfaction, relationship, commitment, functional conflict and costs (Ting et al. 2007; Wang and Yang 2013). In this study, the antecedents of opportunism are the level of competition in the industry as an important environmental factor and the relationship duration as a critical dyadic process factor. We also use variables characterizing two aspects of power: we analyse the effects of market power in dyadic relationships between channel partners and the effects of political power derived from firms' relationships with government agencies. Regarding the behavioural effects of opportunism, we examine the relational conflicts among channel partners in connection with the infringement of business contracts. We agree that a high level of conflict can be detrimental for the performance and quality of relationships (Gaski 1984; Finch et al. 2013).

This chapter seeks to explore inter-firm opportunism among retailers and suppliers in three different consumer industries: grocery, consumer electronics and textiles and apparel products. This multi-sector approach is more generalizable than single industry studies (Crosno and Dahlstrom 2008). Most relevant existing studies are based on cross-sectional data. We use data from three successive surveys of firm managers and thus have the opportunity to trace the main trends from 2013 to 2019. This period includes the economic depression that started in Russia in 2014.

The main research questions are the following: What is the frequency of inter-firm opportunism in respect of explicit violations of contractual terms and conditions? What are the driving factors behind opportunism, and how do they change over time? Are there any differences in the propensity for opportunism across different consumer industries? Finally, does inter-firm opportunism lead to an escalation of relational conflicts?

The structure of the chapter is as follows. We start with the research hypotheses derived from the existing literature, before setting out the main data sources, measures and analytical methods. After presenting the descriptive statistics, we provide the main findings of the regression modelling regarding the antecedents and consequences of opportunistic behaviour. Finally, we discuss our results and draw some conclusions.

Research hypotheses

Opportunistic behaviour can be driven by both external and internal factors. External factors include environmental characteristics. In line with previous studies (Luo 2006; Ting et al. 2007), we assume that environmental volatility increases the uncertainty under which firms operate and can lead to the inability to deliver promised resources or to intentional attempts to enhance their advantage by detrimental means. We used the level of competition in the market as a characteristic of the environment and proposed that competitive pressures might increase opportunism by channel partners (Sa Vinhas and Heide 2015).

H1: Pressure resulting from higher levels of competition from the external economic environment increases opportunism by channel partners.

Internal factors relate to the characteristics and quality of dyadic relationships. Relational contracting theory distinguishes between transactional and relational exchanges and assumes that the creation of stable relationships requires continuity (Macneil 1980; Ivens 2004; Radaev 2015). Thus, the length of relationships represents an inherent element of relational/embedded exchanges. Existing evidence on the effects of relationship duration on opportunistic behaviour is controversial. Some authors show that stable preferential relationships encourage knowledge transfer (Kotabe et al. 2003), increase asset specificity, facilitate mutual commitment and alleviate the risks of opportunism (Gulati and Gargiulo 1999; Ivens 2004; Crosno and Dahlstrom 2008; Lui et al. 2009). Others argue that long-term relationships are more costly (Menard 2004) and may lead to growing opportunism and more conflicts. For example, it was pointed out that 'the more that two companies try to work together, the more conflicting issues will be discovered' (Håkansson et al. 2009, 24). In some cases, durable relationships may become unstable and suffer from greater opportunism and dissatisfaction over time (Klein 1996; Anderson and Jap 2005). At the same time, exchange parties found themselves trapped in close relationships (Grandinetti 2017). Keeping in mind this controversial evidence, we support the insights of relational contracting theory and set out the following proposition.

H2: Relationship duration reduces opportunism by channel partners.

The distribution of market power presents another important characteristic of channel relationships that may influence opportunistic behaviour. Given that power resides in the other's dependency (Emerson 1962), asymmetric dependence might engender opportunism in that it enables less dependent partners to use their market power for detrimental purposes and expropriate resources from more dependent partners (Lusch and Brown 1996; Anselmi and Marquardt 2000). At the same time, opportunistic behaviour could originate from the resistance of the more dependent channel partners to pressure from the partners with the greater bargaining power.

Bargaining power is an important element of market channel power in dyadic relationships. In this study, we define the level of bargaining power in terms of the capacity of channel partners to impose the terms and conditions of business contracts. Thus, opportunism by channel partners indicates the lack of bargaining power of a given firm and its inability to control the actions of the other party during the process of contract negotiation and conclusion. Alternatively, non-compliance with contractual terms could be interpreted as resistance of a given firm to pressures imposed by the more powerful channel partner. In both cases, this power asymmetry might also lead to opportunistic behaviour during the execution of contracts. Here we take one of the potential explanations to hypothesize the following statement.

H3: A lack of bargaining power increases opportunism by channel partners.

Sources of market power are not necessarily confined to dyadic channel relationships. These sources could be derived from a firm's political affiliation with government agencies in their capacity as influential third parties in the market. Relationships with government agencies, especially in emerging economies, may significantly influence opportunistic behaviour in the supply chain (Zeng et al. 2017). More specifically, political ties may have a positive impact by deterring opportunism by channel partners (Zhu et al. 2017). This gives rise to the following hypothesis.

H4: The affiliation of firms with government agencies reduces opportunism by channel partners.

Turning to the consequences of inter-firm opportunism, the latter may influence the firms' performance and the quality of dyadic relationships. It may also lead to relational conflicts, defined here as disagreements between channel partners (Bobot 2011). In previous studies, role deviance and poor communication were recognized as antecedents of inter-firm conflicts (Lumineau et al. 2015). Contract infringement has also been explicated as an influential source of relational conflict in Russia (Radaev 2013). When channel partners go to extremes in their ambivalent relationships and provoke relational conflicts, they create risks of deterioration or even termination of these relationships. Thus, the following statement is suggested:

H5: Opportunism has a direct positive influence on relational inter-firm conflicts.

Data and methods

Data sources

Data were collected from three successive standardized surveys. In total, 2,204 managers completed questionnaires during face-to-face interviews. The surveys were conducted in 2013 with 843 managers, including 424 retailers and 419 suppliers, in 2016 with 684 managers (339 retailers and 345 suppliers) and in 2019 with 677 managers (340 retailers and 337 suppliers).

Because the collection of data on dependence and control from a single source may produce common biases (Provan and Skinner 1989), we used the same questionnaire to survey suppliers and retailers and persuaded channel partners to describe their relationships from opposite sides. We assume that the more discrepancies there are in estimations between the two sides, the more attention should be paid to a given aspect of their relationship (Bloom et al. 2000).

All surveys were conducted in five large Russian urban areas in which modern retailing formats were well developed, including Moscow (central region), Saint Petersburg (north-western region), Yekaterinburg (Ural region) and Novosibirsk and Tyumen (western Siberia region).

Three industries were involved: grocery (1,257 managers), consumer electronics (388 managers) and textiles and apparel (559 managers). Thus, for comparative purposes we have chosen industries dealing with both food and non-food products. We also examined different types of supply chains. Groceries and textiles and apparel are attributed to buyer-driven commodity chains, in which retailers normally have more bargaining power, whereas consumer electronics represents a producer-driven commodity chain, in which suppliers might be more influential (Gereffi et al. 2005).

The sample comprised large companies (28.4 per cent) as well as medium-sized and small enterprises (71.6 per cent), including both domestic and foreign companies operating in Russia.

The same sampling methods were applied in all surveys. Sampling procedures were different with regard to retailers and suppliers. With retailers, we addressed all chain stores (both global and domestic) given that their total number is limited. Thus, retailers were selected from the full lists of chain stores operating in each region. Given their very large number, suppliers were sampled using the international database Ruslana of the Bureau Van Dijk, which contains information on 850,000 companies operating in Russia. Suppliers were randomly selected from this database. Suppliers covered both the manufacturers and distributors of products. All surveys were conducted by the Levada Centre during the same months of November and December to avoid seasonal fluctuations. The basic characteristics of the sample are summarized in Table 6.1.

Table 6.1 Basic sample descriptive statistics, per cent

Companies	Retailers (n = 1,103)	Suppliers (n = 1,101)
Grocery sector	56.3	57.8
Consumer electronics	17.7	17.5
Textiles and apparel	26.0	24.7
Large firms	28.5	28.3
Small and medium-sized firms	71.5	71.7
2013	38.4	38.1
2016	30.7	31.3
2019	30.8	30.6

Measures and analyses

We used 'breach of business contract' as a proxy for inter-firm opportunism. Opportunism presents a clear example of a difficult-to-capture construct. Due to the sensitive and unflattering nature of the issue, we suggested questions about their partners' opportunism rather than about our respondents' own behaviour. We are also fully aware of the fact that the infringement of business contracts might occur for a variety of reasons and that it is hard to determine empirically whether any breach of contractual obligations was the result of dishonest behaviour or merely bad contractual governance and contingent factors. Thus, two additional variables were used to assure that this kind of business practice was associated with opportunistic behaviour per se. These variables were based upon the questions to managers as to whether their channel partners (1) provided distorted information (Yes/No) and (2) breached informal agreements (Yes/No). Data on these issues were collected from the latest survey wave in 2019.

After descriptive analyses, first, we estimated coefficients from a logistic regression model with the existence of breach of contract by business partners in the two years preceding the respective survey as a dichotomic dependent variable (Yes/No). Second, we estimated coefficients from a linear regression model with the percentage of channel partners infringing contracts as a dependent variable.

Regarding the main predictors, external/environmental competition pressure was measured as a perceived level of competition over a certain type of product in a given area (high vs moderate or low). Internal/process factors included relationship duration measured as a percentage of channel partners (retailers or supplier) who worked with a surveyed firm for more than five years.

Following the literature (Brown et al. 1995), we defined marketing channel power as the ability of one channel member to control the decision variables in the marketing strategy of another member at a different level of distribution. This kind of bargaining power was measured on the basis of whether the channel partners were able to impose contractual terms and conditions on a surveyed firm.

With regard to political power, we used the political ties of the surveyed firms as indicated by their receipt of either financial or organizational support from government authorities at the federal, regional or municipal levels in the previous two years. Data on different government agencies and support measures were collected on the basis of eight separate questions. If the surveyed firm received at least one type of support, it was qualified as being affiliated with government agencies.

Control variables included the industry (groceries, consumer electronics or textiles and apparel), the place of the firm in the supply chain (retailer vs supplier), the size of the firm measured on a self-reported basis (large vs medium-sized or small) and the years in which the surveys were conducted (2013, 2016 and 2019).

To examine the consequences of opportunism, we applied a binary logistic regression model, using the existence of conflict with channel partners in the previous two years as a dependent dichotomic variable. The presence and percentage of business partners infringing contractual obligations were examined as the main predictors here in two versions of the same model. The same set of independent and control variables was used. To check the sensitivity of the outcomes, all models were run separately for retailers and suppliers.

Results

Descriptive statistics

The descriptive statistics of the major variables by year and industry are summarized in Table 6.2. The data showed that inter-firm opportunism was still widespread in the industries surveyed. A majority of the firms surveyed faced breaches of contract by their channel partners in the two years preceding the survey. The percentage of managers who reported that their partners had infringed business contracts increased from 74.9 to 76.3 per cent between 2013 and 2016 and to 78.1 per cent by 2019. Non-compliance with contractual terms was more widespread in the grocery sector (80.3 per cent) than in consumer electronics (74.9 per cent) or textiles and apparel (68.7 per cent). In all industries, suppliers were more likely than retailers to report that partners breached business contracts (79.0 and 73.6 per cent respectively).

The percentage of partners breaching business contracts increased from 24.0 to 31.1 per cent between 2013 and 2016, before falling back to 25.9 per cent in 2019, which was still slightly higher than in 2013. Differences across industries were not significant here, accounting for 25–27 per cent in each sector. Again, suppliers reported a higher percentage of partners that behaved opportunistically than retailers (30.3 and 23.9 per cent respectively).

Given that breach of contract is not necessarily associated with calculated efforts to confuse the partner, we used two additional variables – whether channel partners provided distorted information and whether they breached informal agreements – as explicit evidence of opportunistic behaviour. Using data from the 2019 survey, we revealed that these two parameters were positively related to both the existence and the percentage of channel partners infringing business contracts at a high level of significance ($p < .001$). Both indicators of contract infringement were also significantly associated with the existence of relational conflicts with channel partners. Thus, we would argue that the infringement of a business contract may serve as a good proxy for inter-firm opportunism in the case under review.

Turning to the explanatory variables, almost two-thirds of surveyed managers (62.7 per cent) reported that the level of competition was high in all three industries. It was even higher in the years 2013 and 2016 and declined afterwards in 2019, particularly for suppliers in consumer electronics.

Overall, managers preferred more durable contractual relationships. The percentage of channel partners that were working with a surveyed firm for more than five years accounted for 66.8 per cent on average. Relationship duration was particularly important for retailers in the textiles and apparel industry (77.2 per cent) but much less so for suppliers in consumer electronics (57.3 per cent). However, this percentage decreased from 71.8 to 58.5 per cent between 2016 and 2019, especially among suppliers, due to a fall in overall number of long-term partners.

The lack of bargaining power was reported by almost two-thirds of respondents (64.3 per cent), who pointed out that their channel partners were able to impose contractual terms and conditions on them. Overall, suppliers felt much more vulnerable in terms of their comparative bargaining power than retailers did in all industries (71.0 and 57.3 per cent correspondingly), which was particularly true for suppliers in the food industry (76.3 per cent). However, competitive situations improved when the percentage of managers suffering from the imposition of contractual terms decreased from 68.0 to 57.4 per cent between 2016 and 2019 in total (for suppliers from 77.7 to 60.0 per cent).

Not many managers had political ties enabling them to receive either financial or organizational support from government authorities at different levels (6.9 per cent in total, including 7.3 per cent of retailers and 6.4 per cent of suppliers). The frequencies of state support were not sector-specific and demonstrated an explicit downward trend over the years. The percentage of firms receiving support from government agencies decreased from 10.0 to 7.4 per cent between 2013 and 2016 and fell to 2.6 per cent in 2019.

Turning to the effects of opportunism, a significant number of managers pointed to the existence of relational conflicts with their channel partners in the last two years (24.4 per cent in total, including 23.0 per cent of retailers and 25.8 per cent of suppliers). Differences across industries were not significant here. Remarkably, the percentage of managers facing conflicts declined from 29.9 to 22.4 per cent between 2013 and 2016 and showed further decline to 19.6 per cent from 2016 to 2019, implying that the quality of channel relationships was gradually improving.

Results of modelling

We start with the antecedents of inter-firm opportunism and then proceed to its consequences. Table 6.3 summarizes the estimated coefficients from a logistic regression with the existence of channel partners breaching their contractual obligations as a dependent variable and from a linear regression with the percentage of partners violating their contractual obligations within the last two years as a dependent variable. The largest VIF (1.8) suggests no major threat of multicollinearity.

Starting with the environmental factor, competitive pressures increased the probability of contract infringement in line with Hypothesis 1 but only for the presence of opportunistic partners ($p < .01$). The coefficients for the percentage of such partners were not significant, which shows that the effect of the competition level was not robust.

The length of exchange relationships produced a small but significant negative effect on the existence of channel partners breaching contractual obligations ($p < 0.5$) and a more significant negative effect on the percentage of channel partners infringing contracts ($p < .001$). Our Hypothesis 2 was confirmed.

The lack of bargaining power was the most influential factor, providing significant positive effects on both the existence and the percentage of channel partners breaching contractual obligations in line with our Hypothesis 3 ($p < .001$).

Affiliation with government agencies, on the contrary, did not affect the opportunistic behaviour of the channel partners in a significant way. Thus, Hypothesis 4 was not supported by the data.

The place of the firm in the supply chain did not affect the presence of opportunistic behaviours. However, the percentage of partners breaching business contracts was slightly higher for suppliers than for

Table 6.2 Descriptive statistics by years and industries, per cent

	2013	2016	2019	Grocery	Electronics	Textile	Total
High competition	67.8 (69.9–65.8)	66.9 (64.6–69.2)	52.1 (55.5–48.6)	64.0 (64.1–63.9)	59.2 (62.5–55.8)	62.3 (64.0–60.4)	62.7 (63.8–61.6)
Percentage of durable relations (means)	69.2 (69.9–68.4)	71.8 (74.9–69.2)	58.5 (62.2–54.2)	65.2 (63.2–67.0)	64.5 (70.6–57.3)	71.3 (77.2–64.2)	66.8 (68.8–64.7)
Partners impose contractual terms	67.4 (59.8–74.7)	68.0 (57.0–77.7)	57.4 (54.9–60.0)	68.2 (59.3–76.3)	62.8 (59.0–66.5)	56.7 (52.3–61.4)	64.3 (57.3–71.0)
Receive state support	10.0 (13.8–6.4)	7.4 (4.9–9.7)	2.6 (2.2–3.0)	6.9 (6.1–7.6)	7.1 (7.2–6.9)	6.6 (9.6–3.2)	6.9 (7.3–6.4)
Have partners breaching contracts	74.9 (70.9–79.0)	76.3 (70.1–81.9)	78.1 (79.5–76.7)	80.3 (79.0–81.4)	74.9 (73.1–76.6)	68.7 (62.7–75.3)	76.4 (73.6–79.0)
Percentage of partners breaching contracts (means)	24.0 (17.5–30.5)	31.1 (24.5–37.0)	25.9 (27.9–23.9)	27.5 (23.7–30.1)	26.7 (22.2–31.4)	24.6 (21.7–27.8)	26.6 (22.9–30.3)
Have relational conflicts	29.9 (28.5–31.3)	22.4 (19.5–25.3)	19.6 (19.8–19.5)	24.7 (23.0–26.3)	24.4 (26.3–22.4)	23.9 (21.0–26.9)	24.4 (23.0–25.8)

Note: Percentage of retailers and suppliers in parentheses

retailers (p < .05). The size of the firm increased the probability of the presence of opportunistic behaviours (p < .001) but did not affect the percentage of partners practising this kind of behaviour. The type of products did not show a significant effect on the presence and percentage of opportunistic partners with one important exception: the infringement of business contracts was more likely in the grocery sector than in other industries. Positive period effects of the year 2016 were observed with regard to the percentage of opportunistic partners and of the year 2019 with regard to the presence of opportunistic partners (p < .001), while the other effects were not significant.

For the purpose of sensitivity analyses, we ran the same models separately for retailers and suppliers and obtained similar results for all major variables.

Table 6.3 Estimated effect of explanatory and control variables on the existence and percentage of partners infringing business contracts as dependent variables

	Model 1. Existence of partners infringing business contracts	Model 2. Percentage of partners infringing business contracts
Competition level	1.479** (.128)	.026 (1.571)
Relationships duration	.995* (.002)	−.164*** (.025)
Partners impose contractual terms	2.625*** (.126)	.206*** (1.589)
Receive state support	.962 (.235)	−.005 (2.933)
Suppliers/retailers	1.130 (.124)	.055* (1.505)
Size of the firm	1.699*** (.162)	.025 (1.680)
Grocery sector	1.614** (.162)	.001 (2.026)
Textile and apparel	.882 (.174)	−.009 (2.293)
2016	1.215 (.149)	.115*** (1.843)
2019	1.787*** (.156)	.037 (1.858)
R2	.113	.082
Number of observations	1610	1609

Note: Standard errors in parentheses. * p < 0.05, ** p < 0.01, *** p < 0.001

Regarding the consequences of inter-firm opportunism, estimated coefficients from a binary logistic regression using the presence of relational conflicts with channel partners as a dependent variable are presented in Table 6.4.

As suggested in Hypothesis 5, contract infringement was positively associated with relational conflicts with channel partners. The presence of channel partners breaching their contractual obligations had the largest effect on the probability of relational conflict. The effect of the percentage of such opportunistic partners was smaller but still significant ($p < .001$).

The competition level presented a further influential factor affecting the emergence of relational conflicts ($p < .001$). Relationship duration very slightly reduced the probability of relational conflicts ($p < .05$) but this effect was not sustainable. The existence of conflicts was much more affected by the level of the partners' bargaining power, implying that if

Table 6.4 Estimated effect of explanatory and control variables on the existence of conflict with partners as dependent variable

	Model 1	Model 2
Contract infringement^	13.027*** (.309)	1.022*** (.002)
Competition level	2.619*** (.150)	2.867*** (.153)
Relationships duration	.995* (.002)	.996 (.002)
Partners impose contractual terms	2.070*** (.156)	1.975*** (.156)
Receive state support	1.105 (.254)	1.103 (.249)
Suppliers/retailers	1.015 (.135)	.987 (.137)
Size of the firm	1.342* (.145)	1.474** (.145)
Grocery sector	.898 (.185)	1.047 (.187)
Textile and apparel	1.430 (.207)	1.384 (.206)
2016	.585** (.160)	.501*** (.164)
2019	.447*** (.170)	.482*** (.171)
Constant	.023*** (.411)	.095*** (.302)
R^2	.284	.238
Number of observations	1,382	1,382

Note: Standard errors in parentheses. * $p < 0.05$, ** $p < 0.01$, *** $p < 0.001$
^ Existence of partners infringing business contracts in Model 1.
  Percentage of partners infringing business contracts in Model 2.

channel partners had the opportunity to impose contractual terms and conditions, relational conflicts were more likely to emerge. It was not important if the firms received organizational or financial support from government agencies.

The difference between retailers and suppliers was not significant in this respect either. No significant effects of industries were revealed. Firm size was positively associated with the existence of relational conflicts ($p < .05$) but this result was not sustainable and was valid for suppliers only. Finally, significant period effects were observed for the years 2016 and 2019 ($p < .001$), implying that the probability of relational conflicts decreased over the years.

Again, we ran the same models separately for retailers and suppliers to check the sensitivity of outcomes. The obtained results did not deviate from the original model.

Discussion

The results of this study suggest that inter-firm opportunism was widespread across different Russian consumer industries and slightly increased over time. We focused upon behavioural variables and demonstrated that contract infringement was positively associated with the presence of behavioural patterns that signify explicit opportunistic actions, such as supplying distorted information and breaching relational norms. We also examined a variety of antecedents of inter-firm opportunism dealing with external factors and dyadic channel relationships, with a particular emphasis on the length of relationships and the bargaining power of channel partners.

Following the existing literature (Luo 2006; Ting et al. 2007), we assumed that pressures from the external economic environment and environmental uncertainty might increase opportunism. The data showed that a higher level of competition produced pressures in the market and increased the probability of contract infringement, although this effect was not sustainable.

We used relationship duration as an important characteristic of dyadic relationships among channel partners. Contrary to some previous studies (Anderson and Jap 2005; Håkansson et al. 2009; Grandinetti 2017), we concluded that establishing long-term sustainable relationships tended to decrease the level of inter-firm opportunism. Thus, we support the statements of relational exchange theory (Macneil 1980; Gulati and Gargiulo 1999; Ivens 2004; Lui et al. 2009) and argue that transactional exchange increases the risks of opportunism, whereas the length of channel relationships reduces these risks.

A dependence-power advantage is one of the most cited antecedents of opportunism in the inter-firm relationship literature (Hawkins et al. 2008; Wang and Yang 2013). We agree that inter-firm opportunism could originate from the relative dependence on business partners, which might use their market power for detrimental purposes (Emerson 1962; Anselmi and Marquardt 2000). The capacities of channel partners to control critical resources for competitive advantage and impose the terms and conditions of business contracts were considered as a specific form of abuse of power in dyadic relationships. The obtained results showed that a lack of bargaining power was the most influential factor, providing significant effects on both the existence and the percentage of channel partners breaching their contractual obligations.

Previous studies demonstrated that political ties with government agencies, especially in emerging economies, might have a positive impact by deterring opportunism by channel partners (Zeng et al. 2017; Zhu et al. 2017). We revealed that the level of political affiliation of the surveyed firms with government authorities at the federal, regional and municipal levels indicated by receiving financial or organizational support in the consumer markets was low and showed a downward trend over time. Remarkably, we did not obtain any clear evidence that existing political ties were effectively converted into bargaining power. The character of relationships in a dyadic process with channel partners was more important than affiliation with government agencies, which was not very helpful in reducing the propensity of opportunism in the examined case.

Turning to the consequences of inter-firm opportunism, we assumed that contract infringement might lead to relational conflicts, understood as disagreements between channel partners over the execution of contracts (Bobot 2011; Radaev 2013). It was confirmed that both the presence and percentage of opportunistic channel partners breaching their contractual obligations had a direct and sustainable positive influence on the emergence of relational conflicts. The probability of relational conflicts was also significantly affected by the level of market competition as an environmental element and by the level of the partners' bargaining power as an element of the dyadic process. This provided support for the insight that power possessed by one of the channel partners may affect the presence and level of conflict (Gaski 1984). Relationship duration had a smaller impact on the avoidance of relational conflicts, whereas political ties with government agencies were not important at all.

Considering other factors, suppliers suffered more often from the opportunistic behaviours of channel partners than retailers in all surveyed industries. However, the difference between retailers and suppliers was not significant with regard to the emergence of relational conflicts. Larger firms had to face opportunistic behaviour and relational conflicts more often but this result was valid for suppliers only, which was consistent with our previous findings (Radaev 2013). Overall, it implies that bargaining power represents a more influential factor than structural power measured by the size of the firms.

The infringement of business contracts was more often observed in the grocery sector rather than in other industries, while no significant differences across industries were revealed with regard to relational conflicts. Period effects were rather ambivalent, demonstrating a positive impact on the presence of contract infringement and a negative impact on the frequency of relational conflicts over the years. This implies that, on the one hand, non-compliance with contractual terms became a routinized business practice and, on the other, that channel partners increasingly managed to resolve disputable issues of contract execution without the aggravation of mutual tensions.

Conclusion

Our results showed that inter-firm opportunism, measured by the infringement of contracts, was widespread across different industries in the Russian consumer markets.

The length of relationships reduced the incidence of opportunism, whereas the lack of market channel power increased the risks of opportunistic behaviour by business partners. These dyadic process elements had much greater influence on the presence and percentage of channel partners breaching contractual obligations than external competitive pressures and the existence of political ties with government agencies. It also implies that breaches of contract more often indicated an abuse of market power by dominant firms rather than resistance to pressure from firms with less bargaining power.

As for the emergence of relational conflicts, it was mainly affected by inter-firm opportunistic behaviours as an important source of these conflicts. However, obtained data showed that the frequency of relational conflicts decreased over the years, demonstrating that channel partners managed to resolve disputable issues with regard to contract execution more effectively. This implies that despite some tensions provoked by the abuse of bargaining power, the dominant firms restricted their own opportunistic behaviour with regard to more dependent channel partners. Overall, this helps in coping with the ambivalence of exchange relationships and prevents termination of these relationships.

Limitations of the study

The study has some limitations. We have examined only one type of inter-firm opportunism, which is objective, strong and *ex post*, with a clear understanding that opportunism does not necessarily involve the violation of the agreement's explicit terms and that other types of opportunism could be important as well.

We address self-reported data, which have obvious limitations. However, subjective evaluations are highly relevant and very important here because we investigate a politically contested process in which the attitudes of the involved parties matter.

The data on contract infringement did not allow us to distinguish between intentional shirking and the objective inability of channel partners to deliver promised actions and resources due to external factors beyond their control. However, we provided some evidence that breach of contract was directly associated with opportunistic behaviour in the examined case.

The generalizability of obtained outcomes always presents an open question. The collected data were confined to the Russian consumer markets. However, we compared different types of industries to obtain an advantage over a single industry approach.

Acknowledgements

Our fieldwork and analytical work were supported by the Program for Basic Research of the National Research University Higher School of Economics (HSE University).

References

Abosag, Ibrahim, Dorothy Ai-wan Yen and Bradley R. Barnes. 2016. 'What is dark about the dark-side of business relationships?', *Industrial Marketing Management* 55: 5–9.

Anderson, Erin and Sandy D. Jap. 2005. 'The dark side of close relationships', *MIT Sloan Management Review* 46: 75–82.

Anselmi, Ken and Raymond A. Marquardt. 2000. 'A manufacturer's dependence advantage and the reduction in distributor opportunism: The role of a benevolent perspective of governance', *American Marketing Association. Conference Proceedings* 11: 325–37.

Bloom, Paul N., Gregory T. Gundlach and Joseph P. Cannon. 2000. 'Slotting allowances and fees: Schools of thought and the views of practicing managers', *Journal of Marketing* 64: 92–108.

Bobot, Lionel. 2011. 'Functional and dysfunctional conflicts in retailer–supplier relationships', *International Journal of Retail and Distribution Management* 39: 25–50.

Brown, James R., Chekitan S. Dev and Dong-Jin Lee. 2000. 'Managing marketing channel opportunism: The efficacy of alternative governance mechanisms', *Journal of Marketing* 64: 51–65.

Brown, James R., Robert F. Lusch and Carolyn Y. Nicholson. 1995. 'Power and relationship commitment: Their impact on marketing channel member performance', *Journal of Retailing* 71: 363–92.

Crosno, Jody L. and Robert Dahlstrom. 2008. 'A meta-analytic review of opportunism in exchange relationships', *Journal of the Academy of Marketing Science* 36: 191–201.

Emerson, Richard M. 1962. 'Power-dependence relations', *American Sociological Review* 27: 31–41.

Finch, John, Shiming Zhang and Susi Geiger. 2013. 'Managing in conflict: How actors distribute conflict in an industrial network', *Industrial Marketing Management* 42: 1063–73.

Gaski, John F. 1984. 'The theory of power and conflict in channels of distribution', *Journal of Marketing* 48: 9–29.

Gereffi, Gary, John Humphrey and Timothy Sturgeon. 2005. 'The governance of global value chains', *Review of International Political Economy* 12: 78–104.

Grandinetti, Roberto. 2017. 'Exploring the dark side of cooperative buyer–seller relationships', *Journal of Business and Industrial Marketing*, 32: 326–36.

Gulati, Ranjay and Martin Gargiulo. 1999. 'Where do interorganizational networks come from?', *American Journal of Sociology* 104: 1439–93.

Hajda, Jan. 1968. 'Ambivalence and social relations', *Sociological Focus* 2(2): 21–8.

Håkansson, Håkan, David Ford, Lars-Erik Gadde, Ivan Snehota and Alexandra Waluszewski. 2009. *Business in Networks*. Chichester: Wiley.

Hawkins, Timothy G., Terrance L. Pohlen and Victor R. Prybutok. 2013. 'Buyer opportunism in business-to-business exchange', *Industrial Marketing Management* 42: 1266–78.

Hawkins, Timothy G., C. Michael Wittman and Michael Beyerlein. 2008. 'Antecedents and consequences of opportunism in buyer–supplier relations: Research synthesis and new frontiers', *Industrial Marketing Management* 37: 895–909.

Hillcoat-Nalletamby, Sarah and Judith Phillips. 2011. 'Sociological ambivalence revisited', *Sociology* 45: 202–17.

Ivens, Bjoern S. 2004. 'How relevant are the different forms of relational behavior? An empirical test based on McNeil's exchange framework', *Journal of Business and Industrial Marketing* 19: 300–9.

Kang, Bohyeon and Rupinder P. Jindal. 2015. 'Opportunism in buyer–seller relationships: Some unexplored antecedents', *Journal of Business Research* 68: 735–42.

Klein, Benjamin. 1996. 'Why hold-ups occur: The self-enforcing range of contractual relationships', *Economic Inquiry* 34: 444–63.

Kotabe, Masaaki, Xavier Martin and Hiroshi Domoto. 2003. 'Gaining from vertical partnerships: Knowledge transfer, relationship duration and supplier performance improvement in the U.S. and Japanese automotive industries', *Strategic Management Journal* 24: 293–316.

Lui, Steven S., Yin-yee Wong and Weiping Liu. 2009. 'Asset specificity roles in interfirm cooperation: Reducing opportunistic behavior or increasing cooperative behavior?', *Journal of Business Research* 62: 1214–19.

Lumineau, Fabrice, Stephanie Eckerd and Sean Handley. 2015. 'Inter-organizational conflicts: Research overview, challenges, and opportunities', *Journal of Strategic Contracting and Negotiation* 1: 42–64.

Lumineau, Fabrice and Nuno Oliveira. 2020. 'Reinvigorating the study of opportunism in supply chain management', *Journal of Supply Chain Management* 56: 73–87.

Luo, Yadong. 2006. 'Opportunism in inter-firm exchanges in emerging markets', *Management and Organization Review* 2: 121–47.

Lusch, Robert F. and James R. Brown. 1996. 'Interdependency, contracting, and relational behavior in marketing channels', *Journal of Marketing* 60: 19–38.

Macneil, Ian R. 1980. *The New Social Contract: An inquiry into modern contractual relations*. New Haven, CT: Yale University Press.

Menard, Claud. 2004. 'The economics of hybrid organizations', *Journal of Institutional and Theoretical Economics* 160: 345–76.

Paswan, Audhesh K., Tanawat Hirunyawipada and Pramod Iyer. 2017. 'Opportunism, governance structure and relational norms: An interactive perspective', *Journal of Business Research* 77: 131–9.

Provan, Keith G. and Steven J. Skinner. 1989. 'Interorganizational dependence and control predictors of opportunism in dealer–supplier relations', *Academy of Management Journal* 32: 202–12.

Radaev, Vadim. 2013. 'Market power and relational conflicts in Russian retailing', *Journal of Business and Industrial Marketing* 28: 167–77.

Radaev, Vadim. 2015. 'Relational exchange in supply chains and its constitutive elements', *Ekonomicheskaya sotsiologiya (Journal of Economic Sociology)* 16: 81–99.

Sa Vinhas, Alberto and Jan B. Heide. 2015. 'Forms of competition and outcomes in dual distribution channels: The distributor's perspective', *Marketing Science* 34: 160–75.

Smith, Ken G., Stephen J. Carroll and Susan J. Ashford. 1995. 'Intra- and interorganizational cooperation: Toward a research agenda', *Academy of Management Journal* 38: 7–23.

Ting, Shueh-Chin, Cheng-Nan Chen and Darrell E. Bartholomew. 2007. 'An integrated study of entrepreneurs' opportunism', *Journal of Business & Industrial Marketing* 22: 322–35.

Wang, Xuehua and Zhilin Yang. 2013. 'Inter-firm opportunism: A meta-analytic review and assessment of its antecedents and effect on performance', *Journal of Business & Industrial Marketing* 28: 137–46.

Wathne, Kenneth H. and Jan B. Heide. 2000. 'Opportunism in interfirm relationships: Forms, outcomes, and solutions', *Journal of Marketing* 64: 36–51.

Williamson, Oliver E. 1975. *Markets and Hierarchies: Analysis and antitrust implications*. New York: Free Press.

Zeng, Fue, Yunjia Chi, Maggie Chuoyan Dong and Jing Huang. 2017. 'The dyadic structure of exchange partners' governing-agency social capital and opportunism in buyer–supplier relationships', *Journal of Business Research* 79: 294–302.

Zhu, Wenting, Samuel Su and Zhigang Shou. 2017. 'Social ties and firm performance: The mediating effect of adaptive capability and supplier opportunism', *Journal of Business Research* 78: 226–32.

7
Abusive supervision in organizations: Power, dependency and employee voice in labour relations

Evgeniya Balabanova

Introduction

The issue of power in organizations has a long tradition in sociological theory, as well as in industrial relations and management science. The analysis of organizations through the lenses of power and domination made it possible to explore the processes through which elite social groups gain and retain their advantages both within and outside organizations as well as the mechanisms of allocation and distribution of valued resources. While industrial and organizational sociology has been focused more on how power relations shape social structures and contribute to wider societal processes, especially social and economic inequality and discrimination, management science has been more driven by the business logic of ensuring a firm's efficiency and effectiveness. Despite some differences in the sociological and management domains, both rely on the importance of understanding power in organizations and its social and economic effects.

While power can be located in or outside organizations (for a detailed review of the interconnected sites of organizational power, see Fleming and Spicer 2014), sociology has a strong tradition of focusing on the external environments, that is, the social, political and cultural contexts within which organizations reside. The question of power inside organizations – including the struggles within formal organizational boundaries for resources, the systems of control, and the manner of supervising and exercising power and domination over the employees – is most often raised in the framework of the managerial approach. To date, a good deal of literature that stems from the ideas of control over sources of uncertainty and valuable resources proposed by Crozier (1964) and by Pfeffer and Salanick (1974) has focused on power relations between organizational units. Another stream of research refers to employer–employee conflict, primarily focusing on trade unions and other forms of employee collective representation. Finally, a number of studies focus on interpersonal power between individuals. This micro level of analysing power at work, embodied in individual behaviour and attitudinal and emotional reactions, is now highly influenced by psychological approaches. Under these lenses, firstly, the understanding of 'power' is often excessively wide, understood as an actor's general ability to influence another's behaviour. Secondly, psychological approaches focus primarily on personality traits or individual positions in social networks as the main antecedents of power advantages.

To address these two gaps, this chapter goes beyond 'psychological' explanations of power relations in organizations and adopts a sociological perspective on the micro level, or the level of individual behaviour in work roles. My study is based on the Weberian understanding of power, which implies real or potential conflicts of interest and the use of some form of coercion, thus excluding voluntary actions under the processes of social influence.

The micro level of organizational analysis reveals several important features of the ambivalent nature of power. Firstly, power is a necessary condition for achieving organizational goals, mobilizing resources and enhancing performance. It helps to provide regular, predictable and coordinated social interactions, ensures rule compliance and prevents conflicts and anarchy. At the same time, there is also a 'dark side' to interpersonal power which is destructive for organizations. The present study focuses on a phenomenon which embodies the negative aspects of managerial power – 'abusive supervision' (AS), understood here as a 'sustained display of hostile verbal and nonverbal behaviors, excluding physical contact' (Tepper 2000, 178). Abusive supervision leads to a broad range of dysfunctional outcomes – at the individual (e.g., psychological distress, emotional burnout, withdrawal behaviours), team (decline in performance) and organizational (climate of hostility and distrust, low morale among employees) levels (Starratt and Grandy 2010; Tepper et al. 2017). In this way, AS may be considered as an example of the motivational ambivalence of power (Ledeneva 2018): although declared as a means of maintaining order in the workplace and performance enhancement, AS, in fact, is often actually used to strengthen the personal power of managers and/or to camouflage the lack of skills for effective leadership.

Secondly, exercising managerial functions requires administrative and economic resources to foster desirable behaviour on the part of employees. The power to hire and fire and to implement incentives and penalties is often seen as the most important condition for managing people. However, managers' resource advantages create socio-economic dependency on the part of employees and thus may lead to the misuse or abuse of the superiors' power. I turn to the arguments of social exchange theory (SET) (Emerson 1962; 1976), according to which power advantages stem from having valued and deficient resources that other social actors cannot do without and are not able to gain from an alternative source. The SET conception of gaining power seems to be very relevant for the analysis of employment relations. Since the elasticity of demand for labour force is normally associated with the inelasticity of capital and wages supply, employers have power advantages over employees (Poggi 2001). This is especially relevant for the analysis of employment relations in Russia, considering the fact that employees have become increasingly dependent on employers in recent years, thereby tilting the balance of power in the latter's favour (Tikhonova and Karavay 2018). Thus, I address another type of ambivalence (Ledeneva 2018), namely, functional ambivalence of power advantages at the disposal of supervisors. These advantages may provide both positive and negative results; they can be a tool for both increasing and decreasing subordinates' motivation and performance.

Thirdly, AS, being a form of socio-psychological violence, normally assigns the subordinate the role of a passive victim. Managers' abuse of power claims absolute control over employees and demands their unquestioning obedience. Indeed, extant research shows that AS leads to subordinates' emotional burnout and lower levels of self-esteem, thus implying the exercising of predominantly externally driven behaviours of employees. Nevertheless, the latter still have opportunities to oppose the abusive power of their employers and supervisors. Among the resources available to them are their highly valued professional skills, unique expertise (Crozier 1964), social networking and the fact that they have alternatives to their current employers. Moreover, individual employees can restore the balance of power by engaging in proactive 'political behaviour' aimed at accessing valuable organizational resources. Many academics share the idea that organizations are inherently 'political arenas' (Mintzberg 1985), since they are sites for the continuous contestation of employer and employee interests, and the struggle for resources is inevitable in every formal organization. Hence, there is another face of functional ambivalence: although power abuse by managers implies loyalty and obedience from subordinates, the latter may react in a quite opposite way by employing active coping strategies, including, for example, voice behaviour.

To sum up, AS can be seen as embodying the functional and motivational ambivalence of power in organizations in three ways: (1) the ambivalence of the 'positive' and 'negative' sides of managerial power; (2) the ambivalence of the outcomes of managerial power advantages; and (3) the ambivalence of employee reactions to managerial abuses of power.

In recent decades, research on AS has been conducted mainly in the United States and Western Europe. To date, there have been no studies on AS in Russia, except a small-scale exploratory study (Balabanova et al. 2018a). Extant research also focuses primarily on individual-level antecedents of AS, such as the personality traits of supervisors and subordinates and the quality of their relationships, without paying much attention to the socio-economic bases of 'negative' managerial power. Finally, there is still little empirical evidence to suggest that employees subjected to AS do not simply behave as passive victims but try to restore the balance of power through proactive efforts (Wee et al. 2017).

My analysis is based on a sample of 1,100 non-supervisory respondents across 10 industries and nine geographical regions in Russia. It adds to the literature in three ways. Firstly, it sheds light on manifestations of AS as a form of power abuse in the underexplored cultural context of Russia. Secondly, in line with SET propositions, I test the importance of employee economic dependency in predicting AS. Thirdly, my study examines employee voice strategies as proactive reactions to AS aimed at restoring the balance of subordinate–supervisor power relations.

Ambivalence of power in organizations: abusive supervision as a manifestation of 'negative' power

Power is an essential attribute of organizations, a condition for the consistency of interactions and the achievement of organizational goals. Understood as 'the probability that one actor within a social relationship will be in a position to carry out his will despite resistance' (Weber 1968, 53), power is often necessary for the implementation of managerial functions. Over the last two decades, several studies have examined manager–worker power relations. Among these, Radaev (1994; 2009) examined managers' strategies of establishing and legitimizing authority in the Russian context. Being constructed in the intersection of the two axes – the rigidity/flexibility of the administrative hierarchy and the formality/

informality of labour relations – these strategies were described in terms of *bureaucratism, paternalism, partnership* and *fraternalism*. All four strategies refer to 'positive' power as the ability to achieve organizational goals. Likewise, the qualitative study by Balabanova et al. (2018b) described four managerial styles of owners and CEOs in privately owned Russian business organizations (the *wild capitalist, rationalist, passive* and *statist* styles). Although three of the four styles were found to be highly authoritarian and exploitative, all of them were aimed at increasing business profitability in the high power distance context of Russia.

However, a high degree of formal authority and economic resources obtained by managers/supervisors may give rise to the abuse of power. In this case, this produces 'negative power' (Rus 1980; Simon and Oakes 2006), focused on furthering one's personal interests instead of pursuing organizational goals. The negative aspects of managerial power are manifested in the phenomenon of AS (Tepper et al. 2009; 2017; Lian et al. 2012), which is close to other less frequently used terms such as petty tyranny, supervisor aggression, supervisor undermining (Tepper et al. 2017) or bullying (Rainey and Melzer 2021).

The most widely recognized definition of AS – 'sustained display of hostile verbal and nonverbal behaviors, excluding physical contact' – was suggested by Tepper (2000, 178). This understanding implies that AS is a behavioural phenomenon, which includes the discrete, observed actions of a supervisor towards her/his subordinates. Tepper's (2000) AS indicators refer both to overt emotional aggression towards subordinates and to hostility, displayed as psychological pressure, unethical behaviours and rhetoric that might be insulting for subordinates – uncontrolled outbursts, violating promises, refusal of requests, public ridicule or 'sabotage' towards employees.

However, AS is not limited to 'psychological' phenomena which reflect supervisors' poor impulse control. The abuse of power also includes subordinate-targeted behaviours that violate employees' interests related to their day-to-day work activities, material rewards or professional development. Among these are, for example, assigning unachievable tasks, obstructionism, depriving employees of important resources, violating employees' interests, inappropriately blaming employees for others' mistakes, and ignoring or taking credit for achievements. These adverse work-related practices are perceived as offensive and may have the same, if not stronger, damaging effects on employees as 'emotional blowouts' by their supervisors.

Speaking more broadly, this idea behind the classification of AS into two types relates to the understanding that employment relations comprise two main aspects: economic (material, financial) and social (relational, emotional). This division underlies, for example, the well-known classification of psychological contracts (PCs) into transactional and relational (Rousseau 1995). Transactional PCs emphasize transparent obligations associated with monetary rewards, whereas relational PCs include broad, socio-emotional obligations such as support, trust and respect. Following this recognized classification, we propose that AS may also be divided into 'transactional' and 'relational' aspects. However, to date, AS is interpreted mainly from a socio-emotional perspective, without considering the economic ('transactional') aspects of subordinate–supervisor interactions.

To address this gap, I developed indicators of AS which refer to work-related adverse events and day-to-day managerial practices associated with economic resources, which will be presented below.

Ambivalence of administrative and economic resources as sources of managerial power: a condition for management and the basis for the abuse of power

Previous research on AS has been based mainly on psychological, individual-level, theoretical explanations such as social learning theory and workplace role models (Mawritz et al. 2012), conservation of resources theory (Mackey et al. 2013), affective events theory (Eissa and Lester 2017) or leader–member exchange theory (Kim et al. 2019). In line with these approaches, AS is associated with the personality traits or demographic characteristics of the supervisor and/or subordinates. Among these are employees' negative affectivity, low conscientiousness and high neuroticism, young age and short tenure (Tepper et al. 2001; Starratt and Grandy 2010; Zhang and Bednall 2016), and supervisors' Machiavellianism or low emotional intelligence (Wisse and Sleebos 2016; Zhang and Bednall 2016). Other studies focus on other micro-level antecedents of AS, such as perceived supervisor–subordinate dissimilarity and relationship conflict (Tepper et al. 2011).

The general gap in the above-mentioned perspectives is that organizational practices and resources at the disposal of managers receive little attention as antecedents of AS (for exceptions see Mawritz et al. 2014; Zhang and Bednall 2016). These resources are important for implementing core managerial functions such as coordination, motivation and control. At the same time, managers' administrative and economic advantages put subordinates into a vulnerable position, making them dependent on the valued resources which they receive through their interactions with supervisors. In turn, this dependency may become fertile ground for the abuse of superiors' power. As Cook and Rice (2002, 712) explain, 'extreme dependence often invites the abuse of power in social relations, since the power disadvantaged view themselves as having few alternatives'. That is why current research should be complemented by sociological explanations of the nature of AS. For this purpose, SET (Blau 1964; Emerson 1976; Molm 1991) seems to be the most relevant approach, although it is under-regarded at this time.

SET assumes that all social interactions constitute processes of exchange of resources and favours that create mutual obligations (Homans 1958; Emerson 1962; Blau 1964). The balance (perceived equivalency) of these exchanges is the basic condition for the continuation of the interactions. This idea is widely used in research on employee–organization relationships, especially in studies on psychological contracts (e.g., Cropanzano and Mitchell 2005; Coyle-Shapiro and Shore 2007).

If exchanges occur between the owners of unequal resources, the balance is restored through power-dependence relations (Emerson 1962; Gargiulo and Ertug 2014). A 'provider', who controls deficit resources that other people crucially need and cannot get from an alternative source, achieves power over them. 'Providers' are able to impose conditions for delivering resources, to compel those who depend upon them to engage in certain actions, to manipulate by rewards and sanctions, and to convert economic dependency into moral obligations.

Since all formal organizations can be seen as hierarchical social structures characterized by unbalanced employee–employer power relationships, SET can explain many aspects of supervisor–subordinate interactions. The more valuable and indispensable resources a supervisor obtains and the fewer alternative sources there are for a subordinate to acquire these resources, the more personal power a supervisor has over her/his subordinate. These resources may include, for example, basic payments or bonuses, performance appraisals, access to equipment or information, and opportunities for professional training or career promotions. The more personal control a supervisor has over these resources, the more personally dependent a subordinate is. In cases where subordinates do not meet their supervisors' expectations and requirements or where they demonstrate some form of disloyalty, supervisors can cut off subordinates' access to those resources.

Perspectives of power-dependence analysis are mentioned in the literature on aggressive behaviour in organizations. Among these, there is evidence that employees who are mistreated by their supervisors are often powerless because of their resource dependency on their aggressors (Einarsen and Skogstad 1996; Tepper et al. 2009; Sharma 2018). A number of studies examined power asymmetry between managers and their subordinates that derive from fewer resources at the subordinates' disposal. Following Thau et al. (2004), I consider the lack of attractive job alternatives as one of the most reliable indicators of employee dependence. I expect that those with no alternatives at the moment of hiring are more dependent and thus vulnerable to AS. Thus, I formulate the first hypothesis suggesting that low-resource employees are more likely to be subjected to AS.

H1: 'Zero-option' employment positively predicts AS.

'Zero-option' employment is closely connected to job insecurity – a 'perceived threat to the continuity and stability of employment as it is currently experienced' (Shoss 2017, 1914). Since job insecurity increases employee vulnerability, one can expect that employees with high perceived job insecurity are more dependent on their supervisors and this dependency results in supervisors abusing their power. Thus, I propose:

H2: Perceived job insecurity positively predicts AS.

According to previous research, employee dependency is negatively associated with perceived employability, or an employee's perception that they have attractive job alternatives to their current employers (Thau et al. 2004). Indeed, from the SET perspective, it is crucially important that AS is more often experienced by workers scoring low on employability (Tepper 2000). Later, Tepper et al. (2009) associated employee independence with intentions to quit, implying that employees who have concrete plans to leave their organization are less reliant on their current supervisor. Specifically, I hypothesize:

H3: Perceived employability negatively predicts AS.

The next two hypotheses refer to organizational practices that create resource-based employee dependency and power asymmetry between managers and their subordinates. As Martinko et al. (2013) noted, organizational antecedents of AS have still received little direct study. Specifically, to date, there are no studies examining the direct effects of organizational practices such as reward systems on AS.

The literature on meritocracy, defined as a principle that prescribes that only the most deserving are rewarded, gives some idea about how organizational practices are linked with power asymmetry and employee dependency. The opposition between 'meritocratic' and 'anti-meritocratic' principles of social organization in their ability to predict AS could be expected in the area of reward systems (Pfeffer and Fong 2005; Castilla and Benard 2010). Merit- or performance-based criteria of rewards are usually defined at the highest levels of the organizational hierarchy. These criteria imply depersonalized 'rules of the game' and thus give little personal power to a discrete line manager. Contrary to this, if rewards depend upon the subjective evaluations of immediate supervisors, one can expect that the latter will obtain considerable power, since they control an important resource. This informality refers to 'chaotic workplaces' within which managers and workers do not have clear understandings of their work roles or clear procedures for social interactions. The informal, unclear or contradictory expectations and responsibilities facilitate 'laissez-faire' leadership, which is associated with supervisory hostile behaviour as a mechanism to regain power over the labour process (Hodson et al. 2006; Skogstad et al. 2007; Roscigno et al. 2009; Rainey and Melzer 2021). Hence, subordinates' material well-being will depend on their bosses' will, whereby the latter may be tempted to abuse their power. Based on the above, I expect that meritocratic criteria of rewards are negative predictors of AS, while subjective and 'relationship-based' criteria breed AS in organizations:

H4. Performance-based payment negatively predicts AS.

H5. Reward systems based on supervisors' subjective evaluations and supervisor–subordinate personal relations positively predict AS.

Ambivalence of employee responses to abusive supervision: falling victim or breaking the 'spiral of abuse'?

The common narrative in the current literature is that AS, creating detrimental psychological working conditions, is counterproductive for organizations. The overwhelming majority of studies suggest that AS is associated with affective, cognitive and behavioural injury and focus on passive employee reactions to AS such as psychological distress, withdrawal and detachment, emotional burnout, alcohol use or leaving the organization (Bamberger and Bacharach 2006; Tepper et al. 2009;

2017). In general, scholars tend to consider employees subjected to AS helpless victims whose behavioural reactions normally fall within the *exit/loyalty/neglect* options, according to the EVLN (exit-voice-loyalty-neglect) scheme, which was developed by Hirschman (1970) and later by Farrell (1983).

What about the 'political' option from the EVLN scheme, namely, *voice*, defined as 'any attempt ... to change rather than to escape from an objectionable state of affairs' (Hirschman 1970, 30)? In recent decades, voice behaviour has received considerable attention in organizational studies, being understood as employees' proactive upward verbal behaviour, the expression of ideas, information or opinions focused on affecting organizational functional change in the work context and speaking up on important issues and problems in organizations. Notably, this is *upward* communication, that is, it is directed to someone in a higher organizational position (Van Dyne et al. 2003; Maynes and Podsakoff 2014; Morrison 2014).

Existing research suggests different types of employee voice, of which the most important is the distinction between a 'supportive' and a 'challenging' voice (Burris 2012). The first one 'is intended to stabilize or preserve existing organizational policies or practices' (Burris 2012, 853). A supportive voice can be exercised through employee involvement in decision-making processes or discretionary speaking up in response to a threat to the status quo. In contrast, a challenging (or change-oriented) voice 'involves speaking up in ways intended to alter, modify, or destabilize generally accepted sets of practices, policies, or strategic directions that make up the status quo' in organizations (Burris 2012, 852). The latter is riskier for employees since managers often perceive challenging messages as threatening and thus react negatively.

Can we expect voice behaviour from employees faced with AS? Some authors argue that employees who are subjected to AS are less likely to use their voices (Burris et al. 2008; Farh and Chen 2014; Chamberlin et al. 2017) because a psychologically safe environment is a key condition for employees to voice organizational concerns (Detert and Burris, 2007). However, there is an opposite, counter-intuitive assumption that, instead of withdrawal behaviours, employees faced with AS will increase their voice. The arguments for this assumption are as follows. Firstly, employees using a supportive voice may expect their managers to regard them as loyal and thus become more accepting of them (Burris 2012) or, at least, less hostile. Secondly, upward communication may be an active positive coping strategy in response to a stressful environment, specifically aimed at managing the psychological distress caused by AS (Carver et al. 1989), in order to prevent future AS. Thirdly, messages, even challenging ones, may be valuable for an organization, hence voice behaviour can have positive image effects for employees (Burris et al. 2013; Grant 2013). Fourthly, challenging voice behaviour refers to 'political actions' as self-interested behaviour aimed at achieving an actor's objectives (Ferris et al. 2019) and thus may be considered as a way to protect employee interests.

To sum up these arguments in terms of SET, voice behaviour may be a coping strategy which restores the balance of power between managers and subordinates. Voice behaviour may be a way of breaking the 'spiral of abuse' by increasing employees' instrumental value to their supervisors (Wee et al. 2017). 'Value enhancement' may reduce employees' dependency on supervisors and thus restore the balance of power. This is especially important considering that supervisors' power advantage over subordinates is not stable and may change over time; power may shift from one party to another in a workplace (Sturm and Antonakis 2015). When the level of supervisor dependence on the subordinate is higher, the supervisor is more likely to withdraw her/his abusive behaviour towards the subordinate. Thus, we can consider the 'negative' power of managers embodied in AS in terms of functional ambivalence (Ledeneva 2018). Contrary to the expectation of employees' loyalty and obedience, AS may give rise to a counter-intuitive and paradoxical reaction – employee voice as a means to restore employee–employer power symmetry.

From what is known about voice behaviour as a means of restoring the manager–employee power balance, it is reasonable to hypothesize:

H6: AS positively predicts employee voice behaviour.

Method

Sample and procedure

The sampling procedure was based on official data from the Russian Federal State Statistics Service about the population of eight Russian federal districts plus Moscow and the proportions of employees in different industries. Based on these, 10 industries were selected with a prevalence of privately owned industrial and service organizations. The data collection, using standardized face-to-face interviews, occurred in September–November 2018 and was administered by one of the leading Russian polling firms specializing in opinion polls and marketing research.

The obtained sample included 1,100 non-supervisory respondents having completed higher education across 10 industries and nine geographical regions. Respondents were engineers (47 per cent), accountants and other specialists in finance and insurance (23 per cent), non-supervisory managers and administrative staff (17 per cent) and IT specialists (13 per cent). Fifty-five per cent of the participants were men. The average age was 38.6 years old and the average tenure was 6.4 years.

Measures

Abusive supervision

Five 'psychological' indicators of AS were adopted from a shortened version of Tepper's (2000) AS measure (Mitchell and Ambrose 2007). Respondents used a five-point response scale from 1 = 'Never' to 5 = 'Very often'. These widely acknowledged measures have been extended by additional items which refer to the above-mentioned 'transactional', economic-based AS. To validate these measures I conducted a factor analysis. The test returned a two-factor solution which fully corresponded to my theoretical arguments (see Table 7.1). Both factors had satisfactory loadings (above 0.7) with no significant cross-loadings, and the total variance accounted for was 73 per cent.

Antecedents of AS: employee dependency

'Zero-option' employment was measured with a one-item variable. Respondents marked the extent to which they agreed with the statement relating to how they got their current job: 'It was almost the only option of employment for me.'

Perceived job insecurity was measured with one item on a five-point Likert-type scale, asking employees: 'What do you think is the likelihood that you lose your current job?' ('1' stood for 'It is quite unlikely' and '5' stood for 'It is highly possible').

Perceived employability was measured with a three-item measure on a five-point Likert-type scale, asking employees: 'If you lose your current job, how confident are you that you can find another job that would be good enough for you in terms of (1) wage amount, (2) job content, (3) working conditions?'

Performance-based payments were measured with three items on a five-point Likert-type scale, asking employees: 'How much do you think your wage depends upon …?' The items include (1) 'The amount of work you have done'; (2) 'The quality of your work'; and (3) 'Specific outcomes of your work, achieving concrete results'. The Cronbach's α was 0.72.

Table 7.1 Factor analysis results and percentages of respondents faced with AS

Original variables	Two-factor solution: 73% of total variance explained		% of positive answers ('4' plus '5')
	1 'Transactional' AS	2 'Relational' AS	
Violates my interests while distributing work assignments	.822		14
Ignores my merits, achievements and work results	.798		12
Violates my interests while distributing material rewards	.784		15
Hinders my career promotion and professional development in this organization	.758		9
Ignores my proposals and initiatives	.711		11
Puts me down in front of others*		.855	8
Makes negative comments about me to others*		.829	6
Tells me I'm incompetent*		.822	7
Ridicules me*		.740	6
Tells me my thoughts or feelings are stupid*		.720	6
Cronbach's α	.913	.894	

Source: Adapted from Mitchell and Ambrose (2007)

A *reward system, based on the supervisor's subjective evaluations and supervisor–subordinate personal relations*, was measured with one item on a five-point Likert-type scale, asking respondents: 'How much do you think your wage depends upon your personal relations with your supervisor?' where '1' stood for 'Not at all' and '5' stood for 'Strongly depends'.

Consequences of AS: employee voice behaviour

Seven indicators of employee voice were divided into 'supportive' and 'challenge-oriented' types. Respondents were asked: 'Over the last 12 months, have you done the following *voluntarily, without being forced by your supervisors?*' and used a five-point response scale from 1 = 'Definitely no' to 5 = 'Definitely yes' (see Table 7.2).

Table 7.2 Reliability analysis results and percentage of respondents engaged in voice behaviours

'Over the last 12 months, have you done the following *voluntarily, without being forced by your supervisors?*'	Cronbach's α	% of positive answers ('4' plus '5')
Supportive Voice		
Helping your supervisor, proposing solutions for problems that were articulated by the supervisor		38
Making proposals and taking the initiative in your personal work-related issues	0.857	44
Making proposals and taking the initiative in work-related issues in your work unit		31
Making proposals and taking the initiative in work-related issues at company level		28
Challenge-Oriented Voice		
Drawing superiors' attention to the wrongs and problems in your work unit or in the company		27
Speaking up about your critical concerns on work-related issues	0.870	22
Arguing with your superiors, upholding your personal opinions on work-related issues		21

Control variables. I explored the viability of four control variables that could provide alternative explanations for the hypothesized relationships among the constructs. *Subordinates'* and *supervisors' gender* were measured as binary variables (0 = female, 1 = male). *Employee age* and *tenure* were measured in years.

Table 7.3 presents the means, standard deviations and Pearson correlations of the variables in the study.

Analysis and results

Descriptive analysis

The results presented in Table 7.1 suggest, firstly, that AS has two faces – 'transactional' (economic-based, referring to the violation of employees' material interests) and 'relational' (socio-emotional). Secondly, the percentages of respondents indicating '4' or '5' on the scales were interpreted as positive answers and point to the conclusion that Russian professionals are being subjected to AS mainly in its 'transactional' form, while AS as it is traditionally understood, as emotional violence, is experienced by less than 10 per cent of respondents.

Table 7.2 presents an overview of the items used to measure the categories of employee voice and shows that between 28 and 44 per cent of respondents exhibit some forms of supportive voice behaviour, while challenge-oriented voice behaviour is reported less often – by between 21 and 27 per cent of respondents. This is in line with the idea that challenging voice behaviour is less safe and may entail considerable costs for employees.

Table 7.3 shows some important preliminary findings. Firstly, the two types of AS – work-related and socio-emotional – are significantly correlated. We can suppose that if supervisors are engaged in abusive relations with their subordinates, they typically perform both types of AS. Secondly, the two types of voice behaviour – supportive and challenge-oriented – are also highly correlated. Thirdly, interestingly, only one control variable – employee tenure – demonstrates significant bivariate correlations with transactional AS, while the others (subordinate age, subordinate and supervisor gender) do not. Contrary to this, a number of work-related variables significantly relate to AS. Fourthly, none of the three measures of perceived employability shows a significant direct relationship to AS. Thus, Hypothesis 3 – *'Perceived employability negatively predicts AS'* – was not supported.

Table 7.3 Means, standard deviations and correlations

Variables	Mean	SD	1	2	3	4	5	6	7	8	9	10	11	12	13	14	15
1. Employee gender (1 = male)	.55	.48	1														
2. Age	38.65	10.88	-,035	1													
3. Tenure	6.402	4.92	-,014	,543**	1												
4. Supervisor gender (1 = male)	.77	.421	,253**	,075*	,044	1											
5. 'Zero-option' employment	2,58	1,27	-,024	,028	,046	,008	1										
6. Job insecurity	2.63	1.06	-,058	,109**	,028	-,078**	,146**	1									
7. Employability – wage	3,41	1,07	-,018	-,152**	-,125**	-,012	-,164**	-,223**	1								
8. Employability – work content	3,56	1,04	,009	-,151**	-,126**	-,044	-,188**	-,203**	,640**	1							
9. Employability – working conditions	3,48	1,06	,004	-,115**	-,087**	-,064*	-,151**	-,220**	,563**	,682**	1						
10. Performance-based payment (factor score)	0	1	,077*	-,020	-,042	,039	-,082**	-,137**	,087**	,111**	,116**	1					
11. Wage depends upon personal relations with a supervisor	3.07	1.31	,020	-,021	-,005	,004	,050	-,122**	,079**	,078**	,068*	,090*	1				
12. 'Transactional' AS	2.09	.92	,026	,046	,067*	-,024	,166**	,073*	,019	-,039	-,025	-,318**	,212**	1			
13. 'Relational' AS	1.67	.84	,020	,022	,057	-,038	,217**	,033	,041	-,010	,017	-,255**	,204**	,689**	1		
14. Supportive voice	2,88	1,04	,082**	,064*	,027	,121**	-,035	-,204**	,165**	,119**	,062*	,010	,397**	,278**	,243**	1	
15. Challenge-oriented voice	2,52	1,12	,058	,063*	,045	,110**	,055	-,121**	,114**	,075*	,048	-,067*	,354**	,338**	,341**	,702**	1

Note: *, ** Correlations are significant at the 0.05 and 0.01 levels, respectively (two-tailed).

Regression analysis

To test the hypotheses, I performed two separate multiple regression analyses – for transactional and relational AS as dependent variables (Table 7.4). Only those variables which showed significant bivariate correlations with at least one type of AS were included as predictors into the regression models.

In line with H1, 'zero-option' employment is positively related to both types of AS. Perceived job insecurity, although correlated with transactional AS, lost its significance in the regression model, thus not supporting H2. H4, which states that performance-based payment negatively relates to AS, was strongly supported for both types of AS. H5, which states that a reward system based on supervisors' subjective evaluations and supervisor–subordinate personal relations positively relates to AS, was also supported for both types of AS.

To test the hypothesis on the relationship between AS and employee voice behaviour, four multiple regressions were used (Table 7.5). Since the two types of AS are strongly correlated to each other (r = 0.689, p < .001), they were tested as predictors in separate models in order to avoid the problem of multicollinearity. Only those variables which showed significant bivariate correlations with at least one type of voice behaviour were included as predictors in the regression models.

As indicated in Table 7.5, control variables of employees' gender and age lost their significance in regression models. However, interestingly, there is a persistent significance of the supervisor's gender in all regression models, reflecting the fact that subordinates of male

Table 7.4 Regression analysis results for abusive supervision

Predictors	Transactional AS	Relational AS
Tenure	,048	,039
'Zero-option' employment	,120***	,184***
Job insecurity	,039	-,003
Performance-based payment	-,322***	-,259***
Wage depends upon personal relations with a supervisor	,240***	,218***
Adjusted R^2	0.175	0.149
F	48.14	39.71

Notes: ***p < 0.001.

Table 7.5 Regression analysis results for employee voice behaviour

Predictors	Supportive Voice		Challenge-oriented Voice	
	Model 1	Model 2	Model 1	Model 2
Employee gender (1 = male)	,048	,050	,023	,024
Age	,044	,052	,040	,047
Supervisor gender (1 = male)	,112***	,113***	,109***	,113***
'Transactional' AS	,278***		,338***	
'Relational' AS		,246***		,344***
Adjusted R^2	.094	.077	.127	.131
F	29.81	24.29	41.34	42.82

Notes: ***$p < 0.001$.

supervisors are more inclined to speak up. The most important result of the analysis is that, in line with H6, both types of AS positively predict employee voice behaviour. This relationship is stronger for challenge-oriented than for supportive voice behaviour.

Table 7.6 summarizes the key findings of this study.

Table 7.6 Results of testing the hypotheses

H1	'Zero-option' employment positively predicts AS	Supported
H2	Perceived job insecurity positively predicts AS	Not supported
H3	Perceived employability negatively predicts AS	Not supported
H4	Performance-based payment negatively predicts AS	Supported
H5	Reward systems based on supervisors' subjective evaluations and supervisor–subordinate personal relations positively predicts AS	Supported
H6	AS positively predicts employee voice	Supported

Discussion

The current study examined the antecedents and the outcomes of abusive supervision, which embodies the functional and motivational ambivalence of power in organizations: (1) the ambivalence of 'bright' and 'dark' sides of managerial power; (2) the ambivalence of administrative and economic resources as sources of managerial power; and (3) the ambivalence of employee reactions to managerial abuses of power.

My results support one of the key assumptions of SET, namely, that control over valued resources creates unbalanced power relations, thus constituting fertile soil for the perpetration of abusive behaviour. In turn, employees subjected to AS try to restore the balance of power by means of voice strategies, thus supporting Mintzberg's (1985) metaphor of organizations as 'political arenas'. This study addresses several gaps in the literature.

Firstly, the main contribution of the study to the previous literature is that it reveals the leading role of managerial practices in predicting AS in organizations, thus responding to the call to consider the direct organizational antecedents of AS (Martinko et al. 2013). In so doing, I contribute to integrating both sociological and organizational studies perspectives in the analysis of AS. I go beyond individual-level explanations and focus on the institutional conditions of labour, which are objectified in day-to-day work practices. In contrast to the majority of previous studies, I found that the individual characteristics of employees or their bosses do not significantly relate to AS. I reveal that systems of rewards that lack universal performance-based criteria provide fertile ground for AS. When the conditions of payments are left to the informal personal judgements of direct supervisors, work units become a 'preserve', or a 'patrimony', of their heads, thus creating feudal-like relationships, with employees becoming personally dependent upon their supervisors. The ability to control the most valued resource – the size of the salary – promotes the abuse of managers' power. In general, I may conclude that AS is greater under the conditions of anti-meritocratic systems of remuneration, when payments are not performance-based but depend upon subordinates' personal relationships with their superiors. Thus, I employ the ideas of meritocracy in organizations (Petersen et al. 2000; Castilla and Benard 2010), which have not been used in studies on AS at this time.

Secondly, regression models revealed that one more indicator of employee dependency – 'zero-option' employment – also predicts AS. This is in line with the SET propositions (Emerson 1962; Gargiulo and Ertug

2014) that actor A's dependence on actor B is inversely proportional to A's ability to get resources that are critical to A outside of the A–B relationship.

These two findings reveal the motivational and functional ambivalence of power in organizations. As Smelser (1998, 8) proposed, 'dependent situations breed ambivalence'. When speaking about employment relations, we can conclude that supervisors' power advantages provide both positive (performance-enhancing) and negative outcomes, and the latter are embodied in the phenomenon of AS.

Thirdly, the findings lend empirical support to the idea that employees subjected to AS do not always remain passive victims. Rather, they try to restore the balance of power by engaging in proactive voice behaviour. In so doing, they implement two possible strategies. The first one (supportive voice behaviour) is a form of 'active loyalty'. Faced with AS, employees try to demonstrate their conformity to the 'rules of the game' and gain a more positive image, thus expecting more favourable attitudes from their supervisors. The second strategy (challenging voice behaviour) demonstrates employees' readiness to challenge the existing routines. These two strategies, as the analysis revealed, are not opposite but complementary. Both are aimed at employees' *value enhancement*: while still dependent on their supervisors, employees restore the balance of social exchange by making the supervisors more dependent on their skills, opinions and ideas. Moreover, an employee who engages in voice behaviour will be more likely to attract others' attention and, in turn, will increase the likelihood of others viewing the person as competent and group-oriented (Weiss and Morrison 2019). In such a way, voice behaviour may become a strategy of status attainment (Ridgeway and Berger 1986), or an efficient coping strategy in response to AS. Altogether, both voice strategies may lead to breaking the 'spiral of abuse'. That is, employee reactions to AS provide an important though underexplored case of functional ambivalence of power in formal hierarchical organizations. Instead of expected employee victimization and strengthening the personal power of managers, employee voice comes to the fore as a means to create a more symmetrical situation in which the damaging and 'productive' effects of AS coexist. In contrast to most previous studies, I highlight a more balanced view of power relations in organizations, stressing both possible passive and active employee coping strategies in response to AS.

Limitations and future research directions

As with every study, the current one has a number of limitations. Firstly, the data collected in this study are cross-sectional. To fully address this limitation, future research should consider utilizing various research designs (for example, experimental or longitudinal), which could provide further support for the predictive validity of the current study. Secondly, the sample, although it includes 10 industries and nine geographical regions, may not be totally representative of the Russian population. Only non-supervisory respondents who completed higher education and were employed in private-sector organizations were surveyed. Future research should examine the antecedents of AS and employee response strategies among other professional groups, for example, blue-collar workers or public-sector employees.

Acknowledgements

The research was supported by a grant from the National Research University Higher School of Economics (HSE University) through the Program for Basic Research.

References

Balabanova, Evgeniya, Maria Borovik and Veronika Deminskaya. 2018a. 'Abusive supervision: Manifestations, antecedents, and consequences', *Russian Management Journal* 16: 309–36 (in Russian).

Balabanova, Evgeniya, Alexey Rebrov and Alexei Koveshnikov. 2018b. 'Managerial styles in privately owned domestic organisations in Russia: Heterogeneity, antecedents, and organizational implications', *Management and Organization Review* 14: 37–72.

Bamberger, Peter A. and Samuel B. Bacharach. 2006. 'Abusive supervision and subordinate problem drinking: Taking resistance, stress and subordinate personality into account', *Human Relations* 59: 723–52.

Blau, Peter M. 1964. *Exchange and Power in Social Life*. New York: Wiley.

Burris, Ethan R. 2012. 'The risks and rewards of speaking up: Managerial responses to employee voice', *Academy of Management Journal* 55: 851–75.

Burris, Ethan R., James R. Detert and Dan S. Chiaburu. 2008. 'Quitting before leaving: The mediating effects of psychological attachment and detachment on voice', *Journal of Applied Psychology* 93: 912–22.

Burris, Ethan R., James R. Detert and Alexander C. Romney. 2013. 'Speaking up versus being heard: The dimensions of disagreement around and outcomes of employee voice', *Organization Science* 24: 22–38.

Carver, Charles S., Michael F. Scheier and Jagdish K. Weintraub. 1989. 'Assessing coping strategies: A theoretically based approach', *Journal of Personality and Social Psychology* 56: 267–83.

Castilla, Emilio J. and Stephen Benard. 2010. 'The paradox of meritocracy in organizations', *Administrative Science Quarterly* 55: 543–676.

Chamberlin, Melissa, Daniel W. Newton and Jeffery A. LePine. 2017. 'A meta-analysis of voice and its promotive and prohibitive forms: Identification of key associations, distinctions, and future research directions', *Personnel Psychology* 70: 11–71.

Cook, Karen S. and Eric R. W. Rice. 2002. 'Exchange and power: Issues of structure and agency'. In *Handbook of Sociological Theory*, edited by Jonathan H. Turner, 699–719. New York: Kluwer Academic/Plenum Publishers.

Coyle-Shapiro, Jacqueline A.-M. and Lynn M. Shore. 2007. 'The employee–organization relationship: Where do we go from here?', *Human Resource Management Review* 17: 166–79.

Cropanzano, Russel and Marie S. Mitchell. 2005. 'Social exchange theory: An interdisciplinary review', *Journal of Management* 31: 874–900.

Crozier, Michel. 1964. *The Bureaucratic Phenomenon*. Chicago: University of Chicago Press.

Detert, James R. and Ethan R. Burris. 2007. 'Leadership behavior and employee voice: Is the door really open?', *Academy of Management Journal* 50: 869–84.

Einarsen, Ståle and Anders Skogstad. 1996. 'Bullying at work: Epidemiological findings in public and private organizations', *European Journal of Work and Organizational Psychology* 5: 185–201.

Eissa, Gabi and Scott W. Lester. 2017. 'Supervisor role overload and frustration as antecedents of abusive supervision: The moderating role of supervisor personality', *Journal of Organizational Behavior* 38: 307–26.

Emerson, Richard M. 1962. 'Power-dependence relations', *American Sociological Review* 27: 31–40.

Emerson, Richard M. 1976. 'Social exchange theory', *Annual Review of Sociology* 2: 335–62.

Farh, Crystal I. C. and Zhijun Chen. 2014. 'Beyond the individual victim: Multilevel consequences of abusive supervision in teams', *Journal of Applied Psychology* 99: 1074–95.

Farrell, Dan. 1983. 'Exit, voice, loyalty, and neglect as responses to job dissatisfaction: A multidimensional scaling study', *Academy of Management Journal* 26: 596–607.

Ferris, Gerald R., Ellen B. Parker III, Charn P. McAllister and Liam P. Maher. 2019. 'Reorganizing organizational politics research: A review of the literature and identification of future research directions', *Annual Review of Organizational Psychology and Organizational Behavior* 6: 299–323.

Fleming, Peter and André Spicer. 2014. 'Power in management and organization science', *Academy of Management Annals* 8: 237–98.

Gargiulo, Martin and Gokhan Ertug. 2014. 'The power of the weak', *Research in the Sociology of Organizations* 40: 179–98.

Grant, Adam M. 2013. 'Rocking the boat but keeping it steady: The role of emotion regulation in employee voice', *Academy of Management Journal* 56: 1703–23.

Hirschman, Albert O. 1970. *Exit, Voice and Loyalty: Responses to decline in firms, organizations, and states*. Cambridge, MA: Harvard University Press.

Hodson, Randy, Vincent J. Roscigno and Steven H. Lopez. 2006. 'Chaos and the abuse of power: Workplace bullying in organizational and interactional context', *Work and Occupations* 33: 382–416.

Homans, George. 1958. 'Social behavior as exchange', *American Journal of Sociology* 63: 597–606.

Kim, Kyoung Yong, Leanne Atwater, Zahir I. Latheef and Dianhan Zheng. 2019. 'Three motives for abusive supervision: The mitigating effect of subordinates attributed motives on abusive supervision's negative outcomes', *Journal of Leadership and Organizational Studies* 26: 476–94.

Ledeneva, Alena. 2018. 'Introduction: The informal view of the world – key challenges and main findings of the Global Informality Project'. In *The Global Encyclopaedia of Informality, Vol. 1: Understanding social and cultural complexity*, edited by Alena Ledeneva, 1–27. London: UCL Press.

Lian, Huiwen, D. Lance Ferris and Douglas J. Brown. 2012. 'Does power distance exacerbate or mitigate the effects of abusive supervision? It depends on the outcome', *Journal of Applied Psychology* 97: 107–23.

Mackey, Jeremy D., Ellen B. Parker III, Wayne A. Hochwarter and Gerald R. Ferris. 2013. 'Subordinate social adaptability and the consequences of abusive supervision perceptions in two samples', *Leadership Quarterly* 24: 732–46.

Martinko, Mark J., Paul Harvey, Jeremy R. Brees and Jeremy D. Mackey. 2013. 'A review of abusive supervision research', *Journal of Organizational Behavior* 34: S120–37.

Mawritz, Mary Bardes, Robert Folger and Gary P. Latham. 2014. 'Supervisors' exceedingly difficult goals and abusive supervision: The mediating effects of hindrance stress, anger, and anxiety', *Journal of Organizational Behavior* 35: 358–72.

Mawritz, Mary Bardes, David M. Mayer, Jenny M. Hoobler, Sandy J. Wayne and Sophia V. Marinova. 2012. 'A trickle-down model of abusive supervision', *Personnel Psychology* 65: 325–57.

Maynes, Timothy D. and Philip M. Podsakoff. 2014. 'Speaking more broadly: An examination of the nature, antecedents, and consequences of an expanded set of employee voice behaviors', *Journal of Applied Psychology* 99: 87–112.

Mintzberg, Henry. 1985. 'The organization as political arena', *Journal of Management Studies* 22: 133–54.

Mitchell, Marie S. and Maureen L. Ambrose. 2007. 'Abusive supervision and workplace deviance and the moderating effects of negative reciprocity beliefs', *Journal of Applied Psychology* 92: 1159–68.

Molm, Linda D. 1991. 'Affect and social exchange: Satisfaction in power-dependence relations', *American Sociological Review* 56: 475–93.

Morrison, Elizabeth W. 2014. 'Employee voice and silence', *Annual Review of Organizational Psychology and Organizational Behavior* 1: 173–97.

Petersen, Trond, Ishak Saporta and Marc-David L. Siedel. 2000. 'Offering a job: Meritocracy and social networks', *American Journal of Sociology* 106: 763–816.

Pfeffer, Jeffrey and Christina T. Fong. 2005. 'Building organization theory from first principles: The self-enhancement motive and understanding power and influence', *Organization Science* 16: 372–88.

Pfeffer, Jeffrey and Gerald R. Salanick. 1974. 'Organizational decision making as a political process: The case of a university budget', *Administrative Science Quarterly* 19: 135–51.

Poggi, Gianfranco. 2001. *Forms of Power*. Cambridge: Polity Press.

Radaev, Vadim. 1994. 'Four strategies of establishing authority within the firm: Outcomes of the study of Russian entrepreneurs', *Sotsiologicheskii Zhournal* [Sociological journal] 1(2): 149–57 (in Russian).

Radaev, Vadim. 2009. 'How managers establish their authority at the Russian industrial enterprise: A typology and empirical evidence', *Journal of Comparative Economic Studies* 5: 101–24.

Rainey, Anthony and Silvia M. Melzer. 2021. 'The organizational context of supervisory bullying: Diversity/equity and work–family policies', *Work and Occupations* 48: 285–319.

Ridgeway, Cecilia L. and Joseph Berger. 1986. 'Expectations, legitimation, and dominance behavior in task groups', *American Sociological Review* 51: 603–17.

Roscigno, Vincent J., Randy Hodson and Steven H. Lopez. 2009. 'Workplace incivilities: The role of interest conflicts, social closure, and organizational chaos', *Work, Employment and Society* 23: 747–73.

Rousseau, Denise M. 1995. *Psychological Contracts in Organizations: Understanding written and unwritten agreements*. Thousand Oaks, CA: SAGE.

Rus, Veljko. 1980. 'Positive and negative power', *Organization Studies* 1: 3–19.

Sharma, Payal N. 2018. 'Moving beyond the employee: The role of the organizational context in leader workplace aggression', *Leadership Quarterly* 29: 203–17.

Shoss, Mindy K. 2017. 'Job insecurity: An integrative review and agenda for future research', *Journal of Management* 43: 1911–39.

Simon, Bernd and Penelope Oakes. 2006. 'Beyond dependence: An identity approach to social power and domination', *Human Relations* 59: 105–39.

Skogstad, Anders, Ståle Einarsen, Torbjørn Torsheim, Merethe S. Aasland and Hilde Hetland. 2007. 'The destructiveness of laissez-faire leadership behavior', *Journal of Occupational Health Psychology* 12: 80–92.

Smelser, Neil. J. 1998. 'Presidential address 1997', *American Sociological Review* 63: 1–15.

Starratt, Alison and Gina Grandy. 2010. 'Young workers' experiences of abusive leadership', *Leadership and Organization Development Journal* 31: 136–58.

Sturm, Rachel and John Antonakis. 2015. 'Interpersonal power: A review, critique, and research agenda', *Journal of Management* 41: 136–63.

Tepper, Bennett J. 2000. 'Consequences of abusive supervision', *Academy of Management Journal* 43: 178–90.

Tepper, Bennett J., Jon C. Carr, Denise M. Breaux, Sharon Geidern, Changya Hu and Hua Wei. 2009. 'Abusive supervision, intentions to quit, and employees' workplace deviance: A power/dependence analysis', *Organizational Behavior and Human Decision Processes* 109: 156–67.

Tepper, Bennett J., Michelle K. Duffy and Jason D. Shaw. 2001. 'Personality moderators of the relationship between abusive supervision and subordinates' resistance', *Journal of Applied Psychology* 86: 974–83.

Tepper, Bennett J., Sherry E. Moss and Michelle K. Duffy. 2011. 'Predictors of abusive supervision: Supervisor perceptions of deep-level dissimilarity, relationship conflict, and subordinate performance', *Academy of Management Journal* 54: 279–94.

Tepper, Bennett J., Lauren Simon and Hee Man Park. 2017. 'Abusive supervision', *Annual Review of Organizational Psychology and Organizational Behavior* 4: 123–52.

Thau, Stefan, Rebecca J. Bennett, Dagmar Stahlberg and Jon M. Werner. 2004. 'Why should I be generous when I have valued and accessible alternatives? Alternative exchange partners and OCB', *Journal of Organizational Behavior* 25: 607–26.

Tikhonova, Natalia and Anastasia V. Karavay. 2018. 'Dynamics of some indicators of Russians' general human capital in 2010–2015', *Sotsiologicheskie issledovaniya* [Sociological studies] 45(5): 84–98 (in Russian).

Van Dyne, Linn N. A., Soon Ang and Isabel C. Botero. 2003. 'Conceptualizing employee silence and employee voice as multidimensional constructs', *Journal of Management Studies* 40: 1359–92.

Weber, Max. 1968. *Economy and Society: An outline of interpretive sociology*. Berkeley: University of California Press.

Wee, Elijah, Hui Liao, Dong Liu and Jun Liu. 2017. 'Moving from abuse to reconciliation: A power-dependence perspective on when and how a follower can break the spiral of abuse', *Academy of Management Journal* 60: 2352–80.

Weiss, Mona and Elizabeth W. Morrison. 2019. 'Speaking up and moving up: How voice can enhance employees' social status', *Journal of Organizational Behavior* 40: 5–19.

Wisse, Barbara and Ed Sleebos. 2016. 'When the dark ones gain power: Perceived position power strengthens the effect of supervisor Machiavellianism on abusive supervision in work teams', *Personality and Individual Differences* 99: 122–6.

Zhang, Yucheng and Timothy C. Bednall. 2016. 'Antecedents of abusive supervision: A meta-analytic review', *Journal of Business Ethics* 139: 455–71.

8
Beyond the state and digital platforms: (In)formalization of freelance contracting in Russia

Andrey Shevchuk and Denis Strebkov

Introduction

With the advent of information and communication technology, labour markets in which individual providers, such as freelancers, are matched to clients through digital platforms have become a distinctive feature of the new economy. The social regulation of the emerging model referred to as the 'gig economy' falls outside of bureaucratic hierarchies and standard employment relationships, which makes it an important socio-economic and academic issue. Specific configurations and ambivalence of power may shape different models of the gig economy, calling for more research on specific (country and industry) case studies (Codagnone et al. 2018; Thelen 2018). This chapter focuses on the development of the online labour market in Russia. Taking into account the number of registered users on the largest Russian-language freelance platforms, several million people have gained experience of freelancing online (Shevchuk and Strebkov 2021). However, since the very beginning, the Russian-language online labour market has been largely part of the 'shadow economy', based on informal agreements and tax avoidance. Some studies have also reported a high degree of informality in freelance and platform work in other countries, making this phenomenon an interesting topic worthy of investigation (Rodgers et al. 2014; Aleksynska 2021).

From the start, digital platforms also purported to regulate the online labour markets, creating technical infrastructures and implementing the 'rules of the game'. There is a major concern in the literature about the rise of platforms as powerful 'private regulators' that have a huge impact on people's lives (Codagnone et al. 2018). Divergent views either celebrate platforms as entrepreneurial incubators or criticize them for being 'digital cages' and accelerants of precarity (Vallas and Schor 2020). It is also argued that digital platforms have the potential to contribute to transforming informal work into formal employment while facilitating tax compliance and collection thanks to improved traceability (European Commission 2016). However, in Russia, as we will see, the power of online labour platforms is less pervasive and many freelancers have also succeeded in escaping this private regulation.

This chapter investigates the informal freelance economy in Russia by focusing on one dimension of informality – namely, contracting arrangements. First, drawing on a unique data set comprising four waves of Russian Freelance Survey data gathered over a 10-year period (2009–19), we shed light on how freelancers typically enter into agreements with their clients. Particularly, we trace the dynamics of various indicators to see how the situation has changed over time. Drawing this big picture helps improve awareness of persistent informality in the Russian-language online labour market and shows how trends towards formalization are weak and fragile.

Second, we seek to understand which categories of freelancers make agreements of a certain type and investigate the determinants of various contracting arrangements. Who are those rare freelancers who conclude formal legal contracts? Who are those who choose contracting arrangements provided by digital platforms? And how do both groups differ from freelancers who engage in informal transactions? Can using platform arrangements be a first step to concluding written legal contracts or do they present divergent types of formalization? These questions are important because they can shed light on preferences and demand for particular institutional arrangements as well as the barriers and limitations to legalization in the online labour market.

Third, we explore the consequences of various contracting arrangements as exemplified by their ability to curb the opportunistic behaviour of clients. Is there any power in formal legal contracts and platform arrangements compared with informal agreements? Do they help prevent agreement violations and solve various problems with clients? Answering these questions may contribute to a better understanding of persistent informality in the online labour market.

We conclude by discussing the ambivalence of power in the digital freelance economy in Russia.

Contracting in the external labour market: the rise of digital platforms

Understanding work within large bureaucratic organizations and internal labour markets was an important arena for the sociology of work, labour economics and personnel studies in the twentieth century (Doeringer and Piore 1971; Althauser 1989; Osterman 2011). Standard employment systems were characterized by full-time work for an employer organization done on a fixed schedule, at employer-owned locations, under the employer's administrative control, with open-ended employment contracts (Kalleberg et al. 2000). For several decades, commentators have been tracing trends towards the gradual erosion of internal labour markets and non-standard work arrangements, shifting various aspects of work outside the organization (Cappelli 1999; Kalleberg et al. 2003; Ashford et al. 2007). Freelancers have a minimal attachment to firms and represent an extreme form of externalized labour. Conceptually and legally, freelancers do not have employment relationships but act as independent service providers doing discrete work tasks (projects) for multiple clients (Connelly and Gallagher 2006; Cappelli and Keller 2013).[1]

Although many workers are forced into external labour markets, for others, loosening their attachment to organizations provides opportunities to accommodate their desires, preferences and individualized lifestyles (Pink 2001). Highly skilled professionals, in particular, may experience increased work autonomy and greater financial gains by moving into open markets (Barley and Kunda 2004; Osnowitz 2010). However, the contingent relationships between workers and firms in the external labour market beyond the safety net of labour law and collective bargaining are problematic for workers. Theoretically, legal contracts should be used to govern the relationship in external labour markets. Carefully planning the transaction and setting out provisions for future contingencies and potential legal sanctions constitute important elements of formal contracting (Macaulay 1963).[2] However, as we know from various settings, independent contracting in the external labour markets is largely informal and prone to violations of workers' rights (Valenzuela et al. 2006; Bernhardt et al. 2013). Rodgers et al. (2014) reported that only one-third of independent workers in the United States always negotiated formal contracts, and another third did not use contracts at all.[3] Consequently, many independent workers experienced difficulty getting paid (44 per cent), late payment (38 per cent), payment for less than the agreed-upon amount (13 per cent) or were never paid (17 per cent). Moreover, this study also suggested that there was no robust association between the use of formal contracts and difficulty of getting paid (Rodgers et al. 2014). The average US freelancer is cheated out of approximately $5,968 each year, and freelancers in New York State alone are owed between $2.3 billion and $3.7 billion in unpaid wages annually (Baranowski 2018, 441). Osnowitz (2010, 169, 177) also argued that contracts provide no guarantee against opportunism, as freelancers lack collective representation and ready access to legal redress, and they avoid individual litigation, which is expensive and time-consuming. Only 5 per cent of freelancers pursue claims in court to recover payments owed (Baranowski 2018, 441).

The most recent trend is towards the gig economy, short-term on-demand work mediated by digital platforms (Kalleberg and Dunn 2016; Brancati et al. 2019; Huws et al. 2019; Piasna and Drahokoupil 2019). The pioneers of the digitalization of external labour markets were dedicated websites for remote work, which came into existence at around the turn of the millennium. In the literature, these websites are variously referred to as 'freelance online marketplaces' (Aguinis and Lawal 2013), 'crowdwork platforms' (De Stefano 2015) or 'online labour platforms' (Kässi and Lehdonvirta 2018).[4] In contrast to localized gig work (taxi driving, delivery, handiwork, cleaning, etc.), online labour markets comprise work that can be delivered electronically. Huge online labour markets have emerged that operate across spatial and political borders (Kuek et al. 2015). Businesses of various sizes and individual consumers use online labour platforms to gain access to the skills and services they need.

Digital platforms are not mere sites for meeting demand and supply but appear to be genuine market-makers creating a sophisticated technical and regulatory framework for freelance contracting on the internet (Codagnone et al. 2018). To guarantee the fulfilment of contractual obligations, many websites offer 'safe pay' (escrow) options and dispute assistance through arbitration. Escrow is a contractual arrangement common in e-commerce where a third party holds money in a dedicated account until both parties verify the transaction has been completed per the terms set. In the event of disagreement, both parties have the opportunity to turn to a third party for independent arbitration. Overall, digital platforms purport to organize the gig economy and, in many aspects, try to substitute the state in regulating huge labour markets. In search of more autonomy and control, freelancers stay away from bureaucratic hierarchies; however, they confront another employment structure as represented by digital platforms unilaterally imposing the 'rules of the game'.

However, there is evidence that many transactions occur outside platforms, undermining their power. Users (both freelancers and clients) have financial incentives to bypass platforms and contract directly to avoid websites' commissions. Freelancers and clients may use the websites as a resource for gathering data and finding 'leads' instead of as an actual place to conduct business (Snir and Hitt 2003; Radkevitch et al. 2006; Caraway 2010). Several online surveys also revealed that, to get work, freelancers tend to rely more on regular clients and referrals than on strangers from websites (Hackwith 2011; Shevchuk and Strebkov 2018). Finally, involvement in the online labour markets is a matter of degree. Most literature tends to isolate platform work as a distinct phenomenon; however, in real life the boundaries between online and offline freelancing are permeable.

Other factors complicate the state's capabilities to regulate online labour markets, revealing ambivalence of power and contributing to the overall informality of freelance contracting. The very nature of freelance work implies the small-scale production of individual micro-providers. For example, a typical project for website content writers is a small piece of text (about 1,000–2,000 characters) for a price of about $1–2. More complex projects require a considerable degree of flexibility for freelancers and clients to cooperate in knowledge-based and creative co-production (in the fields of ITCs, design or consulting). The fast-paced nature of platform work requires prompt responses in the matching process that may occur a few minutes after the job is posted. Regulatory deficiency is evident as in most cases labour law is not applicable, dedicated regulations governing platform work may be absent or incomplete, and litigation is costly. Long-distance virtual transactions prevent conventional written contracts between distant parties from being concluded, and transnational transactions complicate legal requirements further.

Freelance and platform work in Russia

In the Soviet Union, standard employment in its extreme form was supported by government guarantees of full employment, an imposed obligation to work and a legislative ban on any form of entrepreneurial activity and own-account work beyond state-owned enterprises. As a result, there remained only tiny niches for individual work outside formal organizations in the form of moonlighting (i.e., having a second job), which was entirely informal. Due to economic reforms in the late Soviet Union and after its collapse, independent work emerged as a new phenomenon and a valid option in the Russian labour market. However, many self-employed individuals and entrepreneurs operate in the shadow economy (Chepurenko 2014). They do not obtain a proper legal status, do not declare their economic activity, do not conclude legal contracts and avoid taxes. Persistent informality is also a distinctive feature of the Russian labour market in general (Gimpelson and Kapeliushnikov 2015).

In 2005, the leading Russian-language platform FL.ru (originally Free-lance.ru) was founded, making a key contribution to the development of the online labour market in Russia. FL.ru is a typical general-purpose freelance platform largely for high- and medium-skilled projects in categories such as programming, websites, texts, translating, multimedia, engineering, marketing, legal, consulting and so on. Fl.ru reports having over 1.6 million registered users not only from Russia but also from the other post-Soviet states and other countries (however, not all of them are active). Although there are several dozen Russian-language, online labour platforms (including some big players), FL.ru maintains its long-term dominant position in the online labour market (Shevchuk and Strebkov 2021). As a pioneering platform and genuine market-maker, FL.ru introduced key elements of the regulatory framework which were typical for online labour markets, including the 'safe pay' (escrow) service that was introduced to ensure trust and contract fulfilment. In 2012, to boost revenues from commissions, FL.ru tried to force all users to transact through 'safe pay' but eventually gave up. Protests and significant outflow of users forced FL.ru to leave this service optional. In contrast to many global platforms that rely on algorithmic management to ensure that users conduct their transactions on their site (Bucher et al. 2021), Russian-language platforms do not typically oblige users to do so. Freelance platforms in Russia generate revenues not only from commissions on transactions conducted on their websites but also mainly from payments for advanced accounts and additional services. An interesting situation has emerged, revealing the ambivalence of platform power in the Russian-language online labour market. Digital platforms have created a market infrastructure but are unable to fully reap the benefits. Freelancers and clients actively use websites to advertise themselves and gather information but only a small share of their transactions are carried out on the platforms. This may be explained by a lag in technical capabilities (and algorithmic management), legal deficiencies, competition between platforms, partial involvement of freelancers in platform work and the general widespread informality in the Russian economy, including the labour market.

For many years the new phenomenon of freelance platform work has been virtually ignored by the state, generating a regulative lacuna with neither legislative guidelines nor pragmatic administrative solutions. Labour legislation in Russia is inconsistent and incomplete on many issues, the social protection of self-employed workers in Russia is not feasible and courts follow very formal approaches in labour disputes. The Russian government has made several unsuccessful attempts to tackle the informal economy by introducing privileged tax regimes for self-employed persons (Chesalina 2020).[5] We conclude that the Russian state focuses mainly on tax issues and pays very little attention to other aspects of self-employment and platform work.

Data collection and sample

It has always been more difficult to research non-standard and informal workers quantitatively compared with regular employees, posing serious methodological challenges (Valenzuela et al. 2006; Ashford et al. 2007; Bergman and Jean 2016). We cannot rely on the standard sociological methods based on probability sampling because freelancers belong to hard-to-survey populations (Tourangeau 2014). We apply venue-based sampling, which is typically used to research geographically scattered populations who use certain spaces for regular meetings and congregations (Lee et al. 2014). We use data from the long-term research project 'Russian Freelance Survey' that was conducted on a leading Russian-language platform for online work, FL.ru, regarded as a venue of the target audience (Shevchuk and Strebkov 2021). The sampling assumed that regardless of whether freelancers were registered on other similar platforms, they tended to use the largest and the most developed infrastructure for freelancers on the Russian-language internet represented by FL.ru. To recruit participants, FL.ru administrators sent subscribers emails with invitations to answer the questionnaires and also advertised the surveys on social media. We neither suggested nor provided any incentives for participants. To date, four waves of this survey have been conducted: in 2009, 2011, 2014 and 2019 (see Table 8.1). All waves featured a common methodology for collecting and analysing data, with many questions unchanged between the waves. This provides an opportunity to analyse the dynamics of key indicators over a 10-year period. The questionnaires, which included between 40 and 54 items, covered a wide range of topics, including contracting arrangements and agreement violations. The survey was not restricted to Russian-based workers and attracted Russian-speaking participants from other countries, mainly in the post-Soviet space.

Table 8.1 Overview of the data collection approach and sample size, by survey wave

	2009	2011	2014	2019
Dates of data collection	12 Dec. 2008 – 03 Feb. 2009	25 Feb. 2011 – 29 Mar. 2011	15 Dec. 2013 – 06 Feb. 2014	03 Dec. 2018 – 02 Feb. 2019
Active freelancers	8,613	7,179	10,574	2,055
Number of questions	49	54	40	46
Completing time (median), minutes	13.9	12.8	11.1	11.7

Most of the analysis in this chapter is based on the latest wave of the survey deployed from December 2018 to January 2019. The sample includes 2,055 'active freelancers' who performed their work through online platforms and who completed at least two work projects in 2018. These data are complemented with the data of the previous waves to highlight the dynamics in selected indicators. For regressions, 401 persons were excluded from the analysis due to missing data in at least one of the questions used. Finally, our analytic sample of current active freelancers contained 1,654 respondents.

Divergent paths of (in)formalization

First, we aim to reveal what formal and informal arrangements freelancers rely on while contracting with their clients. To measure the formalization of the agreements, we asked the question 'In what form do you usually make an agreement with your clients?' followed by three alternative items: (1) we draw up an official written contract, (2) we use online platform procedures for arrangements ('safe pay' options) or (3) we have only an informal (written or verbal) agreement. Remarkably, a high level of informality was observed throughout the entire study period. For the first five years, from 2009 to 2014, the share of freelancers who regularly relied on written contracts with their clients was unchanged at 12 per cent (Figure 8.1). And it only rose slightly to 15 per cent by 2019. Since 2014 we have included 'platform procedures' as an option in our survey. For five years, the share of freelancers taking this new opportunity to conclude a formal agreement with their clients has grown by 3 percentage points, from 15 to 18 per cent. Respectively, the share of informal agreements gradually declined over 10 years, from 86 per cent in 2009 to 64 per cent in 2019. Still, almost two in three freelancers rely mainly on informal agreements with their clients.

We conclude that in the online labour market persistent informality was observed throughout the decade. Only a small proportion of freelancers routinely rely on formal arrangements as represented by legal written contracts and platform procedures. Thus, only a slight trend towards formalization exists. It is this that drives our interest in understanding who those people are who are choosing formal contracting arrangements, and how they differ from those relying on informal agreements.

The most intriguing question is why and how freelancers adopt formal arrangements. It is plausible to assume that people may adopt formal arrangements gradually over time. Freelancers may first become acquainted with platform arrangements as they are readily available, easy to use and involve low transaction costs. And after freelancers gain such an experience, they may move to the next level of formalization and conclude written legal contracts. Thus, we posit *a gradual formalization hypothesis* (H1): groups of freelancers using formal contracting

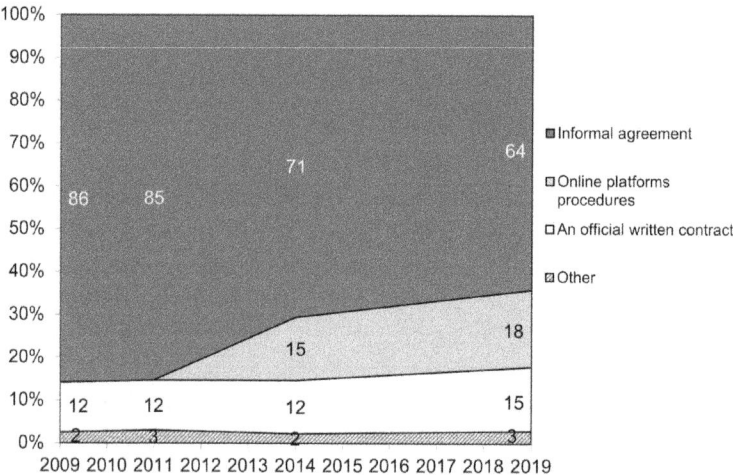

Figure 8.1 Contracting arrangements between freelancers and their clients (percentages), 2009–19.

arrangements, as represented by platform procedures and written contracts, are similar to each other in terms of their personal and professional characteristics, while differing substantially from freelancers relying on informal agreements.

To test this hypothesis, we estimated the association of different social-demographic, job and client characteristics to three types of contracting agreements via a multinomial logistic regression.

All models included a standard set of socio-demographic and job characteristics: sex, age, education level, country of residence, tenure of online platform work, number of projects completed in the last year, weekly hours of work, monthly post-tax income in roubles and the share of freelance work in the total earnings of the individual. In addition, we controlled for specialization in online work (the types of tasks that freelancers do online), which were grouped into six large thematic categories: websites and computer programming; graphic design and creative arts; photography, audio and video; writing, editing and translating; business services (advertising, marketing, consulting, etc.); and engineering.

Regressions also included control variables for the types of clients that online workers deal with. Based on a multiple-choice question, three dummies were used to distinguish individuals, small businesses and medium or large businesses as the types of clients. For Russian freelancers, we controlled whether they work only with local clients or also acquire projects from clients abroad. The mode of communication between freelancers and clients was assessed with the question 'Do you meet with your clients (face to face) while working on a project (e.g., to sign the agreement, discuss some questions, hand over deliverables)?' Responses were made on a five-point Likert scale. To ease the interpretation, we created two dummies: face-to-face contacts and mixed contacts. The category virtual contacts (I never meet with my clients) was the benchmark group.

The job-finding method is a good indicator of the workers' embeddedness in social networks (Granovetter 1995), especially for freelance contracting. We asked the following multiple-choice question: 'How do you usually get projects?' and divided all freelancers into three groups: (1) respondents who exclusively use social ties (such as regular clients, referrals from former clients and referrals from friends and acquaintances), (2) people who tend to rely exclusively on online platforms and (3) freelancers who combine social-channel and platform opportunities for getting job projects.

Descriptive statistics for selected independent and control variables with the specification of reference groups are reported in Table 8.2.

Table 8.2 Means or percentages of variables

	N	Mean or percentage	SD
Types of agreement formalization (%)			
Official contract	241	14.6	
Platform procedures	309	18.7	
Informal agreement	1,104	66.7	
Gender (%)			
Male	962	58.2	
Female (ref)	692	41.8	
Age (years)	1,654	33.39	10.06
Education status (%)			
University education	1,112	67.2	
Absence of university education (ref)	542	32.8	
Freelance tenure (years)	1,654	4.89	4.90
Primary area for freelance work (multiple choice, %)			
Websites/Computer programming	484	29.4	
Graphic design/Creative arts	599	36.4	
Engineering	140	8.5	
Photography/Audio/Video	219	13.3	
Writing/Editing/Translating	473	28.8	
Advertising/Marketing/Consulting	326	19.8	
Working hours per week	1,654	50.37	25.14
Number of projects per year in 2018 (natural logarithm)	1,654	2.94	1.07
Monthly post-tax income in roubles (%)			
90,001 or more	263	15.9	
48,001 to 90,000	438	26.5	
24,001 to 48,000	515	31.1	
12,001 to 24,000	278	16.8	
Less than 12,000 (ref)	160	9.7	

	N	Mean or percentage	SD
Share of freelance work in total earnings (%)			
Less than a third	434	26.2	
About half	217	13.1	
Two-thirds or more	275	16.6	
One hundred per cent (ref)	728	44.0	
Geography (%)			
Russians with clients only from Russia	744	45.0	
Russians with clients from abroad	436	26.4	
Non-Russians (ref)	474	28.7	
Types of clients (multiple choice, %)			
Individuals	1,268	76.7	
Small business	1,286	77.8	
Medium and large business	707	42.7	
Communication (%)			
Face-to-face contacts	233	14.1	
Mixed contacts	237	14.3	
Virtual contacts (ref)	1,184	71.6	
Job-finding method (%)			
Social ties only	464	28.1	
Both social ties and platforms	908	54.9	
Platforms only (ref)	282	17.0	

First, we compared those who usually sign an official contract with freelancers using platform arrangements and informal agreements (Model 1 and Model 2 in Table 8.3). Then, we compared platform arrangements with informal agreements (Model 3 in Table 8.3). The 0.10 level of significance was selected to discuss significant relationships highlighted by significant models. All analyses were conducted using IBM SPSS software version 21.0.

Table 8.3 Multinomial regression results for the types of agreement formalization

	Model 1		Model 2		Model 3	
	Official contract		Official contract		Platform procedures	
	in comparison with (reference category)					
	Platform procedures		Informal agreement		Informal agreement	
	B	S.E.	B	S.E.	B	S.E.
Male (female – ref)	–.43	.23*	–.56	.19***	–.13	.16
Age	–.008	.011	–.001	.009	.008	.007
University education (absence of univ. education – ref)	.41	.23*	.36	.19*	–.06	.15
Freelance tenure	.07	.02***	.01	.02	–.06	.02***
Primary area for freelance work (multiple choice)						
Websites/Computer programming	–.05	.25	.35	.20*	.39	.18**
Graphic design/Creative arts	.59	.24**	.27	.19	–.32	.17
Engineering	.64	.39	.56	.29*	–.08	.31
Photography/Audio/Video	–.20	.30	.14	.25	.34	.20*
Writing/Editing/Translating	–.40	.26	–.24	.22	.16	.18
Advertising/Marketing/Consulting	.51	.25**	.48	.20**	–.03	.19
Working hours per week	.000	.004	.002	.004	.002	.003
Number of projects per year in 2018 (natural logarithm)	–.12	.11	–.01	.09	.11	.07

	Model 1		Model 2		Model 3	
Monthly post-tax income in roubles (less than 12,000 – ref)						
90,001 or more	1.75	.54***	1.90	.48***	.15	.30
48,001 to 90,000	.85	.52	.65	.47	–.20	.26
24,001 to 48,000	.68	.51	.60	.47	–.08	.24
12,001 to 24,000	1.25	.53**	.83	.49*	–.42	.26
Share of freelance work in total earnings (only freelance work – ref)						
Less than a third	–.89	.27***	–.54	.23**	.35	.18*
About half	–.57	.32*	–.42	.26	.16	.22
Two-thirds or more	–.09	.29	–.29	.22	–.20	.21
Geography (non-Russians – ref)						
Russians with clients only from Russia	1.31	.28***	.71	.24***	–.61	.18***
Russians with clients from abroad	.83	.28***	.95	.25***	.12	.17
Types of clients (multiple choice)						
Individuals	–.60	.24**	–.70	.18***	–.11	.18
Small business	.14	.26	–.04	.22	–.18	.17
Medium and large business	.71	.22***	.82	.18***	.12	.16
Communication (virtual contacts – ref)						
Face-to-face contacts	2.03	.36***	1.41	.22***	–.62	.32*
Mixed contacts	1.37	.28***	1.10	.21***	–.27	.23
Job-finding method (platforms only – ref)						
Social ties only	2.45	.41***	.72	.36*	–1.73	.24***
Both social ties and platforms	1.48	.38***	.67	.36*	–.82	.18***
(Constant)	–3.92	.82***	–4.34	.73***	–.42	.46

Notes: * p < .10, ** p < .05, *** p < .01. N = 1,654; Nagelkerke R Square = .317; L.R. X2 (df) = 500 (56)***.

Our analysis reveals that those freelancers who sign an official contract and those who use the platform's procedures are fundamentally different in many ways, while those who conclude informal agreements are approximately in-between the two other groups. Thus, our hypothesis of gradual formalization (H1) has not been supported. It appears that we are dealing with divergent ways of formalization, which do not form a continuum.

Freelancers who sign formal written contracts are more educated, qualified, experienced and professional than others. Usually, they work with a smaller number of projects, but at the same time, their clients are more likely to be medium and large businesses and less likely to be individuals (this group of freelancers tend to carry out larger and longer-term projects). They more rarely use platforms to search for new clients and more often rely on their social networks. This group of freelancers is more likely to live in Russia and meet with clients face to face. They are more likely to specialize in the areas of design, engineering and business services. They also have the highest income level among all freelancers and income from freelance projects makes up the highest share of their total earnings. Women are more likely to sign a formal written contract than men.

The people using dedicated platform arrangements, on the contrary, are more likely to have the lowest freelance tenure, and the lowest level of professional skills. They actively use online platforms to search for clients. More often than others, they do not live in Russia and work with clients from other countries and regions. They are less likely to meet with clients face to face. The share of freelance earnings in their total personal income is the lowest for this group of freelancers. Thus, one can conclude that these people are more likely than others to combine freelancing with a regular job as an employee, that is, moonlighting.

Those who usually rely on informal agreements (either written or verbal) lie between the two previous groups in terms of freelance tenure, professional skills, location, face-to-face meetings with clients, the intensity of using platforms to find new clients and the share of freelance earnings in their total personal income. The only exception is that they are more likely than others to work with individuals and less likely to work with both small and large companies.

The outcomes of (in)formalization: problems and conflicts with clients

Managing an array of short-lived transactions with multiple clients, freelancers routinely encounter various kinds of problems and conflicts when initial agreements are broken or contested.[6]

Agreement violations were measured with the following multiple-choice question: 'In 2018, did you face one or more situations in which a client broke an initial agreement? If yes, in what way?' The possible answers for the respondents to choose from were the following: (1) Changes in initial requirements, specifications and delivery time, (2) Payment delay, (3) Partially unpaid fee, (4) Fully unpaid fee, (5) Other situation, (6) I did not face any of the situations listed above, but I've heard about such cases, and finally (7) I did not face any of the situations listed above and haven't heard about such cases. It should be noted that these self-reported measures are based on subjective understandings of agreements and their violations. However, they may be appropriate given the psychological nature of contracting (Rousseau, 1995).

In 2019, around 70 per cent of Russian-language freelancers reported client-side agreement violations within the last year (Figure 8.2). This proportion remains virtually unchanged over the entire 10-year period under review (71 per cent in 2009, and 72 per cent in 2011).[7] The violations included payment delay (44 per cent), changes in initial

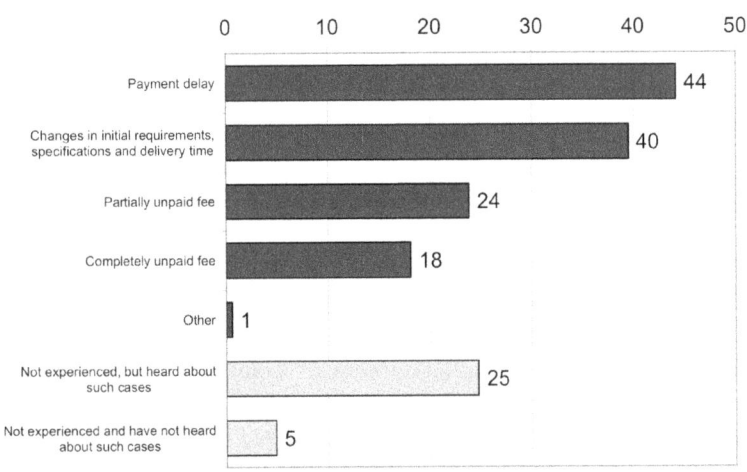

Figure 8.2 Client violations reported in 2019 (percentages).

requirements, specifications and delivery time (40 per cent), and partially unpaid fees (24 per cent) or completely unpaid fees (18 per cent).

It is important to know the final consequences of agreement violations. Success in *resolving problems* was measured with the following multiple-choice question: 'When the initial agreements were broken by the client, did you manage to solve the problem? If yes, how did you manage to do this?' The possible answers for the respondents to choose from were as follows: (1) Through negotiations with the client, (2) The administration of an online marketplace helped to resolve the dispute, (3) Through legal means, (4) Through threats or physical means, (5) Some other way and (6) No, the problems were never solved. Respondents who had not been in conflict situations during the previous year skipped this question. We constructed a new dummy variable coded 1 for respondents who managed to solve their problems in any way, and 0 otherwise ('No, the problems were never solved').

In 2019, 71 per cent of freelancers who suffered from agreement violations were able to resolve these problems successfully (Figure 8.3), showing a marked increase compared with 2009 when only 60 per cent of respondents succeeded in doing so. The vast majority of freelancers handled conflicts through negotiations with clients (57 per cent in 2009 and 64 per cent in 2019). In 2009 only 2 per cent of the freelancers indicated a platform's authority had assisted them in defending their rights, but in 2019 this share increased to 11 per cent. Legally enforcing contracts within the Russian-language freelance market is barely feasible. Only 1 per cent of freelancers were successful in legal action against client violators throughout all four waves of the research. Every year a small group of freelancers (4–5 per cent) applies threats and physical action to enforce their rights. However, 29 per cent reported in 2019 that the problem was never solved.

Do different contract arrangements lead to divergent outcomes in terms of agreement violation and conflict resolution? To test the effects of three contracting arrangements on agreement violations we used a binomial logistic regression. The social-demographic, job and client characteristics in the regressions were the same as in Models 1–3. The only additions were two dummies representing different approaches to the formalization of agreements discussed above. First, we considered the probability of experiencing an agreement violation, measured by the freelancer having experienced at least one problem in the last year (Model 4 in Table 8.4). Then, we analysed how different factors could help freelancers succeed in resolving these problems (Model 5 in Table 8.4). Table 8.4 presents the coefficients in logistic regressions and

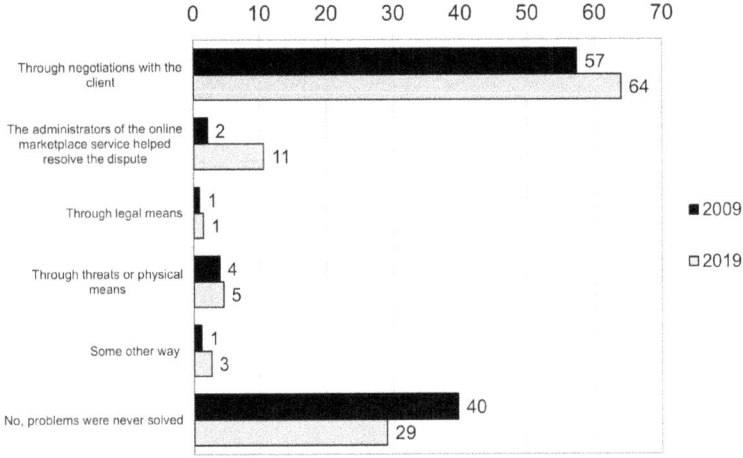

Figure 8.3 Solving problem with clients in 2009 and 2019 (percentages from those who had problems in the previous year).

robust standard errors with the coefficients' statistical significance. The table shows how adding independent variables related to the formalization of agreements, social embeddedness of exchange and mode of communication between freelancers and their clients contributes to predicting the probability of agreement violations and the subsequent resolution of the problems.

The form of the agreement with clients does not make much difference in the likelihood of experiencing violations. Regardless of whether freelancers signed a legal contract or used platform procedures, they have an approximately equal probability of suffering from agreement violations. The crosstab analysis shows us the same result: between 69 and 71 per cent of freelancers in each group faced at least one problem with clients in 2019. Thus, formal procedures fail to safeguard freelancers against agreement violations. But, at the same time, using platform procedures helps freelancers to resolve problems if they occur. Indeed, 78 per cent of workers with a legal contract and 75 per cent of freelancers using platform procedures were successful compared with only 68 per cent of those who rely on informal agreements.

Our analysis also revealed that online platforms are the main sources of problems for freelancers. Although online labour platforms provide freelancers with access to a greater variety of distant clients, they are the riskiest in terms of agreement violations. In contrast, freelancers who work with regular clients or rely only on referrals are less likely to

Table 8.4 Logistic regression coefficients for opportunism and problem-solving

	Model 4		Model 5	
	Some problem situations with clients		Problems not solved	
	B	S.E.	B	S.E.
Male (female – ref)	–.15	.13	–.30	.16*
Age	–.022	.006***	.006	.008
University education (absence of univ. education – ref)	.10	.13	.11	.15
Freelance tenure	.02	.01	–.02	.02
Primary area for freelance work (multiple choice)				
Websites/Computer programming	.06	.15	.11	.17
Graphic design/Creative arts	.13	.14	–.03	.17
Engineering	.02	.22	.26	.28
Photography/Audio/Video	.18	.18	–.53	.23**
Writing/Editing/Translating	–.50	.15***	–.15	.18
Advertising/Marketing/Consulting	.10	.15	–.12	.19
Working hours per week	.002	.002	.003	.003
Number of projects per last year (natural logarithm)	.32	.06***	–.16	.07**
Monthly post-tax income in roubles (less than 12,000 – ref)				
90,001 or more	–.25	.26	–1.03	.31***
48,001 to 90,000	–.05	.23	–.81	.26***
24,001 to 48,000	.01	.22	–.78	.25***
12,001 to 24,000	.22	.23	–.66	.26**

	Model 4		Model 5	
Share of freelance work in total earnings (only freelance work – ref)				
Less than a third	−.42	.15***	−.19	.19
About half	−.35	.18*	−.24	.23
Two-thirds or more	.26	.18	−.04	.19
Geography (non-Russians – ref)				
Russians with clients only from Russia	−.17	.15	.02	.18
Russians with clients from abroad	−.06	.16	.07	.18
Types of clients (multiple choice)				
Individuals	.00	.14	−.10	.17
Small business	.45	.14***	−.08	.18
Medium and large business	.18	.13	−.07	.15
Communication (virtual contacts – ref)				
Face-to-face contacts	.36	.18**	−.58	.24**
Mixed contacts	.44	.18**	−.17	.20
Job-finding method (platforms only – ref)				
Social ties only	−.70	.19***	−.26	.23
Both social ties and platforms	−.07	.18	−.17	.20
Type of agreement with clients (informal – ref)				
Official contract	−.21	.18	−.21	.23
Platform procedures	−.06	.16	−.39	.19**
(Constant)	.57	.39	.76	.49
N	1,654		1,159	
Nagelkerke R Square	.148		.081	

Notes: * $p < .10$, ** $p < .05$, *** $p < .01$.

face different forms of violations. It is well known from the extant literature that social networks help to mitigate opportunism (Shevchuk and Strebkov 2018). However, in this study, we have not found any evidence that social ties between freelancers and clients contribute to resolving problems.

We built analogous regression models for all four waves of the Russian Freelance Survey and obtained very similar and stable results (with only slight differences). In particular, formal procedures (official contract or platform arrangement) were never able to diminish the probability of agreement violations. But they were significantly helpful in resolving problems with clients. Social ties in previous years had a mixed and heterogeneous effect on the probability of agreement violations, but their effect on the resolution process was always positive and significant (Shevchuk and Strebkov 2018).

Conclusion

Contrary to the popular belief that informality is primarily associated with traditional sectors and simple technologies, our research shows how informality thrives in the digital freelance economy (Kovács et al. 2017). Freelance contracting is informal in many ways and according to various definitions. It is a small-scale, mostly individual activity beyond formal organizational structures. It is also informal because it exists in the shadow of state regulation and control; state authorities know little about this sector and cannot effectively tax it. Finally, freelancers rarely rely on institutionalized or formal contracting arrangements and prefer informal agreements.

Our study, which covered a whole decade (2009–19), revealed that the situation in this respect has been changing very slowly. There is little demand for formal contracting arrangements. The safeguarding functions of formal contracting arrangements such as legal contracts and platform procedures are minimal. The data suggest that freelancers choose to use formal arrangements for other reasons, along two divergent paths. More skilled, experienced and accomplished freelancers tend to carry out big and long-term projects for medium and large firms. The more complicated nature of these projects and the bureaucratic structure of these firms may lead to preferences for formal legal contracts. It is noteworthy that freelancers who conclude legal contracts are simultaneously more likely to rely on their social networks to get projects. This means that this group of freelancers possesses greater overall resources as exemplified by both human and social capital. At the same time, novice, low-skilled, inexperienced and part-time freelancers tend to contract for small projects with distant clients (including those from abroad) through platform arrangements. This may suggest that platforms are important for newcomers lacking human and social capital and involved in long-distance (including transnational) transactions. However, the majority of freelancers between high and low ends have no intention to engage in formal contracting. These results contribute to a better understanding of the heterogeneity of platform work and ambivalence of power relations in the digital economy.

The ambivalence of power manifests itself in a failure of manageability and is best grasped through the paradoxes it produces (Ledeneva 2018; Kotelnikova and Radaev in this volume). Although the state is supposed to regulate labour markets, the very nature of online freelancing makes digital platforms more powerful private regulators as they control infrastructure. Freelancers leave bureaucratic hierarchies to gain more autonomy and discretion but confront digital platforms trying unilaterally to impose the 'rules of the game'. Platforms invest in online infrastructure but cannot effectively gain revenues, as freelancers move a significant share of transactions outside these platforms. Freelancers expect contract enforcement and social security but tend to avoid formal contracting and paying taxes, undermining the state regulation. Ultimately, this turns into a vicious circle.

Overall, the study suggests that in Russia neither the state nor digital platforms had enough power to regulate the emerging online labour market and reap all the benefits (in the form of taxes and commissions). Rather, the online labour market developed in line with general patterns of informality in the Russian economy (Morris 2019). The study not only illuminates the failure of the state to regulate the new employment model but also challenges the popular view of platforms as digital cages that exhibit formidable and unrestricted power over workers.

In practical terms, the results of our analysis shed light on the serious challenges facing state initiatives for the legalization of the self-employment and digital freelance economy in Russia. Although it is already an ongoing practice for some other states to have agreements with platforms for the collection of taxes (European Commission 2016), the imperfect power of freelance platforms in Russia also makes this scenario problematic. As for digital platforms, they may continue to lose potential revenue, which deters further investment in this sector. Although informal employment provides some opportunities for workers, in the long run it may curb the further development of the online labour market. If individuals do not see genuine and tangible benefits of having a legal status and platform arrangements, they will continue to eschew any formal contracting. Many challenges regarding working conditions, workers' rights, collective representation and social protection should also be addressed to create positive incentives for workers (Chesalina 2020).

The recognition of ambivalence of power implies the focus on social processes and a variety of paths of development and outcomes (Hajda 1968). Further research should pay more attention to specific (country and industry) case studies and various configurations of power in the gig economy (Thelen 2018).

Acknowledgements

Fieldwork and analytical work were supported by the Program for Basic Research of the National Research University Higher School of Economics (HSE University).

Notes

1. That is why we avoid the term 'employer' in favour of 'client' or 'customer'.
2. The literature on the safeguarding function of contracts is vast (see Schepker et al. 2014 for a review).
3. Another study provided similar estimates that only 28 per cent of freelancers operate under written contracts in the United States (Baranowski 2018, 440).
4. In economic literature they are also referred to as 'online labour markets'. In this chapter, we reserve this term to describe the labour markets as such (not particular websites).
5. In 2019 (after the last wave of our survey), the piloting of a brand new tax regime for the self-employed started in several Russian regions, and in late 2020 it covered the entire country.
6. These situations can be conceptualized as opportunism on the part of clients, defined as any behaviour inconsistent with prior agreements (Williamson 1993; Shevchuk and Strebkov 2018).
7. In 2014, the wording of the question was significantly changed, so the results are not comparable with other waves.

References

Aguinis, Herman and Sola O. Lawal. 2013. 'eLancing: A review and research agenda for bridging the science–practice gap', *Human Resource Management Review* 23(1): 6–17.

Aleksynska, Mariya. 2021. *Digital Work in Eastern Europe: Overview of trends, outcomes, and policy response*. ILO Working Paper. Geneva: ILO.

Althauser, Robert P. 1989. 'Internal labor markets', *Annual Review of Sociology* 15(1): 143–61.

Ashford, Susan J., Elizabeth George and Ruth Blatt. 2007. 'Old assumptions, new work: The opportunities and challenges of research on nonstandard employment', *Academy of Management Annals* 1(1): 65–117.

Baranowski, Caitlin M. 2018. 'Freelance isn't free: The high cost of New York City's freelance isn't free act on hiring parties', *Brooklyn Journal of Corporate, Financial & Commercial Law* 12(2): 8.

Barley, Stephen R. and Gideon Kunda. 2004. *Gurus, Hired Guns, and Warm Bodies: Itinerant experts in a knowledge economy*. Princeton: Princeton University Press.

Bergman, Mindy E. and Vanessa A. Jean. 2016. 'Where have all the "workers" gone? A critical analysis of the unrepresentativeness of our samples relative to the labor market in the industrial–organizational psychology literature', *Industrial and Organizational Psychology* 9(1): 84–113.

Bernhardt, Annette, Michael W. Spiller and Diana Polson. 2013. 'All work and no pay: Violations of employment and labor laws in Chicago, Los Angeles and New York City', *Social Forces* 91(3): 725–46.

Brancati, Cesira Urzì, Annarosa Pesole and Enrique Fernández-Macías. 2019. *Digital Labour Platforms in Europe: Numbers, profiles, and employment status of platform workers*. Luxembourg: Publications Office of the European Union.

Bucher, Eliane Léontine, Peter Kalum Schou and Matthias Waldkirch. 2021. 'Pacifying the algorithm: Anticipatory compliance in the face of algorithmic management in the gig economy', *Organization* 28(1): 44–67.

Cappelli, Peter. 1999. *The New Deal at Work: Managing the market-driven workforce*. Boston: Harvard Business Press.

Cappelli, Peter and Joseph H. Keller. 2013. 'Classifying work in the new economy', *Academy of Management Review* 38(4): 575–96.

Caraway, Brett. 2010. 'Online labour markets: An inquiry into ODesk providers', *Work Organisation, Labour and Globalisation* 4(2): 111–25.

Chepurenko, Alexander. 2014. 'Informal entrepreneurship under transition: Causes and specific features'. In *Soziologie des Wirtschaftlichen: Alte und Neue Fragen*, edited by Dieter Bögenhold, 361–82. Wiesbaden: Springer.

Chesalina, Olga. 2020. 'Social and labour rights of "new" self-employed persons (and in particular self-employed platform workers) in Russia', *Russian Law Journal* 8(2): 49–78.

Codagnone, Cristiano, Athina Karatzogianni and Jacob Matthews. 2018. *Platform Economics: Rhetoric and reality in the 'sharing economy'*. Bingley: Emerald Group Publishing.

Connelly, Catherine E. and Daniel G. Gallagher. 2006. 'Independent and dependent contracting: Meaning and implications', *Human Resource Management Review* 16(2): 95–106.

De Stefano, Valerio. 2015. 'The rise of the just-in-time workforce: On-demand work, crowdwork, and labor protection in the gig-economy', *Comparative Labor Law and Policy Journal* 37(3): 461–71.

Doeringer, Peter B. and Michael J. Piore. 1971. *Internal Labor Markets and Manpower Analysis*. Lexington, MA: Heath.

European Commission. 2016. *Employment and Social Developments in Europe 2016*. Luxembourg: Publications Office of the European Union. Accessed 10 March 2021. http://op.europa.eu/en/publication-detail/-/publication/8d0b1be0-d95d-11e6-ad7c-01aa75ed71a1/language-en.

Gimpelson, Vladimir and Rostislav Kapeliushnikov. 2015. 'Between light and shadow: Informality in the Russian labour market'. In *The Challenges for Russia's Politicized Economic System*, edited by Susanne Oxenstierna, 33–58. London and New York: Routledge.

Granovetter, Mark S. 1995. *Getting a Job: A study of contacts and careers* (2nd edn). Chicago: University of Chicago Press.

Hackwith, Amanda. 2011. *Freelance Confidential*. Lexington, KY: Rockable Press.

Hajda, Jan. 1968. 'Ambivalence and social relations', *Sociological Focus* 2(2): 21–8.

Huws, Ursula, Neil H. Spencer, Matt Coates, Dag Syrdal and Kaire Holts. 2019. *The Platformisation of Work in Europe: Results from research in 13 European countries*. Brussels: Foundation for European Progressive Studies.

Kalleberg, Arne L. and Michael Dunn. 2016. 'Good jobs, bad jobs in the gig economy', *Perspectives on Work* 20(1–2): 10–14.

Kalleberg, Arne L., Barbara F. Reskin and Ken Hudson. 2000. 'Bad jobs in America: Standard and nonstandard employment relations and job quality in the United States', *American Sociological Review* 65(2): 256–78.

Kalleberg, Arne L., Jeremy Reynolds and Peter V. Marsden. 2003. 'Externalizing employment: Flexible staffing arrangements in US organizations', *Social Science Research* 32(4): 525–52.

Kässi, Otto and Vili Lehdonvirta. 2018. 'Online labour index: Measuring the online gig economy for policy and research', *Technological Forecasting and Social Change* 137: 241–8.

Kovács, Borbála, Jeremy Morris, Abel Polese and Drini Imami. 2017. 'Looking at the "sharing" economies concept through the prism of informality', *Cambridge Journal of Regions, Economy and Society* 10(2): 365–78.

Kuek, Siou Chew, Cecilia Paradi-Guilford, Toks Fayomi, Saori Imaizumi, Panos Ipeirotis, Patricia Pina and Manpreet Singh. 2015. *The Global Opportunity in Online Outsourcing.* Washington, DC: World Bank. Accessed 8 December 2021. https://openknowledge.worldbank.org/handle/10986/22284.

Ledeneva, Alena. 2018. 'Introduction: The informal view of the world – key challenges and main findings of the Global Informality Project'. In *The Global Encyclopaedia of Informality. Vol. 1: Towards understanding of social and cultural complexity*, edited by Alena Ledeneva, 1–27. London: UCL Press.

Lee, Sunghee, James Wagner and Richard Valliant. 2014. 'Recent developments of sampling hard-to-survey populations: An assessment'. In *Hard-to-Survey Populations*, edited by Roger Tourangeau, Brad Edwards, Timothy P. Johnson, Kirk M. Wolter and Nancy Bates, 424–44. Cambridge: Cambridge University Press.

Macaulay, Stewart. 1963. 'Non-contractual relations in business: A preliminary study', *American Sociological Review* 28(1): 55–67.

Morris, Jeremy. 2019. 'The informal economy and post-socialism: Imbricated perspectives on labor, the state, and social embeddedness', *Demokratizatsiya: The Journal of Post-Soviet Democratization* 27(1): 9–30.

Osnowitz, Debra. 2010. *Freelancing Expertise: Contract professionals in the new economy.* Ithaca, NY: Cornell University Press.

Osterman, Paul. 2011. 'Institutional labor economics, the new personnel economics, and internal labor markets: A reconsideration', *Industrial and Labor Relations Review* 64(4): 637–53.

Piasna, Agnieszka and Jan Drahokoupil. 2019. *Digital Labour in Central and Eastern Europe: Evidence from the ETUI Internet and Platform Work Survey.* Brussels: ETUI Research Paper-Working Paper. Accessed 8 December 2021. https://www.etui.org/node/31891.

Pink, Daniel H. 2001. *Free Agent Nation: How America's new independent workers are transforming the way we live.* New York: Warner Books.

Radkevitch, Uladzimir, Eric van Heck and Otto Koppius. 2006. *Buyer Commitment and Opportunism in the Online Market for IT Services.* ERIM Report Series Research in Management. Accessed 14 October 2014. http://repub.eur.nl/pub/7903.

Rodgers, William M., Sara Horowitz and Gabrielle Wuolo. 2014. 'The impact of client nonpayment on the income of contingent workers: Evidence from the freelancers union independent worker survey', *Industrial and Labor Relations Review* 67(Sup 3): 702–33.

Schepker, Donald J., Won-Yong Oh, Aleksey Martynov and Laura Poppo. 2014. 'The many futures of contracts: Moving beyond structure and safeguarding to coordination and adaptation', *Journal of Management* 40(1): 193–225.

Shevchuk, Andrey and Denis Strebkov. 2018. 'Safeguards against opportunism in freelance contracting on the internet', *British Journal of Industrial Relations* 56(2): 342–69.

Shevchuk, Andrey and Denis Strebkov. 2021. *Freelance Platform Work in Russia, 2009–2019.* ILO Working Paper No. 38. Geneva: ILO. Accessed 8 December 2021. http://www.ilo.org/global/publications/working-papers/WCMS_815254.

Snir, Eli M. and Lorin M. Hitt. 2003. 'Costly bidding in online markets for IT services', *Management Science* 49(11): 1504–20.

Thelen, Kathleen. 2018. 'Regulating Uber: The politics of the platform economy in Europe and the United States', *Perspectives on Politics* 16(4): 938–53.

Tourangeau, Roger. 2014. 'Defining hard-to-survey populations'. In *Hard-to-Survey Populations*, edited by Roger Tourangeau, Brad Edwards, Timothy P. Johnson, Kirk M. Wolter and Nancy Bates, 3–20. Cambridge: Cambridge University Press.

Valenzuela, Abel, Nik Theodore, Edwin Meléndez and Ana Luz Gonzalez. 2006. *On the Corner: Day labor in the United States.* Los Angeles: Center for the Study of Urban Poverty, University of California, Los Angeles.

Vallas, Steven and Juliet B. Schor. 2020. 'What do platforms do? Understanding the gig economy', *Annual Review of Sociology* 46(1): 273–94.

Williamson, Oliver E. 1993. 'Opportunism and its critics', *Managerial and Decision Economics* 14(2): 97–107.

9
Power struggles and quality construction in the market for municipal rental housing in Sweden

Elena Bogdanova

Introduction

Despite its name, since the 1990s the public rental sector in Sweden has undergone growing marketization, and according to researchers in the fields of economics and politics it is highly neoliberalized today (Hedin et al. 2012; Lind 2015). At the same time, it is still highly regulated compared with other countries, as it is comprised of two coexisting policy regimes that aggravate each other but without negating each other (Christophers 2013, 888). This hybridization gives rise to the ambivalent structural positions of core market actors: municipal housing companies are still responsible for creating and supporting housing as a public good but are obliged to act as profit-driven firms.

Empirically, I analyse how increasing the 'standard' and presenting it as higher-quality housing gives housing companies the justification to significantly raise rents, and my focus is thus on how tenants are trying to oppose the 'luxury' renovation of their rental apartments. I analyse the case study of the process of public participation in a housing renovation project in Gothenburg, Sweden. Housing policy in Sweden is an example of how partial marketization and liberalization can create conditions for ambivalent power relations in the market.

Political power and the Swedish 'public goods' housing system

Municipal housing in Swedish literally translates as 'public good' and municipal companies as 'public goods companies' and is an example of the attempt to introduce market, and therefore power, relations into the previously public domain. Municipal housing is comprised of older housing stock in the city centres, buildings from the 'record years' of the post-war industrial growth and recently produced housing. Bengtsson (2015, 25) describes its central functions as 'the responsibility of local municipalities (communes) for housing provision, the central role of organisations in the housing market, a system of rent-setting, and specific rules and market prerequisites for other types of ownership'. The definition of housing as a specific regime with defined rules, state strategies and interest groups reveals a high degree of institutionalization of housing in Sweden.

Between 1963 and 1973 the Swedish government implemented the 'Million Homes Programme', which aimed at providing affordable modern housing for all. The mass construction of industrialized prefabricated houses started in 1961, and the period between 1961 and 1975 is often referred to as the 'record years' (Hall and Vidén 2005, 303). About half were owned by municipal housing companies. The record wave of construction was heavily subsidized by state loans, and, as several authors have pointed out, the rents never reflected the costs of construction.

In both municipal and private rental markets rents are defined through collective bargaining between property owners and their organization and the Union of Tenants. These negotiations were framed by the so-called use value system (*bruksvärdesystemet*), which means that rent levels in municipal housing also affect possible rent levels in the private rental sector, which is based on agreement between the owner and the Union of Tenants. The use value of an apartment is derived from the following features: size, level of modernization, layout, location inside the building, the standard of repair and sound insulation. Access to an elevator, laundry, waste pipe, separate storage space, good maintenance, garage and parking lot can also increase an apartment's use value (*Sveriges domstolar*). The presence or absence of one of these features in a particular building defines its standard, and the respective value is reflected in the rent level.

The role of the use value system is crucial in cases of building renovations. In the past decade the local authorities in Gothenburg have sought to 'redevelop' the most vulnerable suburbs in the city. To achieve this, the city proposed a package of constructions and renovations, including acute renovation of the existing municipal housing.

Theoretical framing and previous research

My theoretical considerations are framed by two strands of the literature. The first is discussions among social movement scholars about power and its enforcement in the process of urban development and deliberation. The second is the framing of the concepts of value and worth in the field of economic sociology. I argue that the combination of these two lines of research enriches the field of economic sociology by providing new dimensions of power in the valuation process.

Theoretically, positions of stakeholders can be described as sociologically ambivalent (Merton 1976) as they have to perform several conflicting roles associated with their status as public companies (Merton 1976, 10). Hajda (1968, 23) addressed social structural ambivalence as 'contradictory pulls of ties between individuals, positions, and groups'. He pointed out that this ambivalence is most visible in periods of social dislocation and connected the latter several processes, including urbanization and transformation of local markets into national and world markets. Housing markets in most central cities in Europe are bearing the effects of globalization and financialization.

> In every social situation the individual acts as a species of marginal men: he is in part alienated from the situation, in part embracing the situation as a given condition, and in part stimulated by the situation to surpass it or at least determine it. He not only confronts a 'social reality,' he also creates it by his own actions. (Hajda 1968, 27)

The consultation process in housing renovations represents this structural social ambivalence – bureaucrats and engineers from the managing companies, representatives of the union of tenants, and tenants – all three groups are alienated, conditioned by the situation or are trying to determine it at different stages of the consultation process where they are trying to establish the value and worth of proposed renovations.

According to the European conventions, housing is a human right, and therefore any actions that could lead to the loss of housing cause immediate protests. There is a large body of literature that has already approached the problem of renovation of housing built in the 1960s and

1970s and problems connected to this process. The focus was mostly on the social and economic effects that renovation processes have on different social groups: gentrification in connection with extreme rent increases, densification and 'renoviction' (Baeten et al. 2017; Thörn 2020). Densification relates to overpopulated apartments, and 'renoviction' is displacement caused by renovation. The 'violations' used by property owners to obtain renovation approval from tenants were extensively studied by Polanska et al. (2019) and Polanska and Richard (2019) in connection with tenants' protest movements. These violations can be 'the violent practices of making invisible; withholding information; threat, or threat of force and sanctions; inaccessibility of the housing company; and rule by division' (Polanska and Richard 2019, 16).

Renovation in connection with urban planning and deliberation is often discussed in relation to different stakeholders and their positions. Different frameworks provide a positional and structural analysis of participation mechanisms, stakeholders and the effects of participation as well as risks related to different levels of public involvement (Arnstein 1969; Fung 2006). Arnstein (1969), in her most cited work, 'A ladder of citizen participation', proposed the model of empowerment through deliberation, also known as the 'ladder' of empowerment: manipulation, therapy, informing, consultation, placation, partnership, delegated power and citizen control. The steps of the ladder describe different degrees of stakeholder involvement, from passive dissemination of information to active involvement.

In the Swedish context, Stenberg (2018), following the concept of 'black boxes', analysed macro and micro actors in the dialogue process. In her analysis of the 'Consultation model of renovation', she discusses four dilemmas that still prevent tenants from exercising more power in the decision-making process (Stenberg 2018). These dilemmas were formulated based on interviews with representatives of housing companies: tenants' beliefs about the costs of the renovation, the timing of the planning (before the consultation, the generalized image of tenants does not match the profile of tenants who are actually occupying the apartments) and the evaluation of the tenants' ability to participate in the renovation process (Stenberg 2018, 19). Baeten et al. (2017) describe displacement through renovation as a profit-making strategy by public and private companies.

The policy of democratizing the planning process created the need for new ways of involving the broader public in the process of legitimizing judgements and decisions, 'which includes the contestation and negotiation of value as well as its diffusion, stabilization, ritualization, consecration, and institutionalization' (Lamont 2012, 205). While social movements and planning research provide us with the framework for understanding the ambivalent power positions of different stakeholders, the economic sociology literature helps us frame the concepts of quality, value and worth in relation to renovation.

Valuation in a situation of quality uncertainty is one of the central problems of market coordination, along with competition and cooperation. In the field of sociology of markets the success of valuation is believed to be possible when market agents share stable reciprocal expectations shaped by the social, cultural and institutional macro-structures in which the markets themselves are embedded (Beckert 2009). The problem of the quality and standard of housing is related to the power positions of different stakeholders. These positions are ambivalent and, as I show in the coming sections, the stakeholders are 'constructing' and 'deconstructing' the quality of seemingly standardized products. The tenants have to make value judgements in situations of uncertain quality and price, knowing that their choice can affect rent-setting. They are trying to reopen the 'black boxes' analysed by Stenberg (2018). Callon and Latour (1981) referred to these as 'leaky' black boxes that the macro actors are sitting on to protect their power, which in relation to building renovation will serve as a metaphor for further analysis: the details about plumbing, ventilation or economic calculations are often 'black-boxed' while less 'technical' questions are left out.

In standard markets, valuation is often viewed as calculation, a part of rational decision-making. To assure correct calculations, Callon et al. (2002) propose qualifying and positioning socio-technical devices that help to distribute cognitive competence. Agents define characteristics of a good 'by a combination of characteristics that establish its singularity' (Callon et al. 2002, 198). They are continuously involved in qualification of the products. There are also 'market professionals' who are involved in co-production of singular and objectified properties, and who, with the help of classification, clustering and sorting, make products comparable and different (Callon and Muniesa 2005). Market transactions are thus based on the processes of qualifications and requalifications of things and include an open list of qualities that can be taken into consideration.

While for Callon et al. (2002) a process of qualification is more important than its result, in the framework developed by Karpik (2010), the main focus of attention is on certain configurations in which the quality of products is important, rather than the process of (re) qualification (Callon et al. 2002, 215). Karpik proposed a concept of 'calculative judgment devices' that are cognitive supports in the process of valuation. Calculative judgement devices are 'practices that combine … teaching, persuading, and seduction' (Karpik 2010, 44). They reduce the cognitive deficit that market agents experience under uncertainty of product quality. In contrast to Callon, where the 'devices' sort, classify and cluster available characteristics of objects, calculative judgement devices produce 'oriented knowledge'.

> Judgment devices offer *oriented knowledge,* and implicitly or explicitly they set the conditions the consumer must respect in order for an adjustment between the product and the consumer to be satisfying. They qualify simultaneously both product and client – which means that the third party literally constructs the exchange relationship. (Karpik 2010, 51)

This approach implicitly implies the concept of power that the market professionals can exercise over consumers. Not only the goods but also actors are qualified and evaluated, and cognitive 'supports' become cognitive constraints. In a classical sense this market is operating under conditions of quality uncertainty as defined by Knight (1921) as a lack of information on which the calculation of probabilities can be based. It can also be viewed as epistemic (Dow and Werlang 1994), substantive and procedural (Dosi and Egidi 1991), or uncertainty connected to complexity (Beckert 1996). Tenants are in the situations of lack of available data (how much specific renovations will cost them) or inability to measure certain variables (for instance, technical need for renovation). Other stakeholders exploit the uncertainty of product quality to argue for the complexity of the renovation and subsequent rent increase.

Tenant participation and opportunities to affect quality judgements

Rent-setting is a process of negotiation between property owners and their organizations and the Union of Tenants, and it is part of the above-mentioned Swedish housing policy (Bengtsson 2015). Every year the representatives of owners and their organizations and the Union of Tenants negotiate the yearly rent increase. This negotiation is framed by the 'use value model', and the rent levels are defined – even for existing private rentals. During this negotiation the maximum rent increase is decided for all tenants in a specific municipality, and both private and public companies have to abide by the decision. In the case of annual rent increase, companies are not allowed to make significant hikes. Another situation leading to rent rise is the substantial renovation of a building that leads to an increase in the 'standard' of the property. In this case, the housing company can negotiate a substantial one-time rent increase for all apartments in a specific project. Interventions in apartments' physical conditions are governed by a second process in which tenants are directly involved through their participation in the negotiations.

If a housing company needs to renovate parts of an apartment or building through regular maintenance, they do not need tenants' approval, and in such cases they cannot demand a high rent increase. Maintenance covers changes to the infrastructure and utilities, and whatever the scale of the maintenance work, this is not considered to constitute an improvement in the standard of the property. This, in combination with the requirement to be profitable, gives owners incentives to generate income by carrying out renovations that lead to an improvement in the standard of the property.

In 2014, after active protests against extreme rent rises, the Union of Tenants developed a 'Consultation model for renovation', aimed at improving tenants' participation. This model increased the power of tenants and resulted in more explicit process thinking and a closer connection between the tenant consultation and rent negotiation (Stenberg 2018, 5).

If tenants do not grant approval, the owner can come up with a new renovation proposal or appeal to the rent tribunal. Historically, rent tribunals in Sweden take the property owner's side, even if this results in transaction costs for the housing company as well as possible reputational losses (Stenberg 2018). Therefore, many companies prefer to reach an agreement with tenants before starting the legal procedure. At this stage, the tenants and the housing companies are the two interest groups involved in the negotiations, which will be discussed more below.

Following Callon and Latour (1981), Stenberg (2018) approaches the concept of power in the consultation process in terms of 'black boxes' and looks at how micro-actors can become macro-actors in the renovation process. 'Black boxes' are devices or practices that are opaque for outsiders because their content is often regarded as technical. Stenberg (2018) further shows that macro-actors are 'black-boxing' some elements for the micro-actors, and in order to change the power balance, the latter have to reopen those boxes. Opening the black boxes and redefining them is a challenge for the tenants. As they are granted influence over and participation in the renovation, consultation is often limited to technicalities, such as choosing the finishing of interiors. Tenants have no direct involvement in the rent negotiations, and therefore they try to act within the space that is available to them – discussions about the quality and standard of apartments. They are empowered by law but disempowered by procedures and the content of deliberation.

Method

This case study is part of a larger research project entitled 'Renovation and participation: towards an ecologically, socially and economically sustainable Million Programme?', funded by the Swedish research agency FORMAS. The research was conducted in three Swedish cities, Stockholm, Uppsala and Gothenburg, by a team of researchers from different universities. The author is a member of the Gothenburg research team and personally participated in the collection of empirical data together with other researchers. The empirical material for this chapter is based on the ethnographic observations of negotiations between two municipal housing companies in Gothenburg and tenants who are included in the 'consultation group', representing the interests of all tenants in the properties subject to renovation. I am also using documents including presentation materials used by the housing companies; information that they sent out to the tenants before, during and after the consultation meetings; presentations and documentation provided by the Union of Tenants (Hyresgästförening); and information that self-organized tenants sent to their neighbours.

The 15 ethnographic observations were conducted by three members of the research groups, and we attended all the meetings between the housing companies, the Union of Tenants and the consultation groups. Each meeting lasted a minimum of one to a maximum of two and a half hours. In Case 1 there was more than one researcher present at the majority of the meetings; in Case 2 one researcher was present at all meetings. The author personally participated in different meetings in both cases. For ethical reasons meetings were not recorded on audio or video, but all participating researchers made extensive notes during the meetings. Research group members working on the same empirical cases shared their notes and discussed the process after each observation.

The initial contact was made through the umbrella organization that is central to both housing companies included in the case study. We first conducted pilot interviews with the persons who are responsible for the renovation projects in the respective companies and asked them for an opportunity to trace one or several participatory dialogues within their projects from the initiation of the project until the end of the renovation.

Although all the activities of the municipal housing companies should be open to the public, we sought the consent of all the parties to trace the observation (tenants, housing company as well as Union of Tenants) and informed all the participants about the project and requested their permission to be present as researchers at the consultation group meetings. These presentations were made at several initial meetings so that all participants knew who we were.

The following stakeholders have specific interests in the consultation process: tenants, housing companies, activist groups, local politicians, tenants' association and the rent tribunal. In this chapter I focus on the consultation group meetings, mediated by the representatives of the Union of Tenants. Empirical data consist of ethnographic observations, interviews and document analysis of the consultation process regarding the renovation of two areas of Gothenburg.

Case 1. North-eastern Gothenburg

Case 1 is located in one of the areas in the north-east of Gothenburg that was built as part of the Million Homes Programme during the 1960s. A particular renovation project that we observed concerned condominiums comprised of more than 200 apartments. According to the information provided by the housing company during the informational meeting with the tenants, smaller-scale maintenance and renovation had been done earlier, including the addition of balconies and the renovation of the facades in 2001. The formal consultation process started with a general information meeting in May 2019, in which about 80 tenants participated. At this meeting the housing company made a presentation of their plans to renovate the apartments and informed the tenants about the possibility to become a member of the 'consultation group' to negotiate the details of renovation. Already at the first meeting tenants protested against the uncertainty of rent increase and expressed doubts about the transparency of the whole process. The consultation group was heterogeneous; younger people and pensioners, and tenants with native languages other than Swedish, signed up to participate.

Case 2. Northern Gothenburg

The project studied in the second case was also comprised of high-rise buildings where the balconies and the facade had been renovated within the previous decade. Specific to this case is that several buildings are reserved for seniors. The consultation process started in October 2019 but was organized differently from the beginning. Instead of a general information meeting, the housing company sent out information about the planned renovation to all tenants and invited them to participate in a 'reference group'. Therefore, the first meeting between the housing company and the tenants was a 'reference group' meeting. At this meeting the representatives of the housing company also gave a presentation of their plans and informed tenants about their rights and opportunities. The majority of the participants in this case were over 55 years old, speaking fluent Swedish.

Ambivalence in deliberative processes

Organization of consultation: black-boxing standard, quality and prices of renovation

The stages of the consultation process are described in detail by Stenberg (2018). She also argues that there are several dilemmas that are related to the black-boxing of different aspects of renovation. There is a time gap between the negotiation of the renovation in terms of quality between the housing company and the tenants, and the rent-setting negotiation between the housing company and the Union of Tenants. This means that the tenants are involved in the quality negotiations without knowing the future costs. Stenberg refers to this as a Catch 22 situation (Stenberg 2018): the tenants want to talk about the costs, but it is not possible before they agree on the scale of renovation.

The housing companies have several reasons not to reveal the possible rent increase: they have to negotiate the rent increase with the Union of Tenants and do not want to trigger the protests that are likely to arise when the figure is announced. In some meetings with tenants they can refer to the procurement system and claim that they do not know how much the project will cost. But this relates to another dilemma that Stenberg (2018) describes: the tenants believe (and the housing companies do not directly contradict this belief) that the rent increase depends on the costs of renovation. However, according to the use value model, there is no connection between the costs of renovation and the rent-setting. The rents are set according to a specific valuation principle, not according to what the renovation is worth or its quality.

During the first meeting in Case 1, the housing company presented the following 'interests' that are vested in the process: management, social aspects, freedom of choice and law. 'Quality' was a central factor in each of them. Management should consider the quality of life, economic questions and the environment. Security and the right to stay at the same apartment define the social aspects. Freedom of choice was framed as the freedom to choose a higher standard of living and, legally, rent should be adjusted to reflect a new standard (Case 1, Information meeting 1, Presentation by the housing company, 2019). At the same meeting, in line with Stenberg (2018), the housing company explained that the negotiation of the rent would happen after the 'consultation group' meetings. Similarly, in Case 2 representatives of the housing company referred to the rent negotiation as a 'question for the distant future' which would be resolved between the housing company and the Union of Tenants. When tenants asked about the puzzling situation of making choices before knowing the price, the answers were defensive: 'We will not make any shock increases' and 'We stand for the collective' (Case 2, Educational meeting, 2019).

Despite the earlier renovation of facades of the buildings, the inside of the apartments in both cases was not significantly different from the time of construction and some tenants continually complained at different meetings about the bad living conditions in their apartments. In different years some maintenance was done to the apartments, and in Case 2 tenants could always upgrade their interiors (e.g., replace the kitchen or parts of it) individually, with a respective rent increase. However, in both cases, a major renovation of the entire utilities infrastructure (water, drainage, electricity and ventilation) is required. As mentioned above, these renovations are not grounds for a rent increase and should be covered by the funds that tenants have paid, based on a share of their monthly rent, since the properties were built. But as I discussed above, the large-scale replacement of the utilities infrastructure creates an opportunity for the housing company to intervene in matters that are regarded as setting the standard of an apartment: primarily, the finishing of bathrooms and kitchens.

While in both cases all communications presented the renovation as an immense undertaking, given the scale of the changes, the content of the consultation group meetings was limited to the choice of the interior finishing and the members were told that all the technical solutions should be trusted to experts: 'Some things you can influence, but in some things you have to trust our engineers' (Case 1, Information meeting 1, 2019). The appeal to the expertise of the experts and the refusal to discuss technicalities with the tenants is one of the black-boxing strategies discussed by Stenberg (2018). In Case 2 the representative of the housing company did provide some explanations (Case 2, Educational meeting,

2019) but usually finished his explanation with 'now it is getting too technical'. The refusal to go into specific details about the need for a new ventilation system, or wiring, or a choice of pipe replacement resulted in the tenants repeatedly questioning these technicalities.

Tenants' strategies to reopen the black boxes

'Quality debt' vs 'luxury renovation'

During the meetings with tenants and the consultation groups the same question was raised several times: why is the current bad condition of the housing not considered in the rent negotiation? One tenant pointed out that hardly any maintenance work had been carried out in the years following the construction of the properties, and all the attempts to steer the discussions towards future or even present maintenance often reached a dead end (Case 1, Information meeting 1, 2019). This question was specifically raised every time the representatives of the housing company were trying to explain that they needed to raise the standard because the current quality of the apartments was poor. What tenants generally asked for can be seen as a demand to 'fix the past', maintain the 'status quo' and start negotiations from that point. By doing this, the tenants tried to open up the box of the 'increase in standard'. They pointed to the fact that the actual increase in standards would cover the period long before the suggested renovation, and the costs thus should be borne by the owners.

At the same time the housing companies often tried to redirect the process into the future: 'Think about young people who will move into your apartments in the future. You are not only deciding for yourselves, you are deciding for them. Do you think the current quality standard of your apartment will be reasonable in twenty years?' (Case 2, Information meeting 1, 2019).

The representatives of the profit-driven, future-oriented companies were trying to keep the 'standard' box closed by making it a future concern, while tenants were trying to keep it open and redefine it as a 'past debt'. As some of the tenants put it, the necessary renovations were not done in the 30 years since they moved in, and the 'needs' did not justify the rent increase because this should constitute a 'renovation debt' to the tenants (Case 1, Meeting with the Union of Tenants, 2019). The reduced quality of the housing at present cannot justify the high costs and rent increase.

While housing companies presented freedom of choice as the choice between different levels of rent increase, tenants insisted on closing the quality gap created by bad maintenance and paying past debts before implementing improvements. Several times in Case 1 the tenants suggested lowering the rents first because of the deterioration in quality, and then starting the consultation process. In none of the cases did the housing companies explain the principles of the use value model and the particulars of the improvement in standards. While the majority of the tenants did not use knowledge about the model in their argumentation, it is possible to assume that the improvement of the quality standard compared with the period of construction was not perceived by the tenants as such. For the tenants, the quality standard is perceived as lower than at the time of construction, and they often expressed their satisfaction with the 'older' standard but wished it were better maintained. The perceived difference between the quality of the housing at present (poor because of bad maintenance), initially (at the time of construction) and the proposed renovation creates a discrepancy in the value judgements by the housing companies and the tenants, where the housing company does not acknowledge the existing 'renovation debt'.

Between the 'wants' and the 'needs'
As mentioned above, the increase in standards can be used as one of the strategies by profit-driven companies to increase the value of their property, and to raise rents. But the condition to consult with the tenants forces them to frame it as a necessity. There are two strategies to do this: to claim that there is an acute 'need' for certain changes, and to persuade the tenants that it is something they 'want'.

In the cases at hand this framing differed from the beginning of the dialogue process. While in Case 1 the changes in quality were presented as 'needs', in Case 2 they were formulated as something the tenants would 'wish for'. Therefore, in Case 1 the whole renovation strategy focused on the necessary technical improvements to pipes and other parts of the utilities infrastructure, and the standard increase as a by-product of these; in Case 2 the focus from the beginning was on the better quality of the finishing of the apartments, while the technical aspects should be 'left to engineers'. The needs in Case 2 were not presented as improving the poor quality and deterioration, but rather as modernizing and improving the quality of the future everyday life of the current tenants and the coming generations of tenants. Altogether the strategy of the housing company in Case 2 was to create the image of a 'caring host' who gives the tenants an opportunity for a better life.

Being embedded in the past (needs) and the future (wants), the two strategies produced different responses from the tenants. In particular, the 'need' created a direct and negative response from the tenants at the first information meeting in Case 1 (Case 1, Information meeting 1,

2019). Several tenants who participated in the information meeting and later in the consultation group meetings claimed that they had spent significant periods of their lives in the buildings in question. Their perception of quality and needs was connected to the 'maintenance debt' – the underperformance in maintenance over decades – and understanding that they had already paid the costs of the renovation by paying rent. 'They were cheating us all these years, now we have to say "stop"' (Case 1, Meeting with the Union of Tenants, 2019). 'Where is all the money we paid you with our rent?' (Case 1, Information meeting 1, 2019). Tenants did not want higher standards; they wanted the current standard to be better quality.

The appeal to 'needs' came from different stakeholders in the process. The housing companies framed it as 'we do not do more than is needed' (Case 1, Information meeting 1, 2019). The representatives of the Union of Tenants referred to the needs when justifying the necessity for tenants to participate in the process: 'It is you who should influence, not a consultant or a company, you know what your needs are' (Case 1, Meeting with the Union of Tenants, 2019). 'The consultation group represents you ... You know the area better and what is needed' (Case 1, Meeting with Union of Tenants, 2019). In both citations we see how the needs are spatially anchored in the personal experiences of the tenants. They are symbolically empowered as hands-on experts who have first-hand knowledge of the quality of housing and the improvements needed. In Case 2 the 'need' was articulated as a no-choice option. While the tenants could choose tiles and floors, and their opinions were welcomed, the hardware, 'pipes', electricity and ventilation were presented as non-negotiable interventions. The power over the quality judgements remained on the side of the housing company.

One for all: collective bargaining about quality

Another theme that emerged from the analysis of the negotiations in relation to quality is the difference between collective needs and wants, and potential individual preferences. Both housing companies and tenants referred to and problematized this issue: while the tenants often expressed their claims as a collective, the housing companies referred to the interests of each particular tenant, and thus to possible 'discrepancies' in judgements of quality (Case 1, Information meeting, 2019). When some of the tenants referred to their individual preferences, both the Union of Tenants and the housing companies started to appeal to 'the collective'.

Housing companies often appeal to selflessness in the interests of all abstract tenants, for instance, young people who will move into the apartments in 10 to 20 years' time and who will want a modern apartment. The idea of the collective covers not only the present tenants but also future generations. The housing company is interested in having one negotiation partner – 'a generalized tenant' – and, even if they claim that all individual interests should be met, they prefer to have one decision for all. The Union of Tenants also refers to the collective as the most viable strategy to achieve consensus with the housing companies. In Case 2 the representatives of the Union of Tenants explicitly recommended collective bargaining with the housing company so as to avoid the rent tribunal (Case 2, Meeting with Union of Tenants, 2019).

The individual–collective divide reveals itself in different forms. Firstly, participation in the consultation group means representing the interests of all tenants, but the procedure by which this group is formed often prioritizes those who are concerned in the first place for their own future and often about some 'special situation', often without explaining what the situation is (Case 1, Meeting with the Union of Tenants, 2019). Secondly, the collective interest of all tenants should be accounted for, but housing companies tend to refer to an abstract 'future tenant' in the long run. Thirdly, tenants start worrying about possible opportunism by their neighbours: 'Shall we all pay for those who want more?' (Case 1, Question from the tenants, Meeting with Union of Tenants, 2019).

In Case 2 the housing company referred to the members of the consultation group as 'the ambassadors of all tenants' who had to make responsible decisions (Case 2, Educational meeting with housing company, 2019). The idea of being an ambassador was not well received by several participants in the consultation groups, partly because they were there to protect their personal interests and partly because they did not want to make 'wrong' decisions for others. 'I do not know what others want, how can I decide for everyone?' (Case 1, Meeting with the Union of Tenants, 2019). It became clear at one of the meetings that tenants do not have contact with the majority of their neighbours (Case 2, Educational meeting with housing company, 2019), and some were worried about their names and contact information being distributed to other tenants. While everyone wanted to have the power to influence their own future, the idea of bearing the responsibility to decide for all tenants was not as desirable in Case 2.

Even if the consultation group were to agree on the scale of the renovation, the housing company still needs written approval from every tenant, and if some tenants do not agree, the whole consultation process reaches a stalemate. During one of the 'reference group' meetings a representative of the housing company described another case where the consultation group and the owner reached an agreement on the scale and details of renovation, but another group of tenants who did not participate in the consultations started a protest, so they had to start all over.

Conclusion

The consultation process with tenants is built on the idea that they should have the power to participate in the decision-making about their future housing. However, by separating issues in time (past and future) and content (interior finishing and hardware), the housing companies are reducing tenants' power to make judgements about the quality of the interior finishing. The tenants are often excluded from a whole range of decisions, including hardware (pipes, electricity, water) and economic sustainability. In this situation tenants choose the strategy of reopening the 'leaky black boxes' (Callon and Latour 1981, 286) or shifting the discussion into areas beyond the agenda set by the managing company. Firstly, they try to prevent the increase in standards by shifting attention from the standard to quality. Tenants refer to 'debt' as a calculable category, and instead of being seated on the 'black box' packed by the macro-actors, they 'requalify' the standard and quality of the housing into what is calculable for them. Secondly, they refer to the ambivalent position of the companies as public good providers and shift the discussion into the human rights area, organizing protests against 'black-boxing'. At several meetings the attempts to discuss the current renovation project completely failed because tenants switched the conversation to the 'renovation debt' and other problems originating in the past, the general situation on the rental market, and political decisions. The ambivalent role of the managing companies opens up an opportunity for negotiations outside the areas left for the tenants after the technical issues have been 'black-boxed'. The fusion of the formal consultation process (attempts at requalification and recalculation) with the protest and social organizations (shifting outside the area of black-boxing) creates a new judgement device that addresses the ambivalence of power positions in the market.

Acknowledgements

This chapter is based on the results of the research project at the University of Gothenburg, 'Renovation and participation: towards an ecologically, socially and economically sustainable Million Programme?', funded by the Swedish research agency FORMAS DrN: 2018-00191.

References

Arnstein, Sherry R. 1969. 'A ladder of citizen participation', *Journal of the American Institute of Planners* 35(4): 216–24.
Baeten, Guy, Sara Westin, Emil Pull and Irene Molina. 2017. 'Pressure and violence: Housing renovation and displacement in Sweden', *Environment and Planning A: Economy and Space* 49(3): 631–51.
Beckert, Jens. 1996. 'What is sociological about economic sociology? Uncertainty and the embeddedness of economic action', *Theory and Society* 25(6): 803–40.
Beckert, Jens. 2009. 'The social order of markets', *Theory and Society* 38: 245–69.
Bengtsson, Bo. 2015. 'Allmännyttan och bostadspolitiken i går, i dag och i morgon: institutionella förutsättningar i förändring' ['Public good and housing policy yesterday, today, and tomorrow: institutional conditions in change']. In *Nyttan Med Allmännyttan* [Benefits of the public good], edited by Tapio Salonen, 25–47. Stockholm: Liber.
Callon, Michel and Bruno Latour. 1981. 'Unscrewing the big leviathans: How do actors macrostructure reality'. In *Advances in Social Theory and Methodology: Toward an integration of micro and macro sociologies*, edited by Aaron Cicourel and Karin Knorr, 277–303. Boston, London and Henley: Routledge & Kegan Paul.
Callon, Michel, Cécile Méadel and Vololona Rabeharisoa. 2002. 'The economy of qualities', *Economy and Society* 31(2): 194–217.
Callon, Michel and Fabian Muniesa. 2005. 'Economic markets as calculative collective devices', *Organization Studies* 26(8): 1229–50.
Christophers, Brett. 2013. 'A monstrous hybrid: The political economy of housing in early twenty-first century Sweden', *New Political Economy* 18(6): 885–911.
Dosi, Giovanni and M. Egidi. 1991. 'Substantive and procedural uncertainty', *Journal of Evolutionary Economics* 1(2): 145–68.
Dow, James and Sérgio Ribeiro da Costa Werlang. 1994. 'Nash equilibrium under Knightian uncertainty: Breaking down backward induction', *Journal of Economic Theory* 64(2): 305–24.
Fung, Archon. 2006. 'Varieties of participation in complex governance', *Public Administration Review* 66: 66–75.
Hajda, Jan. 1968. 'Ambivalence and social relations', *Sociological Focus* (Kent, Ohio) 2(2): 21–8.
Hall, Thomas and Sonja Vidén. 2005. 'The Million Homes Programme: A review of the great Swedish planning project', *Planning Perspectives* 20(3): 301–28.
Hedin, Karin, Eric Clark, Emma Lundholm and Gunnar Malmberg. 2012. 'Neoliberalization of housing in Sweden: Gentrification, filtering, and social polarization', *Annals of the Association of American Geographers* 102(2): 443–63.
Karpik, Lucien. 2010. *The Economics of Singularities*. Princeton: Princeton University Press.
Knight, Frank H. 1921. *Risk, Uncertainty and Profit*. Boston: Houghton Mifflin.
Lamont, Michèle. 2012. 'Toward a comparative sociology of valuation and evaluation', *Annual Review of Sociology* 38: 201–21.
Lind, Hans. 2015. 'A monstrous hybrid: A comment on Brett Christophers' Interpretation of Swedish Housing Policy'. Working Paper Series, Department of Real Estate and Construction Management & Centre for Banking and Finance (CEFIN), KTH Royal Institute of Technology 15/4.
Merton, Robert K. 1976. *Sociological Ambivalence and Other Essays*. New York: Free Press.
Polanska, Dominika, Sarah Liz Degerhammar and Åse Richard. 2019. *Renovräkt! hyresvärdars makt (spel) och hur du tar striden*. Stockholm: Verbal.
Polanska, Dominika and Åse Richard. 2019. 'Narratives of a fractured trust in the Swedish model: Tenants' emotions of renovation', *Culture Unbound: Journal of Current Cultural Research* 11(1): 141–64.
Stenberg, Jenny. 2018. 'Dilemmas associated with tenant participation in renovation of housing in marginalized areas may lead to system change', *Cogent Social Sciences* 4(1): 1528710.
Sveriges domstolar. 'Bruksvärde'. Accessed 12 December 2021. https://www.domstol.se/amnen/hyra-bostadsratt-och-arrende/hyra-av-bostad-och-lokal/skalig-hyra/bruksvarde/.
Thörn, Catharina. 2020. '"We're not moving": Solidarity and collective housing struggle in a changing Sweden'. In *Gentrification Around the World: Vol. 1,* edited by Jerome Krase and Judith DeSena, 175–95. Cham: Palgrave Macmillan.

10
Private authority in regulating markets: Power dynamics around free prior and informed consent (FPIC) in forestry and the oil industry in Russia

Maria S. Tysiachniouk, Sara Teitelbaum, Andrey N. Petrov, and Leah S. Horowitz

Introduction

In the twenty-first century, with the increased pace of globalization, decentralization and marketization, natural resource governance is evolving rapidly. This chapter focuses on private authority in its effort to regulate markets of renewable and non-renewable resources. Theoretically, the chapter builds on the governance generating network (GGN) theory to explain power shifts in the process of interplay of actors involving global institutions, civil society and companies' networks in fostering the implementation of sustainability standards in Russia. The chapter analyses power dynamics surrounding the introduction of free prior and informed consent (FPIC) to Russian institutional and organizational environments in Forest Stewardship Council (FSC) certification and in the oil sector. It elucidates the operation of globally designed private instruments implemented locally in the context of more fluid, dynamic and partly deterritorialized societies.

Non-state actors, such as non-governmental organizations (NGOs) and transnational corporations (TNCs), are playing a greater role in both global decision-making and decision implementation (Campbell 2004; Boström and Garsten 2008; Haufler 2009, 140). This results in private-sector engagement, specifically through voluntary standards and self-regulation (Bartley 2007; Auld et al. 2009; Khanna and Brouhle 2009; King and Toffel 2009). Therefore, private authorities have become effective agents of institutional change in regulating markets (Mayer and Gereffi 2010; Vogel 2010). They have changed the rules of the game by redistributing power, changing the norms and discourses of market actors, and fostering corporate social responsibility (CSR) towards the environment and local and Indigenous Peoples' communities (Tysiachniouk 2012).

Private authorities such as the FSC, the Marine Stewardship Council and the Aquaculture Stewardship Council have fostered voluntary certification schemes. Through such certification opportunities and CSR actions, 'fictitious commodities', perceived in the early literature as having little to no market value (Polanyi 1944), such as ecosystems, biodiversity and the rights of workers and local/Indigenous communities, are disembodied from self-regulating markets and re-embedded in society (Langthaler and Schüßler 2019; Postel and Sobel 2019). These so-called fictitious commodities are acknowledged in a 'sensitive' market niche in which producers voluntarily agree to put a price on fictitious goods and consumers are willing to pay a premium for these goods. Practically speaking, these voluntary schemes verify companies' production practices, such as the presence/absence of child labour exploitation, fair salaries for workers, respect for Indigenous Peoples' rights, biodiversity conservation and a low carbon footprint. Certification allows companies to receive positive feedback in niche markets where consumers care about environmental and social issues and express their preferences by purchasing goods with sustainability labels (Wirth 2009 ; Oosterveer et al. 2014; Giacomarra et al. 2016). One of two case studies in this chapter focuses on the FSC, which aims to preserve biodiversity, promote economically feasible companies and foster Indigenous/local communities' rights.

Other businesses, for example those operating in markets perceived as unsustainable (such as oil and mining), have adopted selective global standards (Escobar and Vredenburg 2011). Successful naming and shaming by NGO networks may result in reputational risks and the loss of investors, with sudden and significant losses of power and resources. Global standards, when adopted, can protect companies from reputational risks and serve as markers to demonstrate production sustainability and respect for Indigenous/communities' rights. Our second case study focuses on FPIC implementation in the oil sector on Sakhalin Island, where FPIC is connected to the policy commitments of large international organizations such as the World Bank (WB) and International Finance Corporation (IFC).

FPIC is a requirement within multiple certification schemes (Buxton and Wilson 2013). FPIC has become a central element of international policy-making towards strengthening the rights of Indigenous Peoples, especially within resource development. However, very few nations have enshrined FPIC in law, thereby putting certification schemes such as that of the FSC at the forefront of implementation. FPIC invokes the power of Indigenous communities to refuse or accept resource development activities on their traditional territories based on their right to self-determination. Each component of FPIC confers specific meaning. 'Free' refers to consent given without coercion, intimidation or manipulation. 'Prior' means that consent is sought well in advance of project approval. 'Informed' refers to the need to share pertinent information regarding the scope and impacts of the project. 'Consent' is a collective decision made by rights holders through a community-sanctioned decision-making process (Papillon and Rodon 2017). However, in practice FPIC remains a contested norm due to differences in interpretation and shortcomings in implementation (Tysiachniouk et al. 2021). Due to the strong normative position of FPIC in defence of Indigenous Peoples' rights, there is evidence of ambivalence and friction between the policy sphere and the localized settings where FPIC is implemented. Understanding this interplay and the nature of FPIC interpretation and implementation in a private regulatory setting represents a key aim of this study.

Russia, in terms of its socio-economic characteristics, represents an ideal case study for analysing private authorities' introduction of FPIC within the forest and oil sectors. Firstly, given the limited citizen involvement in natural resource governance in Russia, as in a majority of post-Soviet economies, there is reason to question the suitability of new FPIC requirements as instruments to enhance local/Indigenous engagement and promote the implementation of their customary environmental rights. Secondly, it is particularly valuable to investigate how a non-state regulatory instrument such as FPIC is received by stakeholders in the statist society of Putin's Russia. Russia has not ratified the International Labour Organization (ILO) Convention 169 on Indigenous Peoples, and the state exercises ownership over natural resources, such as forests and oil deposits, that could be leased (as in the case of forestry) or licenced for extraction (as in the oil sector) to private industry. However, companies operating in Russia must still adhere to FPIC and other internationally recognized standards to operate in the global market.

This chapter presents a cross-sectoral comparison of private actors' efforts to require FPIC for forest and oil businesses in Russia, with a focus on the interplay of global, national and local actors in its implementation.

We compare how FPIC was received and implemented by companies in two settings: within the forestry sector's FSC standard development process; and in the oil industry, where FPIC compliance is a WB and IFC requirement. We focus on the FPIC negotiations process between economic, social and environmental actors in the standard development group (SDG) in FSC Russia and compare it with oil companies' FPIC interpretation and implementation on Sakhalin Island. More specifically, this chapter seeks to answer the following questions: what are the power dynamics between global and local actors in governing resource extraction in Russia? How do power struggles between stakeholders in Russia affect how global standards are adjusted to Russian institutional and organizational environments? To what extent are global standards influencing Indigenous Peoples' rights in Russia? Does ambivalence of power, meaning inconsistent behaviour resulting from divergent norms within a shared institutional environment (Merton 1976), pose problems for the implementation of FPIC? Through an analysis of power dynamics (Haugaard 2012), we examine how power is exercised in the national adaptation and local implementation of FPIC and how such dynamics shape the rights afforded to Indigenous/local communities.

Our study reveals that ambivalence, for example, conflicting norms and counter-norms, associated with particular positions is created through the presence of competing conceptions of FPIC, which are often difficult to reconcile with contextual conditions in place during adoption and implementation of the standard. The presence of a strong normative definition of FPIC is interpreted by economic actors as a type of power over them, forcing them to comply while at the same time extending power for Indigenous and local communities, providing a mechanism for enhancement of their rights.

The theoretical framework

The theoretical framework is based on the governance generating networks (GGN) theory that examines private authority in regulating markets (see Figure 10.1).

The GGN theory serves as a useful lens for analysing the development of global standards that operate within dynamic and varied networks at multiple scales (Tysiachniouk 2012; Tysiachniouk and McDermott 2016; Tysiachniouk et al. 2018; Henry and Tysiachniouk 2018). A GGN is comprised of three elements: (1) the nodes of global governance design, in which global policies and standards develop; (2)

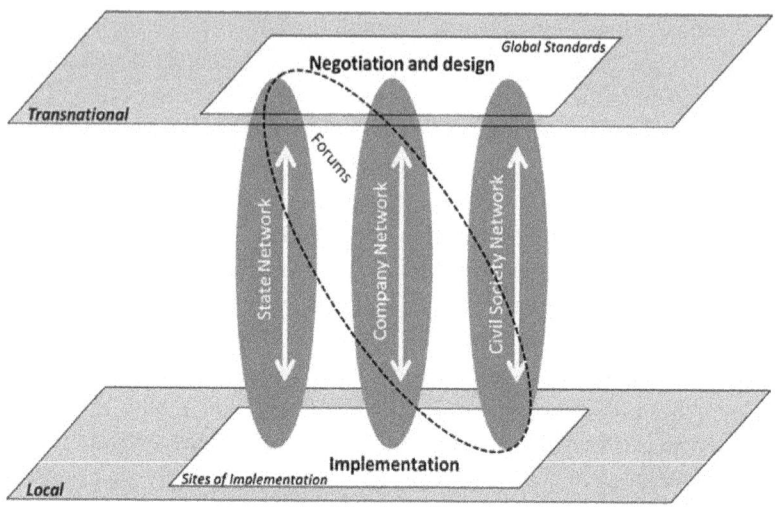

Figure 10.1 Governance generating network.

negotiation forums, where stakeholders develop and modify standards; and (3) implementation sites, where global standards transform into practices (Tysiachniouk 2012). Actors within the GGN's structure exercise ambivalent, contradicting and conflicting dimensions of power that interact in ways that can be described in terms of *power over, power for* and *power together* (or *power with*) (Haugaard 2012). *Power over* is associated with an ability to dominate or coerce which is often, although not always, exercised at the expense of one party. *Power for* involves monetary or non-monetary benefits to certain actors, such as enhancement of their rights and/or their empowerment. *Power together* describes the ability of GGNs to link transnational space to spaces of places (Haugaard 2012). Ambivalence of norms and interests fosters a productive way of exploring dynamic actor interactions and constant power struggles among global-to-local actors. Through this process GGNs generate social change both transnationally and locally. The outset of GGNs, such as social movements or NGO-led market campaigns, can happen bottom-up. In order to set new global standards, GGNs address appeals and requests to company headquarters, retail stores and investment banks (Tysiachniouk 2012). GGNs can also be manifested top-down for collective action, when transnational actors, such as standard-making organizations and TNCs that adopt these standards, implement global standards locally to compel institutional amendments in spaces of places (Tysiachniouk et al. 2018). Lastly, there are certification scheme-based GGNs (FSC, for example), characterized by a consistent bilateral exchange of information between local and transnational actors (Tysiachniouk and McDermott 2016). Through negotiation forums at different levels, these actors pursue their interests and seek compromise. Power struggles along with negotiations determine the generation mechanism that allows for the institutionalization and implementation of new rules both globally and locally.

The power within GGNs is distributed unevenly between actors operating at different levels of the spatial hierarchy. GGNs with top-down patterns see power exercised through core standards that limit network actors' involvement and become gatekeeping entities. These standards determine the interaction between actors within the GGN, and power is exercised by the imposition of the rules of inclusion (Tysiachniouk 2012). Large holding companies engage in voluntary certification schemes and, through them, gain access to new 'sensitive' niche markets and become 'responsible producers'. The introduction of FPIC represents a new means of influencing decision-making with the potential to alter negotiated dynamics at both local and global levels. International investment banks, some international corporations and the FSC all adopted FPIC in part because of international bottom-up NGO market campaigns and Indigenous environmental and human-rights protests. In turn, this encouraged the creation of international principles limiting the extractive industries' impacts on Indigenous Peoples and local communities (Tomlinson 2019).

In an international institutional and normative framework, the FSC, TNCs and investment banks have adopted global standards regarding Indigenous rights. Upon the agreement of 143 countries, the UN Declaration on the Rights of Indigenous Peoples (UNDRIP) added more binding language that called for the 'Free Prior and Informed Consent' of Indigenous Peoples regarding activities affecting Indigenous rights. When certain UN processes and international fora, such as the 2010 United Nations Framework Convention on Climate Change, adopted FPIC, FSC standards extended FPIC to more generally address the rights of 'local communities' rather than exclusively those of Indigenous Peoples. This expansion partially reflected debates over the definition of indigeneity and the appropriateness of the term in diverse country contexts and especially in Russia. Examining FPIC negotiations and implementation provides an important illustration of how power dynamics are being shaped by actors and institutions in global rule-making at multiple scales. In both forest and oil sector GGNs, FPIC was introduced through 'top-down' directives to be implemented locally. Forest companies which commit to the FSC certification scheme must comply with its standards (including FPIC requirements), and non-compliance may result in certificate revocation and, therefore, loss of access to environmentally and socially sensitive markets. In the oil sector, FPIC emerged as foreign investors, shareholders and international companies required it. Global standards usually encourage overcompliance with existing national standards, imposing new requirements on economic actors and simultaneously enhancing rights and empowering Indigenous/local communities. Through overcompliance, private authority, therefore, is becoming an effective force in natural resource governance, with the state losing its hegemony yet maintaining its power.

Methodology

We used qualitative in-depth semi-structured interviews, participant observation and document analysis. We chose the forestry and oil sectors because of the shared presence of FPIC requirements, yet differences in private authority involvement in governance. In the forestry sector global standards for Indigenous Peoples' rights are part of the certification scheme, while in the oil sector they are part of foreign direct investment requirements and/or global commitments of TNCs. Differences in governance by private authority determine the differences in power dynamics around FPIC.

We created separate interview guides for company representatives, Indigenous leaders, NGOs and government officials. Each interview took 30 to 90 minutes and was recorded, transcribed and coded. To study FPIC in the context of the FSC, we conducted interviews in Bonn, Germany, with FSC staff (8), with representatives of the SDG in Russia (26) as well as with actors involved in testing FPIC implementation in specific localities. Members of the SDG included representatives of Russia's Social, Environmental and Economic chambers. We also interviewed FSC Russia board members who were actively involved in discussing issues related to FPIC (see Table 10.1). Interview questions revolved around the following issues: process approach and dynamics, priority issues brought forward regarding FPIC, forms of engagement, and levels of satisfaction with the process and final indicators. An iterative process was used to identify and organize data around key themes such as definitions and meanings ascribed to FPIC, perceptions of FPIC, quality of negotiation processes, key challenges to a shared articulation of FPIC and satisfaction with final indicators. Interviews took place in 2018–19.

Table 10.1 Research on FPIC in the framework of FSC

Environmental Chamber	Economic Chamber	Social Chamber	FSC staff	FSC non-member stakeholders	FSC-international staff/board/experts
11	5	4	2	1	8

Within the oil sector, we chose Sakhalin Island as a case study, as implementation of FPIC was clearly stated there by transnational consortium operators. Research on Sakhalin Island was carried out in September 2013 and August 2015, with several interviews conducted in Houston, Texas, in 2018 at companies' head offices. These in-depth, semi-structured interviews involved representatives of oil companies (e.g., Sakhalin Energy and ExxonMobil), environmental NGOs, Indigenous Peoples associations and Indigenous-led local NGOs. In addition, the study analysed global standards related to FPIC required by the FSC, WB and IFC. To assess companies' commitment to global standards, we also analysed a variety of documents pertaining to companies' CSR policies, Global Reporting Initiative (GRI) reports and other publications related to corporate relations with Indigenous communities (see Table 10.2).

Table 10.2 Research on FPIC in oil and gas sectors on Sakhalin Island

Oil companies	State	Civil society
Exxon Neftegaz Limited and ExxonMobil-9 (including Sakhalin and Houston offices)	State agencies in Sakhalin-6	Sakhalin Environmental Watch-2
Sakhalin Energy-6	Local municipal administration in Sakhain-8	Indigenous Peoples' associations and Local Indigenous led NGOs-4
Rosneft-1		Local residents 29

Results

FPIC and the FSC certification scheme in Russia: power struggles around standard development

The FSC seeks to promote sustainable forest management through the development and application of an international standard covering social, economic and environmental dimensions. Globally, Russia has the largest number of FSC-certified forest management territories (see Figure 10.2). Therefore, FPIC, when implemented, should enhance citizen rights in many local communities, and especially in Indigenous settings.

The FSC standard is based on an international set of principles and criteria, which are adapted to national contexts through the development of national indicators. In 2012, a revised international standard was approved, which included expansive requirements regarding FPIC, applicable to both Indigenous Peoples (Principle 3) and local communities (Principle 4). This prompted a revision process led by national offices, including FSC Russia, in order to bring national indicators in line with international requirements. For the first time, FSC International also provided a set of International Generic Indicators (IGIs), designed to guide national standards and enhance consistency across jurisdictions. The Russian revision process was based on the creation of a standard development group consisting of FSC members in equal numbers and representing economic, social and environmental interests (see Figure 10.2). Each chamber holds equal voting power within the FSC governance standard development process. Our work focused on analysing the process of adapting FSC International's FPIC-related requirements to the Russian national FSC standard.

For FSC Russia, the new FPIC indicators represented a significant departure. Prior to 2012, the FSC standard required forestry companies to reach an 'agreement' with Indigenous Peoples and to consult with local communities. Even this level of engagement proved difficult for forestry companies due to a number of contextual constraints present in Russia. For example, forestry companies holding large leases were often required to consult between 70 and 140 rural communities on a single certified territory. Communities were often unfamiliar with the FSC process and the forest management plan, requiring additional outreach by forestry companies to raise awareness, respond to complaints, and designate and preserve places of social significance called High Conservation Value forests

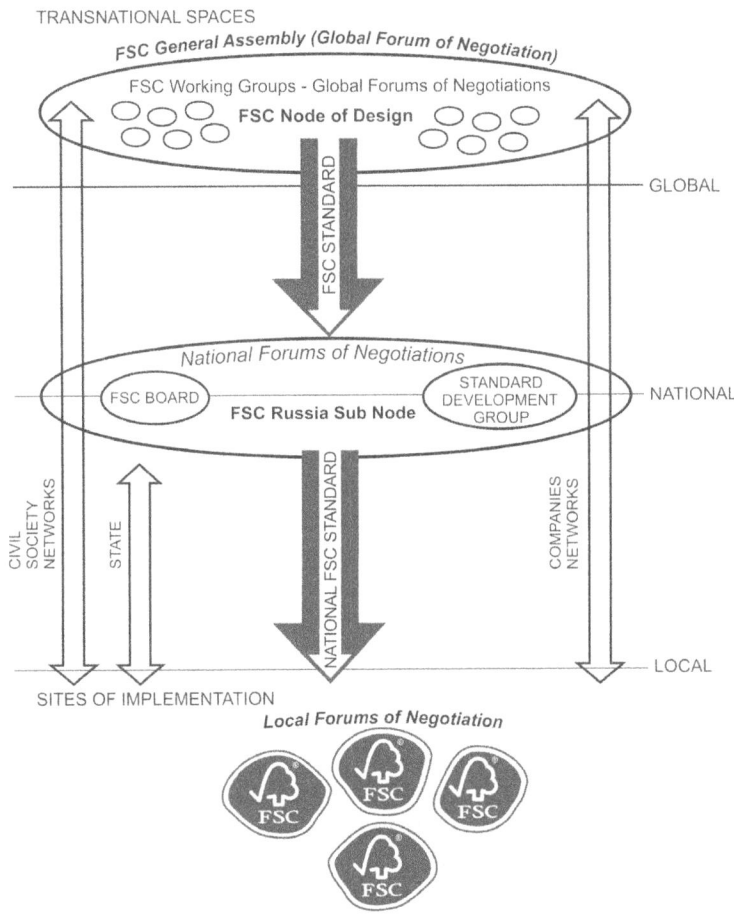

Figure 10.2 Power dynamics in the process of development of the new national FSC standard.

(HCV-5-6) (Tysiachniouk 2012). The new FPIC requirements differed from this 'consultative' approach, requiring forestry companies to engage Indigenous and local communities in an FPIC process and culminating in the explicit granting (or withholding) of consent. This process should include the identification of rights holders, the documentation of rights and impacts from forestry activities and the negotiation of mutually agreeable conditions (Tysiachniouk et al. 2021). Its introduction proved controversial within the standard development process in FSC Russia due to conflicting interpretations of norms between the Economic and Social chambers, and variable positions with regards to its relevance. Members of the Social Chamber supported the new FPIC requirements and were hopeful that the more stringent requirements would help redress some of the weaknesses seen in the implementation (see Figure 10.3).

Therefore, members of the Social Chamber insisted on high eligibility for FPIC and for it to be applied to both local and Indigenous communities. These members saw the new FPIC requirements as an opportunity for greater empowerment, or *power for*. Members of the Economic Chamber met the international FPIC requirements with scepticism and frustration as they considered them to be ill-fitting, externally imposed and designed without sufficient consideration for the particularities of the Russian context: a type of *power over* dynamic. Transaction costs were a major consideration for members of the Economic Chamber, who expressed concerns that the financial and administrative burden of FPIC requirements would be unmanageable. Furthermore, there were concerns that FPIC would be interpreted by Indigenous and local communities as commensurate with a type of veto over forestry operations that could lead to intractable negotiations and unreasonable financial requests, and potentially create delays and interruptions to logging operations. For example, one member of the SDG argued: 'It is frightening [for companies] that the local population can give consent to logging, or can quickly withdraw it ... It is frightening that this may be the subject of blackmail by the population, some extortion.'[1] Thus, for members of the Economic Chamber, the introduction of the new and more prescriptive FPIC requirements was an imposition, where the international level was seeking to exert a type of *power over* forestry companies (Haugaard 2012). The standard development process was also bogged down in a struggle around the FPIC application scope, that is, which communities would be eligible for FPIC arrangements. According to the international standard and IGIs, FPIC was required for Indigenous Peoples and local communities with customary or legal rights in the forest. The FSC definition of Indigenous Peoples is based on the UN definition and relevant mostly for postcolonial countries. The previous Russian FSC standard used an expansive definition of Indigenous rights holders, based mainly on self-identification. Not only groups officially recognized by the Russian state could qualify as Indigenous. For example, the FSC Russian standard considered multicultural groups, such as Pomor people living on the shore of the White Sea, to be Indigenous because of

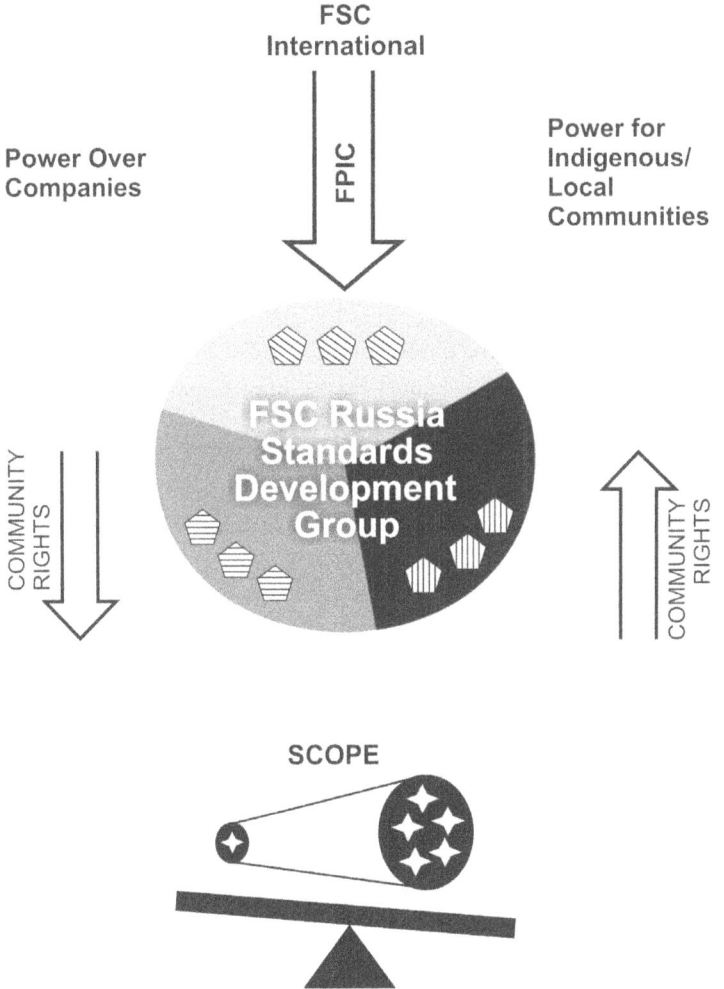

Figure 10.3 Interactions between members of the SDG in the process of negotiations.

their dependence on forest resources. This contrasted with Russian national legislation, which limited official recognition to 'Indigenous Small-Numbered Populations of the North and Far East in the Russian

Federation' (fewer than 50,000 people). The existing standard also recognized customary rights deemed illegal under Russian legislation. In the standard development process, members of the Economic Chamber intended to revise the guidelines that determined to whom the rights applied and what those rights entailed. The consolidated opinion of the Economic Chamber was that FPIC procedures should not apply to people who rely on the land by hunting and gathering, since customary rights are currently protected by law. Because the Forest Code covers these rights, the Economic Chamber proposed removing the right to foraging activities from the FPIC standard.

The economic actors expected that the implementation of FPIC would require the employment of social experts and increased transaction costs. They were also concerned that Indigenous/local communities may not be able to advance the process effectively due to the lack of capacities or political organization in some communities. For example, it would be unclear with whom to sign the FPIC agreement and who is the leader in the village. SDG members stated: 'When we speak with our Indigenous people, with our local people, it's very difficult to say that everywhere it's really clear who is the leader, even the informal leader. Because even the Indigenous population is so fragmented.'[2]

Alongside supporters from the Environmental Chamber, FSC social experts from the FSC board organized the field testing of the FPIC requirements in different regions of Russia, specifically in the Tver oblast, the Komi Republic and the Arkhangelsk region. Several teams of experts visited local communities on FSC-certified territories to evaluate the applicability of the FPIC requirements, including who qualifies as a 'rights holder', who is eligible for an FPIC process and with whom to sign FPIC agreements. These social experts described the exercise as challenging but concluded that, with considerable effort on the part of companies, it would be possible to apply the FPIC requirements. This did not convince members of the Economic Chamber, however, who continued to mobilize arguments around transaction costs and insufficient community capacity.

Members of the SDG grappled with these issues throughout the process of developing the Russian standard, with increasing tensions and conflict between the Social and Economic chambers. The Environmental Chamber remained divided on FPIC. Throughout the process, the Social Chamber maintained its position of support for a strong interpretation of FPIC, which aligned with the FSC's language and international norms. The Economic Chamber also developed a unified position, which sought to either remove FPIC or significantly reduce its scope and/or applicability. The Economic Chamber became increasingly organized, adopting a variety of arguments and strategies. This included demands to revisit the FSC definition for the identification of Indigenous Peoples, which relied on a combination of self-identification, some social organization and dependence on natural resources for subsistence. They also pushed for stronger alignment between the FSC's approach and Russian legislation.

After lengthy debates, a 'weak' compromise was reached. FPIC was maintained in both Principles 3 and 4. This was an important victory for the Social Chamber, which can be explained, at least in part, by the FSC's governance structure, which provides balanced voting rights across chambers, thereby equalizing less powerful actors with more powerful ones. The Social Chamber also benefited from the support of FSC International, which shares a conception of FPIC based in international human rights discourse. However, the Economic Chamber also achieved some gains. An Appendix was added to the Russian standard, laying out a number of conditions for and exceptions to the FPIC application, with the potential to significantly reduce its scope. Recognition of customary rights, for example, is limited to activities which do not conflict with the law. FPIC processes need not apply in situations where the requirement to obtain FPIC from Indigenous or local communities is in conflict with other consequences of the FSC standard, such as in the case of significant job losses, or when obtaining FPIC will lead to a conflict either between the forestry company and other FPIC rights holders or between different groups of rights holders (Tysiachniouk et al. 2021).

The new Russian standard was approved by FSC International in September 2020, but the power struggles around the FPIC application in Russia continue.

FPIC in Russia's oil sector: power struggles around benefit sharing

For extractive industries, FPIC is mandatory only in countries that ratified the ILO Convention 169 on Indigenous Peoples. However, Russia and many other oil- and gas-extractive countries did not ratify it (Buxton and Wilson 2013; Stammler and Ivanova 2016). The Russian government argues that following the ILO standards would infringe upon Russian law because all land in Russia belongs to the state and cannot be owned by any ethnic group. However, there are Russian laws that acknowledge the rights of Indigenous Peoples and require consultations in order to conduct extractive activities (Gassiy and Potravny 2019; Tysiachniouk et al. 2020). The rights to land and resources are guaranteed for the Indigenous Peoples of Russia in Article 69 of the Russian Constitution, in the Land Code and in other more specific legislative acts. According to the Federal

Law 'On the Guarantees of the Rights of Indigenous Small-Numbered Populations of the North and Far East in the Russian Federation' (1999), Indigenous Peoples can use land for traditional economic activities. They also have the right to receive compensation for damages to their traditional livelihoods. According to the law 'On the Territories of Traditional Nature Use of Indigenous Small-Numbered Peoples of the North, Siberia and Far East of the Russian Federation' (2001), companies operating in areas with designated Territories of Traditional Nature Use have to obtain consent before engaging in resource extraction and must pay compensation (Sulyandziga 2019). The Federal Law 'On the Ecological Expert Review' (1995) provides guidelines for the environmental impact assessment process, which lacks provisions for assessing socio-economic and cultural impacts (Wilson and Stammler 2016). Regional regulations are sometimes established to close gaps in the federal legislation.

The IFC, along with the WB and the European Bank for Reconstruction and Development (EBRD), require recipients of their loans to adhere to the ILO 169 and UNDRIP standards. Russian companies, as borrowers from the EBRD and other investment banks, are required to sign agreements with the Indigenous Peoples and establish benefit-sharing mechanisms or Indigenous Peoples' Development Plans (Tysiachniouk et al. 2018; Wilson and Stammler 2016). Given the nature of the Russian legislation, investors' growing expectations and mounting pressure from regional governments, and sometimes from civil society, oil companies often opt to develop benefit-sharing agreements. Benefit sharing, formally defined as the distribution of monetary and non-monetary benefits generated through the resource extraction activity (e.g., Thuy et al. 2013), represents one aspect of CSR but does not necessarily imply the recognition of FPIC. The mechanisms of benefit sharing vary considerably within Russia (Tysiachniouk et al. 2020), but they often reflect the power struggles between companies, authorities and Indigenous Peoples placed in the context of global standards and expectations. In certain cases, such benefit-sharing agreements are 'labelled' as FPIC (Wilson 2016),[3] although the practice is not universal. For example, in the Komi Republic, the oil and gas company Lukoil Komi in 2015 signed an agreement with the Indigenous association Izviatas, representing Komi Izemtsi people, who are not recognized by the Russian government as an Indigenous group (Tysiachniouk et al. 2018; Loginova and Wilson 2020). The terms specified in the agreement seem comparable with FPIC (Goloviznina 2019).

Sakhalin case study

In this section, we analyse oil consortiums' FPIC implementation on Sakhalin Island in the Russian Far East. The Sakhalin-1 and Sakhalin-2 projects are held by consortia of international companies, whose operators have declared their commitment to FPIC (see Figure 10.4).[4]

Oil company-driven GGNs on Sakhalin Island are atypical for Russia, as transnational oil and gas companies adopted global standards and committed themselves to implementing FPIC standards despite the differences between the Russian context and those of other countries, state co-ownership of Russian companies and state-driven policy in the oil sector. At the same time, the companies in these consortia were not influenced by Soviet-type practices of social responsibility, in which state-owned companies were involved in building all community infrastructure and constantly filling gaps in the state budget (Wilson 2016; Tulaeva and Tysiachniouk 2017; Tysiachniouk et al. 2018).

The process of introducing FPIC in Sakhalin created both dissonance and ambivalence concerning prevailing interests and values, due to the presence of countervailing and multi-scalar forces. Along with a set of global standards, FPIC implementation started after the rise of a social movement called the Green Wave campaign (2004–6), which formed against intense oil development on the island (Roon 2006; Novikova 2014). An international campaign against damages to the Pacific grey whale population and to salmon stocks started in late 1990 and involved the Russian NGO Sakhalin Environment Watch, in partnership with the California-based NGO Pacific Environment and the Russian Green Party. A relatively small number of NGOs involved in collective action became engaged in power struggles with large oil companies, contesting the legitimacy of their activities and introducing new multi-scale power dynamics. The bottom-up campaign exercised *power together* against oil consortia by targeting investment banks interested in financing the further expansion of the Sakhalin-2 project (CEE Bankwatch 1997; Bradshaw 2008).

Simultaneously, Indigenous-led campaigns emerged, exercising collective action within a *power with* dynamic. Grievances were related to damages to salmon rivers and reindeer herding and the destruction of Nivkh sacred sites. In 2004, Indigenous Peoples requested financial compensation for the damage to their traditional way of life (Graybill 2013). In 2005, around 300 people, including members of Indigenous organizations, Greenpeace, the World Wide Fund for Nature (WWF) and local environmental NGOs (Sakhalin Environment Watch and Green

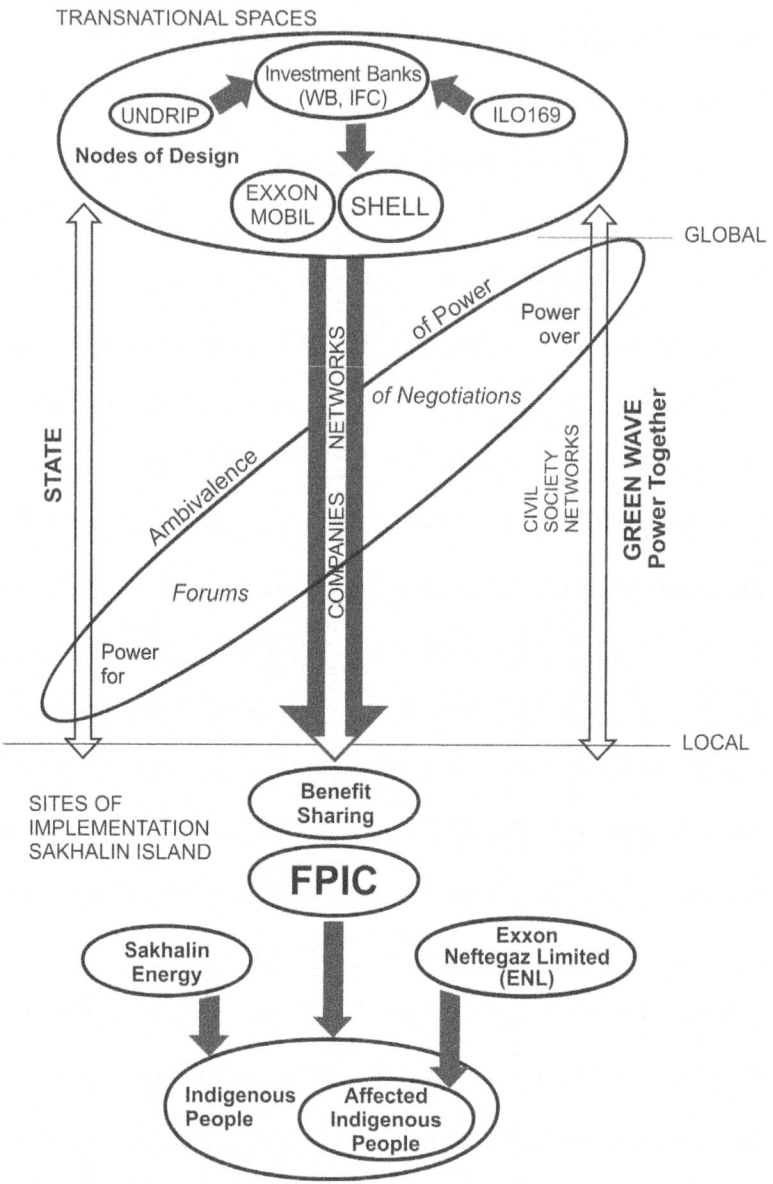

Figure 10.4 Governance generating network: Sakhalin case study.

Patrol), protested for several days against unsustainable oil construction.[5] The movement against companies grew internationally and 146 NGOs operating in 22 countries, including 80 Russian NGOs, WWF, Greenpeace, Rainforest Action Network, BANKTrack and Friends of the Earth, pressured international financial lenders on both environmental and Indigenous rights issues (Lee 2005). Supported by the local government, another petition was sent to the EBRD in 2016 demanding a calculation of the environmental damage and loss of fish stock due to the construction of a liquefied natural gas plant. In January 2007, as a result of the campaign, the EBRD finally denied a loan of $300 million to the Sakhalin-2 project. In this way, actors involved in bottom-up GGNs successfully exercised power by targeting the transnational nodes (banks), allowing them to exercise a degree of *power over* the Sakhalin-2 consortium.

As a result of the Green Wave campaign, Sakhalin Energy adopted multiple sustainability standards, including FPIC implementation, when Royal Dutch Shell (then a key shareholder) committed to apply it to all its global operations and, by doing so, empowered FPIC rights holders. The Sakhalin-2 project found new investors when Sakhalin Energy started implementing sustainability standards.

The Sakhalin-2 project relied on international financial institutions for financial support and therefore experienced more pressure after the Green Wave campaign than Sakhalin-1, which used ExxonMobil funds. However, ExxonMobil's global commitments and Sakhalin Energy's commitments are similar. When interacting with Indigenous Peoples, both companies comply with the IFC Performance Standards on Environmental and Social Sustainability, UNDRIP, ILO Convention 169 and the WB Operational Policy and Bank Procedure on Indigenous Peoples.[6] Both companies participate in the UN Global Compact and the GRI. Both operators are committed to FPIC, but in the documents related to operations on Sakhalin Island, only Sakhalin Energy explicitly emphasizes its implementation of FPIC. Therefore, the power of the standards developed can significantly change companies' practices at implementation sites, empowering Indigenous actors through private authority.

Sakhalin Energy established a tripartite partnership between the state, Indigenous Peoples and the company in 2006, while ENL established a similar partnership only in 2012. Prior to Gazprom purchasing shares from Royal Dutch Shell in 2007, the Sakhalin-2 consortium mostly used Shell's social policies and standards (Wilson 2016, 77) yet did not declare FPIC implementation on Sakhalin Island. For example, Indigenous NGO Kykh-Kykh (The Swan) served as an intermediary for redistributing Sakhalin Energy's money, coming via the 'Supplemental Development of

Traditional Culture Fund'. A social fund also provided money for healthcare and education (see Figure 10.5).

After the Green Wave campaign, in 2006, as recommended by the IFC, Sakhalin Energy started the Sakhalin Indigenous Minorities Development Plans (SIMDPs), each lasting for five years. These plans were set up as part of a tripartite partnership between the Indigenous Peoples, the regional government and Sakhalin Energy. They listed multiple global standards and fully satisfied international lenders.

FPIC has been incorporated into SIMDP-2, and since then, Indigenous Peoples have had the opportunity to determine the grant competition winners and, via this mechanism, distribute Sakhalin Energy's money to beneficiaries. The company stated:

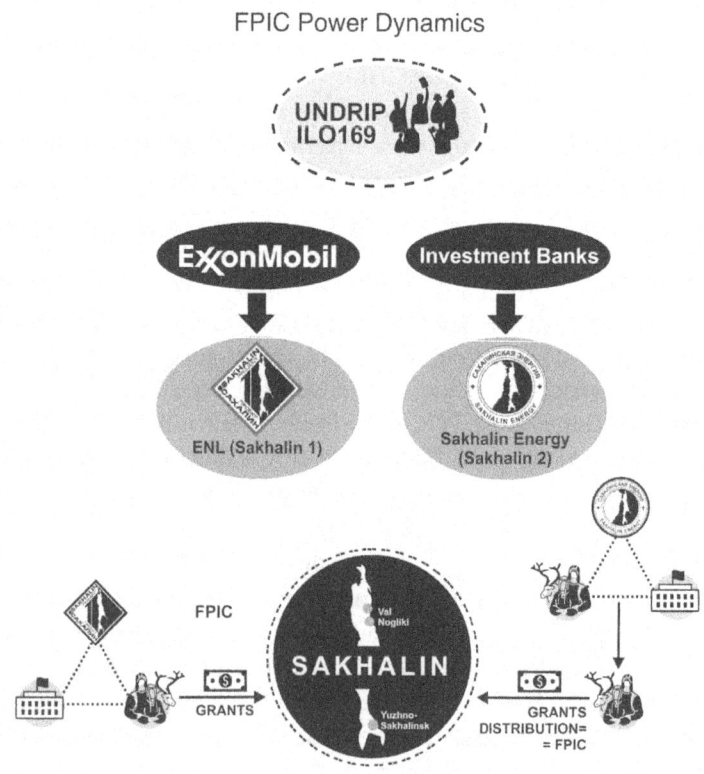

Figure 10.5 Power dynamics in the process of FPIC implementation.

SIMDP is based on the international standards concerning Indigenous peoples and including FPIC, which was recorded in the UN Declaration on the Rights of Indigenous Peoples (2007) and is included in the new Performance Standard 7 on Indigenous Peoples of the International Finance Corporation (IFC). Sakhalin Energy has become the first industrial company to apply this standard successfully when interacting with society.[7]

FPIC implementation gives limited rights to Indigenous Peoples (Mahanty and McDermott 2013). Both ENL and Sakhalin Energy inform Indigenous communities about their operations and employ local Indigenous observers to monitor grey whale populations (Sakhalin-2) or to observe offshore oil exploration and its influence on fish (Sakhalin-1). The companies employ local liaisons and have grievance procedures for companies' possible impacts on Indigenous livelihoods, fish stocks or reindeer herding activities. However, the power the companies yield to Indigenous 'rights holders' is limited. Indigenous Peoples cannot halt any oil operations or influence companies' plans. Despite global standards, the state and oil companies remain major 'power holders' on Sakhalin.

Negotiation forums in GGNs adjust and decide how global standards will regulate companies' activities on implementation sites. The tripartite partnership agreements became major negotiation forums where the Indigenous Peoples have a say on how to spend grant money. On Sakhalin Energy's agreement, the Indigenous Peoples are given full authority to distribute grants. This is how Sakhalin Energy sees FPIC implementation and Indigenous Peoples' empowerment. In the ENL partnership agreement, all three entities (Indigenous Peoples, the regional government and the company) are involved in grant decisions. Importantly, ENL does not label this process as FPIC implementation. Except for ExxonMobil's global commitments, there are no ENL indications related to FPIC implementation on Sakhalin. Because of its reliance on investment from international banks, Sakhalin Energy holds annual third-party evaluations by international and local teams of experts. Indigenous grantees comment on SIMDP implementation and the distribution of funds. Sakhalin Energy provides support to Indigenous Peoples throughout Sakhalin Island, while ENL only supports Indigenous Peoples living near the company operation sites.

In general, Sakhalin residents have positive opinions of both Sakhalin Energy and ENL but acknowledge that Sakhalin Energy provides funds for projects on the whole island (Wilson 2016). Indigenous informants highlight that Sakhalin Energy funds traditional family businesses, in contrast to ENL, which only funds organizations. Sakhalin Energy's SIMDPs empowered Indigenous enterprises; however, the Indigenous Peoples find these funds insufficient. The framework of tripartite partnership with Sakhalin Energy allows Indigenous Peoples to make decisions on the distribution of funds; however, this causes conflicts and power struggles in communities: 'In Nogliki there are many disputes over funding because Indigenous people allocate money to their friends and do not listen to expert groups, which leads to resentments when the committee is changed.'[8] There are fewer conflicts in ENL's distribution of funds, as there are three entities to blame, not only the Indigenous decision-makers. Residents assessed ENL's grant process as convenient and mostly criticized the company because distributed funds go only to the affected communities.

As we can see, the oil production GGNs described in this case study adopted standards from the global nodes of governance design and are successfully implementing many of these standards on Sakhalin. However, the implementation of FPIC reflects Russian peculiarities; the implementation process redefines FPIC through benefit sharing. Sakhalin Energy's FPIC implementation mainly focuses on how to distribute funds allocated to support Indigenous communities and not on management of the land and waters shared by the oil company and the Indigenous Peoples. This type of agreement is not equivalent to UNDRIP's conception of FPIC, since the arrangements on Sakhalin do not explicitly allow for community decision-making regarding resource development. Rather, the situation on Sakhalin reflects a 'watered down' interpretation of FPIC more closely resembling consultative forms of engagement, impact assessments and benefit sharing through project funding.

Discussion

Our study of the FSC GGN reveals ambivalence created through the presence of competing conceptions of FPIC, which are often difficult to reconcile with contextual conditions in place during the adoption and implementation of standards. This is compounded by the presence of global actors acting across different scales. Different interpretations of FPIC as a norm create ambivalence of power between actors. Thus, Economic Chamber members interpret the introduction of a strong normative FPIC definition, for example within the FSC's IGIs, as a type of *power over*, requiring them to comply with an FPIC formulation seen as top-down, ill-adapted to cultural conditions and bringing unacceptable transaction costs. Simultaneously, FSC International's FPIC requirements represented *power for* Indigenous and communities' rights and therefore were supported by the Social Chamber and partly by the Environmental Chamber, exemplifying the ambivalence of power within the FSC GGN (Haugaard 2015).

The ambivalence of attitudes towards FPIC were manifested in power struggles experienced during SDG negotiations. The FSC structure equalized power among FSC actors and allowed compromise. Continuous negotiation platforms were essential in adjusting and interpreting FPIC, narrowing the scope of the ambivalence of power. Economic actors were especially resistant to stringent global FPIC requirements and made coordinated efforts to diminish and restrict FPIC applicability in Russia. For example, the members of the SDG, representing economic interests, revisited previously approved notions of who qualified as Indigenous as per the FSC standard, who could be considered as rights holders and how to define customary rights. They tried to use Russian national legislation to avoid overcompliance in implementing FSC. Further, they tried to diminish the scope of eligibility for FPIC and make its application as restrictive as possible (Tysiachniouk et al. 2021). Social actors mobilized FPIC as an opportunity to enhance local/Indigenous rights. Power struggles were ongoing across the hierarchy of scales. Actors from FSC International, as well as social actors from FSC Russia, tried to strengthen the FPIC requirements.

After several years of negotiations, a compromise was reached. The 'weak' consensus was only reached because FSC internal rules do not allow economic actors to overrule environmental or social ones. Thus, while the global marketplace did provide a degree of empowerment to local/Indigenous communities, this was tempered by the types of mitigative measures achieved by the Economic Chamber within negotiations. Our findings also show that a strong normative push from the international level does not guarantee the enhancement of Indigenous rights. For example, economic actors utilized the standard negotiation process to propose narrowing the scope of the local and Indigenous communities whose rights qualify for protection.

Our study of oil GGNs also showed the ambivalence of power exercised by the interplay of global and local actors. The bottom-up Green Wave market campaign against investment banks exercised *power together* (*power with*) (Haugaard 2012). The top-down part of the GGN originating from the investment banks exercised *power over* the Sakhalin-2 consortium and *power for* Indigenous people, who received both rights and resources. As a result of these power struggles, the Sakhalin-2 consortium was required to implement FPIC. The FPIC requirement, discussed and accepted through global and local GGN negotiation forums, became a step forward in the implementation of Indigenous rights despite its meaning being significantly weakened.

The companies on Sakhalin have different dynamics surrounding the adoption of FPIC. After NGOs and Indigenous groups opposed to oil development on Sakhalin launched the Green Wave campaign, investment banks imposed stringent requirements on Sakhalin Energy's oil consortium (Tysiachniouk et al. 2018). Sakhalin Energy adopted these requirements, including FPIC, and developed FPIC implementation procedures. However, their conception of FPIC did not represent a process of granting or withholding consent for oil development. Indigenous Peoples could make decisions on how to distribute the company's allocated funds but did not have broader decision-making authority. Another Sakhalin oil fields operator, ENL, adopted CSR policies that do not directly reference FPIC and utilized a limited interpretation of the CSR mandate. This tendency to adopt restrictive definitions of FPIC has been observed elsewhere (Yaffe 2018; Papillon and Rodon 2019).

However, in both the FSC GGN and oil consortium-driven GGNs, the power of global standards provided support for the enhancement of local/Indigenous rights in implementation sites, such as in FSC-certified forest management units and places of oil extraction on Sakhalin Island. The normative power of Indigenous People's rights was articulated in campaigns against unsustainable production practices. The UNDRIP and ILO 169 conventions, adopted by companies, also highlighted rights and brought some social change by allocating more power to Indigenous Peoples.

In the case of the FSC, the overall process represented a multi-scalar power struggle that was going on in multiple formal and informal negotiation forums inside and outside the SDG and global to local forums of FSC Russia and FSC International. Structural considerations, such as national legislation, are not the only important factors in comparative research on introducing new standards to institutional and organizational environments (Judge-Lord et al. 2020; Vogel 2010). The negotiation forums and implementation sites play roles at multiple scales in exercising power and agency in the process of introducing social change (Tysiachniouk et al. 2021).

In cases such as the FSC, efforts to implement FPIC in specific sites may foster new power struggles on the local level, where FPIC must be interpreted and adjusted to the needs and desires of local/Indigenous communities. FSC-certified companies may contest such power struggles.

Therefore, power struggles in FPIC implementation will continue on both national and local scales. While promoting corporate reflexivity and sensitivity to the needs of local societies, the process of commodifying Indigenous and local rights is not unproblematic for the parties involved.

We found very different power dynamics in the oil and gas sectors. In oil GGNs, only companies that are borrowing money from international financial institutions or whose foreign headquarters adhere to UNDRIP and ILO 169 make an effort to implement FPIC-like arrangements in Russia. In the Sakhalin case study, Indigenous Peoples demanded ethnological expertise with subsequent compensation for damage. Only Sakhalin Energy, a company registered on Sakhalin, clearly states its implementation of FPIC (Tysiachniouk et al. 2018). However, with existing FPIC arrangements, the Indigenous communities acquire an opportunity to distribute a fixed amount of money allocated by the company in the form of grants to local communities. UN representatives and shareholders of Sakhalin-2 companies, as well as third-party reviewers, seem to agree with FPIC implemented in such a particular way (Tysiachniouk et al. 2018). Therefore, forums of negotiation between the Indigenous Peoples focus on fund distribution. Indigenous Peoples are familiar with company operations and can complain through established grievance mechanisms, set up independently from FPIC, or via Indigenous liaisons located in the settlements. With the Sakhalin-style FPIC implementation, companies act under the power imposed by lenders and global norms while providing local/Indigenous communities with very limited opportunities for empowerment. Our chapter demonstrates that, in this case, the power of private economic actors prevails.

Conclusion

Historically, GGNs in the form of market campaigns were important for persuading companies to adopt different kinds of sustainability standards. The integration of social requirements raised expectations regarding corporate behaviour, leading to the creation of new relationships and more complex power dynamics between Indigenous/local communities and corporate entities. As has been shown in this chapter, this includes a complex interplay of actors at various scales. For example, in the FSC and Sakhalin case studies, market campaigns against unsustainable business operations were instrumental in pushing for the establishment of private regulatory approaches. Historical worldwide market campaigns were extremely important for promoting the adoption of the UNDRIP guidelines and ILO 169 by all large financial lending institutions, such as the EBRD, WB and others, which in turn became the key nodes of governance design through private authority. Adoption of these global standards by banks and investors allowed bottom-up market campaigns, such as Sakhalin's Green Wave, to be successful and foster changes to companies' practices in the sites of implementation.

Generating the capacity of GGNs, both historical and those described in this chapter, is determined by shifting power dynamics in the networks involved, which can result in ambivalent effects. When a voluntary certification scheme, such as the FSC, is well established, the role of NGO-led market campaigns, that is, bottom-up GGNs, diminishes since there is an effective instrument that can separate sustainable markets from non-sustainable markets. With an established FSC scheme, the top-down part of the GGN, linking transnational and local places, plays a major role in governing forest management in FSC implementation sites. This was apparent in the coercive ability of the international norm, which, through the IGI design, required a certain level of conformance to what is an internationally sanctioned principle. The ambivalence of power, that is, *power over* the companies and *power for* local communities, of the top-down standards enforced through private authority becomes increasingly important. However, pushback from industrial actors on the ground, who are accustomed to contextually bound interpretations, can create dissonance and ambivalence of power. In this study, this push–pull between international networks and local actors was very evident.

The power struggles that we bring to light in this chapter involve a complex dynamic of actors on multiple scales. The situations in specific cases of FPIC implementation depend on the histories of NGO- and Indigenous-led market campaigns in the form of GGNs stretching from the implementation sites to the global nodes of design. Therefore, the cases described in this chapter are not only about an ambivalence related to the coexistence of opposing forces, such as industry and civil society, but also about tensions between international and national forums of negotiation.

The chapter demonstrated an increasing role of private actors in promoting Indigenous Peoples' rights using market instruments. This is especially important in countries with vast natural resources, such as Russia, that have not ratified ILO Convention 169. In global sustainability standard certification schemes, private actors are taking the lead in fostering FPIC application. The same tendency is observed in policies of lending institutions in the mineral extraction sector, where certification schemes do not exist. Therefore, the private authority's role in global policy setting is increasing.

One of the limitations of this study is that we were not able to do a comparative analysis of FPIC implementation in forest and oil sectors by specific TNCs. FPIC was introduced to Russia earlier in the oil sector than in the forestry sector. Future research will help show how FPIC implementation in Russia and beyond will play out in specific forest management units and the political agency this will afford Indigenous and local communities. More research is needed to understand how FPIC implementation is evolving in the oil and gas sectors and if and how it will shape public policy under pressure from private actors.

Acknowledgements

This research was supported by the NWO, the Netherlands Organization for Scientific Research, Arctic Program ('Developing benefit sharing standards in the Arctic', No. 866.15.203), a Finnish Academy project ('Confronting sustainability: governing forests and fisheries in the Arctic', No. 333231), the National Council for Eurasian and East European Research ('National interests and transnational governance: Russia's changing environmental policy', No. 827-06), the Swedish research council FORMAS (Grant no. 2017-00826), the Social Sciences and Humanities Research Council (Grant no. RNH01176) and a Kone Foundation grant ('Diversities of the environmental movement in Russia', No. 202005986).

We are very thankful to Lena Richter and Brittany Bondi for editing this manuscript and to Alexandra Orlova and Sofia Beloshitskaya for illustrating our work.

Notes

1. Manager of a transnational logging company, member of the SDG, St Petersburg, 14 September 2018.
2. FSC board member representing Environmental Chamber, Moscow, 24 October 2019.
3. Sakhalin Energy. 'Sakhalin indigenous minorities development plan'. Accessed 9 June 2020. http://www.sakhalinenergy.ru/en/social/programmes/simdp/.
4. Sakhalin Energy. 'Sakhalin indigenous minorities development plan'. Accessed 9 June 2020. http://www.sakhalinenergy.ru/en/social/programmes/simdp/.
5. Hannah Jones, 4 February 2011, 'Indigenous Peoples in Sakhalin, Russia, campaign against oil extraction, 2005– 2007'. Accessed 2 April 2020. https://nvdatabase.swarthmore.edu/content/indigenous-peoples-sakhalin-russia-campaign-against-oil-extraction-2005-2007.
6. ExxonMobil. (2018). 'Indigenous peoples'. Accessed 9 June 2020. https://corporate.exxonmobil.com/Community-engagement/Working-with-communities/Indigenous-peoples; Sakhalin Energy (2016). *Sakhalin Indigenous Minorities Development Plan: Five-year SIMDP3*, p. 15. Accessed 9 June 2020. http://simdp.com/uploads/files/SIMDP2016_ENG.pdf.
7. Sakhalin Energy. 'Sakhalin indigenous minorities development plan'. Accessed 9 June 2020. http://www.sakhalinenergy.ru/en/social/programmes/simdp/.
8. Interview with Indigenous resident from the village Nogliki, August 2015.

References

Auld, Graeme, Cristina Balboa, Steven Bernstein and Benjamin Cashore. 2009. 'The emergence of non-state market-driven (NSMD) global environmental governance'. In *Governance for the Environment: New perspectives*, edited by Magali A. Delmas and Oran R. Young, 183–218. New York: Cambridge University Press.

Bartley, Tim. 2007. 'Institutional emergence in an era of globalization: The rise of transnational private regulation of labor and environmental conditions', *American Journal of Sociology* 113(2): 297–351.

Boström, Magnus and Christina Garsten. 2008. 'Organizing for accountability'. In *Organizing Transnational Accountability*, edited by Magnus Boström and Christina Garsten, 1–26. Cheltenham: Edward Elgar.

Bradshaw, Michael. 2008. 'The Sakhalin saga: Energy, politics and the environment', *Soundings* 40: 56–68.

Buxton, Abbi and Emma Wilson. 2013. 'FPIC and the extractive industries: A guide to applying the spirit of free, prior and informed consent in industrial projects'. International Institute for Environment and Development Issue Paper. London: IIED.

Campbell, John L. 2004. *Institutional Change and Globalization*. Princeton: Princeton University Press.

CEE Bankwatch Network. 1997. 'Bankwatch Coordinators Joined Letter to EBRD and OPIC on Proposed Sakhalin II Project, 1 December 1997'. Accessed 24 August 2016. http://bankwatch.org/our-work/projects/sakhalin-ii-oil-and-gas-extraction-russia.

Escobar, Luis and Harrie Vredenburg. 2011. 'Multinational oil companies and the adoption of sustainable development: A resource-based and institutional theory interpretation of adoption heterogeneity', *Journal of Business Ethics* 98(1): 39–65.

Judge-Lord, Devin, Constance L. McDermott and Benjamin Cashore. 2020. 'Do private regulations ratchet up? How to distinguish types of regulatory stringency and patterns of change', *Organization & Environment* 33(1): 96–125.

Gassiy, Violetta and Ivan Potravny. 2019. 'The compensation for losses to Indigenous peoples due to the Arctic industrial development in benefit sharing paradigm', *Resources* 8(2): 71.

Giacomarra, Marcella, Antonio Galati and Maria Crescimanno. 2016. 'The integration of quality and safety concerns in the wine industry: The role of third-party voluntary certifications', *Journal of Cleaner Production* 112: 267–74.

Goloviznina, Marina. 2019. 'Indigenous agency and normative change from below in Russia: Izhma-Komi's perspective on governance and recognition', *Arctic Review* 10: 142–64.

Graybill, Jessica. 2013. 'Mapping an emotional topography of an ecological homeland: The case of Sakhalin Island, Russia', *Emotion, Space and Society* 8: 39–50.

Haufler, Virginia. 2009. 'The Kimberley process certification scheme: An innovation in global governance and conflict prevention', *Journal of Business Ethics* 89(4): 403–16.

Haugaard, Mark. 2012. 'Rethinking the four dimensions of power: Domination and empowerment', *Journal of Political Power* 5(1): 33–54.

Haugaard, Mark. 2015. 'Concerted power over', *Constellations* 22(1): 147–58.

Henry, Laura and Maria Tysiachniouk. 2018. 'The uneven response to global environmental governance: Russia's contentious politics of forest certification', *Forest Policy and Economics* 90: 97–105.

Khanna, Madhu and Keith Brouhle. 2009. 'The effectiveness of voluntary environmental initiatives'. In *Governance for the Environment: New perspectives*, edited by Magali A. Delmas and Oran R. Young, 144–82. New York: Cambridge University Press.

King, Andrew and Michael Toffel. 2009. 'Self-regulatory institutions for solving environmental problems: Perspectives and contributions from the management literature', *Governance for the Environment: New perspectives,* edited by Magali A. Delmas and Oran R. Young, 98–115. New York: Cambridge University Press.

Langthaler, Ernst and Elke Schüßler. 2019. 'Commodity studies with Polanyi: Disembedding and re-embedding labour and land in contemporary capitalism', *Österreichische Zeitschrift für Soziologie* 44(2): 209–23.

Lee, Julian 2005. 'Squaring off on Sakhalin: A "glocal" NGO campaign against big oil'. Centre for Applied Studies in International Negotiations working paper.

Loginova, Julia and Emma Wilson. 2020. 'Our consent was taken for granted'. In *Regulation of Extractive Industries: Community engagement in the Arctic*, edited by Rachael Lorna Johnstone and Anne Merrild Hansen, 156–84. London: Routledge.

Mahanty, Sango and Constance McDermott. 2013. 'How does "free, prior and informed consent" (FPIC) impact social equity? Lessons from mining and forestry and their implications for REDD+', *Land Use Policy* 35: 406–16.

Mayer, Frederick and Gary Gereffi. 2010. 'Regulation and economic globalization: Prospects and limits of private governance', *Business and Politics* 12(3): 1–25.

Merton, Robert King. 1976. *Sociological Ambivalence and Other Essays*. New York: Free Press.

Novikova, Natalia. 2014. *Okhotniki i neftyaniki: issledovanie po yuridichescoy antropologii* [Hunters and oil workers: research on legal anthropology]. Moscow: Nauka.

Oosterveer, Peter, Betty Adjei, Sietze Vellema and Maja Slingerland. 2014. 'Global sustainability standards and food security: Exploring unintended effects of voluntary certification in palm oil', *Global Food Security* 3: 220–6.

Papillon, Martin and Thierry Rodon. 2017. 'Indigenous consent and natural resource extraction: Foundations for a made-in-Canada approach'. IRPP Insight 16.

Papillon, Martin and Thierry Rodon. 2019. 'From consultation to consent: The politics of Indigenous participatory rights in Canada'. In *The Prior Consultation of Indigenous Peoples in Latin America: Inside the implementation gap*, edited by Claire Wright and Alexandra Tomaselli, 261–76. London: Routledge.

Polanyi, Karl. 1968. 'The self-regulating market and the fictitious commodities: Land, labor, and money'. In *Primitive, Archaic, and Modern Economies: Essays of Karl Polanyi*, edited by George Dalton, 26–37. Garden City, NY: Anchor Books.

Postel, Nicolas and Richard Sobel. 2019. 'Corporate social responsibility (CSR): An institutionalist Polanyian analysis', *Society and Business Review* 14(4): 381–400.

Roon, Tatiana. 2006. 'Globalization of Sakhalin's oil industry: Partnership or conflict? A reflection on the *etnologicheskaia ekspertiza*', *Sibirica* 5(2): 95–114.

Stammler, Florian and Aitalina Ivanova. 2016. 'Resources, rights and communities: Extractive mega-projects and local people in the Russian Arctic', *Europe-Asia Studies* 68(7): 1220–44.

Sulyandziga, Liubov. 2019. 'Indigenous peoples and extractive industry encounters: Benefit-sharing agreements in Russian Arctic', *Polar Science* 21: 68–74.

Thuy, Pham Thu, Maria Brockhaus, Grace Wong, Sinarra Januarti, Tjajadi Lasse Loft, Cecilia Luttrell and Samuel Assembe Mvondo. 2013. 'Approaches to benefit sharing: A preliminary comparative analysis of 13 REDD+ countries'. Working Paper CIFOR 108. Accessed 14 December 2021. https://www.cifor.org/publications/pdf_files/WPapers/WP108Pham.pdf.

Tomlinson, Kathrin. 2019. 'Indigenous rights and extractive resource projects: Negotiations over the policy and implementation of FPIC', *International Journal of Human Rights* 23(5): 880–97.

Tulaeva, Svetlana and Maria Tysiachniouk. 2017. 'Benefit-sharing arrangements between oil companies and indigenous people in Russian Northern regions', *Sustainability* 9(8): 1326.

Tysiachniouk, Maria. 2009. 'Conflict as a form of governance: The market campaign to save the Karelian Forests'. In *The Changing Governance of Renewable Natural Resources in Northwest Russia*, edited by Soili Nysten-Haarala, 169–96. London: Ashgate.

Tysiachniouk, Mara. 2012. *Transnational Governance through Private Authority: The case of the Forest Stewardship Council certification in Russia*. Wageningen: Wageningen Academic Publishers.

Tysiachniouk, Maria, Laura Henry, Machiel Lamers and Jan van Tatenhove. 2018. 'Oil and indigenous people in sub-Arctic Russia: Rethinking equity and governance in benefit sharing agreements', *Energy Research & Social Science* 37: 140–52.

Tysiachniouk, Maria and Constance McDermott. 2016. 'Certification with Russian characteristics: Implications for social and environmental equity', *Forest Policy and Economics* 62: 43–53.

Tysiachniouk, Maria, Constance McDermott, Antonina Kulyasova, Sara Teitelbaum and Marine Elbakidze. 2021. 'The politics of scale in global governance: Do more stringent international forest certification standards protect local rights in Russia?', *Forest Policy and Economics* 125: 102407.

Tysiachniouk, Maria, Andrey Petrov and Violetta Gassiy. 2020. 'Towards understanding benefit sharing between extractive industries and Indigenous/local communities in the Arctic'. *Resources* (Special Issue). Accessed 16 March 2022. https://mdpi-res.com/d_attachment/resources/resources-09-00048/article_deploy/resources-09-00048.pdf.

Vogel, David. 2010. 'The private regulation of global corporate conduct: Achievements and limitations', *Business & Society* 49(1): 68–87.

Wilson, Emma. 2016. 'What is the social licence to operate? Local perceptions of oil and gas projects in Russia's Komi Republic and Sakhalin Island', *The Extractive Industries and Society* 3(1): 73–81.

Wilson, Emma and Florian Stammler. 2016. 'Beyond extractivism and alternative cosmologies: Arctic communities and extractive industries in uncertain times', *The Extractive Industries and Society* 3(1): 1–8.

Wirth, David. 2009 'The International Organization for Standardization: Private voluntary standards as swords and shields', *Boston College Environmental Affairs Law Review* 36: 79–102.

Yaffe, Nathan. 2018. 'Indigenous consent: A self-determination perspective', *Melbourne Journal of International Law* 19(2): 703.

11
How brand holders have deprived counterfeiting of legitimacy in Russia since the early 2000s

Zoya Kotelnikova

Introduction

Copyrights, patents and trademarks gained significant importance for the transnational corporate economy in the twentieth century (Hart 2010). The peak of trademarks' popularity coincided with the rapid growth of counterfeit goods, making up 5–7 per cent of total international trade (International Anticounterfeiting Coalition 2008; Kotelnikova 2008). In general, counterfeiting refers to 'a range of illicit activities linked with the trademark infringement' (OECD 2007, 8). Not only individual entrepreneurs but also entire nations were involved in the production and distribution of counterfeit goods, mainly due to the abundance of cheap labour and the global diffusion of technology coupled with the absence of restrictive legislation (Bamossy and Scammon 1985).

The increasing share of counterfeit goods in world trade pushed some developed countries to redouble their efforts to protect major brand owners through global policy diffusion in the wave of liberalization in the late twentieth century (Sell 2003; Dobbin et al. 2007; Archibugi and Filippeti 2010). As a result, 50 developing countries adopted international intellectual property (IP) laws and started policing intellectual property rights in the 1990s (Hart 2010). Similarly, in the early 1990s, Russia signed 18 major international treaties on intellectual property rights (IPR)[1] and adopted special legislation on IPR.[2] Moreover, the new Constitution of the Russian Federation affirmed IPR protection as a constitutional right in 1993.

Despite the adoption of IPR laws, Russian markets were heavily affected by counterfeiting, particularly in the 1990s. Due to the shocking proportion of fakes, international experts noted that 'Russia has the dubious honour of being one of the world's worst intellectual property offenders' (Eugster 2010, 131). Counterfeited goods included clothes, cigarettes, medicine, food, automobile parts, computer software, mobile phones and wristwatches. In some product categories counterfeit goods accounted for 70–80 per cent of retail turnover (e.g., sportswear) (Radaev et al. 2008).

By the late 2000s, however, the proportion of counterfeit goods had decreased significantly to 10–20 per cent of Russian retail trade turnover (Radaev et al. 2008; 2010). According to the Property Rights Alliance, Russia's IPRI score increased, placing it sixth in the Central Eastern Europe and Central Asia region in 2007.[3] Nevertheless, what caused such dramatic changes in the scope and structure of counterfeit trade in Russia still remains unknown.

The chapter aims to reconstruct, from a bottom-up perspective, how the emerging markets changed under the increasing globalization of the corporate economy. It is based on two premises. Firstly, transnational corporations were a powerful force driving the significant reduction of counterfeit goods in local markets. Secondly, their IPR protection strategies were complicated since globalization of national markets inevitably generated ambivalence – the coexistence of opposing forces – in behaviour (Hajda 1968, 21).

Thus, picking the postulate of ambivalence, I focus on how global firms secured their intellectual property rights in Russian markets between the early 2000s and 2010s. For this purpose, I examine brand holders' contradictory attitudes towards fakes because evidence exists that the coexistence of brand manufacture and counterfeit production is beneficial for both parties (Saviano 2008); I analyse the strategies applied by transnational companies to convert their economic resources into political influence; and I demonstrate how they interacted with the authorities and private security firms to make the Russian market toe the global line.

This chapter is structured as follows. It starts by setting out the theoretical premises drawn from the literature, describing how firms protect their property rights and indicating two origins of social ambivalence. Next, the data and methods employed are presented. In the results section, I present the main research findings on how global companies contributed to reducing counterfeit goods in local markets. The chapter concludes with a discussion of how ambivalence and power are intertwined in markets.

Three approaches to property rights protection in the economy

Trademarks, along with patents and copyrights, refer to intellectual property, which has its distinctive features. Unlike tangible objects, which exist independently of private property rights, intangible assets are 'constituted directly through law, and exist because of law' (Carruthers 2015, 129). This makes the legal order critically important to those who own trademarks and other intangible assets. Trademarks are traditionally governed by civil law, which guarantees trademark owners exclusive rights to use them for commercial purposes.

In the context of IP, legislation is necessary but not sufficient. Intellectual property enforcement is even more important, as it reflects how legality is socially experienced. As Johns explains, '[i]t takes shape not only through the stipulation of laws and treaties, but also through actions societies take to put those laws and treaties into effect in homes, offices, factories, and colleges' (2009, 497). Besides, IP law enforcement practices do not work properly without social legitimacy (Carruthers and Ariovich 2004). Intellectual property 'exists only as it is recognized, defended and acted upon' (Johns 2009, 497).

Three approaches to property rights protection can be found in the literature (Markus 2012). Firstly, economic actors privately secure their property rights with the help of their reputation, supported by repeated social interactions, community power and societal culture. Economic obligations are thus enforceable without recourse to the law or coercion (Portes and Sensenbrenner 1993). Secondly, a third party possessing coercive resources (e.g., state or mafia) is committed to enforcing the economic actors' property rights. Since the state specializes in coercion, it is highlighted as being uniquely qualified to ensure compliance with all kinds of rules (Carruthers and Ariovich 2004), while economic actors appear to be the mere recipients of policy-making (Markus 2012). Thirdly, economic actors can secure their property rights through alliances with stakeholders, including neighbouring communities, the labour force, and foreign actors, such as investors, media, non-governmental organizations and governments (Markus 2012, 249). Alliances are defined as 'groups with common interests'. Joining informal or institutionalized alliances, members accumulate the common resources, which allow for restraining potential aggressors, imposing financial or political types of costs on the latter (Markus 2012, 249).

Markus (2012, 249) emphasizes that 'the literature tends to neglect the potential that firms have to improve PR security *at the company level*', treating the state as 'the only actor able to enforce property rights'. The alliance-based argument was empirically shown to be influential in post-communist countries, where alliances with stakeholders around firms matter because they reduce threats from the state as well as private predators (Markus 2012).

This chapter follows a bottom-up perspective, with a particular focus on the work of building alliances conducted by global brand owners to protect their intellectual property rights.

The two origins of ambivalence in post-communist countries

The existing literature indicates that under special circumstances, ambivalence moves to the fore (Hajda 1968). In the context of post-communist countries, ambivalence can be conceived as an experience of the blurred boundaries between public and private regulation generated from both 'transition' and globalization.

The transition economies are characterized by an increase in private and informal forms of regulation due to the imperfectness of both state and market. In the case of weak or failing states that cannot maintain property rights, businesses and citizens wishing to protect their property rely on 'private' enforcement services (mafia) (Volkov 2002; Carruthers and Ariovich 2004) or alliances with stakeholders around firms (Markus 2012). A weak state is expected to be disciplined by economic actors (Markus 2012, 248). Meanwhile, market failures push businesses and citizens to increase cooperation with government agencies through both formal communication (e.g., business association as corporate–state interface) and informal practices (e.g., mutual informal assistance) to eliminate market imperfectness (Ledeneva and Shekshnia 2011; Yakovlev and Govorun 2011). This business–state cooperation may take many forms. For example, in the mid-2000s, Russia saw how mafia was displaced by horizontal networked structures of representatives of various state law enforcement bodies which engaged in law enforcement entrepreneurship (Volkov 2018).

The growing global governance structures which play a pivotal role in disciplining national markets should also be taken into account. Not only do brand holders operate at both the global and local levels, but also the intellectual property defence industry has become globalized and transformed from dispersed and discrete businesses into a coherent and high-technology enterprise combining the interests of states, corporations, multinationals and world bodies (Johns 2009, 498–9). For example, in its economic policy agenda, the 2007 G8 summit addressed the global problem of IPR protection. The year 2004 saw the first Global Congress on Combating Counterfeiting and Piracy convened by the World Customs Organization and Interpol, with the support of the World Intellectual Property Organization. In 2002 Interpol created an Intellectual Property Crime Action Group (Kotelnikova 2008). This intellectual property defence industry which came into existence in the 2000s contributed to the decreasing dependency of individual enterprises on the nation state (Cavusgil 1993).

Emerging markets and global governance problematize the traditional basis of legal promulgation and rule enforcement (Carruthers 2015, 128), contributing to a shift away from public law-making towards private law-making and, thus, to the blurring boundaries between public and private authorities.

Data and methods

This chapter draws on 90 in-depth interviews collected by the author and research fellows from the National Research University Higher School of Economics (HSE University) within several consecutive research projects from 2003 to 2016 (headed by Vadim Radaev),[4] including 16 interviews collected in 2003, 21 interviews in 2008, 19 interviews in 2010, 14 interviews in 2011 and 20 interviews in 2016. Among the 90 interviews, 51 were carried out with managers of transnational companies and 39 with representatives of enforcement authorities and legal experts, including customs inspectors, officials of the Ministry of Internal Affairs, IPR lawyers, representatives of private security firms and business associations dealing with counterfeiting problems (see Table 11.1).

Informants were recruited through the contacts of the trade associations RusBrand, the Association of European Business and the Association of Trading Companies and Manufacturers of Electrical Household and Computer Equipment (Association RATEK).

Brand holders were largely represented by global multi-branded manufacturers and marketers promoting a wide range of consumer and professional products across the world. Participating in the interviews, brand holders' representatives were asked to limit the topic to the products and brands which were the most vulnerable to infringements. The observed transnational companies comprised 12 fast moving consumer goods

Table 11.1 Characteristics of the interviews

Informant Type	Year/Number					Total
	2003	2008	2010	2011	2016	2003–16
Brand holders	16	11	6	8	10	51
Government	—	1	1	1	3	6
Trade associations	—	1	4	—	1	6
Enforcement authorities	—	4	2	2	—	8
Private security firms	—	2	2	1	2	7
Law firms	—	2	3	1	3	9
Patent attorney	—	—	1	—	—	1
Logistics company	—	—	—	1	1	2
Total	16	21	19	14	20	90

(FMCG) market segments: food and drink (coffee, mineral water, tea, etc.), medicine, sportswear, alcoholic beverages, tobacco products, cosmetics, perfume, body care products, hygiene care products, cleaning and detergents, batteries, razor blades, insect repellent, fur coats, home appliances and consumer electronics. Thus, the scope of this survey is limited to FMCG goods. The interviewed brand holders primarily represented the proactive market leaders; small businesses and copyright infringers were not covered by the projects. The average interview length was 60 minutes. In some cases, interviews were repeated.

The interview analysis was based on flexible coding, implying a three-step process: indexing and cross-case memos, applying analytical codes and examining the cross-case reliability of thematic codes (Deterding and Waters 2021).

Dedoose was used as the QDA (qualitative data analysis) software package to process the interview transcripts, including writing memos, coding data with thematic labels, adding organizational demographic information and so forth.[5]

Additionally, this chapter provides judicial and legal statistics extracted from the Supreme Court of the Russian Federation, the Arbitration Court of the Russian Federation and the Federal Customs Services of Russia to visualize some dynamics.

Research findings

The history of markets for counterfeit goods in Russia went through three distinctive stages. The first stage, between 1992 and 2001, was characterized by a significant gap between legality and legitimacy in relation to counterfeit goods: despite the existing IP laws adopted in the early 1990s, IP infringements were widespread and socially accepted. The unauthorized use of trademarks was not considered a crime by most consumers, authorities and entrepreneurs. The second stage started in 2002, when the 1992 Law of the Russian Federation on Trademarks, Service Marks and Appellations of Origin of Goods was amended. Between 2002 and 2008, global brand holders were successful in combating fakes, collaborating with the public authorities and establishing proper IPR policing practices in Russia. In 2008 the new Part IV of the Civil Code came into force and replaced a number of previous specialized IP laws. The third stage started in 2008, since which time global brand owners have faced new challenges: the Eurasian Customs Union was set up, a series of economic and political crises arose and so forth.

Brand holders' ambivalent attitudes towards fakes

Brand holders' behaviour towards counterfeiting is ambivalent. At the initial stage, rather than actively defending their intellectual property rights, some global manufacturers disregarded counterfeiting because fakes promoted their brands and developed consumer loyalty to their products in a new market.

> All sorts of sunglasses produced by French and Italian firms ... they said that they did not care a jot about it – counterfeit what you want. ... On the contrary, it was important for us that our trademarks were becoming popular, and then we would enter the markets ... (Director, business association, 2007)

Entering the Russian market, most branded manufacturers were reluctant to inform consumers that their goods were being counterfeited. As fakes are a socially sensitive issue, the brand holders were fearful that consumers would stop buying their goods and switch to their competitors' brands, knowing that fakes were in the FMCG markets. Moreover, in markets for medicines, regulators had a right to withdraw goods of a given brand from the market if fake pharmaceuticals were found in commercial circulation.

> The problem is as follows: if I begin to shout that I have a lot of fakes, the consumer is pushed to think that it would be better to not deal with me. S(he) will go to another guy who does not yell, giving the impression that (s)he has no problem. So, when we raise the issue of fakes in the media, it is better to do so on behalf of an association, thus not distorting consumers' perceptions. This problem is then ... a problem of society but not of the given company. (Top manager, British multinational consumer goods company, owning over 400 brands, 2003)

Brand holders also recognized that counterfeits cannot be driven out of the market by means of economic competition alone. Fakes are several times cheaper than the genuine goods, presenting a profitable business with a low risk of being punished, especially in the 1990s when fakes were socially legitimized. Given that legal institutions did not work properly in the country, the costs of fighting counterfeiters under civil law were too high for those companies.

> In some cases, they [lawyers] said 'yes, you can do that but it will cost so much, take a lot of time, and take a toll on your nerves. Make a decision by yourself.' So, we decided not to bother. (Top manager, American multinational manufacturer of household cleaning supplies and other consumer chemicals, 2003)

Thus, brand holders have been reluctant to fight counterfeiting openly and on their own, looking for alternative anti-counterfeit policies. At first, they started working with law firms and private security firms.

Applying private force

The global companies considered the operational and investigative activities needed to fight infringers as too labour-intensive, time-consuming and expensive to undertake on their own. Therefore, they outsourced the work to law firms and private security firms which assisted them with the prosecution of counterfeiters. Law firms were specialized in protecting the brand holders' IP rights (trademark registration, pre-trial and in-court dispute resolution, representing brand holder interests in the legal field, etc.), while private security firms were mainly involved in search and operational tasks, such as market monitoring, collection of evidence, raids, detention and so forth. The brand holders chose law firms and private protection agencies to deal with on the basis of recommendations received from business networks, associations and public enforcement authorities.

> Interviewer: How do you select these private security companies? Informant: Now we have recommendations from the association. Back [in the early days of] ... security companies, we had recommendations from militia ... (Top manager, American global manufacturer and marketer of consumer and professional products, 2003)

Generally, law firms and private security firms in collaboration with brand holders considered their main task to be applying pressure to markets and making them toe the line. Law firms and private protection agencies provided full-scale services in brand protection through their contacts with a wide range of public enforcement authorities and courts. Specifically, the services provided by law firms and private protection agencies included market research and market monitoring, consulting and costs evaluation, trademark registration, searching and detecting, evidence gathering, test purchases, detention, enforcement (pre-trial and in-court), storage of confiscated counterfeit goods, dealing with public enforcement authorities and overseeing the destruction of counterfeit goods.

Dealing with transnational companies, local law and security firms also began to embed themselves into the global intellectual property defence industry.

> I gave a presentation in Japan, they studied security firms ... All of us were invited to Japan to engage with this thing ... There I gave an interview with all broadcasting companies. (Head, local private security firm, 2008)

Exercising collective power

Subsequently, brand holders turned to the use of political power and coercive resources. They established business associations with their direct competitors and forged informal alliances with stakeholders, including state regulators and public enforcement agencies.

> I think that, thus, we can have influence at the legislation level, on the state and power elite. You know, I cannot stay at customs every day; therefore, it is necessary to create the atmosphere and system which would control all those things. Through common efforts, we

> can solve the problem. We have something to negotiate. We have big money, large sales, and we can influence it. (Top manager, Swiss multinational food and drink company, 2003)

Combating the counterfeit markets, the brand holders used business associations as formal and depersonalized structures to transform their economic power into political influence through collective movements.

There were two special reasons pushing brand holders to conduct collective actions. Counterfeiters produced and distributed fakes of popular brands owned by different companies at the same time. The transnational companies whose IPR were infringed had to join forces during investigations and trials against violators. Brand holders that actively fought counterfeiters caused other companies to join their efforts, because counterfeiters easily switched to brands that were poorly protected.

Joining the trade associations, the brand holders pursued a variety of aims. The brand holders coordinated their activities against counterfeiting (e.g., consolidation of partial interests and development of common plans). They lobbied government ministries and the State Duma. They engaged in regular dialogue with enforcement authorities in order to develop mechanisms of efficient control. Finally, with the help of business associations, the global brand holders were able to make their efforts visible to the state regulators and consumers.

> We cheer and salute that associations and other organizations are established to fight against counterfeit goods. Because we, along with our department, have solved the problems in Moscow and St. Petersburg, but we cannot overcome two things – we cannot amend the legislation in Russia, and we cannot individually resolve the problem with falsified goods across all of Russia. (Top manager, largest producer of natural mineral waters in the countries of the CIS and the Baltic states, 2003)

Turning from private interests to the public good

The brand holders considered that the interests of the authorities were much closer to their own than to those of consumers in the context of the fight against counterfeiters.

> [I]t is reasonable that what should be done is at the level closest to our experience, i.e. it could be our partners – people who are

> engaged in retailing or it could be trade inspections, at the level of Customs, those who are to some degree involved in the provision of our goods to the final consumer … (Top manager, American manufacturer of batteries, 2003)

At first, the state regulators had no incentives to intervene in the process, preferring that the brand holders dealt with counterfeiters via private channels.

> I don't think the government agency is interested in that. I mean I have to continue to do it in a private way. We have to use a private lawyer, private security. (Top manager, American global manufacturer and marketer of consumer and professional products, 2003)

In the early 2000s, the general political context became conducive to brand holders pressuring public authorities from the bottom up because Russia was seeking to enter the World Trade Organization. The branded manufacturers tried to convince the public authorities that counterfeiting had led to significant losses for the state budgets because infringers did not pay taxes, fees and customs duties. It was also necessary to protect citizens from potential health hazards related to the low quality of fake goods. They pushed the authorities to reframe counterfeiting not only as a problem that private branded manufacturers faced but also as a form of social harm that concerned the whole of society. In this way, they sought to transfer the struggle against counterfeiting from the domain of partial commercial interests to the domain of public goods, so that the government would also be motivated to take responsibility.

> [C]ounterfeiting is primarily a social problem; this is a problem of the state. (Head, local private security firm, 2008)

Brand holders were not keen to leave it to the government agencies to solve the problem (even more, they were against being mere recipients of the state policy). Rather, they put the problem of intellectual property rights at the forefront of government officials' minds. The transnational companies realized that when using political resources they obtained more control over consumer markets, which they could manage privately in order to secure their intellectual property rights and profits.

> The only thing I'm afraid of – no matter how it happens – is that the state will say in a whisper that the problem of enforcement of

intellectual property constitutes an argument among economic actors. In other words, the state will extricate itself further and further and end up just being an arbitrator. And yet what we want is for the state to directly demonstrate and use its force. On the one hand, we want to initiate the force, but, on the other, we want be a part of this process, but without having to face the problem alone. (Top manager, American multinational supplier of sports footwear, apparel, equipment, accessories and services, 2008)

Providing information and expertise is one of the key tools for brand holders to influence the state regulators. The transnational companies collect empirical data on how markets work regularly. They also have a staff of sales representatives operating on local markets, reporting on the discovery of fakes. The brand holders periodically initiated research initiatives in cooperation with reputable research institutions to measure the number of counterfeiters, to estimate losses in state budgets and so forth. All the mentioned efforts to monitor markets allowed the brand holders to impress on officials how acute the problem of counterfeiting was in Russia.

Results of the public force utilization

The brand holders indicated that an improvement to the existing legislation was a priority for future collaboration. The existing IP laws were deemed compatible with international standards but were not fully effective, as some of the procedural issues were vague. For example, the brand holders had been working on two amendments, introducing (1) a sanction to destroy confiscated counterfeit goods, which judges would be able to prescribe, and (2) a right to confiscate equipment that was rented by infringers to manufacture fakes. The brand holders used two main mechanisms to amend laws: political lobbying organized through business associations and targeted work with law firms. The cumulative efforts of the brand holders resulted in numerous amendments to the Administrative Code, the Code of Administrative Misdemeanours, the Criminal Code and the Criminal Procedure Code in the 2000s.

> Interviewer: So, amendments to the legislation are a priority?
> Respondent: Above all ... Principally, the legislation is normal, just normal mechanisms need to be elaborated. Instructions are needed. Subordinate acts and other things are needed to work properly. This is the first thing. (Top manager, American supplier of safety razors and other personal care products, 2003)

It is worth noting that all those amendments generally implied two things: firstly, the tightening of sanctions against copyright violators, and secondly, the expansion of law enforcement authorities' powers, allowing them to prosecute IPR infringers under administrative and criminal law (for more details, see Radaev et al. 2008; 2010; International Intellectual Property Alliance 2008).

In the anti-counterfeiting context, the brand holders dealt with enforcement agencies on a regular basis. However, the companies can be divided into several groups, depending on how they were involved in working with the enforcement authorities. Some companies preferred to contact the enforcement authorities directly, having their own departments and staff responsible for personalized work with the enforcement authorities. Other companies chose an alternative strategy, preferring to deal with the enforcement authorities indirectly – with the help of business associations, private protection agencies and law firms. Furthermore, from their headquarters, the global managers decided to coordinate this work with enforcement authorities themselves and not involve local management. There was also a third group of brand holders who took all available opportunities to establish and maintain relationships with enforcement authorities, working with them both directly and indirectly.

> We have our own special department for combating fake goods, in which we work in two directions: with the state trade inspection and with the Ministry of Internal Affairs. We make full use of both channels. All the information that is generated from our marketing research, we have purposely passed to enforcement authorities over the last three years, primarily to the department responsible for combating economic crimes, and, in cooperation with the trade inspection, we conducted market audits, etc. – we tried to use to the full all the opportunities that those two channels and the legislation provided. (Top manager, largest producer of natural mineral waters in the countries of the CIS and the Baltic states, 2003)

> We deal with the Ministry of Trade, as the trade inspection responsibility resides there, and with the regional department for combating economic crimes – with all, but not always directly, we sometimes work with help of intermediaries – lawyers, let's say law firms, business associations, etc. (Top manager, American supplier of safety razors and other personal care products, 2003)

Each company developed its own strategy, depending on the nature of the problems it faced, on its relations and contacts with enforcement authorities, on the experience it had accumulated and on its subjective perceptions of the effectiveness of the work of a given enforcement authority. Some brand holders decided to focus on working with customs officials because they had problems with imported fakes. Other brand holders chose to contend with the fakes circulating in retail, thus cooperating more intensively with trade inspections. Still other brand holders opted to take action against the manufacturers of fakes themselves, soliciting assistance from the Ministry of Internal Affairs. Finally, there was a small group of activists among the brand holders who preferred to deal with all the enforcement authorities simultaneously.

Generally, brand holders worked with enforcement authorities in the following ways: providing them with marketing information; conducting joint raids; providing expert knowledge on how to distinguish fakes from genuine goods; establishing working groups and committees; developing joint mechanisms of problem solving; conducting educational initiatives; and issuing information leaflets, recommendations and so forth.

One of the important aspects of the brand holders' work with enforcement authorities was educational activities. Brand holders held training sessions and seminars for enforcement authorities to improve their knowledge and skills concerning intellectual property matters. They also published information leaflets, guidelines, instructions and protocols in order to make the policing practice easier for public authorities.

> Just three years ago, many companies started their work in this direction. They began to conduct active seminars and training sessions for the Higher School of Militia, for the Academy of the Ministry of Internal Affairs, and for the Federal Customs Service ... At those regional and all-Russian conferences, we gave presentations to and educated customs officials ... Since 2004, active work has been undertaken. We conducted educational seminars for judges as well as for the Prosecutor's Office. The Prosecutor General's Office of the Russian Federation actively joined that initiative. (Top manager, British multinational consumer goods company, owning over 400 brands, 2008)

Moreover, the brand holders, in cooperation with the enforcement authorities, developed institutional mechanisms for dealing with counterfeiters. One of these was the Customs Register for Objects of Intellectual Property introduced in 1999. Additionally, brand holders provided customs officials with 'efficient prices', indicating the threshold below which no one company could import goods into the Russian Federation.

As a result, brand holders managed to activate the public force against counterfeiters, thus reducing the amount of fake goods in Russian markets. The number of legal cases initiated by public enforcement authorities and brand holders against the illegal use of registered

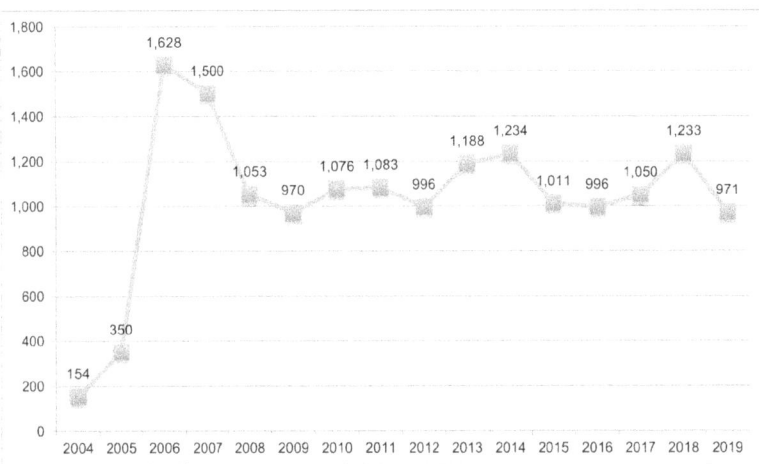

Figure 11.1 The number of legal cases initiated by Customs against illegal use of trademarks, 2004–19. Source: Federal Customs Service of Russia data.

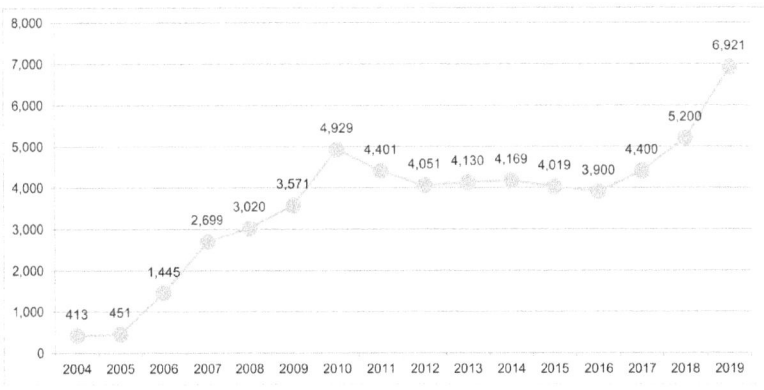

Figure 11.2 The number of arbitration courts trials against administrative violations (illegal use of trademarks), 2004–19. Source: Arbitration courts data.

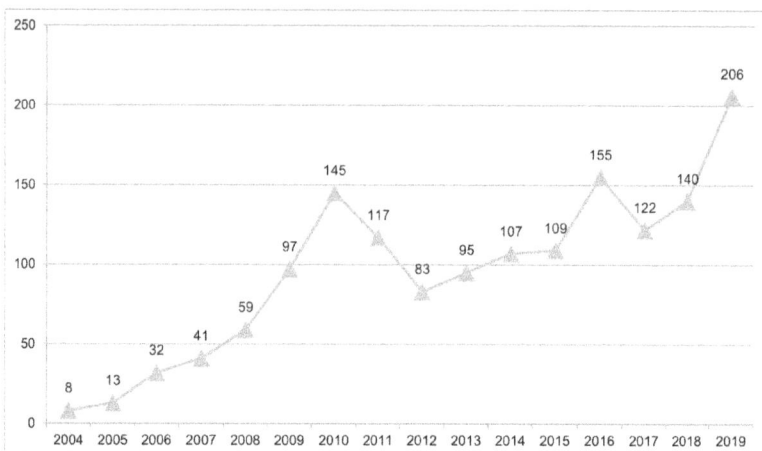

Figure 11.3 The number of market dealers sentenced under Article 180, Part 1 of the Criminal Code (illegal use of trademarks), 2004–19. Source: Data of Judicial Department under the Supreme Court of the Russian Federation.

trademarks increased severalfold in the mid-2000s (see Figures 11.1–11.3). For example, with some fluctuations, the number of legal cases initiated by Federal Customs against the illegal use of trademarks increased sixfold (from 154 to 971), the number of arbitration court trials against administrative violations was nearly 17 times higher (from 413 to 6,921) and the number of market dealers sentenced under Article 180, Part 1 of the Criminal Code was almost 26 times higher (from 8 to 206) between 2004 and 2019.

Discussion and conclusions

Property and politics are necessarily intertwined, as 'the right to control, govern, and exploit things entails the power to influence, govern, and exploit people' (Carruthers and Ariovich 2004, 23). Intellectual property is very peculiar since it exists only thanks to the law and its enforcement. In this sense, social legitimacy is crucial, providing a basis for the formal order to exist.

It should be stressed that brand holders' attitudes towards counterfeits are ambivalent in several ways. Firstly, they perceive counterfeit goods in terms of both loss and profit, implying that counterfeiters may harm the registered trademarks, but at the same time they make the brands more recognizable and more valuable among consumers (Saviano 2008), given that some people knowingly buy fakes (see also Crăciun 2012). Secondly, branded manufacturers are forced to hide from consumers the truth about how widespread counterfeit goods are in the market, not wishing to lose potential consumers who do not want to purchase fake products by chance. Thirdly, the brand holders oscillate between two poles: whether counterfeiting is a private problem of a given company or whether this is an issue the state has to deal with.

The situation for the brand holders intending to secure their intellectual property was even more complicated due to the under-institutionalized conditions of the Russian transition economy. It appeared to be costly, inefficient and harmful to the brands for companies to take action against counterfeiters on their own through the civil legislation in collaboration with private security firms.

All the above pushed global brand holders to seek access to political resources (the threat of physical coercion, to use Max Weber's term) to solve their partly commercial issues caused by unfair competition from counterfeiters. The brand holders needed collective power (Parsons 1963) to raise collective awareness and demand social changes.

To exercise their collective power, the transnational companies joined together to form trade associations – depersonalized supra-market structures that helped them make anti-counterfeit measures socially visible. Our findings are consistent with previous research demonstrating that 'business associations (especially the industry-wide and "leading" ones) consolidate the most active, advanced companies and act as collective representatives of their interests' (Yakovlev and Govorun 2011, 21).

In addition to collective movements organized within markets, transnational companies forged informal alliances with the authorities. Forging alliances was possible due to the bounded solidarity (Portes and Sensenbrenner 1993) emerging between branded manufacturers and authorities against copyright infringers. Branded manufacturers did a lot to reframe the anti-counterfeit struggle as a public good rather than a private one. For these purposes, economic actors employed such mechanisms as defining common group interests (Dobbin and Jung 2016, 176) and educational activities – to promote new patterns of feeling, thinking and acting towards an issue. The brand holders also lobbied for numerous legal amendments, contributing to the expansion of the powers of the public enforcement authorities in relation to IPR infringements. All the above contributed to changing the boundaries between illegitimacy and legitimacy towards trademarks as intellectual property.

Brand holders' motivational ambivalence towards counterfeiting resulted in the emergence of 'power with' those who possessed private and public coercive resources to exercise indirectly 'power over' those who infringe their IPR. Thus, firms exercise their power in markets ambivalently, turning power into a 'silent' and invisible dimension of economic action.

Our research findings contribute to the discussion that previous studies tended to underestimate the potential of economic actors and to overestimate the opportunities of the state to secure property rights, by preferring top-down concepts to bottom-up ones (Ledeneva and Shekshnia 2011; Markus 2012). From a bottom-up perspective, private and public enforcement were discovered to be not so much choice alternatives for businesses but rather two poles between which economic actors oscillate to protect their property.

Acknowledgements

Support from the Basic Research Program of the HSE University is gratefully acknowledged.

I am particularly grateful for the extremely helpful comments on the early drafts of this chapter provided by Alena Ledeneva and Vadim Radaev. I also appreciate the feedback from the participants of the international workshop 'The varieties of power in the economy' (HSE, Moscow, Russia, 3–4 July 2020), where the first draft of this chapter was presented. This chapter is based on interviews which were collected during a series of research projects conducted between 2003 and 2016. I appreciate the support from the project team members including Vadim Radaev (2003, 2008, 2010, 2011 and 2016), Svetlana Barsukova (2003, 2008 and 2010), Vladimir Karacharovskiy (2003), Alexander Kurakin (2010), Maxim Markin (2011), Elena Nazarbaeva (2011), Elena Berdysheva (2016) and Natalia Conroy (2016).

Notes

1. The Universal Copyright Convention, the Berne Convention for the Protection of Literary and Artistic Works, the Paris Convention for the Protection of Industrial Property, the Madrid Agreement on the International Registration of Trademarks, the Protocol to the Madrid Agreement and others.
2. The 1992 Law of the Russian Federation on Trademarks, Service Marks and Appellations of Origin of Goods, the 1992 Patent Law of the Russian Federation, the 1993 Copyright Law and Neighboring Rights of the Russian Federation and others.
3. International Property Rights Index. Accessed 9 March 2022. https://www.internationalpropertyrightsindex.org/country/russia.

4 'Scales of grey imports and counterfeits in Russian FMCG markets' initiated by RusBrand (2002–3); 'Changes in the scales and the forms of the struggle with counterfeits in Russian FMCG markets' initiated by RusBrand (2008); 'The primary trends in the counterfeit markets and the potential impact by the Customs Union' initiated by RusBrand (2010); 'The impact of parallel import legalization on FMCG markets' initiated by RATEK and RusBrand (2011); 'Main forms of illicit goods turnover in the Russian FMCG markets and their countermeasures' initiated by RusBrand (2016–17).
5 Dedoose. Accessed 9 March 2022. http://www.dedoose.com/.

References

Archibugi, Daniele and Andrea Filippeti. 2010. 'The globalisation of intellectual property rights: Four learned lessons and four theses', *Global Policy* 1(2): 137–49.
Bamossy, Gary and Debra L. Scammon. 1985. 'Product counterfeiting: Consumers and manufacturers beware', *Advances in Consumer Research* 12(1): 334–40.
Cavusgil, S. Tamer. 1993. 'Globalization of markets and its impact on domestic institutions', *Indiana Journal of Global Legal Studies* 1(1): Art. 5. Accessed 9 March 2022. https://www.repository.law.indiana.edu/ijgls/vol1/iss1/5.
Crăciun, Magdalena. 2012. 'Rethinking fakes, authenticating selves', *Journal of the Royal Anthropological Institute* 18(4): 846–63.
Carruthers, Bruce G. 2015. 'Economy and law: Old paradigms and new markets'. In *Re-Imagining Economic Sociology*, edited by Patrick Aspers and Nigel Dodd, 127–47. Oxford: Oxford University Press.
Carruthers, Bruce G. and Laura Ariovich. 2004. 'The sociology of property rights', *Annual Review of Sociology* 30(1): 23–46.
Deterding, Nicole M. and Mary C. Waters. 2021. 'Flexible coding of in-depth interviews: A 21st century approach', *Sociological Methods and Research* 50(2): 708–39.
Dobbin, Frank and Jiwook Jung. 2016. 'The fourth dimension of power'. In *Re-Imagining Economic Sociology*, edited by Patrick Aspers and Nigel Dodd, 174–94. Oxford: Oxford University Press.
Dobbin, Frank, Beth Simmons and Geoffrey Garrett. 2007. 'The global diffusion of public policies: Social construction, coercion, competition, or learning?', *Annual Review of Sociology* 33(1): 449–72.
Eugster, Esprit. 2010. 'Evolution and enforcement of intellectual property law in Russia', *Washington University Global Studies Law Review* 9(1). Accessed 9 March 2022. https://openscholarship.wustl.edu/law_globalstudies/vol9/iss1/5.
Hajda, Jan. 1968. 'Ambivalence and social relations', *Sociological Focus* 2(2): 21–8.
Hart, Keith. 2010. 'Intellectual property rights'. The Memory Bank. Accessed 19 March 2021. http://thememorybank.co.uk/papers/intellectual-property/.
International Anticounterfeiting Coalition. 2008. 'About counterfeiting: Get real – the truth about counterfeiting'. Accessed 25 August 2008. http://www.iacc.org/counterfeiting/counterfeiting.php.
International Intellectual Property Alliance. 2008. '2008 Special 301 Report: Russian Federation 109'. Accessed 19 March 2021. https://ustr.gov/archive/assets/Trade_Sectors/Intellectual_Property/Special_301_Public_Submissions_2008/asset_upload_file141_14486.pdf.
Johns, Adrian. 2009. *Piracy: The intellectual property wars from Gutenberg to Gates*. Chicago: University of Chicago Press.
Kotelnikova, Zoya. 2008. 'Goods with fake faces: Why owners of trademarks contribute to counterfeiting', *Journal of Economic Sociology = Ekonomicheskaya sotsiologiya* 9(4): 30–48.
Ledeneva, Alena and Stanislav Shekshnia. 2011. 'Doing business in Russia: Informal practices and anti-corruption strategies', *Russie.Nei.Visions* 58. Accessed 19 March 2021. https://www.ifri.org/sites/default/files/atoms/files/ifriledenevashekshniaengcorruptionrussiamarch2011.pdf.
Markus, Stanislav. 2012. 'Secure property as a bottom-up process: Firms, stakeholders, and predators in weak states', *World Politics* 64(2): 242–77.
OECD. 2007. *The Economic Impact of Counterfeiting and Piracy: executive summary*. Paris: OECD. Accessed 19 March 2021. http://www.oecd.org/dataoecd/13/12/38707619.pdf.

Parsons, Talcott. 1963. 'On the concept of political power', *Proceedings of the American Philosophical Society* 107(3): 232–62.

Portes, Alejandro and Julia Sensenbrenner. 1993. 'Embeddedness and immigration: Notes on the social determinants of economic action', *American Journal of Sociology* 98(6): 1320–50.

Radaev, Vadim, Svetlana Barsukova and Zoya Kotelnikova. 2008. 'Markets for counterfeit goods in Russia', *Analytics of Laboratory for Studies in Economic Sociology* 2. Moscow: Higher School of Economics Publishing (in Russian).

Radaev, Vadim, Svetlana Barsukova, Zoya Kotelnikova and Alexander Kurakin. 2010. 'Main trends in markets for counterfeited goods and the Eurasian Customs Union's potential in influencing them'. *Analytics of Laboratory for Studies in Economic Sociology* 7. Moscow: Higher School of Economics Publishing (in Russian).

Saviano, Roberto. 2008. *Gomorrah: A personal journey into the violent international empire of Naples*. New York: Picador.

Sell, Susan K. 2003. *Private Power, Public Law: The globalization of intellectual property rights*. Cambridge: Cambridge University Press.

Volkov, Vadim. 2002. *Violent Entrepreneurs: The use of force in the making of Russian capitalism*. Ithaca, NY: Cornell University Press.

Volkov, Vadim. 2018. *State or Price of Order*. Saint Petersburg: The Publishing House of the European University at St Petersburg (in Russian).

Yakovlev, Andrei and Andrei Govorun. 2011. 'Industrial associations as a channel of business–government interactions in imperfect institutional environment: The Russian case'. Centre for Comparative Economics Working Paper 116. Accessed 19 March 2021. https://ssrn.com/abstract=1918137 or http://dx.doi.org/10.2139/ssrn.1918137.

12
Academic excellence through homogenization? Gaining legitimacy from the strategic positioning of top-ranked universities

Ivan Pavlyutkin and Anastasiia Makareva

Introduction

As ways of differentiating between institutions in higher education systems, national and global rankings have introduced a stratified frame of vertical positioning for universities, based on their performance and reputational assessment (Altbach 2018; Rindova et al. 2018). As part of the general trend towards quantification and commensuration in the world of organizations, rankings make it possible to compare different universities according to common metrics (Espeland and Stevens 1998). As a result, various local and national universities can be socially categorized and publicly recognized by virtue of their position in the global rankings and be divided into high-, middle- or low-status groups (Stensaker et al. 2019).

On the one hand, the impact of global rankings is undeniable – as Marginson (2007) suggests, global university rankings impact the behaviour of a variety of actors and institutions both within and outside the field of academia to an unprecedented extent; a similar vision has also been supported by Altbach (2012). Additionally, Hazelkorn (2017) focuses particular attention on the ways in which university rankings have come to have a significant impact upon different environments. On the other hand, from the time global rankings were first introduced, they have hurt the collective feelings of many university communities worldwide, meaning that some of them came under pressure to redouble their efforts to implement new initiatives aimed at improving their positions, as their status honour was at stake (Yudkevich et al. 2016). Global rankings, in turn, have been criticized by scholars and university administrators for their weak methodology, irrelevance and volatility, rigidity and other negative effects that consequently emphasized the injustice and subjectivity of this form of differentiation (Pusser and Marginson 2013).

Nowadays, rankings take advantage of the power they exercise and possess and have hence become influential tools for political and economic mobilization in many countries. This can be seen in the special programmes of academic excellence that governments have introduced with the aim of entering the closed status group of elite universities (Froumin and Lisyutkin 2015; Hazelkorn 2015). Today hundreds of universities from various countries are involved in the status game known as the 'global academic race' – not only are they ranked but they also act as if they were, are and will be ranked. Global and national rankings along with awards, ratings and accreditation became toolkits for the social construction of university organizational status (Brankovic et al. 2019). This means that ranking universities is not a one-time act but rather the accumulation of ranks over time, a process that has an influence on the construction of the organization's status. Drawing their power from the global field of higher education rankings has become a source of ambivalence for universities. The rankings prompt many national universities to become 'catching up organizations' and to formulate their institutional ambitions in order to enter the desired status group of global leaders. In turn, this can lead to contradictions in organizational identity regarding the relationship between external strategic priorities and the expectations of the intra-university community, which can be discussed in terms of 'autonomy or dependence' (Elken et al. 2016; Pavlyutkin and Yudkevich 2016).

The strategic positioning of universities is the other side of the process of constructing an organization's status. Recognized as a professional management tool in higher education (Hardy et al. 1983), strategic plans play an important role both in decision-making and, furthermore, in the internal legitimation of various ideas and rationales inside the academic community. The transformation of universities into institutional environments and instruments of public media also questioned their external legitimacy (Meyer and Rowan 1977) and demanded another type of strategic positioning, reflecting upon the relationship between the internal community and the self-representation of the university in the wider society (Drori and Honig 2013). As a strong external reputational force for universities from different status groups, global rankings became an important mechanism for constructing an organization's status (Brankovic 2019) and it is currently hard to ignore them in the process of strategic planning (Altbach 2016). Today, public strategic positioning has become a general organizational ritual, which gives universities a sense of internal and external legitimacy that eventually resonates with their position in the global ranking.

In this chapter, we argue that the strategic positioning of universities reflects the ambivalence of power in the global field of higher education. As soon as leading national and regional universities, embedded in various institutional contexts, enter the global academic race, they experience incompatible normative expectations or double standards while managing their legitimacy. By taking part in the competition for 'academic excellence' that results in the global rankings, lower-ranked universities gain their legitimacy from the rationalized myth applying the 'racing model' to their strategic positioning. They expect to close the gap between themselves and the highly ranked universities, but the latter group gains their legitimacy from other sources. This results in the double thinking of what it means to be world-class – to race or to lead?

Theoretical framework

The pervasion of the notion of ambivalence into social science experienced the influence of theoretical reflections and empirical studies about the academic organization. More than 50 years ago, R. Merton consolidated the concept of ambivalence in sociology, through his studies of scientists. The result of his research, based on the analysis of biographical memoirs, was that scientists constantly have to manoeuvre between contradictory normative expectations (norms and counter-norms), which brings stress, inner conflicts and a sign of malintegration of the social institution (Merton 1973). For example, contradictions based on the internalized values of originality and humility lead to tensions when it comes to the request for recognition of the scientific contribution, because disinterestedness and 'organized scepticism' have little in common with the quest for public recognition of someone's academic achievements. Reflections on ambivalence and ambiguity have become an integral part of the debate about the nature of the organization of colleges and universities. Ambivalence of leadership and the decision-making process at universities and colleges is emphasized through the notions of 'organizational anarchy', 'garbage can model of choice', 'loose coupling system' and 'management fad' (Cohen et al. 1972; Weick 1976; Birnbaum

1988). It is important to note that the definition of a university as a deeply ambivalent institution is interpreted not as a kind of organizational dysfunction. Being partly progressive but at the same time a conservative social organization, the university community develops defence mechanisms as a strategic reaction to organizational change (Weiler 2005). In this sense, the concept of ambivalence helps to explain the dual nature of the academic organization. At the same time, when global rankings gained power and started influencing the institutions of public recognition and national reputation, organizational changes became more radical and transformative for many universities. Ongoing trends demand reflections on the ambivalence of power of global rankings, as they have become the source of contradictory normative expectations in the global field of higher education and of the quest for strategic responses by leading national universities.

On the basis of new institutionalism in organizational analysis and from the perspective of the ambivalence of power, this chapter will test competing hypotheses on the relationship between top universities' positions in the global rankings and their strategic positioning.

The general question which has been discussed since global academic rankings became an influential instrument in the field of higher education is whether they create an 'iron cage' for universities from different cultural localities and force them to apply standardized governance and educational models which lead to the general homogenization of the field of higher education. Moreover, the expansion of rankings is also associated with the general abstraction and disembeddedness of universities from societies (Pavlyutkin and Yudkevich 2016; Ramirez 2020).

More intensive interactions and exchanges between universities from different parts of the world – creating regional and international associations and coalitions, holding global conferences and opening programmes in academic governance, rising global and national ranking agencies – all enforce the process of structuration and normative density in the global field of higher education.

Being highly ranked in the global academic rankings or showing progress in academic racing can provide various benefits for specific universities and create an attractive image for others. As a result, this leads to the establishment of international patterns of similarities based on strong norms emerging from global higher educational narratives. Influential ideas and attractive models to emulate, such as those of 'world-class' or 'flagship' universities, spread around the world and force national states to initiate institutional programmes of academic excellence and relevance (Salmi 2009; Douglass 2016).

'Excellence' and 'engagement' as organizational frames for universities

The notion of the world-class university became dominant in the higher education sector in the 2000s–2010s, although the idea of excellence was defined as a 'watchword of the University' much earlier by Bill Readings (1996). From this perspective, it becomes relevant as a manifestation of the bureaucratic form in reaction to the decline of the ideological power of the nation state. Consequently, in searching for the meaning of their activities in the new age, universities take this from the external world of production and come to the idea of excellence and quality enhancement. This idea was fully criticized by Readings (1996) and other scholars, but the expansion of national and then global academic rankings empowered this idea further and made it increasingly widespread among academic bureaucrats. As a result, the idea of academic excellence was implemented as a desired model by governments and universities in many countries. It is hard today to identify a clear definition of what it means to be 'world-class', not least due to the existence of various critiques of the model and its applicability. At the same time, there are several references which highlight its key visions, concepts and features (Altbach and Salmi 2011). 'World-class' refers, in general, to academic excellence in teaching and research of high impact, a concentration of academic talents (students and faculty) and a university's international or global involvement, which can be represented by its participation and progress in academic rankings. One of the introducers of the concept identified the list of features of world-class: '(a) a high concentration of talent (faculty members and students); (b) abundant resources to offer a rich learning environment and to conduct advanced research; and (c) favorable governance features that encourage leadership, strategic vision, innovation, and flexibility and that enable institutions to make decisions and manage resources without being encumbered by bureaucracy' (Salmi 2009, 7). The conceptual model of 'academic excellence' has been operationalized and implemented in a number of university development programmes funded by governments from different countries including Germany, China, Singapore, Russia and others (Froumin and Lisyutkin 2015). Relying on and taking into consideration the best practices of academic excellence approached through various cases of top universities, the followers or 'catching up universities' prepared their proposals in order to fit this influential and successful (as measured by its sustainability) framework. Hence, excellence can be considered today as one of the normative ideals or rationalized myths which impact both the ranking and strategic positioning of universities across the world. Specific examples were selected to support this claim (Ramirez 2010; Ramirez and Tiplic 2014).

The new flagship university was introduced to some extent as an alternative framework because the conceptual model of academic excellence was highly criticized for its national and regional irrelevance and low degree of engagement in national economies and local communities. As a case in point, in their analysis of some 50 national higher education systems, de Rassenfosse and Williams (2015) referred to the 'inherent conflict' between the singular focus of some governments (especially in small-population countries) on rankings and the desire and need for greater engagement with local communities. As Douglass has emphasized in his book on the flagship model,

> the New Flagship University profiled is not, and could never be, a wholesale repudiation of rankings and global metrics, or of the desire for a global presence. The model is compatible with the World Class University (WCU) focus on research productivity but aims much higher to help articulate a larger purpose. And national and regional relevance and international engagement are mutually compatible goals—indeed the markers of the best universities. (Douglass 2016, 40)

In comparison with the vision of excellence, the idea of engagement is directly related to the provision of public good and serving the communities that are central to the university. It assumes that the university strategy might be developed for the benefit of society in general and its people in particular. According to this vision, the university is striving not only for research excellence and to gain an academic reputation but also to engage with society and contribute to the sustainability of its development.

A recent study of the third mission pursued in the strategic plans of top-ranked, middle-ranked and non-ranked universities revealed that 'top globally ranked institutions are generally less explicit about their commitment to the third mission relating to their geographic setting compared to mid/low and unranked institutions' (Lee et al. 2020, 236). Following these authors, one can ask whether universities' increasing dependence on ranking schemes influences the extent to which public good and community engagement are represented in their strategic vision.

Is strategic positioning of universities a source of organizational homogenization?

As with a university's position in the global rankings, it has been shown that strategic positioning today has become more prone to external pressures, being, on the one hand, embedded in the demand for accountability (Fumasoli et al. 2015) and, on the other, represented as a branding and marketing tool (Hartley and Morphew 2008). Hence, university strategic plans become a way to balance external expectations and institutional ambitions (Stensaker et al. 2019). Considering the arguments of enhancing external legitimacy and the general structuration of organizational fields as sources of isomorphic influence, one can argue that today for various universities their position in the ranking and strategic positioning are both the result of and part of the process of building legitimacy in an external environment that leads to organizational homogenization.

From the perspective of isomorphism, such a transition signifies an attempt at the structuration of the global organizational field, using rankings, associations and other means of network development responsible for the maintenance of the global field's infrastructure. What deserves particular attention here is the way the field is framed, concerning the fact that by definition, a field exists within providential arrangements. Consequently, to assess the performance of a field and the frameworks it creates, the mechanics of institutional isomorphic alternation (DiMaggio and Powell 1983) depict and explain the behavioural patterns of universities' decision-making reflected in their strategies. As a case in point, the development of university strategy not only concerns the initial aims and objectives from the perspective of a separate institution but also, through a competitive environment in which universities operate as actors, is an expression of a thorough analysis of its opponents' strategies. In this regard, the ambitions that universities embed in their strategies create the overall conditions for homogenization, which universities use to search for legitimacy in the global organizational field of education.

At the same time, it should be noted that homogenization alone cannot derive its power immediately and thus faces a variety of constraints related to both the intentions and the efforts of individual organizations as well as to the general social order and social structure of the sector. Along with growing similarities, studies that explain the differentiation process in various fields have gained tremendous prominence. For example, Riesman introduced the concept of a 'snake-like possession' to show that institutions placed differently in the social structure will be engaged in distinct strategic behaviours (Riesman 1958; Stensaker et al. 2019). The sources of this differentiation may be of a different kind, including institutional norms and selective demands for ideas, aspirations for a recognized status distance of leading actors, or closed circles of interorganizational communication and exchange (Fligstein 1996; Hartley and Morphew 2008).

As an example, the recent debate around two strong competing visions or models of universities embedded two sides: 'world-class universities' and 'flagship universities'. Both types are represented by universities across different regions of the world (Douglass 2016). The aspiration for a recognized status distance, resulting in a different ranking and strategic positioning, is driven by the interest of leading organizations to reproduce the existing stable social order, where they acquire the status of a trendsetter and rule-giver (Fligstein 1996). At the same time, it can also become a desirable incentive to distinguish oneself not only from leaders (or highly ranked universities) and outsiders but also within the leading group if actors are competing for a dominant position in the field.

On the level of education as a field, the process of homogenization, despite being closely tied to the structural level of analysis of organizational forms, could also be embedded in the patterns of strategic positioning. At the same time, the structure is not always present in its 'pure form', due to its dependency upon such factors as government politics, ideology, public actors and a range of other factors dictating their own rules of the game. Therefore it cannot be taken as a fully objective constant, always serving the expectations of multiple participants. This leads to the implications of new institutionalism, which sets out the rationale behind the behaviour of universities as actors in the institutional field. Accordingly, the process considered implies significant adjustments to the dominant norms, while simultaneously preserving the values and ambition of the actor. The duality of the conditions set by the framework of new institutionalism consequently accounts for the ambivalence occurring in the field, which, in turn, unleashes both the competitiveness of actors and their mutual interdependence. As a result, while trying to give everyone a good dressing-down, universities are playing an ambivalent game: while they are becoming similar to each other in terms of their organizational structure, bureaucracies and objectives, they remain in competition by counteracting each other in pursuit of dominance in the field.

In the case of university strategies, the ambivalence of performance is created by power relationships (e.g., competition) (Musselin 2018). By developing and publishing strategies, universities highlight the key focus areas of their performance, as a social value and a contribution to society. Using such means of representation as excellence, engagement and sustainability, universities consequently can claim government support or other means of assistance (Sutphen et al. 2019).

From this it could be inferred that the global field of education is becoming more structured. This notion is supported by the homogenization of the field, which not only embodies organizational forms but also concerns the strategic positioning of universities. Consequently, it leads to the assumption that the frames and patterns applied by universities involved in ranking games create the ambivalence of power within the field.

Data and sampling

To form the sample of universities' strategic plans we used data on ranking positions and strategic documents gathered from open sources: the websites of universities and ranking agencies. The final sample consists of 33 strategic documents of universities ranked from 1 to 150 according to three main global ranking agencies – ARWU, THE and QS (see Table 12.1). As not every university in the top 150 put their strategic plan online

Table 12.1 Sample list of universities

No	University	Ranking group	Position	Country
1	Oxford University	Highly ranked	Stable	UK
2	MIT	Highly ranked	Stable	US
3	Imperial College	Highly ranked	Stable	UK
4	Yale University	Highly ranked	Stable	US
5	ETH Zurich	Highly ranked	Stable	Switzerland
6	Karolinska Institute	Highly ranked	Stable	Sweden
7	University of British Columbia	Highly ranked	Stable	Canada
8	University of Melbourne	Highly ranked	Variable	Australia
9	University of Copenhagen	Highly ranked	Variable	Denmark

No	University	Ranking group	Position	Country
10	University of Edinburgh	Highly ranked	Variable	UK
11	University of Tokyo	Highly ranked	Variable	Japan
12	University of Illinois at Urbana-Champaign	Highly ranked	Variable	US
13	Oslo University	Middle-ranked	Stable	Norway
14	University of California, Davis	Middle-ranked	Stable	US
15	University of Helsinki	Middle-ranked	Stable	Finland
16	Utrecht University	Middle-ranked	Stable	Netherlands
17	Boston University	Middle-ranked	Stable	US
18	McGill University	Middle-ranked	Variable	Canada
19	University of Sydney	Middle-ranked	Variable	Australia
20	King's College	Middle-ranked	Variable	UK
21	Geneva University	Middle-ranked	Variable	Switzerland
22	Australian National University	Middle-ranked	Variable	Australia
23	Vienna University	Low-ranked	Stable	Austria
24	Lund University	Low-ranked	Stable	Sweden
25	University of Warwick	Low-ranked	Stable	UK
26	University of Amsterdam	Low-ranked	Stable	Netherlands
27	Georgia Institute of Technology	Low-ranked	Stable	US
28	Chinese University of Hong Kong	Low-ranked	Variable	China
29	Cardiff University	Low-ranked	Variable	UK
30	Rutgers University	Low-ranked	Variable	USA
31	University of Hong Kong	Low-ranked	Variable	China
32	Alberta University	Low-ranked	Variable	Canada
33	Tohoku University	Low-ranked	Variable	Japan

as an open document, the final sample consisted of those files that were available and downloadable.

All the universities in the sample were divided into six groups determined by two indicators. The first is belonging to one of the top groups in the global academic ranking – the top 50, top 50–100 or top 100–150. The second is the degree of variation in the university's position in the ranking over a 15-year period according to ARWU. We studied the strategic plans to identify not only similarities and differences between differently ranked universities in one period but also the extent to which different institutions climb or fall down the rankings or stay the same over time.

Looking at the dynamics of university rankings, one can identify that some universities have stable rankings over time (less than 5–15 points change) and some of them show a radical change in their ranking (more than 50–100 points change). If we divide the universities ranked from 1 to 150 into three groups, we can see that the last group (top 101–150) is the most volatile over time as it consists of universities that changed their ranking positions by 30–150 points. The opposite is true of the first group (top 50), which has been quite stable over time – few universities have left or joined the group over the last 10 years, although there are several exceptions. We can assume that some of the exceptions are racing universities, which did a great deal in order to break through the borders of the tight group of the top universities. At the same time, some universities lost their positions and joined the lower-ranked groups. As a result, each of the three top groups (as defined in 2019/20) consists of two types of universities: those with a stable ranking and those with a more variable position.

The final sample of universities includes universities from different countries and world regions: Asia (Japan, China), North America (United States, Canada), Oceania (Australia), Western Europe (United Kingdom, Germany, Austria, Switzerland, Netherlands) and Northern Europe (Norway, Sweden, Finland, Denmark). It is important to consider that most of them are leading national institutions which boost their countries' visibility and reputation. Moreover, of course, they are part of local territories and communities.

We assume that the public-facing strategic positioning of universities takes into account several dimensions, which are partly related to status positioning on the global field and partly to their positioning on the home territories. It reflects a situation of ambivalence when universities, to become leading institutions, gain their legitimacy from different sources.

Group-level hypothesis

Relying on previous studies, we assume that differences or similarities in the strategic positioning (patterns) of top universities can be explained by their belonging to self-regulated status groups based on (1) ranking group (top 50/top 100/top 150), (2) stability in the ranking system over time (stable/variable) and (3) regional and global institutional norms (insiders/outsiders).

- H1: Highly ranked and lower-ranked universities from the top 150 will differ in their strategic positioning templates as they gain legitimacy from different sources.

- H2: Highly ranked universities (top 50) will have more in-group similarities in their strategic positioning than the middle- (50–100) and lower-ranked groups (100–150).

- H3: Middle-ranked universities (50–100) are more diffuse in terms of their strategic positioning templates than highly ranked (top–50) or lower-ranked ones (100–150). There are no shared strategic patterns in the group and no clear conceptual boundaries between them and other groups of universities.

- H4: 'Fast-falling' and 'fast-rising' universities will have more similarities in their patterns of strategic positioning than those with a more stable position regardless of their affiliation with the ranking group inside the top 150.

- H5: Universities from similar institutional contexts (involvement in national academic excellence programmes) will have more similarities in patterns of strategic positioning than those from different contexts.

- H6: Highly ranked universities represent an indifferent vision for academic excellence (success in rankings) in their strategic positioning.

Data analysis

The sampled and selected strategic plans are not of the same kind. They differ in length, visual inserts, planning periods, visual structure (headlines) and so forth. It should be assumed that all the strategies highlight the importance of research and teaching as core activities. At the same time, they put them both into different frameworks that can be identified by analysing various keywords. Keywords in strategic plans can be determined as organizational signs and scripts, which are the result of the reflexive work of their writers. They also work as tools for the public representation of universities in the organizational fields and reflect their institutional vision of the external environment and strategies for gaining legitimacy (Suchman 1995; Stensaker et al. 2019).

To test the hypothesis on the differences and similarities in the strategic positioning of leading universities, we conducted a two-step data analysis. It relies on open and axial coding procedures. The analysis starts with open coding, whereby we identify keywords which bind the narrative of the strategic text. The result of the open coding procedure leads to the definition of several dimensions of strategic positioning which form the groups of codes. We identified several groups of codes and built core categories, which will be the focus of the axial coding and counting. The list of categories with examples of codes is presented in Table 12.2.

After identifying core keywords, we analysed how they are presented in the whole sample of strategic texts. We assume that the frequency of keywords mentioned reflects the degree of attention that the university pays to the particular issue in its strategy: the more often a keyword is mentioned, the more important the issue is in a particular strategy. If a strategy contains more words relating to global or

Table 12.2 Key categories of universities' strategic positioning

Key Categories	Codes
Strategic vision	excellence (excellence, excel, quality, world-class) / engagement (engagement, engage, contribution, communities) / sustainability (sustainability, sustain)
Area of strategic positioning	global (international) / national (country) / local (city, area, communities)
Core activities	teaching / research / innovation / service / learning
Openness	partnership / collaboration

international than national or regional dimensions, for example, this reflects the university's strategic priorities.

As a result, we counted the frequency and keyword ratios to find different weights inside the strategic texts and between the texts. The procedure was simple. We counted the frequencies of keywords mentioned, divided them by the overall number of words in the text and ranged them by university strategies.

Excellence = excellence + quality + ranking + world-class / N
Engagement = engagement + contribution + relevance + benefit / N

In addition to the main counts we also collected the results by keywords related to the openness of the university (partnerships, collaborations) and area of positioning (global, local, national).

Conceptual frameworks of the strategic visions

The analysis of the sampled strategic plans provides the complex range of core categories and codes which frame the conceptual vision of university activities. For example, teaching, learning and research are still considered to be core activities of many universities. Nevertheless, the conceptual models of these activities, that is, the meaningful frames of representation, will be different for universities from different regions and institutional and cultural contexts. Two of these conceptual models today are known as competing: these are the notions of 'academic excellence', representing the idea of a 'world-class university', and 'engagement', representing the idea of a 'flagship university'.

What is worth mentioning is that both conceptual models consist of their own keywords, signifying their area of expertise and key salient issues. The vocabulary of excellence includes such codes as world-class, first-class, best quality, talents, global leadership, rankings and centres of excellence. The vocabulary of engagement, in turn, involves the codes community, contribution, public good, local, benefit society and social impact. Such codes form the corpus of the strategic framework and make it meaningful. This does not mean that the codes from different models are mutually exclusive in the strategy of individual universities. One of the findings from the analysis of the strategic plans is that some universities in the sample focused purely on excellence or engagement conceptual models, while others created fusion models combining keywords from different vocabularies.

Looking at the strategic plans of the sampled universities from different world regions and ranking groups, one can find that excellence is one of the core categories that frames the strategic vision and university activities. Mainly it appears in the parts of the texts which define the university's goals, mission and vision.

An obvious example for this is the strategic plan of Warwick University, which is lower ranked in the top 150 but has a stable position, entitled 'Excellence with purpose'. In the main body of the text, one can find 'excellence' as a keyword, which marks the purpose of the university: 'The core purpose of our University – furthering the excellence of our research and education'.[1]

The same vision runs through the plan of Zurich University, which is highly ranked in the top 150. Various factors were mentioned in the strategic plan as challenges for 'the institutions' ability to thrive, attract the world's best talent, perform high-impact research and provide first-class education for future students'.[2]

The University of Tokyo, which is highly ranked but lacks a stable position in the ranking group, formulated its Vision 2020 to 'set forth two basic principles for fulfilling this mission: excellence and diversity'.[3]

The University of Sydney was classified as a university in the middle-ranked group in the top 150 that several times in the last decade crossed the threshold into the top 100. It prioritizes strategic investment in excellence to enable its academics to foster excellence in education and research according to 'world standards'.[4] In the plan of the university, one can also find an emphasis on international rankings as reflections of the university's reputation and global leadership:

> Our international rankings reflect our reputation for global leadership in research and education. The university is ranked 45th in the world in the 2015–16 QS World University rankings; first in Australia and 14th globally in the QS Graduate Employability Rankings 2016; 56th in the 2015 Times Higher Education World University Rankings; in the 101–150 band of the 2015 Academic Ranking of World Universities (ARWU); and 51st in the 2016 US News and World Report Best Global Universities Rankings.[5]

At the same, looking at the strategic plans of the sampled top universities we found that the conceptual model of engagement is represented unequivocally in only a few of them.

As an example, the strategic plan of the University of Melbourne, which is in the top 50 universities in the world, put engagement as a sense-making concept for university development: 'Engagement connects our learning and research work with communities, helping us to achieve academic aspirations and create economic, social and cultural value. Engagement is a vow to relevance, connections and public-spirited actions'.[6]

The University of California, Davis, which is in the top 100 universities in the world, also presents engagement as one of its key goals: 'Support our community, region, state, nation and world through mutually beneficial and impactful partnerships that reflect a firm commitment to our mission and increase the visibility and reputation of the university'.[7]

At the same time, most of the universities in the sample put codes from both the 'excellence' and 'engagement' vocabularies at the core of their strategic vision. For example, the strategic document of the University of Alberta is entitled 'For the Public Good' and its aim is 'to empower and enable each member of the University of Alberta to build, experience, excel, engage, and sustain'.[8]

The University of British Columbia, which is a highly ranked university, puts engagement as the core category in its strategic vision but also highlights the importance of academic excellence:

> This plan describes the strong connections between these themes and the core areas that continue to define what we do as a public university: People and Places, Research Excellence, Transformative Learning and Local and Global Engagement. It also emphasizes our enduring focus on academic excellence and on Indigenous engagement, sustainability and wellbeing. Our relationship with Indigenous people and communities is central to the university; we hold profound commitments to reciprocity, knowledge curation and development.[9]

Testing the group-level hypothesis on strategic positioning

In the second step, we tested the group-level hypothesis on the similarities or differences in universities' strategic positioning. We take into account that the selected strategies are implemented by the universities from the top 150 ranking category but at the same time they represent different regions and institutional contexts, different ranking groups (highly ranked, middle-ranked, low ranked) and different degrees of variability in academic racing (over the last 10 years).

Since we found that it is hard to find representatives of the pure conceptual models in the strategic texts (excellence or engagement), we conducted a quantitative analysis by comparing the ratio of the keywords related to excellence or engagement in each strategy, whereby we show the degree of strategic orientation towards one of the two visions – excellence or engagement – by conducting a quantitative analysis of the codes of representation. The results are presented in Table 12.3.

Regarding the formulated hypotheses (H1, H2, H3), we found that the conceptual models of university strategies were different for highly ranked and low-ranked top institutions. While the strategic visions of the highest-ranking group consist of more keywords from the engagement model, the lowest group in the sample represents mainly the excellence vision. We cannot claim a strong negative correlation between the measures of engagement and excellence, but comparing the two models at different universities shows quite a clear distinction between the groups. The results show that the leading universities in the world do not focus on academic excellence in their strategic positioning as much as catching up universities do. On the contrary, the lower you are in the ranking, the greater is the eagerness for global engagement. In addition, contrary to the second hypothesis, we found that in the highest-ranking group there is less homogeneity in terms of strategic positioning. Five out of the 12 strategic plans are not related to the engagement model. One of the strategies (Yale) is based on the concept of sustainability, which is close to the engagement model, and another (MIT) we entitled 'global collaboration', although it should be compared to the fusion model, as a combination of both excellence and engagement. Still, the question is whether it can be defined as a distinct model, separate from the engagement model. Three strategic plans are closer to the academic excellence model. At the same time, there is no strategic plan in the low-ranking group that contains the pure engagement model.

An interesting result was found at the intersection of two dimensions: global/national/local and openness to partnership/collaboration. Both engagement and excellence models vary according to the degree of partnership orientation and embeddedness in the local, national and global areas. This means that the engagement model may involve partnerships that may take not only local but also national and global orientations.

As for the third hypothesis (H3), we found that the strategic positioning of middle-ranked universities did not consistently comprise any special features but rather contained a mix of different orientations and models associated in part with the highest-ranked group and in part with the lowest one.

Table 12.3 General models of strategic positioning based on the counting of keywords (by groups of universities)

Number	Stable/Variable	Ranking group (High/Medium/Low)	University	Engagement	Excellence	Sustainability	Partnership	Collaboration	International	National + country	Local + area	Conceptual model
1	S	H	Oxford University	0.95	0.6	0.31	0.77	0.34	0.63	0.26	0.35	Engagement + Partnership
2	S	H	MIT	0.64	0.22	0.07	0.27	0.35	2.37	0.22	0.04	Engagement + Collaboration
3	S	H	Imperial College	0.44	0.57	0.11	0.3	0.4	0.42	0.3	0.1	Academic excellence + Collaboration
4	S	H	Yale University	0.3	0.11	1.78	0.18	0.18	0.13	0.06	0.29	Sustainability
5	S	H	ETH Zurich	0.45	0.42	0.12	0.14	0.24	0.61	0.31	0.01	Fusion
6	S	H	Karolinska Institute	0.42	0.39	0.28	0.37	0.57	1.15	0.37	0.14	Engagement + Partnership
7	S	H	University of British Columbia	0.58	0.34	0	0.34	0.39	0.44	0.26	0.61	Engagement + Partnership
8	V	H	University of Melbourne	0.94	0.49	0.39	0.4	0.2	0.63	0.33	0.14	Engagement + Partnership
9	V	H	University of Copenhagen	0.71	0.56	0.05	0.17	0.59	1.26	0.52	0.05	Engagement + Partnership
10	V	H	University of Edinburgh	0.58	0.25	0.47	0.38	0.21	0.68	0.25	0.85	Engagement + Partnership
11	V	H	University of Tokyo	0.24	0.53	0.03	0	0.35	0.7	0.41	0	Academic excellence + Collaboration

Number	Stable/Variable	Ranking group (High/Medium/Low)	University	Engagement	Excellence	Sustainability	Partnership	Collaboration	International	National + country	Local + area	Conceptual model
12	V	H	University of Illinois at Urbana-Champaign	0.38	0.42	0.03	0.38	0.15	0.41	0.22	0.5	Engagement + Partnership
13	S	M	Oslo University	0.28	0.69	0.05	0.06	0.02	1.06	0.46	0.15	Academic excellence + Collaboration
14	S	M	University of California, Davis	0.48	0.3	0.09	0.33	0.18	0.29	0.17	0.12	Engagement + Partnership
15	S	M	University of Helsinki	0.26	0.48	0.8	0.29	0.44	0.85	0.29	0.07	Global collaboration
16	S	M	Utrecht University	0.31	0.17	0.19	0.04	0.29	0.6	0.31	0.08	Fusion
17	S	M	Boston University	0.11	0.33	0.08	0	0.14	0.21	0.53	0.13	Fusion
18	V	M	McGill University	0.31	0.22	0.25	0.18	0.25	1.1	0.2	0.8	Engagement
19	V	M	University of Sydney	0.35	0.49	0.06	0.28	0.14	0.24	0.26	0.09	Academic excellence
20	V	M	King's College London	0.54	0.25	0.14	0.59	0.22	0.95	0.32	0.8	Engagement + Partnership
21	V	M	Geneva University	0.21	0.42	0	0.14	0	0.9	0.14	0.14	Fusion
22	V	M	Australian National University	0.68	0.87	0.04	0.1	0.1	0.3	0.94	0.02	Fusion
23	S	L	Vienna University	0.22	0.22	0.04	0.07	0.03	0.63	0.25	0.03	Fusion

Number	Stable/Variable	Ranking group (High/Medium/Low)	University	Engagement	Excellence	Sustainability	Partnership	Collaboration	International	National + country	Local + area	Conceptual model
24	S	L	Lund University	0.42	0.35	0.21	0.14	0.63	0.9	0.21	0	Global collaboration
25	S	L	University of Warwick	0.23	1.41	0.31	0.61	0.27	0.99	0.34	0.27	Academic excellence + Collaboration
26	S	L	University of Amsterdam	0.4	0.64	0.17	0.26	0.07	0.85	0.31	0.24	Academic excellence
27	S	L	Georgia Institute of Technology	0.22	0.45	0.06	0.22	0.13	0.96	0.36	0.12	Academic excellence
28	V	L	Chinese University of Hong Kong	0.4	0.38	0.32	0.13	0.1	0.78	0.56	0.33	Fusion
29	V	L	Cardiff University	0.45	0.83	0.11	0.5	0.11	0.13	0.67	0.5	Fusion
30	V	L	Rutgers University	0.23	0.84	0.07	0.07	0.07	1.61	0.58	0.36	Academic excellence
31	V	L	University of Hong Kong	0.44	0.49	0.16	0.44	0.44	0.56	0.38	0.22	Academic excellence + Collaboration
32	V	L	Alberta University	0.86	0.66	0.53	0.39	0.23	0.94	0.83	0.45	Fusion
33	V	L	Tohoku University	0.31	0.35	0.05	0.13	0.35	0.94	0.07	0.08	Fusion
				0.43	0.43	0.23	0.26	0.25	0.74	0.37	0.24	

We found little support for the fourth hypothesis (H4) concerning the difference between 'fast-moving' and 'stable' universities. Although one might think that the fast-moving universities in the rankings would be more oriented towards the fusion model due to their ambitions and uncertainty, whereby they multi-task and implement competing visions of university development, the gathered data do not support this. Our data did, however, support the fifth hypothesis (H5), which can be seen as contradicting the first and second. If we look at the final table, we identify fewer North American universities which implemented the excellence model. The arguments here might relate to different institutional contexts and facilitating factors. European and Asian universities are more involved in national excellence programmes than North American institutions. In addition, many US universities are more dependent on states and land grant obligations than their European counterparts. The difference in institutional norms influencing top universities may explain the difference in the concepts used in strategic positioning. The last hypothesis (H6) is supported, although it does not mean that the highest-ranked universities totally ignore rankings.

At the same time, as we have shown that the vision for engagement is more widespread in the elite group than in the lowest group, we can argue that originally world-class universities do not gain their power and legitimacy from the world-class models.

Conclusion

Our comparative study of strategic positioning among the world's top 150 universities revealed several important observations.

It is hard to find representatives of only one conceptual model in the strategic positioning of universities. Top universities involved in academic racing allocate and combine conceptual keywords from different competing models, as they meet incompatible normative expectations. To compare the strategies of top universities by the degree of excellence or engagement orientations, the keywords from both vocabularies were counted. The analysis leads to an unexpected result: universities belonging to the highest-ranking group are more oriented towards the engagement vision than universities in the lower-ranking group, which are more oriented towards the excellence model. Since universities depend on their institutional environments, representing one or the other model in their strategic plans becomes a way of managing legitimacy.

The ambivalence of power of global academic rankings is manifested in the fact that, in order to gain legitimacy, leading universities as organizational actors are forced to manoeuvre between conflicting normative expectations. Once introduced as instruments for the comparative evaluation of universities in different regions of the world, academic rankings became powerful geopolitical tools which enforce the structuration of the global field of higher education and provide benefits for progress on the track to excellence. The processes of structuration and institutional change in global higher education are accompanied by the competition of influential ideas, such as excellence, engagement and sustainability. They are translated on the national level and become institutionalized as conceptual frames through the creation and realization of various developmental programmes for universities. The result of this institutional translation reflects the strategic positioning of leading universities, which present their visions and organizational ambitions. On the one hand, leading national universities are expected to be involved in academic racing and to compete for higher organizational statuses in the global field of higher education. On the other hand, they are expected to generate public goods and to engage in the development of national economies and societies. Becoming world-class for many leading universities means first of all becoming a 'catching up university', whereby they derive their legitimacy by applying the 'racing model' in their strategic positioning. According to the results of our study, this is not the same as being a leading university, which means representing the ideas of engagement.

Notes

1. 'Strategic direction to 2030', 18. https://warwick.ac.uk/about/strategy/hp-contents/university_of_warwick_strategy.pdf.
2. 'Strategy and Development Plan 2021–2024', 6. https://ethz.ch/en/the-eth-zurich/portrait/strategy.html.
3. 'Announcement of the University of Tokyo: Vision 2020', 1. https://www.u-tokyo.ac.jp/content/400035617.pdf.
4. 'The University of Sydney 2016–20 Strategic Plan', 12. https://www.sydney.edu.au/content/dam/intranet/documents/strategy-and-planning/strategic-plan-2016-20.pdf.
5. 'The University of Sydney 2016–20 Strategic Plan', 12. https://www.sydney.edu.au/content/dam/intranet/documents/strategy-and-planning/strategic-plan-2016-20.pdf.
6. 'Engagement at Melbourne 2015–2020', 2. https://about.unimelb.edu.au/__data/assets/pdf_file/0021/15348/Engagement-at-Melbourne-2.pdf.
7. 'To boldly go: A strategic vision for UC Davis', 40. https://leadership.ucdavis.edu/sites/g/files/dgvnsk1166/files/files/page/Strategic%20Plan_0.pdf.
8. 'For the public good', 1. https://www.ualberta.ca/strategic-plan/index.html.
9. 'Shaping UBC's next century', 4. https://strategicplan.ubc.ca/wp-content/uploads/2019/09/2018_UBC_Strategic_Plan_Full-20180425.pdf.

References

Altbach, Philip G. 2012. 'The globalization of college and university rankings', *Change: The Magazine of Higher Learning* 44(1): 26–31.
Altbach, Philip G. 2016. *Global Perspectives on Higher Education*. Baltimore, MD: Johns Hopkins University Press.
Altbach, Philip G. 2018. 'World-class universities and higher education differentiation: The necessity of systems'. In *World-Class Universities: Towards a global common good and seeking national and institutional contributions*, edited by Yan Wu, Qi Wang and Nian Cai Liu, 56–69. Leiden: Brill.
Altbach, Philip G. and Jamil Salmi (eds). 2011. *The Road to Academic Excellence: The making of world-class research universities*. Washington DC: World Bank.
Birnbaum, Robert. 1988. *How Colleges Work: The cybernetics of academic organization and leadership*. San Francisco, CA: Jossey-Bass Publishers.
Brankovic, Jelena. 2019. 'The status games they play: Unpacking the dynamics of organisational status competition in higher education', *Higher Education* 75(4): 695–709.
Brankovic, Jelena, Leopold Ringel and Tobias Werron. 2019. 'Theorizing university rankings: A comparative research perspective'. Working Paper SFB 1288, No. 2. Accessed 16 March 2022. https://doi.org/10.4119/unibi/2939561.
Cohen, Michael D., James G. March and Johan P. Olsen. 1972. 'A garbage can model of organizational choice', *Administrative Science Quarterly* 17(1): 1–25.
De Rassenfosse, Gaétan and Ross Williams. 2015. 'Rules of engagement: Measuring connectivity in national systems of higher education', *Higher Education* 70(6): 941–56.
DiMaggio, Paul J. and Walter W. Powell. 1983. 'The iron cage revisited: Institutional isomorphism and collective rationality in organizational fields', *American Sociological Review* 48(2): 147–60.
Douglass, John Aubrey (ed.). 2016. *The New Flagship University: Changing the paradigm from global ranking to national relevancy*. Cham: Springer.
Drori, Israel and Benson Honig. 2013. 'A process model of internal and external legitimacy', *Organization Studies* 34(3): 345–76.
Elken, Mari, Elisabeth Hovdhaugen and Bjørn Stensaker. 2016. 'Global rankings in the Nordic region: Challenging the identity of research-intensive universities?', *Higher Education* 72(1): 781–95.
Espeland, Wendy Nelson and Mitchell L. Stevens. 1998. 'Commensuration as a social process', *Annual Review of Sociology* 24(1): 313–43.
Fligstein, Neil. 1996. 'Markets as politics: A political-cultural approach to market institutions', *American Sociological Review* 61(4): 656–73.
Froumin, Isak and Mikhail Lisyutkin. 2015. 'Excellence-driven policies and initiatives in the context of Bologna process: Rationale, design, implementation and outcomes'. In *The European Higher Education Area: Between critical reflections and future policies*, edited by Adrian Curaj, Liviu Matei, Jamil Salmi, Hanne Smidt, Remus Pricopie and Peter Scott, 249–65. Cham: Springer.
Fumasoli, Tatiana, Romulo Pinheiro and Bjørn Stensaker. 2015. 'Handling uncertainty of strategic ambitions: The use of organizational identity as a risk-reducing device', *International Journal of Public Administration* 38(13–14): 1030–40.
Hardy, Cynthia, Ann Langley, Henry Mintzberg and Janet Rose. 1983. 'Strategy formation in the university setting', *Review of Higher Education* 6(4): 407–33.
Hartley, Matthew and Christopher C. Morphew. 2008. 'What's being sold and to what end? A content analysis of college viewbooks', *Journal of Higher Education* 79(6): 671–91.
Hazelkorn, Ellen. 2015. *Rankings and the Reshaping of Higher Education: The battle for world-class excellence*. Cham: Springer.
Hazelkorn, Ellen. 2017. 'Rankings and higher education: Reframing relationships within and between states'. Centre for Global Higher Education working paper 19. Accessed 16 March 2022. https://www.researchcghe.org/perch/resources/publications/wp19.pdf.
Lee, Jenny J., Hillary Vance, Bjørn Stensaker and Sowmya Ghosh. 2020. 'Global rankings at a local cost? The strategic pursuit of status and the third mission', *Comparative Education* 56(2): 236–56.

Marginson, Simon. 2007. 'Global university rankings: Implications in general and for Australia', *Journal of Higher Education Policy and Management* 29(2): 131–42.

Merton, Robert K. 1973. *The Sociology of Science: Theoretical and empirical investigations*. Chicago: University of Chicago Press.

Meyer, John W. and Brian Rowan. 1977. 'Institutionalized organizations: Formal structure as myth and ceremony', *American Journal of Sociology* 83(2): 340–63.

Musselin, Christine. 2018. 'New forms of competition in higher education', *Socio-Economic Review* 16(3): 657–83.

Pavlyutkin, Ivan and Maria Yudkevich. 2016. 'The ranking game on the Russian battlefield: The case of the Higher School of Economics'. In *The Global Academic Rankings Game: Changing institutional policy, practice, and academic life*, edited by Maria Yudkevich, Philip G. Altbach and Laura E. Rumbley, 171–94. New York: Routledge.

Pusser, Brian and Simon Marginson. 2013. 'University rankings in critical perspective', *Journal of Higher Education* 84(4): 544–68.

Ramirez, Francisco. 2010. 'Accounting for excellence: Transforming universities into organizational actors'. In *Higher Education, Policy, and the Global Competition Phenomenon*, edited by Laura M. Portnoi, Val D. Rust and Sylvia S. Bagley, 54–75. Basingstoke: Palgrave.

Ramirez, Francisco. 2020. 'The socially embedded American university: Intensification and globalization'. In *Missions of Universities: Past, Present, Future*, edited by Lars Engwall, 131–61. Cham: Springer.

Ramirez, Francisco and Dijana Tiplic. 2014. 'In pursuit of excellence? Discursive patterns in European higher education research', *Higher Education* 67(4): 439–55.

Readings, Bill. 1996. *The University in Ruins*. Cambridge, MA: Harvard University Press.

Riesman, David. 1958. *Constraint and Variety in American Education*. Lincoln: University of Nebraska Press.

Rindova, Violina P., Luis L. Martins, Santosh B. Srinivas and David Chandler. 2018. 'The good, the bad, and the ugly of organizational rankings: A multidisciplinary review of the literature and directions for future research', *Journal of Management* 44(6): 2175–208.

Salmi, Jamil. 2009. *The Challenge of Establishing World Class Universities*. Washington, DC: World Bank.

Stensaker, Bjørn, Jenny J. Lee, Gary Rhoades, Sowmya Ghosh, Santiago Castiello-Gutiérrez, Hillary Vance, Alper Çalıkoğlu and Ivan Pavlyutkin. 2019. 'Stratified university strategies: The shaping of institutional legitimacy in a global perspective', *Journal of Higher Education* 90(4): 539–62.

Suchman, Mark. C. 1995. 'Managing legitimacy: Strategic and institutional approaches', *Academy of Management Review* 20(3): 571–610.

Sutphen, Molly, Tone Dyrdal Solbrekke and Ciaran Sugrue. 2019. 'Toward articulating an academic praxis by interrogating university strategic plans', *Studies in Higher Education* 44(8): 1400–12.

Weick, Karl E. 1976. 'Educational organizations as loosely coupled systems', *Administrative Science Quarterly* 21(1): 1–19.

Weiler, Hans N. 2005. 'Ambivalence and the politics of knowledge: The struggle for change in German higher education', *Higher Education* 49(1): 177–95.

Yudkevich, Maria, Philip G. Altbach and Laura E. Rumbley (eds). 2016. *The Global Academic Rankings Game: Changing institutional policy, practice, and academic life*. New York and London: Routledge.

13
One man's pill is another man's poison: Ambivalence of definitional power – the case of breast cancer drugs in Russia

Elena Berdysheva

Introduction: the sacred power of the profane and vice versa

Cancer morbidity poses problems of population survival, places a high economic burden on society and exacerbates social inequality, not to mention the painful fate of cancer patients. The policy on cancer in European death-denying societies (Livne 2014; Price and Cheek 2007) faces the ambivalence of life and death. The principle of saving individual lives at any cost by means of innovative medical technologies turns out to be a new utopia for contemporary healthcare policy. Given that cancer cannot be cured with the most expensive pills, its expansion problematizes the subjection of death to medical authority and appeals to state authority, which uses medicine as an instrument of social control and political management (Lantz and Booth 1998). Public funds are actively redirected to programmes that improve the quality of life of cancer patients (through psychological assistance, rehabilitation and palliative care) and develop infrastructure for early cancer detection and prevention.

About 1,500 people are diagnosed with cancer every day in Russia. In 2019, 3.9 million Russians, representing 2.6 per cent of the population, were living with cancer diagnoses. Every year this figure increases by

500,000 people (Kaprin et al. 2020). Diagnoses related to advanced (III and IV) stages of cancer – when a patient sees a five-year survival rate as the ultimate dream – comprise 37.4 per cent of diagnoses. However, the vector of Russian policy on oncological diseases, contrary to global trends, is aimed at expanding access to innovative domestic chemotherapy by using public funds, while the problem of the quality of life of cancer patients remains in the shadows. The aim of this chapter is to show that the current vector of Russian cancer policy is determined by the political and economic interests of the government and the interests of the domestic pharmaceutical companies affiliated with the government in the field of public healthcare. To examine the situation, I use the concept of definitional power, which marks the ability of the dominant institutional actors to achieve the cognitive legitimacy of their decisions and manage public policy in accordance with them. When it comes to managing cancer, definitional power deals with the contradiction between life and death. The implementation of definitional power in practice does not remove this contradiction but balances it in the best or worst way. This ineradicable ambivalence lurks in the resulting balance. At the same time, the very concept of ambivalence allows us to see how the positive side is organized and what lies beside it (Koreckaya 2021).

The qualitative empirical study that underlies this chapter began with an assessment of the epidemiological significance of the creation of a biosimilar version of the innovative Swiss drug for breast cancer treatment in Russia. We have revealed that the mechanisms for bringing this drug into the drug procurement market were largely corrupt.

The purpose of the study has therefore shifted to the identification of the main power holders of the definitional power, the principles they follow and the interests they seek to further. Our main objective is to demonstrate that the mechanisms and principles of governance which have fuelled the optimistic story about the Russian counterpart to the effective Swiss drug for breast cancer treatment are contributing to the fact that the Russian healthcare system is increasingly lagging behind similar systems in the Western developed countries. In a broader sense, this study is intended to contribute to a scholarly debate on the role of meaning-making in the configuration of power relations and group interests (Dobbin and Jung 2015) in contemporary market society (Sandal 2012).

This chapter is structured as follows. First, I clarify the theoretical and methodological foundations of the empirical research. Then, I disclose the biography of the domestic drug T+ rus for the treatment of breast cancer in Russian public procurement and describe the power network in the Russian government which drives the promotion of this product.

Further, I demonstrate that at the level of practice, this promotion is ensured by the protectionism of Russian manufacturers in healthcare, which is managed by the government. The state authorities in Russia define what is good and what is bad for cancer management in the country. Supported by the market success of innovative domestic drugs, these definitions legitimize the state's power and allow the authorities to disperse public money as they want. Having described how cancer policy in Russia is becoming a tool for expanding distribution channels for Russian cancer drugs, I move on to a discussion of the shadowy side of the pharmacological strategy for fighting cancer. I demonstrate that both at the level of the Russian field of oncological care and at the level of contemporary trends in the fight against cancer, the pharmacological strategy is oriented towards localized, autarkic and costly technological development. The profane interests of power networks in the Russian governmental system distort the national project of control over the cancer morbidity and thereby belittle the sacred basis for the legitimacy of its power.

Theoretical framework: market valuation of social worth

Within the frame of technocratic capitalism, the public authorities increasingly draw upon rationality and human nature rather than military power, manipulation or hoaxes to obtain legitimacy (Haugaard 2012, 47). Instead of competing for power to promote their own interests, rival social groups now seek the right to define the essence of these interests (Dobbin and Jung 2015). Such power can be denoted as definitional (Smith 2007; Dubuisson-Queiller 2013). In market societies, definitional power justifies the social worth of goods and generates the meanings and rules, priorities and values that legitimate politically embedded economic practices. This power deals with the ambivalence of the sacred and the profane (Kajua 2003) which takes place when monetary valuation touches upon socially entangled issues (Fourcade 2011, 57–9). For example, in early 2015 the cancer drug I discuss in this chapter cost about $2,055 per package, or about $20,545 for a course of treatment. Is this amount of money worth an extra three to five years of life for one patient if we speak about spending from public funds? 'Secularization does not imply the extinction of the sacred in society but goes hand in hand with the emergence of secular forms of the sacred' (Beckert 2011, 112). Definitional power refers to the sacred in order to implement the secular. The performative effect of power is produced by disciplinary practices (Koreckaya 2021). Under monetary capitalism, these disciplinary practices may be subject to market actors whose primary interest is profit. Definitional power establishes practical solutions within biopolitics and is reproduced through them. To compare and evaluate the social worth of these solutions, it is necessary to identify the practices with the help of which the effect of power relations is produced here and now (Raffnsøe et al. 2014). The ambivalence of power is visibly manifested precisely in the zone where those in power set up the practices for dispersing it. The chosen practical solution suppresses competing alternatives. At the practical level, the implementation of definitional power remains ambivalent.

Ambivalence indicates the social contradictions which complicated social scenarios may face at the level of practice, for example, when power drives the desire both to exert influence and to strengthen one's own position. Ambivalence does not refer to hidden manipulation and it is not about obvious dysfunctionality that can be easily repaired (Koreckaya 2021). It is a litmus test for evaluating practices, which allows one to track and compare the alternatives. The interests of the majority often threaten those of the minority. Ambivalence highlights the criteria for definitions of different group interests. To identify and evaluate these definitions, I use these criteria in combination with the sociology of knowledge approach to discourse. The latter is based on the constructivist ideas of Berger and Luckmann and Foucault's genealogy of discipline power (Keller 2005; 2011). Using this approach to analyse the control of public discourse highlights how group interests can be defined and manipulated.

Methodology: case study of a bestselling drug in Russian discourse

The chapter is based on ethnographic data, qualitative analysis of Russian media within the framework of the sociology of knowledge approach to discourse and desk-based marketing research relating to T+'s market biography in Russia. The discourse analysis of T+'s history in Russian social media was contextualized and complemented with expert interviews with three marketing specialists, one medical representative from a pharmaceutical company, three oncologists, two representatives of governmental agencies, one representative of a non-profit charitable foundation for helping cancer patients and one private healthcare consultant. Open-access interviews with relevant institutional actors on innovative cancer drugs were also assessed, allowing us to critically evaluate the assumptions developed during the research.

The empirical base for the evaluation of the discourse devoted to T+ in the Russian media was accumulated through the media monitoring and analysis system 'Medialogia'. The research was limited to statements relating to T+ in two pro-government newspapers (*Rossiiskaya Gazeta* and *Komsomolskaya Pravda*), two 'more liberal' newspapers (*Kommersant* and *Novaya Gazeta*) and a leading industry publication (*Farmazevticheskii Vestnik*). A keyword search on T+, Gswiss and Brus in the period from January 2011 to January 2021 generated 355 statements, which I used for the analysis.

Secondary data were actively used to identify the context and to get the full picture, including official documents, opinion journalism devoted to the studied drug, media materials, print and video interviews with representatives of government departments, pharmaceutical companies, scientists, leading oncologists of the country, data of medical and pharmacoeconomic studies of the investigated drug and cancer drug market analytics published in the industry press.

In line with the sociology of knowledge approach to discourse analysis, I identified the most influential actors in the field and traced their efforts in relation to self-positioning, the meanings they use to indicate this social problem, the emotional hue of their statements and the values they appeal to when justifying their decisions.

Findings

The total volume of the Russian pharmaceutical market in 2020 exceeded $33.1 billion, which was 9.8 per cent higher than in 2019.[1] Overall, the Russian pharmaceutical market is dominated by global companies, who account for two-thirds of total sales, and therefore remains strongly dependent on imports.[2] In 2020 the share of foreign-made drugs amounted to 56 per cent in value terms. The share of drugs locally produced by global pharma was 44 per cent (in value terms). The share of domestically produced medicines represents one-third of sales and is expected to increase to 36.4 per cent by 2024. Domestic manufacturers are still nearly absent in the segment of innovative original drugs, selling 11 per cent of such medicines. Nevertheless, the procurement volume of medicines manufactured in Russia is growing (+19 per cent in 2020).

State procurement is critically important for the Russian pharmaceutical market. By the end of 2019, its share reached 30–35 per cent.[3] In 2020, purchases of pharmaceuticals for budget-funded medical centres increased by 23.5 per cent to reach $5.4 billion.

Cancer drugs are the ultimate market leaders among medical products, accounting for 12 to 17 per cent of all sales, according to various estimates. This group of drugs remains the most heavily state-funded part of the pharmaceutical supply programme in Russia. In 2020, about 41.9 per cent of the total amount of state support was directed to their procurement. For the future, there are positive market expectations associated with the implementation of the National Cancer Control Strategy until 2030 and the relevant regional programmes, in which 16 Russian regions are involved.

The shifts in the procurement structure in favour of drugs for oncology therapy has led to a remarkable increase in the weighted average package cost of drugs procured for the needs of budget-funded hospitals in Russia. In 2020, the cost increased on average by 40.1 per cent compared with the previous year. The weighted average cost per package of imported drugs is three to four times higher than the weighted average cost of domestically produced packages.

The Russian pharmaceutical market is led by global companies. Sanofi, Novartis and Bayer are found at the top of the ranking of drug manufacturers. In the government procurement segment, two domestic manufacturers and one global company take the lead: Pharmstandard (5.8 per cent), Roche (4.9 per cent) and Biocad (4.7 per cent). All top manufacturers have a high share of drugs for treatment of oncological diseases.

Market interests in centralized Russian healthcare

Those working in healthcare explain that the healthcare system in Russia is dominated by the state. The government manages public health in a paternalistic manner for political purposes.

> No politician dares to propose market reforms in medicine but promising the people the best medicine for free is a guarantee of a high rating.[4]

On the one hand, the healthcare system is categorized as a budget sector, where spending plans are prioritized over rationality and results.

> We can always read what has been planned. And then you read the report – 100 were planned, 99 were fulfilled. And what happened to medicine itself this year? How many people have you cured? What

are the practical results of all this turbulent activity? You will not get this information anywhere.[5]

On the other hand, according to the interviews, the Russian government seeks to invest as much of the budget funds as possible into the domestic technological industries and to reduce the technology gap between Russia and developed capitalistic economies. In the context of healthcare, it provides institutional preferences for domestic pharmacological manufacturers for the procurement of drugs for public healthcare under the mask of the fight against cancer in Russia.

The National Strategy for the Fight against Cancer is one of the most resource-intensive areas of the National 'Healthcare up to 2030' programme in Russia. It was the first document in the country to prioritize cancer as a public health problem. The Strategy publicly vows to use the extra funds earmarked for the fight against cancer to produce innovative domestic drugs.

The legislative regulation of cancer care is adopted at the level of the Russian government, as well as drug turnover and clinical-economic efficacy.[6] The Department of State Regulation of the Circulation of Medicines acts like the National Institute for Health and Clinical Excellence in the United Kingdom and unlike the Federal Drug Administration in the United States, which acts as an independent agency. It establishes the list of vital and essential medicines. Without medicines from this list, sick people will either die or their disease will progress, leading to significant shortening of life, disability, development of severe complications and/or significant decrease in the quality of life. In 2018, the vital and essential medicines list was expanded to include 20 anti-tumour drugs. In cooperation with the Federal Antimonopoly Service, the Department of State Regulation of the Circulation of Medicines controls manufacturers' maximum selling prices for the drugs included in this list. The state cannot purchase drugs which do not comply with official standards of treatment approved by the Russian Ministry of Health and Social Development. The list of vital and essential medicines should be connected with the clinical recommendations for public medical centres. Budget funds that go to the market of state orders are institutional money. They can only be spent on drugs which are included in the treatment protocols approved by the state. In 2020–1, clinical guidelines for oncology received official status for the first time. The formation of clinical guidelines and lists of vital and essential drugs led to an increase in the share of expensive treatment regimens. For 2020–1, 16 domestic drugs entered the list. Accordingly, their procurement also increased by 46 per cent compared with the previous year on average.[7]

The physical availability of these drugs will also be improved with the opening of about 420 outpatient cancer care centres in Russia by the year 2024. According to the federal Fight against Cancer programme, the outpatient centres will increase detection rates of early-stage cancer and improve oncological care rates in the country. However, insiders describe these centres as 'just for show' ('*smena vyvesok*'), intended to bring drug therapy closer to patients' place of residence.

For imported drugs that enter the Russian healthcare system, the Department of State Regulation of the Circulation of Medicines requires that additional clinical trials are conducted with Russian patients. Local clinical tests bring additional money to the state commissions. They also raise the price of the imported drugs, while price is the main criterion for selecting applications in the tender competition on the procurement market. Foreign drugs suffer from the 'odd man out' rule: when at least two market offers from Eurasian Economic Union countries come up for procurement auction, the imported medicine is rejected.

Thus, the domestic pharmaceutical sector has gained a privileged position in Russia and secured its business interests in the cancer care field.

Revolution by 'new Russian pharma': domestic biosimilar launch

In 2013, Russian biotechnological company Brus launched the first 'made in Russia' biosimilar of the original drug Swiss T+ and, called it T+rus. This event is particularly important given that it was the outcome of a remarkable scientific discovery. This discovery legitimized the opportunity for biosimilar drugs to enter the market alongside original drugs.

The pharmaceutical market is structured by generic competition. The original drug usually opens a new class of medicine. It is protected by patents which last on average 10–15 years to constitute the return on investment in research and development. The worth of an innovative drug should be clarified to the stakeholders – government agencies, hospitals, doctors and others. 'Customer development' starts when a pill is under development. In the case of drugs such as T+rus, the whole process takes at least five to seven years before the drug enters the market.

Biosimilars emerge from original drugs which cannot be copied because they have complex molecular structures. The efficacy, safety and pharmacokinetic tests demonstrate no differences between biosimilars and the original drug. Contrary to the imported original drug, the domestic biosimilar escapes the costs of local registration. In addition, bringing a biosimilar to market is cheaper as its clinical reputation relies on the reputation of the original drug.

The case of the Russian T+ indicates that the cost of biosimilars is 20–30 per cent lower than that of the original drugs. In 2016, the Brus company applied for re-registration and came up with a voluntary initiative to reduce the purchase price for 13 of its drugs by up to 30 per cent.

Russian T+ has replaced the Swiss T+ in the list of vital and essential medicines in Russia. Being on this list of official standards guarantees stable and predictable demand.

> The main thing is to get onto the list of mandatory drugs, and then you can forget about the product: everyone just begins to prescribe it.[8]

The lower price of T+rus allows it to compete with Swiss T+ in the markets of developing countries. It is a rare situation in which Russia can export advanced technological products instead of unprocessed fossil fuels. Russia's pharmaceutical industry development plan to 2030 involves a twofold increase in drug exports from the country, up to $1 billion, compared with $540 million in 2017.

Russian T+ fights against breast cancer, a disease which threatens 'sisters, wives and mothers'.[9] The main social expectation promoted within its customer development programme involves the invention of a miraculous pill that redefines cancer as a manageable biological weakness of the modern human being, armed with scientific knowledge. The pharmaceutical company rewrites cancer from being a death sentence to a chronically runny nose.

> Cancer will soon become as chronic and as common as the flu. In 10–20 years, everyone in the industry is confident of this. In my opinion, nature is so wise that it constantly discards us as a species. Primates live for 30 years. Nature gave us a body with resources designed for 30 years. And we used to live like that. Most simply, we did not live to the age when cancer comes to the fore. The body is not designed for the length of life we would like to have. If we have exhausted our resource, we are no longer needed for nature. But we are human. And our body is being taken over by a life form which we do not understand. We do not accept this situation. Therefore, we must fight. We pharmacists, provide ammunition to doctors who are at the forefront of the fight against cancer. We are not in a race with a cell. We are in a race with the nature. Nature decides that this individual is no longer needed. But we struggle against this injustice inherent to us by nature.[10]

The invention of Russian T+ marks a significant success of the power networks driven by Russia's authoritarian government system in a symbolic game in the market economy. The innovative drug made by the centralized economy is cheaper than its market ancestor despite all historical evidence that markets, not governments, have become the main driver of innovations and social progress in the twenty-first century. Russian T+ supports the political image of Russia as an outpacing national state that is coping with the second epidemiological transition.

Cancer drugs, economic development and power networks

In 2018, social media discovered a Word document outlining the strategy of the Ministry of Industry and Trade for the development of the pharmaceutical industry in Russia, which had been written by an employee of the pharmaceutical company Brus. The company justified itself by the fact that it was only sending its suggestions to the ministry.[11]

Brus was included among the top 10 largest actors in the Russian pharmaceutical market in 2019, with a 2.1 per cent share and residence in the special economic zone 'St Petersburg'.[12] The company identifies itself as part of the 'New Russian Pharma'. Its founder and CEO participates in the Expert Council for the Development of Competition in the Social Sphere and Healthcare at the Federal Antimonopoly Service of Russia; holds membership in the Health Board of the Federation Council Committee on Social Policy; and belongs to the Subcommission on the Circulation of Medicines and the Board of Directors of the Association of Pharmaceutical Manufacturers of the Eurasian Economic Union. In 2019, by decree of Russian President Vladimir Putin, the CEO of Brus was awarded the medal of the Order 'For Merit to the Homeland' II degree.

In 2019, the largest amount of the healthcare budget was spent on the purchase of T+rus – $82 million. In comparison with the expenditures in 2018, this figure increased by 115 per cent.

Today the founder and CEO of Brus owns a 30 per cent share of the company. Fifty per cent of Brus belongs to Phrus holding. Currently, more than half of the drugs on the vital and essential medicines list come from just these two domestic pharmaceutical companies.[13] In 2019, $952 million was spent on the purchase of anti-tumour drugs; in 2020, the federal budget for them almost doubled, reaching $1.6 billion. In 2016 only $452 million was spent on chemotherapy.[14] The experts attribute the change in the procurement structure in favour of domestic oncological drugs to a leading Russian politician and economist who has served as Deputy Prime Minister of Russia for Social Policy, Labour, Health and Pension Provision since 2018. For the last 10 years, the Russian media has accused the cabinet of this politician of lobbying the pharmaceutical business associated with a communication ('friendship') with the CEO of Phrus, a stakeholder in Brus.[15] The chairman of Phrus holding regularly denies counterclaims of 'friendship' with the former Deputy Prime Minister of Russia, former Minister of Industry and Trade and the husband of the Deputy Prime Minister of Russia for Social Policy, Labour, Health and Pension Provision. Our experts interpret the position of Phrus and Brus in the state drug procurement market as an 'effective business–state partnership within paternalistic healthcare'.

> To survive in Russian pharmaceuticals, you need to go to work to the Ministry of Health and the Ministry of Industry. Everyone sat in these corridors, but Brus's CEO was the one to win; and not because he knew how to sit and wait properly, but because he took risks.[16]

The entry of the Russian pharmaceutical company into the market with a competitive innovative drug brings political and tax credits.

Brus's T+ results meet the aims of the National Pharmaceutical Industry Development Project. The Russian Ministry of Industry and Trade has been implementing an import substitution policy in the pharmaceutical industry since 2009. The development of strategically significant drugs is an explicit benchmark against which the success of the Federal Target Program's strategy can be measured. The share of domestic drugs on the vital and essential medicines list is projected to grow to 93 per cent by 2024. The $146 million in funding of the corresponding state programme has increased by another $64 million.[17]

The Russian government system has told the public that it is trying to manage public resources more efficiently. It has vowed to implement at least five tasks simultaneously: firstly, to fulfil the lowest social guarantees with minimal costs; secondly, to collect additional taxes and increase revenues from the export of drugs; thirdly, to strengthen the country's economy and promote its development through technological breakthroughs; fourthly, to reduce dependence on foreign partners; and fifthly, to strengthen its internal and external status as a modern developed country.

> No healthcare system will cover everything on pharmaceutical companies' wish lists. This is an endless race. This is, firstly, a

> mechanism aimed at providing leadership: we have it, and you do not. You are the second grade, and we are the first. And, secondly, it resonates with such an important social component: 'Can we make sure that our people do not die, or can we not?'[18]

The face of amiability between the Russian state and 'New Russian Pharma' reveals their mutual satisfaction with the work of the network-based governance pattern (Ledeneva 2013). The case of T+ illustrates how *sistema* in Russia is increasing its own stability by redefining the success of loyal (*'svoih'*) companies as evidence of social modernization in the country. 'Fighting cancer at any cost' remains the dominant value for national cancer care in Russia. The pharmacological monopoly associates life chances with access to drugs and narrows the space for 'reasonable' responses to cancer diagnosis available to patients in Russia. Pharmacological discourse in Russia proposes a particularistic solution to the public management of cancer, as if cancer were not a cultural symbol of the weakening of modern healthcare institutions in the face of postmodern diseases (Weiss 1997; Bach 2009), and as if developed nations were not seeking healthcare institutions which may provide wholistic, human-centred solutions. But a pharmacological monopoly is more in line with the current political regime in Russia. Coordination between the state and promising 'New Russian Pharma' brings notable results. However, in terms of modernization of cancer care in Russia, these results build walls, not bridges.

Behind the facade of domestic pharma success

T+rus is part of a medical revolution in cancer treatment. What is rarely discussed, however, is that this revolutionary system for distributing benefits to society has become 'a funnel'[19] instead of a pyramid: fewer people in need have a greater chance of success. Basing the national management of cancer on an innovative chemotherapy drug, Russia is opting for a widely criticized model of cancer care which rests on late detection, extensive and expensive interventions, and short life expectancy of the sick.

> The healthcare system, voluntarily or involuntarily, is locked into treating neglected cases because they are more expensive, and the system gets more money for them. The city authorities can say: 'Let's invest more money in early diagnosis of cancer.' But the

leading enterprise in the structure of the Ministry of Health in this area is the oncological centre – as a specialized institution. And it does not benefit from early diagnosis, which belongs to the outpatient stage. It benefits more from treatment and consultative care.[20]

In synergy with the National Pharma Development Project, the National Health Project gravitates towards a high-cost model, forcing the rise of ever-increasing production and turnover of innovative domestic drugs. It employs pharmacologic methods of cancer management that receive social criticism (Davis 2015). The system cannot assimilate this criticism, as the practices of the dominant power network performatively reinforce negative inertia. Nevertheless, the overoptimism about cancer expressed by pharmaceutical companies and adopted by the state does not consider the fact that drug therapy is the only one frontline on which the battle is raging.

> Cancer treatment neither begins nor ends with chemotherapy. It's a complicated story. Now the clinical process is broken and fragmented because it is beneficial for some actors. At least in Russia, expensive chemotherapy is a great engine for a car with square wheels.[21]

The World Health Organization classifies the Russian Federation as an upper-middle-income country.[22] This status comes with recommendations to raise annual investment in cancer prevention and treatment programmes to $8.15 per capita by 2030. Given the protracted worldwide economic crisis, the ever-increasing social support for the fight against cancer is becoming less affordable. This triggers the parity of price and social value of innovative chemotherapy.

> It is extremely difficult to justify the high social value of an innovative oncological drug if an ampoule is offered for $100, which will extend the patient's life for a month, and he will spend it in the intensive care unit taking strong painkillers and sedatives recognizing that this is only for a month.[23]

In 2020 in Russia, the average cost of cancer treatment in a 24-hour hospital increased by 30 per cent, and in a day hospital by more than 50 per cent.[24] The more exclusive the *personalized* treatment is, the more it costs. The picture gets complicated when the multiplicity and heterogeneity of oncological diseases are observed. Experts talk about at least 100 varieties of cancer. By fuelling demand for innovative drugs, pharmaceutical companies encourage society with promises that they will discover a cure in the future that will make cancer no more serious than having a runny nose. However, making cancer more bearable is not the same as making efforts to avoid it in the first place. According to our experts, the logic of wider public provision of drug therapy corresponds with the demographic key performance indicators of death rates from causes of death driving public health policy in the country. Considering this, the declarative aim 'to make breast cancer a condition that will not affect the cause of death' may be read as Wittgenstein's language game, while the real practice relates to the management of public statistics for political purposes. The discourse about the social and market value of innovative cancer therapy is a discourse of promises, not guarantees. Pharmaceutical companies openly say that even in the most optimistic cases, innovative drugs introduced to the market are aimed at prolonging life, not curing cancer (Howard et al. 2015). The pharmaceutical line in the fight against cancer is aimed primarily at 'buying time till the more promising drug will be invented'. Cancer drugs' premium prices clash with the logic of scarcity (Bach 2009; Kerasidou 2019). The latter brings to the social arena an 'existential premise that life has an end, people are mortal, and there are limits to what can be done to prolong life' (Livne 2014, 906).

The results of my study support the hypothesis that public resources in Russia are distributed by power authorities 'through diffuse networks rather than following market principles, and benefit those who adapt and manipulate the blurred line between the public and the private, now known as bureaucrats-turned-businessmen' (Ledeneva 2013, 20). Definitional power is at the core of this process. *Sistema* has a monopoly to define its choice as a positive trend, but in fact it cares about the enhancement of monopoly state capitalism in the country. It maintains the demand for domestic innovative drugs via the national policy on oncological diseases. The system of governance distributes the budgetary financial flows according to these corrupted definitions, achieves corrupted goals and feels legitimate and entitled to rule. The interrelations between cancer policy and pharmaceutical industry policy make cancer a driver of demand for commercial products. Anti-cancer policy turns into a profitable business. Commercial interests obscure the real interests of people who do not want to live comfortably with an oncological diagnosis, but rather do not want to have cancer at all (Sulik 2010).

Discussion

The results obtained on the implementation of innovative cancer policy provide an empirical illustration of the thesis that 'the economic growth and stability of Putin's Russia is detrimental to Russia's development in the long term' (Ledeneva 2013, 22). The story of the Russian innovative biosimilar for the Swiss cancer drug illustrates the ambivalence of definitional power. As far as Russian cancer policy is concerned, this power is distributed between government authorities and loyal domestic pharmaceutical companies.

In the academic literature, all relationships between business and the state are regarded with scepticism (Yakovlev 2015). At best, they are explained as economic development projects (Block 1986; Fligstein and Stone Sweet 2002). At worst, they are interpreted as a merger of business and the state in an attempt to capture one by the other (Shleifer and Vishny 2002). A compromise approach is the model of exchanges between administrative and business elites (Frye 2002; Tkachenko et al. 2017), which promotes the reproduction and sustainability of dominant groups in politics via institutional corruption (Zvyagintsev and Barsukova 2006; Barsukova 2019). Incorporating the concept of definitional power allows us to go beyond the talk of officials manipulating their administrative power in such exchanges to extract additional private rents. Using ambivalence as a criterion of quality for the order generated by this power, one can observe exactly how social perceptions of the social groups' interests are distorted.

The political system in Russia refers to the network state model where the government intersects with private interests' networks. Following Alena Ledeneva, in this chapter the data obtain meaning when this system is labelled and interpreted as *sistema* (Ledeneva 2013, 19–20). The reliance on domestic pharmacology as the main strategy for this policy is dictated by the ties of certain Russian pharmaceutical companies with senior government officials. The latter shape the institutional environment to provide these firms with preferential treatment not only over global competitors, but also over other cancer care agents. The Russian political choice in favour of a pharmacological strategy of fighting cancer is both good and evil at the same time.

On the one hand, the alliance between the state and national pharmacological companies is improving the country's cancer treatment situation. More patients can get innovative medicines through public healthcare. This sacred side contributes to the discussion that informality should be recognized as a resource (Ledeneva 2013; 2018).

On the other hand, favourable treatment of the domestic pharmaceutical business by senior officials supports the hype over expensive domestic cancer drugs in Russia. Differentiation of cancer control strategies in Russia runs counter to the interests of the dominant power network. The governance system acts not as a stakeholder, but as a short-run beneficiary of the pharmacological strategy of policy on cancer. The facade of the policy articulates the fulfilment of social obligations to the population and strengthens the ideological propaganda of the growing power of the state. In fact, it conceals the corruption schemes which allow dominant political actors to dispose of public funds at their discretion and legally (Inozemtsev 2018, 145). Paradoxically, the corruption schemes in their turn produce positive externalities for a group of cancer patients. And we return from profane to the sacred. Ambivalence of power refers to a controversy between the sacred and the profane, the purity and danger which lurk within the practices of power implementation (Kajua 2003; Koreckaya 2021).

Conclusion

Political reliance on innovative cancer therapy in the fight against cancer is inherently ambivalent in Russia. The system organizes a local technological breakthrough corruptly and reports it as a systemic improvement. This strengthens its position in the short term, together with hopes for the competitiveness of the Russian economy in non-commodity sectors. However, the ways in which the local breakthrough is provided appear ambivalent. Extremely expensive and rare innovations cannot provide a capacity for global competitiveness in the field of high-tech healthcare systems. Delivering extra funds for the production of domestic innovative drugs as a major strategy against cancer does not lead to a significant improvement of the oncological care system in Russia. With enormous efforts and budget spending, such a strategy largely looks like a performance aimed at demonstrating the sovereign power of the authoritarian state.

Acknowledgements

The fieldwork and analytical work for this chapter were supported by the Basic Research Program of the National University Higher School of Economics (HSE University).

Notes

1. Russian Pharmaceutical Market Trends in 2020 (Report by Deloitte). Accessed 10 December 2021. https://www2.deloitte.com/content/dam/Deloitte/ru/Documents/life-sciences-health-care/russian/russian-pharmaceutical-market-trends-2020.pdf (in Russian).
2. Pharmaceutical market of the Russian Federation - will the state help us? (Report by National Rating Agency). Accessed 10 December 2021. https://www.ra-national.ru/ru/node/63747 (in Russian).
3. Pharmaceutical market of Russian Federation in 2021 (Report by Alpharm). Accessed 10 December 2021. https://alpharm.ru/ru/analytics/farmacevticheskiy-rynok-rf-q1-2021 (in Russian).
4. Expert interview for this research. 2021. Maryana, private healthcare consultant, Moscow, Russia.
5. Open access interview with Artem Gapeev, the General Director of the Ilyinsky Hospital, Moscow, Russia. Accessed 10 December 2021. https://www.facebook.com/medicine2024/videos/331550171202652.
6. Federal Law No. 61-FZ 'On Drug Circulation'. Accessed 10 December 2021. http://www.consultant.ru/document/cons_doc_LAW_99350/.
7. Vademecum Analytics. Oncological Service in Russia. Infrastructure and Budgets. 2021. Accessed 10 December 2021. https://vademec.ru/news/2021/02/12/ostavte-zayavku-na-priobretenie-issledovaniya-onkologicheskaya-sluzhba-rossii-infrastruktura-i-byudzh/ (in Russian).
8. Expert interview for this research. 2019. Fedor, medical representative, marketing specialist, Transnational Pharmaceutical Company, Moscow, Russia.
9. Open access interview. The future is happening in our laboratories. Dialogue with CEO of Brus. 2018. Accessed 10 December 2021. https://www.youtube.com/watch?v=rpzhsCHX2-4 (in Russian).
10. Open access interview. The future is happening in our laboratories. Dialogue with CEO of Brus. 2018.
11. The Biocad manager turned out to be the author of the document with the pharmaceutical strategy of the Ministry of Industry and Trade. Accessed 10 December 2021. https://www.rbc.ru/society/09/07/2018/5b3f93509a79475d92da135e (in Russian).
12. Life after Arbidol: how Viktor Kharitonin has conquered the pharmaceutical market. Accessed 10 December 2021. https://www.forbes.ru/milliardery/288203-zhizn-posle-arbidola-kak-viktor-kharitonin-zavoeval-rynok-farmy (in Russian).
13. Report on the Segment of Drugs Procurement, AlPharm Research Agency, 2018. Accessed 10 December 2021. https://alpharm.ru/sites/default/files/alpharm_obzor_segmenta_goszakupok_na_fr_i-iii_2018_.pdf (in Russian).
14. Vademecum Analytics. Oncological Service in Russia. Infrastructure and Budgets. 2021.
15. From officials to pharmacists. Accessed 10 December 2021. https://www.vedomosti.ru/business/articles/2015/01/15/iz-chinovnikov-v-farmacevty (in Russian).
16. Open access interview. How an ex-banker sells billions of drugs to the state and creates a vaccine against COVID-19. Dialogue with CEO of 'Brus', 9 September 2020. Accessed 10 December 2021. https://www.forbes.ru/biznes/408589-kak-eks-bankir-prodaet-gosudarstvu-lekarstv-na-milliardy-i-sozdaet-vakcinu-ot-covid-19 (in Russian).
17. Vademecum Analytics. Oncological Service in Russia. Infrastructure and Budgets. 2021.
18. Expert interview for this research. 2020. Vitaliy, marketing specialist, Russian Pharmaceutical Company, Moscow, Russia.
19. Open access interview. 2020. Dialogue with Nikolay Zhukov, oncologist, Head of the Department of the Dmitry Rogachev's National Medical Research Center. Accessed 10 December 2021. https://www.kp.ru/daily/27074.7/4146759/ (in Russian).
20. Expert interview for this research. 2021. Anna, private healthcare consultant, Moscow, Russia.
21. Open access interview. 2020. Dialogue with A. Gapeev, CEO of Ilyinsky Hospital, Moscow. Accessed 10 December 2021. https://www.facebook.com/2279843975430408/videos/331550171202652 (in Russian).
22. WHO country cooperation strategy at a glance: Russian Federation. Accessed 10 December 2021. https://www.who.int/publications/i/item/WHO-CCU-18.02-Russian-Federation.
23. Expert interview for this research. 2019. Mihail, oncologist, Gercen'c Institute, Moscow, Russia.
24. Vademecum Analytics. Oncological Service in Russia. Infrastructure and Budgets. 2021.

References

Bach, Peter B. 2009. 'Limits on Medicare's ability to control rising spending on cancer drugs', *New England Journal of Medicine* 360: 626–33.

Barsukova, Svetlana. 2019. 'Informal practices of big business in the post-Soviet period: From oligarchs to "kings of state orders"', *Demokratizatsiya: The Journal of Post-Soviet Democratization* 27: 31–50.

Beckert, Jens. 2011. 'The transcending power of goods: Imaginative value in the economy'. In *The Worth of Goods: Valuation and pricing in the economy*, edited by Jens Beckert and Patrick Aspers, 106–28. Oxford: Oxford University Press.

Block, Fred. 1986. 'Political choice and the multiple logics of capital', *Theory and Society* 15: 175–92.

Davis, Courtney. 2015. 'Drugs, cancer and end-of-life care', *Social Science and Medicine* 131: 207–14.

Dobbin, Frank and Jiwook Jung. 2015. 'The fourth dimension of power: Social construction of interest in the new economic sociology'. In *Re-Imagining Economic Sociology*, edited by Patrick Aspers and Nigel Dodd. https://doi.org/10.1093/acprof:oso/9780198748465.003.0008

Dubuisson-Queiller, Sophie. 2013. 'From qualities to value: Demand shaping and market control in mass consumption markets'. In *Constructing Quality: The classification of goods in markets*, edited by J. Beckert and C. Musselin, 247–67. Oxford: Oxford University Press.

Fligstein, Neil and Alec Stone Sweet. 2002. 'Constructing markets and politics: An institutionalist account of European integration', *American Journal of Sociology* 107: 1206–43.

Fourcade, Marion. 2011. 'Price and prejudice: On economics and the enchantment (and disenchantment) of nature'. In *The Worth of Goods: Valuation and pricing in the economy*, edited by Jens Beckert and Patrick Aspers, 41–62. Oxford: Oxford University Press.

Frye, Timothy. 2002. 'Capture or exchange? Business lobbying in Russia', *Europe-Asia Studies* 54: 1017–36.

Haugaard, Mark. 2012. 'Rethinking the four dimensions of power: Domination and empowerment', *Journal of Political Power* 5: 35–54.

Howard, David H., Peter B. Bach, Ernst R. Berndt and Rena M. Conti. 2015. 'Pricing in the market for anticancer drugs', *Journal of Economic Perspectives: A Journal of the American Economic Association* 29: 139–62.

Inozemtsev, Vladislav. 2018. *Nesovremennaya Strana: Rossiya v Mire Dvadtsat' Pervogo Veka* [Outdated country: Russia in the world of the twenty-first century]. Moscow: Alpina Publisher.

Kajua, Rozhe. 2003. *Mif i Chelovek. Chelovek i Sakral'noe* [Myth and man. Man and the sacred]. Moscow: OGI.

Kaprin, Andrey, Valeriy Starinskij and Galina Petrova. 2020. 'Sostoyanie Onkologicheskoj Pomoshchi Naseleniyu Rossii v 2019 Godu' [The conditions of public cancer care in Russia in 2019]. Accessed 16 March 2022. https://glavonco.ru/cancer_register/%D0%9F%D0%BE%D0%BC%D0%BE%D1%89%D1%8C%202019.pdf.

Keller, Reiner. 2005. 'Entering discourses: A new agenda for qualitative research and sociology of knowledge', *Qualitative Sociology Review* 8: 46–75.

Keller, Reiner. 2011. 'The sociology of knowledge approach to discourse (SKAD)', *Human Studies* 34: 43–65.

Kerasidou, Angeliki. 2019. 'Empathy and efficiency in healthcare at times of austerity', *Health Care Annals* 27: 171–84.

Koreckaya, Marina. 2021. *Ambivalentnost' Vlasti: Mifologiya, Ontologiya, Praksis* [The ambivalence of power: mythology, ontology, praxis]. St Petersburg: Aleteiya.

Lantz, Paula M. and Karen M. Booth 1998. 'The social construction of the breast cancer epidemic', *Social Science and Medicine* 46: 907–18.

Ledeneva, Alena. 2013. *Can Russia Modernise? Sistema, power networks and informal governance*. Cambridge: Cambridge University Press.

Ledeneva, Alena. 2018. 'The substantive ambivalence: Relationships vs. use of relationships'. In *The Global Encyclopaedia of Informality, Vol.1: Understanding social and cultural complexity*, edited by Alena Ledeneva, 31–5. London: UCL Press.

Livne, Roi. 2014. 'Economies of dying: The moralization of economic scarcity in U.S. hospice care', *American Sociological Review* 79: 888–911.

Price, Kay and Julianne Cheek. 2007. 'Avoiding death: The ultimate challenge in the provision of contemporary healthcare?', *Health Sociology Review* 16: 397–404.

Raffnsøe, Sverre, Marius Gudmand-Høyer and Morten Thaning. 2014. 'What is a dispositive? Foucault's historical mappings of the networks of social reality', Copenhagen Business School Working Paper, Frederiksberg. Accessed 18 March 2022. https://research-api.cbs.dk/ws/portalfiles/portal/58811258/Raffnsoe.pdf.

Sandel, Michael J. 2012. *What Money Can't Buy: The moral limits of markets*. New York: Farrar, Straus and Giroux.

Shleifer, Andrei and Robert W. Vishny. 2002. *The Grabbing Hand: Pathologies and their cures*. Cambridge, MA: Harvard University Press.

Smith, Charles. 2007. 'Markets as definitional practices', *Canadian Journal of Sociology* 32: 1–39.

Sulik, Gayle A. 2010. *Pink Ribbon Blues: How breast cancer culture undermines women's health*. New York: Oxford University Press.

Tkachenko, Andrey, Andrey Yakovlev and Aleksandra Kuznetsova. 2017. '"Sweet deals": State-owned enterprises, corruption and repeated contracts in public procurement', *Economic Systems* 41: 52–67.

Weiss, Meira. 1997. 'Signifying the pandemics: Metaphors of AIDS, cancer, and heart disease', *Medical Anthropology Quarterly* 11: 456–76.

Yakovlev, Andrey. 2015. 'State–business relations in Russia after 2011: "New deal" or imitation of changes?'. In *The Challenges for Russia's Politicized Economic System*, edited by Susanne Oxenstierna, 59–76. Abingdon: Routledge.

Zvyagintsev, Vasiliy and Svetlana Barsukova. 2006. 'Mekhanizm "politicheskogo investirovaniya", ili kak i zachem biznes uchastvuet v vyborakh i oplachivaet partiynuyu zhizn' [The mechanism of 'political investment', or how and why business participates in elections and pays parties]. *Journal of Economic Sociology = Ekonomicheskaya sotsiologiya* 2: 8–22.

14
'Russian Parmesan, even better than the original': Exploratory research into organic farmers' valuation strategies

Tamara Kusimova

Introduction

In 2014, a former IT manager, Oleg Sirota, sold his business and moved to the countryside, took out a loan and hired two refugees from eastern Ukraine; a year later, he opened the 'Russian Parmesan' creamery (*The Economist* 2016).[1] Mr Sirota glorifies Vladimir Putin's political course and promises to create a monument to Barack Obama and Angela Merkel for their sanctions against Russia, since they created so many opportunities for local farmers and foodies.[2] Mr Sirota is not alone in his initiative. A whole new generation of individual farmers-cum-entrepreneurs harbours the ambition to respond to the challenges of import substitution. Their marketing genius attracted worldwide attention due to a specific mixture of patriotic pro-Russian narratives with the progressive concepts of eco-friendly entrepreneurship and back-to-the-land lifestyles, bringing Russian organic farmers close to their Western counterparts from alternative food movements (Hille 2014; Matthews 2016; Chapple and Churmanova 2017). Another key feature they share with their Western counterparts is the emphasis on authenticity: the products they make are unique and *Russian*, even though they look like substitutes of now unavailable Italian Parmesan and other imported goods. The idea of food authenticity, however, is known for its ambivalent nature. Commonly understood as the link between a particular dish and a specific place and time (Weiss 2011, 74), the production of unique products with their own *terroir* has become a global industry in its own right, with its own bureaucratic regulations and standardization procedures, and political and market actors with their own specific interests (Pietrykowski 2004; Pratt 2008; Monterescu 2017). Authenticity, indeed, is the new source of value in the economy of experiences (Banet-Weiser 2012).

Drawing on the idea of food as a cultural commodity (Appadurai 1981, 495; 1988) – an object of valuation that embodies the relations of power between the global and the local, industrial and rural, singular and mass production – I examine farmers' strategies for enhancing the symbolic value of their products. What makes their products unique, and how do they explain their considerably higher prices? In addressing this question, the chapter has the following structure. It begins with a discussion of popular narratives of food sovereignty and the general tension between the global and the local, in response to which a whole niche of authentic food has emerged. It then offers a critical examination of the 'authentic national food' concept from a historical and sociological perspective. Following that, I demonstrate how the ambivalence of authenticity is productively used in the new Russian farmers' valuation strategies. The empirical part of this research is based on materials collected during master's thesis preparation at the Department of Sociology and Social Anthropology at the Central European University in spring 2019.

Food movements: between populism and elitism

Our daily nutritional needs automatically turn us into participants of the global food order, since the ingredients of our meals come from all over the world through global supply chains – sets of actors interlinked for subcontracting and outsourcing the process of production (Phillips 2006, 38; Tsing 2009, 148). The history of agricultural development is inseparable from its sad consequences, including colonialism, slavery and interdependence between the 'core' Western countries and less developed regions that provide cheap labour and material resources (Mintz 1986; Mintz and Du Bois 2002; Friedmann 2005; McMichael 2009). While the ideas of sustainable development and organic farming are at the peak of their popularity, the adverse effects are still an inevitable part of this industry, as the fair-trade organic market itself has become the subject of multiple regulations and certifications that force small and medium-sized businesses to either adapt or merge with more prominent market players (Friedmann 2005; Gille 2009; Aistara 2018). Labour studies into the food industry reveal race and gender aspects and low-paid jobs in the peripheral zones of global capitalism (Tsing 2009; Besky and Brown 2015). Various forms of inequality generated by the global food order have resulted in food sovereignty movements – initiatives which are aimed at re-localizing food systems and enforcing measures against the negative impacts of neoliberal policies (Friedmann 2005; Phillips 2006; Pratt 2008). Originated as peasant initiatives, they were quickly incorporated into populist governments' strategies in Latin America, Central and Eastern Europe and, to some extent, Russia, due to the popularity of these narratives among working-class and rural voters (Mamonova 2016; 2019; Mamonova and Franquesa 2019).[3]

While some food justice movements unite around left-wing political and labour agendas, others demonstrate an impressive ability to commercialize their ideas. Among the latter, the Slow Food movement deserves special attention for two reasons: its initiatives are popular in Russia,[4] and its ideology is centred around the idea of *authenticity* – one of the most controversial in sociological terms, but an analytically productive category in food studies. From the Slow Food perspective, fast-food chain restaurants are the embodiment of all the worst qualities that food can possess: cheap, fast, standardized and full of additives; according to the Slow Food philosophy, food should not be a commodity; instead, the environmentally friendly, sustainable production of organic food endemic to a particular region should be a socializing ritual that sustains the local community (Pietrykowski 2004, 311). Generally, the global–local opposition is the core dichotomy for alternative food movements (Pietrykowski 2004, 310; Pratt 2008). Since its establishment, the Slow Food movement has been continuously criticized for becoming an exclusive institution and commercial brand; exploitative labour relations still exist in the quality segment and many farmers cannot afford to adhere to the Slow principles due to the higher costs of 'clean' production (Peace 2008; Pratt 2008, 68; Philippon 2015).

The popularity of food justice movements and the ambivalent relationships between the *global* and the *local* in a world bound by supply chains have created a niche for a new type of ethical entrepreneurship. As Gourevitch (2011) notes, the valuation of local, ethically produced food resembles the valuation of wine, as it is based on the production of singularities (Gourevitch 2011, 86). What are the mechanisms of valuation in local food, if one cannot try it before buying? Firstly, certificates and labels can be adopted (e.g., Fairtrade, Slow Food,

Non-GMO) with a signalling function that will convey social values attractive to customers.[5] Secondly, another way to attribute value to a unique good is to tell the story behind it (Bogdanova 2011, 152). Since every meal puts us in a complex network of cultural meanings, local food has a specific message behind it: a message of identity, belonging and *authenticity* (Anderson 2005; Pratt 2008).

Ambivalent authenticities: valuation strategies in a global era

Authenticity is commonly understood as an association between a particular food tradition, geographical space and time (Weiss 2011, 74). Nevertheless, archaeological and historical evidence shows that, firstly, nutrition patterns poorly coincide with national borders, and secondly, food traditions were shaped by patterns of trade and migration long before the first nation states emerged (Anderson 2005; Phillips 2006). If this is true, why and how do certain foods become exclusively associated with specific nations, ethnic groups and cultural traditions?

The link between social group belonging and food preferences is confirmed by evolutionary psychology and biology (Rozin et al. 2007). Stable associations arise during primary socialization in childhood; they are consolidated through widely shared social representations – elements of collective memory transmitted in the form of written and oral stories (Rozin 1990; 1996; Holtzman 2006; Boyer 2018). The process of food identity formation became markedly pronounced in the age of nation states in the eighteenth and nineteenth centuries when a culinary canon turned into an essential element that unites the nation, and cookbooks became codified sets of traditions, written in one particular language to strengthen the imagined community in Anderson's sense (Anderson 1991; K. Ferguson 2004; 2012; P. P. Ferguson 2010). The French term *terroir* perfectly conveys the idea of authenticity – it means a specific combination of geographical characteristics, climatic conditions and history that contribute to the product's exceptionality (Trubek 2008; Monterescu 2017).

Since the establishment of the culinary canon is a modern-era phenomenon, the idea of food authenticity should be critically assessed (A. Weiss 2011; B. Weiss 2012). There is a billion-dollar industry behind the idyllic representations of ancestral traditions: authenticity has been turned into a gastropolitical issue that has already become the object of regulation and conventionalization.[6] Hungary creates its unique *Hungarikum* (Gille 2009),[7] France fights for its *foie gras* (DeSoucey

2010; 2016) and EU countries develop their appellation labelling (Barham 2003). As Ichijo and Ranta (2016) point out, the idea of authentic food has stakeholders who recognize its scope for meaning-making and its features and who find means to identify and protect it.

The complexities generated within the global food order are hard to fit into one frame. Instead of looking for ways these contradictions are logically resolved in the minds of individuals participating in the production, distribution and consumption of selected goods, it is fruitful to address the way those contradictions coexist in a state of ambivalence, which Bauman (1991) named as the main companion of the condition of postmodernity and late capitalism (Jovanović 2016, 2; Ledeneva 2014, 19). In Robert Merton's (1976) classic definition, ambivalence arises from incompatible normative expectations (Merton 1976, 6). Shaped by the tension between the global and local power structures, the industry of authentic organic food requires its producers to adhere to mutually exclusive requirements: to be both locally responsible and globally competitive; to be both unique and standardized; to be independent and to be able to cooperate with the large market (e.g., retailers) and governmental structures to receive institutional and financial support. Nevertheless, I would argue that producers of authentic food, in the end, tend to benefit from this ambivalence, using the local–global tension as the source of additional value in communication with customers and key stakeholders on the market.

The unique story behind the product embeds it in a web of meanings and values, turning it into an authenticated and personalized object (Bogdanova 2011, 153). In an affluent consumer society, authenticity and value go hand in hand, since a unique narrative turns every product – from an antique painting to a bottle of wine – into a singularity, a valuable cultural commodity, significantly increasing its price (Aspers and Beckert 2011; Beckert 2011; Bogdanova 2011; Beckert et al. 2017). Research on valuation is focused on how and based on which criteria individuals evaluate certain goods and practices, considering them (un-)worthy and (un-)desirable, and which strategies social agents use to manage these evaluations (Lamont 2012). Since the market is the arena of social interaction (Beckert 2009, 246), consumers and local stakeholders, in turn, must recognize the manufacturer's inherent meanings – they must understand why this product is valuable, which, in some cases of wine and food, requires special skills and cultural capital (Pratt 2008; Aspers 2009; Beckert et al. 2017). Thus, coordination in the market of unique goods arises between different modes of evaluation (Beckert 2009; Lamont 2012).

Food studies in Russia: state of the art and new perspectives

Three different gastropolitical trends in post-socialist Russia attract our attention. First of all, shock therapy and the opening of Russian markets gradually normalized the new 'Western' consumer desires and practices of rationalized shopping (Jung 2009) and differentiating between 'the taste of necessity' and 'the taste of luxury' (Oushakine 2000). Despite the abundance of new goods, former citizens of the socialist bloc have not escaped nostalgia for Soviet food in the post-socialist states and Russian diasporas (Boym 1995; Holak et al. 2007; Barney 2009; Klumbytė 2010; Holak 2014; Goering 2017). Finally, as the gradual spread of nationalist ideologies in post-socialist Russia and the search for identity in the former Soviet republics revived discussions over national traditions, attempts to find opposition to 'rootless' McDonald's and Snickers attracted scholarly attention (Caldwell 2002; Manning and Uplisashvili 2007). The topic of alcohol occupies a separate niche in cultural (Herlihy 2001; Schrad 2014) and sociological research (Nemtsov and Vågerö 2011; Radaev 2017; Radaev et al. 2020). Despite the presence of studies focused on the material aspects of contemporary Russian patriotism (Gurova et al. 2017; Kalinina 2017), food issues have received almost no attention (with the exception of Barsukova 2017; Yormirzoev et al. 2019).

Opportunities for new socio-cultural research on food and related consumption practices have opened up over the past decade, thanks to the growing role of discourses of food security and self-sufficiency. Even though Russia was moving towards import substitution and protectionist policies before 2014, the food embargo marked the symbolic break-up with the Western countries (Wegren 2014; Wegren et al. 2017; Barsukova 2018). It transformed the very cultural categories around food by dividing the content of supermarket shelves into 'us' and 'them': overnight, imported products disappeared from the supermarket shelves, and excavators destroyed leftovers of imported food in a potlach-like ritual, all featured in evening news programmes (*The Economist* 2015). 'War and cheese' – an ironic allegory to *War and Peace* – accurately conveys the patriotic fever that swept the Russian media in 2014–15 (*The Economist* 2016). Individuals missing *zapreschenka* were labelled as liberals ready to sell their homeland for *jamón* by patriotic media.[8] In 2019, the National Association of Meat Producers appealed to the Deputy Prime Minister to ban individuals from bringing meat and dairy products from foreign countries. In response to the public's bewilderment, the Miratorg company's head (a prominent import substitution lobbyist) distinguished himself by suggesting that everyone should think about their 'homeland instead of jamón and cheese' (BBC News Russia 2019). Opinion polls recorded a marked change in the ideological climate and a 'rally-around-the-flag' effect: for instance, in 2014 (right after the sanctions), 79 per cent of respondents supported the embargo (FOM 2014); over the next years, the share of respondents believing the embargo policy is justified hovered around 82 per cent (FOM 2016; 2017; Kazun 2016). The government framed the new policy as an opportunity for the country to develop its agricultural industry and food market (Barsukova 2016; 2018)

The evolution of post-Soviet agricultural policy in Russia is a history of a change in the general political line from the radical market liberalism of the 1990s to state patronage and support of the agricultural sector in the 2010s (Barsukova 2018; Wegren et al. 2018). Land privatization and attempts to create a new class of individual (or family) farmers – 'effective' managers of their private property – were remarkably unsuccessful and led to a continuous decline, making food and agriculture the least developed sector of the economy (Barsukova 2016). The consolidation of small farms into large agro-holdings characterized the last two decades (Davydova and Franks 2015). The market structure was solidified by the agricultural holdings' dependency on regional and federal authorities, making most of them inseparable from the state, since a substantial part of them operate as a form of public–private partnership of bureaucratic-market type (Barsukova 2016, 66). As in any Russian business under significant state influence, embeddedness in networks of informal relationships (*sistema*) plays a major role in establishing contacts and partnerships (Ledeneva 2013; Barsukova 2019). The latter is vital for small independent producers since access to financial support and avoiding bankruptcy is often possible only through being embedded in *sistema* (for example, through membership in a central committee of a leading political party or a major business association) (Ledeneva 2013).

By 2012, family farms and individual entrepreneurs produced only 9 per cent of the country's gross agricultural production (Davydova and Franks 2015, 135). The latest available data on the post-embargo period show that in 2015, about R6 billion was allocated to support individual farms; in 2016, R14 billion was earmarked for distribution (Barsukova 2016, 68). While the major market players are still the embargo's primary beneficiaries, individual farmers are supported via targeted measures (Wegren et al. 2018). For instance, the Moscow oblast' administration allocated over R300 million in the form of grant-based financial aid (*Dairy News* 2020).

Despite the apparent superiority of large companies that can fill supermarket shelves faster and cheaper, Moscow and the nearby regions observed a notable increase in festivals and marketplaces with various local producers' goods. The 'marginal minority'[9] of individual organic farmers in Russia is the main target of this research's empirical part. Apart from the general interest in the phenomenon of authenticity in food and its use in valuation strategies, there are other reasons why these entrepreneurs should be studied as a new, emerging structural element of the Russian economy: the niche is growing on the back of increased interest in eco-friendly lifestyles and craft goods, especially in the 16–30 age group (Gudkov et al. 2020). Moreover, patriotic fervour turned some farmers, such as the already mentioned Mr Sirota, into significant public figures lobbying for their interests in various state-associated organizations.

Methodology

Based on the existing theories mentioned above, it can be assumed that not only entrepreneurs' personal imaginaries will shape the way they narrate the story behind their products. Therefore, to understand the valuation strategies they employ, one must also ask them about how they see their place in the market, where they have to coexist with the large agro-industrial holdings and state policies. The empirical part of this chapter is based on field research conducted in April 2019. The grounded theory methodology was chosen as the most suitable way of performing an exploratory study (Milliken 2010). Four criteria were used to select the most vivid cases of individual farmers working with organic Russian food:

1) Their marketing strategy should emphasize localness, 'Russianness' and their products' purity.
2) Those projects should have an articulated 'social mission', or, at least, clear statements about their ideas.
3) They should cooperate only with other small-scale producers and stay outside of extensive supply chains.
4) They should have a visible media presence.

Overall, five cases were selected. Since the number of personal in-depth interviews with the informants was limited, they were combined with the ethnographic participant observation in the farm-to-table restaurant owned by one of the informants and secondary sources analysis. The latter included interviews, social media publications, official websites and, in one case, a public blog. All personal in-depth interviews lasted from two to three hours; the names of respondents have been changed. All of the research took place in Moscow, and all the farmers in the selected cases were from Moscow and the Moscow region.

The imaginary value: authenticity and armchair nostalgia

What is authentic Russian food? In interviews, this question was asked to understand how the entrepreneurs define Russian food and what they mean by authenticating their products. When asked about the origin of these recipes, my informants pointed to historical cookbooks and traditions.

> *Kisel'* is usually perceived as a starchy drink you are given in the school canteen. However, this is not a drink but a dish made of different ingredients. *Kisel'* with pea is something like hummus. And sweet *kisel'* made from oats is like a Russian answer to panna cotta. (Alexander, farmer, owner of the cooperative and the farm-to-table-restaurant)

Pre-revolutionary origins united all of them; the selectivity of ingredients is marked not only by the period but also by their simplicity and association with the peasant diet. Moreover, my respondent shared his plans to organize a food festival in Pereslavl-Zalesskiy, combined with a major religious holiday. From a historical point of view, the stable association between Russian cuisine, Christianity and the peasant diet occurred first in conscious attempts to construct a national culinary canon in the Russian Empire (Smith 2011; 2012).

Yet the regular variety of goods presented at the farmers' shops, whether my respondent's shop or the famous cheesemaker Oleg Sirota's project, consists of consumer categories much more familiar to the average customer's taste: yoghurt, milk or bread.[10] With these details in mind, I argue that in this case, authenticity is not about the food itself. Instead, it is constructed through historical performance – references to pre-revolutionary heritage in recipes on the website and in restaurants, marketing strategies and visual design. In his research on valuation, Beckert (2011) speaks of an imaginative performance of goods 'that evoke fantasies based on symbolic associations with desired events, people, places, or values' (Beckert 2011, 110).

Claiming historical authenticity means giving goods a specific type of imaginative value recognized by consumers and other stakeholders, such as authorities who provide 'patriotic' grants to farmers. Valuation strategies are shaped through specific cultural repertoires – sets of symbols, associations and collective symbolic representations (Beckert 2011; Lamont 2012). Popular representations include, for example, associating modern farmers with the traditions of Russian merchants. In his blog, Oleg Sirota writes:

> Friends! Our cheeses are on Red Square! Each time, being here next to the counter, I have fantastic feelings of belonging to the peasants and merchants who brought their goods, cheeses, sausages, bread for hundreds of years. It turns out that we are continuing their glorious traditions; we have something to be proud of and should not be ashamed of our great grandfathers! (Oleg Sirota, personal blog)[11]

Appealing to the merchant tradition was common among Orthodox entrepreneurs (Fomina 2020) and early Soviet entrepreneurs – shuttle traders and the first members of trade cooperatives (Skvirskaja 2018). Utopian images of Moscow, the city of 'priests and traders', and nostalgic narratives about Russian merchants are a sort of response to the lack of official entrepreneurial culture in the Soviet Union, where the official state ideology condemned profit-seeking and labelled it as speculation (Skvirskaja 2018, 548). Goods with imaginative value can take us to other places and create so-called armchair nostalgia – nostalgia for a time in which we never lived (Bogdanova 2011, 172). The visual design and marketing strategies of the entrepreneurs I interviewed and of the most media-savvy farmers, such as Oleg Sirota or German Sterligov, refer us to a pre-revolutionary peasant utopia.[12] On a larger scale, the Tsarist nostalgia became a widespread cultural phenomenon after the so-called conservative turn in Russian politics in 2014 – precisely the year when the food embargo attracted media attention to the farmers (Laruelle 2016). Concurrently, turning to pre-revolutionary imagery does not automatically turn a farmer into a Russian nationalist. In symbolic strategies of enhancing the commodity's value, individuals use culture as a toolkit – a flexible set of established cultural representations that help them communicate with other social agents on the market (e.g., consumers and the state) (Beckert 2009; 2011).

'Not like Soviet food': constructing the positional value

Against the background of Soviet nostalgia, the lack of references to Soviet culinary heritage attracts attention. Researchers of food nostalgia in former socialist countries regularly point to its paradoxical nature – people tend to miss foods from the past despite the traumatic experience associated with stagnation, empty food shelves and poor service (Kaspe 2008). Taking these collective representations into account, entrepreneurs from the premium segment try to avoid negative associations. In one of his online articles, the head of the organic farmers' cooperative compares 'a Soviet citizen without a clan and a tribe' with the global consumer today (Akimov 2016). What united Soviet and Western citizens was the consumption style set by mass industrial production; food was certified and standardized, provided by the large-scale supply chains. Organic farm products, which, like wine, claim the status of a delicacy, have a positional value – it signals the belonging to a particular class, and its audience should distance themselves from the mass-produced food of poor quality (Beckert 2011; Beckert et al. 2017).

As noted earlier, leaving aside authenticity performances, we can see that the new Russian farmers' assortment combines familiar products and 'Western' specialities. It is unlikely that Russian inhabitants knew of yoghurts, gluten-free bread, or ricotta and burrata cheeses from ancient times. Nevertheless, we regularly see Russian surrogates of such foreign products. Their prices are also striking – the average Russian Parmesan is more expensive than its European counterpart brought into Russia in a suitcase (of course, excluding the transportation costs).

It is not a coincidence that organic farming enterprises offering their domestic analogues to Parmesan began to grow close to big cities. According to statistics, 54.4 per cent of the Russian middle class lives in large Russian cities, with every 10th representative living in Moscow; the core of the middle class that meets all necessary characteristics is only 7 per cent of the population (Tikhonova 2019). The upper-middle class, whose purchasing power grew during the 2000s, acquired what Bourdieu calls the 'taste for freedom' – the ability to choose and perceive food not only as a way to satisfy basic needs but also as a social practice that brings pleasure (Bourdieu 1986, 178; Ochs et al. 1996, 8; Tikhonova 2016, 104). In his work on culture and symbolic violence in contemporary Moscow, Mikhail Iampolski (2018) gives a vivid illustration of upper-middle class Muscovites' reaction to the food embargo: 'A friend of mine put smuggled cheese on the table, for which he paid a triple price by saying: "We will not let you bring us back to the USSR!"' (Iampolski 2018, 127). The logic of distinction and symbolic boundaries is the key to understanding such irritation – limiting the freedom of choice in consumption is perceived as a return to the 'world of necessity' associated with the Soviet Union (Iampolski 2018).

The logic of freedom (in contrast to the logic of necessity) and taste makes the middle class more sensitive to symbolic elements of consumption, that is, to different types of valuation (Bourdieu 1986; Lamont 1992). Recognition of this guides the farmers featured in this study: in their niche, they compete for the opportunity to sell a product with the highest imaginary and positional value. The latter is expressed through the construction of symbolic boundaries between the consumer of a mass product, equalized to the Soviet citizen, and connoisseurs whose cultural and economic capital allows them to understand what *real* healthy food is and to try new exotic things.[13]

Sistema and beyond

The food embargo of 2014 may look like a radical movement towards food sovereignty, attempting to re-localize the food system; yet in respondents' perception, the current agricultural policy is a continuator of Soviet gigantism. The patriotic facade of import substitution has turned into a cultural representation which, firstly, is well integrated into the idea of confrontation with the West; secondly, is popular with the general public; and thirdly, is used by both large-scale producers and individual farmers to attract attention and receive development grants and other financial assistance (Barsukova 2017; 2018). Nevertheless, as was noted in the previous parts of the chapter, the market structure faced little change, and individual farmer-entrepreneurs remain a marginal phenomenon. In such conditions, the references to authenticity are constructed through the opposition between the large-scale and traditional craft modes of production, giving the products an imaginary and positional value.

> If you look at the fundamental part of this, it seems that the agro-industrial complex as a part of the business … its beneficiaries are not the people related to the territory they use. It is a fundamental thing. They aggregate vast spaces, including many ecosystem elements, create some products, and make money out of it. It does not mean that these people are evil. They may be great owners, but they are self-interested. It is understandable. Their interests are

related to profits. Not to the space they use ... They say: 'Yes, it may be bad for the environment, but you have to prove this. And I do not care much because I live thousands of kilometres away and have never been to these places.' (Alexander, entrepreneur, farmer, owner of the cooperative and the farm-to-table restaurant)

The tension between the global and the local expressed by the respondent is conflated with the general critical narrative regarding food supply chains, common among both activists and academic circles (Carrier 2008; Tsing 2009). When asked what the fair organization of the industry would look like, one of the respondents referred to the historical case of a pre-revolutionary merchant from the Arkhangelsk region, who invested all surplus in the development of his native village. Another interviewee referred to a story about Nicholas II, who, presumably, had enough skills to grow food in his garden. The emphasis on localization and personalization, as opposed to the regular supermarket food's anonymity, plays a significant role in enhancing its symbolic value. While authenticity and localness give goods the imaginative value of the desired, intangible idea of a better, fair world with better food, the positional value occurs through comparing the *real food* for those who understand and the mass-market *commodities* for less sophisticated ones.

> – And what about the scale of production?
> – This is the key. What do we produce: food or commodities? Sometimes there is more control in the factories. But it also means additives. Just another ideology, you know. (Sergey, small-scale entrepreneur in organic farming)

Although working in a specific niche and defining their authenticity against the backdrop of the large-scale food suppliers is a vital economic and symbolic strategy, the respondents acknowledge the advantage of the current food policies:

> What I've seen ... What is going on? We worked at a cheese festival this summer. It was a real bomb. There were so many producers. And people who were interested in it. They travelled to Europe and knew all these cheeses. And they went to a [local, Russian] cheese fair and spent a lot of money there. (Igor, small-scale entrepreneur, sells organic products made of pumpkin)

At the end of August 2021, after a long period of sanitary restrictions, a festival of farm products, 'Cheese! Feast! Peace!', took place in the vicinity of Moscow.[14] Oleg Sirota was its main organizer, PR manager and host. Small local producers of cheese, honey, dairy and traditional Russian food were positioned alongside large sponsoring companies (for instance, with Zolotaia Balka),[15] and the key guest of the first days of the festival was Andrey Vorobyov, the current governor of the Moscow region.[16] Accompanied by the cases above, I argue that this situation illustrates the ambivalence structurally embedded in producing authentic organic foods. On the one hand, the positional value that signals the proper values to the customers is acquired by opposing large structures of agro-industrial production; authenticity, in this case, represents a symbolic opposition to the structural power of corporate capitalism and the state, which are strongly interrelated in the Russian case and constitute what Ledeneva (2013; 2014) calls *sistema*. On the other hand, only within the *sistema* is it possible to achieve significant commercial results, including the vital access to new markets and large retailers' shelves. The situation of dependence produces ambivalence and the ability to incorporate contradictory dispositions (Smelser 1998), or 'pragmatic doublethink' (Ledeneva 2014).

Concluding remarks

The mere existence of erstwhile unimaginable products such as Russian Parmesan may puzzle some international readers of this chapter. Nevertheless, the deconstruction of authenticity shows how various cultural representations, popular at the moment, become means of increasing product value and commercial profit and an essential tool in negotiations with the state and other structures built into the system that allocate resources in the market. In a broader context, this finding allows us to enrich our understanding of such phenomena as rural populism in Central and East European countries. Farmers may use patriotic or nationalist rhetoric not because of their personal views, but because that is how market power works – counting on state support, one cannot afford not to be patriotic. Taking the market as an arena of social interaction aimed at mutual coordination (Aspers 2009; Beckert 2009), farmers use different strategies to communicate with potential stakeholders, including customers, and enhance their symbolic value. The first strategy, which I call nostalgic performance, refers to the construction of uniqueness through references to symbolic representations of Russian heritage and culture. The second strategy is to draw symbolic boundaries between the unique farmers' dishes that nourish the body and mass-produced food associated with industrial supply chains. As Bogdanova (2011) shows, in the construction of quality, stories about the product and the market environment are equally important since ascribing value to a particular commodity means comparing it with others. The respondents regularly did this by drawing the line between Soviet and Russian, local and global, and mass production and the specific market niche they belong to. In this context, the successors of Soviet mass production are agro-industrial holdings that control most of the market and from which individual farmers distinguish themselves on a symbolic and practical level, thus forming a separate market niche.

Notes

1. This chapter is based on the dissertation submitted in partial fulfilment of the requirements for the degree of Master of Arts at the Department of Sociology and Social Anthropology, Central European University. For the dissertation text, see Kusimova (2019).
2. For more information, see the documentary by Ben Garfield about Russian Parmesan (English subtitles): *Meet a Russian Man Who Built a Cheese Factory in the Snowy Wilderness | War and Cheese*. (2017). Accessed 24 September 2020. https://www.youtube.com/watch?v=WG3Vc0OltNw.
3. The notions of fair trade, food sovereignty and food security intersect, and the search for differences between them would be a topic for a separate research project. In this chapter, the terms are used as synonyms because all of them (1) emphasize the local origin of the products, (2) declare opposition to neoliberal food regimes and (3) emphasize the need for fair wages for workers.
4. By 2018, nearly 1,500 convivia in 160 countries were established. See, for instance, Slow Food International, 'Where We Are'. Accessed 11 March 2021. https://www.slowfood.com/about-us/where-we-are/; Slow Food International, 'Convivia in Russia'. https://www.slowfood.com/nazioni-condotte/russia/. One of the respondents belongs to this movement and regularly participates in their events.
5. This research took place when there was no official certification of organic products in Russia. As of 1 January 2020, the Federal Law 'On Organic Products' came into force, which will allow producers to obtain official confirmation of their status.
6. In 1984, Arjun Appadurai coined the term '*gastropolitics*' to grasp the variety of relations of power, identity and belonging embodied in food (Appadurai 1981, 495).
7. Hungarikum: 'a unique product, marketed and protected as originated in Hungary and embodying national traditions' (Gille 2009, 59).
8. *Zapreschenka* (from *zapret*; English: prohibition): a slang word used for food products banned in the Russian market since 2014.
9. One of my informants' description of his role on the market.
10. 'Magazin' [Shop]. Istrinskaya Syrovarnya Olega Siroty [Oleg Sirota's Istra Creamery]. Accessed 12 March 2021. https://parmezan.ru/shop/; 'Vitrina' [Showcase]. LavkaLavka. Accessed 12 March 2021. https://lavkalavka.com/; 'Magazin' [Shop]. Internet-Magazin Krestyanskih Prodktov Bratyev Sterling [The Sterling brothers' peasant food shop]. Accessed 12 March 2021. http://sterling.market.
11. Oleg Sirota's personal blog in Telegram. Accessed 10 March 2021. https://t.me/sirotaoleg/1173.
12. Probably, the most extreme case of utopian-messianic imagery is German Sterligov's Sloboda: 'Ofitsialny Site Germana Sterligova' [German Sterligov's official webpage]. Accessed 12 March 2021. http://sterligoff.ru/.

13. It is worth noting the farmers featured in this chapter had promising careers before they started their businesses, which means, in particular, that they could afford to take risks in terms of costs. Of the modest number of those with whom I conducted in-depth interviews, two had entrepreneurship experience even before turning to organic products. My third interviewee, my host during the ethnographic part, was a well-known journalist in Moscow. Regarding the authors of publications used as secondary sources, Oleg Sirota is a former IT entrepreneur, and German Sterligov was a well-known businessman in the 1990s. Considering this fact and their orientation towards the demands of the middle-class population of nearby large cities, this phenomenon should be examined as part of rural gentrification instead of the general rural population (Mamonova and Sutherland 2015).
14. 'Syr! Pir! Mir!' [Cheese! Feast! Peace!]. Accessed 30 September 2021. https://parmezan.ru/events/syr-pir-mir-2021/.
15. Zolotaia Balka is one of the largest wineries in Crimea. Since 2015, it has received numerous additional investments for modernization and expansion of production. For more information, see 'Nasha Istoriya. Zolotaia Balka' [Our history. Zolotaia Balka]. Accessed 30 September 2021. https://zolotaiabalka.ru/company/history/.
16. Oleg Sirota's personal blog in Telegram. Accessed 30 September 2021. https://t.me/sirotaoleg/3361.

References

Aistara, Guntra A. 2018. *Organic Sovereignties: Struggles over farming in an age of free trade*. Seattle: University of Washington Press.

Akimov, Boris. 2016. 'Chto Znachit Byt' v Oppozitsii?' [What does it mean to be in opposition?], *LAVKALAVKA Newspaper*, 29 September. Accessed 12 March 2021. http://web.archive.org/web/20170618041108/https://lavkagazeta.com/slowfood/chto-znachit-byt-v-oppozicii/.

Anderson, Benedict. 1991. *Imagined Communities: Reflections on the origin and spread of nationalism*. London: Verso.

Anderson, Eugene N. 2005. 'Food and borders: Ethnicities, cuisines, and boundary crossings'. In *Everyone Eats: Understanding food and culture*, edited by Eugene N. Anderson, 186–209. New York: New York University Press.

Appadurai, Arjun. 1981. 'Gastro-politics in Hindu South Asia', *American Ethnologist* 8: 494–511.

Appadurai, Arjun. 1988. *The Social Life of Things: Commodities in cultural perspective*. Cambridge: Cambridge University Press.

Aspers, Patrik. 2009. 'Knowledge and valuation in markets', *Theory and Society* 38: 111–31.

Aspers, Patrik and Jens Beckert. 2011. 'Value in markets'. In *The Worth of Goods: Valuation and pricing in the economy*, edited by Jens Beckert and Patrik Aspers, 3–32. Oxford: Oxford University Press.

Banet-Weiser, Sarah. 2012. *Authentic™: The politics of ambivalence in a brand culture*. New York: New York University Press.

Barham, Elizabeth. 2003. 'Translating terroir: The global challenge of French AOC labeling', *Journal of Rural Studies* 19: 127–38.

Barney, Timothy. 2009. 'When we was red: Good bye Lenin! And nostalgia for the "everyday GDR"', *Communication and Critical/Cultural Studies* 6: 132–51.

Barsukova, Svetlana. 2016. 'Dilemma "fermery-agroholdingi" v kontekste importozameschenia' [The dilemma of the 'farmers vs. agricultural holdings' in the context of import substitution], *Social Sciences and Contemporary World* 5: 63–74.

Barsukova, Svetlana. 2017. 'Consumer patriotism: How Russians "vote with their rubles" for great power status', *Russian Analytical Digest* 207: 8–12.

Barsukova, Svetlana. 2018. 'Food and agriculture'. In *Russia: Strategy, policy and administration*, edited by Irvin Studin, 241–55. London: Palgrave Macmillan.

Barsukova, Svetlana. 2019. 'Informal practices of big business in the post-Soviet period: From oligarchs to "kings of state orders"', *Demokratizatsiya: The Journal of Post-Soviet Democratization* 27: 31–49.

Bauman, Zygmunt. 1991. *Modernity and Ambivalence*. Ithaca, NY: Cornell University Press.

BBC News Russia. 2019. 'Hamon nuzhno est v Ispanii: biznes daet sovety rossiiskim gurmanam' [Jamon must be eaten in Spain: business gives advice to Russian gourmets], 30 April. Accessed 12 March 2021. https://www.bbc.com/russian/news-48104977.

Beckert, Jens. 2009. 'The social order of markets', *Theory and Society* 38: 245–69.

Beckert, Jens. 2011. 'The transcending power of goods: Imaginative value in the economy'. In *The Worth of Goods: Valuation and pricing in the economy*, edited by Jens Beckert and Patrik Aspers, 106–27. Oxford: Oxford University Press.

Beckert, Jens, Jörg Rössel and Patrick Schenk. 2017. 'Wine as a cultural product: Symbolic capital and price formation in the wine field', *Sociological Perspectives* 60: 206–22.

Besky, Sarah and Sandy Brown. 2015. 'Looking for work: Placing labor in food studies', *Labor: Studies in Working Class History of the Americas* 12: 19.

Bogdanova, Elena. 2011.'Valuing the past: The constitution of the antiques market in Russia'. Doctoral thesis, Universität zu Köln. Accessed 11 March 2021. https://kups.ub.uni-koeln.de/5084/1/bogdanova.pdf.

Bourdieu, Pierre. 1986. *Distinction: A social critique of the judgement of taste*. London: Routledge.

Boyer, Pascal. 2018. *Minds Make Societies: How cognition explains the world humans create*. New Haven, CT: Yale University Press.

Boym, Svetlana. 1995. 'From the Russian soul to post-communist nostalgia', *Representations* 49: 133–66.

Caldwell, Melissa L. 2002. 'The taste of nationalism: Food politics in postsocialist Moscow', *Ethnos* 67: 295–319.

Carrier, James G. 2008. 'Think locally, act globally: The political economy of ethical consumption'. In *Hidden Hands in the Market: Ethnographies of fair trade, ethical consumption, and corporate social responsibility*, 31–51. Bingley: Emerald Group Publishing.

Chapple, Amos and Ksenia Churmanova. 2017. 'Sanctions and the Russian farmer', *Radio Free Europe/Radio Liberty*. Accessed 10 March 2021. https://www.rferl.org/a/sanctions-and-the-russian-farmer/28658608.html.

Dairy News. 2020. 'Poryadka 330 million rublei v vide grantov vlasti Podmoskovia vydelili na podderzhki fermerskih hoziaistv v etom gody' [Approximately 330 million rubles in the form of grants were allocated by the Moscow Region authorities to support farms this year], 24 April. Accessed 24 September 2020. https://www.dairynews.ru/news/poryadka-330-mln-rubley-v-vide-grantov-vlasti-podm.html.

Davydova, Irina and Jeremy Franks. 2015. 'The rise and rise of large farms: Why agroholdings dominate Russia's agricultural sector', *Mir Rossii* 24: 133–59.

DeSoucey, Michaela. 2010. 'Gastronationalism: Food traditions and authenticity politics in the European Union', *American Sociological Review* 75: 432–55.

DeSoucey, Michaela. 2016. *Contested Tastes: Foie gras and the politics of food*. Princeton: Princeton University Press.

The Economist. 2015. 'The bonfire of the vans of cheese', 15 August. Accessed 10 March 2021. http://www.economist.com/news/europe/21661031-famine-prone-country-tests-its-citizens-loyalty-destroying-food-bonfire-vans.

The Economist. 2016. 'War and cheese', 7 April. Accessed 10 March 2021. https://www.economist.com/europe/2016/04/07/war-and-cheese.

Ferguson, Kennan. 2012. 'Intensifying taste, intensifying identity: Collectivity through community cookbooks', *Signs: Journal of Women in Culture and Society* 37: 695–717.

Ferguson, Priscilla Parkhurst. 2004. *Accounting for Taste: The triumph of French cuisine*. Chicago: University of Chicago Press.

Ferguson, Priscilla Parkhurst. 2010. 'Culinary nationalism', *Gastronomica* 10: 102–9.

FOM. 2014. '"Produktoviye sanktsii". Otnoshenie rossiyan' ['Food sanctions'. Attitude of Russians]. FOM.ru, 27 August. Accessed 10 March 2021. http://fom.ru/Ekonomika/11688.

FOM. 2017. 'Vospriyatie sanktsiy i anti-sanktsiy' [The perception of sanctions and anti-sanctions]. FOM.ru, 14 February. Accessed 22 March 2021. http://fom.ru/Ekonomika/13192.

FOM. 2018. 'Sanktsii' [Sanctions]. FOM.ru, 8 July. Accessed 22 March 2021. http://fom.ru/Ekonomika/12740.

Fomina, Victoria. 2020. '"How to earn a million in the glory of God?": Ethics and spirituality among Orthodox entrepreneurs in contemporary Russia', *Anthropological Quarterly* 93: 27–55.

Friedmann, Harriet. 2005. 'From colonialism to green capitalism: Social movements and emergence of food regimes'. In *New Directions in the Sociology of Global Development*, edited by Frederick H. Buttel and Philip McMichael, 227–64. Bingley: Emerald Group Publishing.

Gille, Zsuzsa. 2009. 'The tale of the toxic paprika: The Hungarian taste of Euro-globalization'. In *Food and Everyday Life in Postsocialist Eurasia*, edited by Melissa L. Caldwell, 97–128. Bloomington: Indiana University Press.

Goering, Laura. 2017. 'Marketing Soviet nostalgia: The many faces of Buratino', *Gastronomica* 17: 88–101.

Gourevitch, Peter. 2011. 'The value of ethics: Monitoring normative compliance in ethical consumption markets'. In *The Worth of Goods: Valuation and pricing in the economy*, edited by Jens Beckert and Partik Aspers, 87–105. Oxford: Oxford University Press.

Gudkov, Lev, Natalia Zorkaya, Ekaterina Kochergina, Karina Pipiya and Alexandra Ryseva. 2020. 'Rossijskoe "Pokolenie Z": Ustanovki i Cennosti' [Russia's 'Generation Z': attitudes and values]. Friedrich-Ebert-Stiftung. Accessed 10 March 2021. http://library.fes.de/pdf-files/bueros/moskau/16134.pdf.

Gurova, Olga, Ekaterina Kalinina, Jessie Labov and Vlad Strukov. 2017. 'Patriotic (non) consumption: Food, fashion and media: An introduction', *Digital Icons: Studies in Russian, Eurasian and Central European New Media* 16: 1–7.

Herlihy, Patricia. 2001. *The Alcoholic Empire: Vodka and politics in late imperial Russia*. Oxford: Oxford University Press.

Hille, Kathrin. 2014. 'Russian agriculture struggles to meet self-sufficiency challenge', *Financial Times*, 19 August. Accessed 10 March 2021. http://www.ft.com/intl/cms/s/0/776c7c6a-2782-11e4-ae44-00144feabdc0.html#axzz3oZVOwNLa.

Holak, Susan L. 2014. 'From Brighton Beach to blogs: Exploring food-related nostalgia in the Russian diaspora', *Consumption Markets & Culture* 17: 185–207.

Holak, Susan L., Alexei V. Matveev and William J. Havlena. 2007. 'Nostalgia in post-Socialist Russia: Exploring applications to advertising strategy', *Journal of Business Research* 60: 649–55.

Holtzman, Jon D. 2006. 'Food and memory', *Annual Review of Anthropology* 35: 361–78.

Iampolski, Mikhail. 2018. *Park Kul'tury: Kultura i Nasilie v Moskve Segodnya* [Park Kul'tury: culture and violence in today's Moscow]. Moscow: Novoe Izdatelstvo.

Ichijo, Atsuko and Ronald Ranta. 2016. *Food, National Identity and Nationalism: From everyday to global politics*. Basingstoke: Palgrave Macmillan.

Jovanović, Deana. 2016. 'Ambivalence and the study of contradictions', *HAU: Journal of Ethnographic Theory* 6: 1–6.

Jung, Yuson. 2009. 'From canned food to canny consumers: Cultural competence in the age of mechanical production'. In *Food and Everyday Life in the Postsocialist World*, edited by Melisa L. Caldwell, 29–53. Bloomington: Indiana University Press.

Kalinina, Ekaterina. 2017. 'Becoming patriots in Russia: Biopolitics, fashion, and nostalgia', *Nationalities Papers* 45: 8–24.

Kaspe, Irina. 2008. '"Syest' Proshloe": Ideologia i Povsednevnost Gastronomicheskoy Nostalgii' ['To eat the past': ideology and daily life of the Soviet culinary nostalgia]. In *Puti Rossii: Kultura – Obshestvo – Chelovek. Materialy XV Mezhdunarodnogo Sympoziuma* [Russia's Ways: Culture – Society – Human, Materials of the XV International Symposium], edited by Alexander M. Nikulin, 1–11, Moscow: Logos.

Kazun, Anastasia. 2016. 'Rally around the flag and the media: case of economic sanctions', *Demokratizatsiya: The Journal of Post-Soviet Democratization*, 24: 327–50.

Klumbytė, Neringa. 2010. 'The Soviet sausage renaissance', *American Anthropologist* 112: 22–37.

Kusimova, Tamara. 2019. 'The (re-)invention of new Russian cuisine: Gastropolitics in the post-embargo Moscow'. Master's thesis, Central European University. http://www.etd.ceu.edu/2019/kusimova_tamara.pdf.

Lamont, Michele. 1992. *Money, Morals, and Manners: The culture of the French and the American upper-middle class*. Chicago: University of Chicago Press.

Lamont, Michèle. 2012. 'Toward a comparative sociology of valuation and evaluation', *Annual Review of Sociology* 38: 201–21.

Laruelle, Marlene. 2016. 'The three colors of Novorossiya, or the Russian nationalist mythmaking of the Ukrainian crisis', *Post-Soviet Affairs* 32: 55–74.

Ledeneva, Alena. 2013. *Can Russia Modernise? Sistema, power networks and informal governance*. New York: Cambridge University Press.

Ledeneva, Alena. 2014. 'Economies of favors or corrupt societies?', *Baltic Worlds* (blog), 29 April. Accessed 10 March 2021. https://balticworlds.com/economies-of-favors-or-corrupt-societies/.
Mamonova, Natalia. 2016. 'Naive monarchism and rural resistance in contemporary Russia', *Rural Sociology* 81: 316–42.
Mamonova, Natalia. 2019. 'Understanding the silent majority in authoritarian populism: What can we learn from popular support for Putin in rural Russia?', *Journal of Peasant Studies* 46: 561–85.
Mamonova, Natalia and Jaume Franquesa. 2019. 'Populism, neoliberalism and agrarian movements in Europe: Understanding rural support for right-wing politics and looking for progressive solutions', *Sociologia Ruralis* 60: 710–31.
Mamonova, Natalia and Lee-Ann Sutherland. 2015. 'Rural gentrification in Russia: Renegotiating identity, alternative food production and social tensions in the countryside', *Journal of Rural Studies* 42: 154–65.
Manning, Paul and Ann Uplisashvili. 2007. '"Our beer": Ethnographic brands in postsocialist Georgia', *American Anthropologist* 109: 626–41.
Matthews, Owen. 2016. 'Moscow is enjoying a wonderfully unexpected renaissance of local cuisine', *Newsweek*, 24 January. Accessed 10 March 2021. https://www.newsweek.com/2016/02/05/strange-delightful-renaissance-moscow-cuisine-418847.html.
McMichael, Philip. 2009. 'A food regime genealogy', *Journal of Peasant Studies* 36: 139–69.
Merton, Robert King. 1976. *Sociological Ambivalence and Other Essays*. New York: Free Press.
Milliken, P. Jane. 2010. 'Grounded theory'. In *Encyclopedia of Research Design*, edited by Neil Salkind, 548–53. Thousand Oaks, CA: SAGE.
Mintz, Sidney W. 1986. *Sweetness and Power: The place of sugar in modern history*. New York: Penguin Books.
Mintz, Sidney W. and Christine M. Du Bois. 2002. 'The anthropology of food and eating', *Annual Review of Anthropology* 31: 99–119.
Monterescu, Daniel. 2017. 'Border wines: Terroir across contested territory', *Gastronomica* 17: 127–40.
Nemtsov, Alexandr and Denny Vågerö. 2011. *A Contemporary History of Alcohol in Russia*, translated by Howard M. Goldfinger. Stockholm: Södertörns Högskola.
Ochs, Elinor, Clotilde Pontecorvo and Alessandra Fasulo. 1996. 'Socializing taste', *Ethnos* 61: 7–46.
Oushakine, Serguei Alex. 2000. 'The quantity of style: Imaginary consumption in the new Russia', *Theory, Culture & Society* 17: 97–120.
Peace, Adrian. 2008. 'Terra madre 2006: Political theater and ritual rhetoric in the slow food movement', *Gastronomica* 8: 31–9.
Philippon, Daniel. 2015. 'How local is slow food?', *RCC Perspectives* 1: 7–12.
Phillips, Lynne. 2006. 'Food and globalization', *Annual Review of Anthropology* 35: 37–57.
Pietrykowski, Bruce. 2004. 'You are what you eat: The social economy of the slow food movement', *Review of Social Economy* 62: 307–21.
Pratt, Jeffrey. 2008. 'Food values: The local and the authentic'. In *Hidden Hands in the Market: Ethnographies of fair trade, ethical consumption, and corporate social responsibility*, edited by Geert de Neve, 53–70. Bingley: Emerald Group Publishing.
Radaev, Vadim. 2017. 'Crooked mirror: The evolution of illegal alcohol markets in Russia since the late socialist period'. In *The Architecture of Illegal Markets: Towards an economic sociology of illegality in the economy*, edited by Jens Beckert and Matías Dewey, 218–41. Oxford: Oxford University Press.
Radaev, Vadim, Yana Roshchina and Daria Salnikova. 2020. 'The decline in alcohol consumption in Russia from 2006 to 2017: Do birth cohorts matter?', *Alcohol and Alcoholism* 55: 323–35.
Rozin, Paul. 1990. 'Acquisition of stable food preferences', *Nutrition Reviews* 48: 106–13.
Rozin, Paul. 1996. 'Sociocultural influences on human food selection'. In *Why We Eat What We Eat: The psychology of eating*, edited by Elizabeth D. Capaldi, 233–63. Washington, DC: American Psychological Association.
Rozin, Paul, Matthew B. Ruby and Adam B. Cohen. 2007. 'Food and eating'. In *Handbook of Cultural Psychology*, edited by Dov Cohen and Shinobu Kitayama, 447–8. New York: Guilford Press.
Schrad, Mark Lawrence. 2014. *Vodka Politics: Alcohol, autocracy, and the secret history of the Russian state*. Oxford: Oxford University Press.

Skvirskaja, Vera. 2018. '"Russian merchant" legacies in post-Soviet trade with China: Moral economy, economic success and business innovation in Yiwu', *History and Anthropology* 29: 48–66.

Smelser, Neil J. 1998. 'The rational and the ambivalent in the social sciences', *American Sociological Review* 63: 1–16.

Smith, Alison Karen. 2011. *Recipes for Russia: Food and nationhood under the tsars*. DeKalb: Northern Illinois University Press.

Smith, Alison Karen. 2012. 'National cuisines'. In *The Oxford Handbook of Food History*, edited by Jeffrey M. Pilcher, 444–60. New York: Oxford University Press.

Tikhonova, Natalia. 2016. 'Vozmozhnosti i Modeli Potrebleina Srednego Klassa' [Opportunities and consumption patterns of the middle class]. In *Sredniy Klass v Sovremennoi Rossii: Opyt Mnogoletnikh Issledovaniy* [The middle class in contemporary Russia: based on the experience of many years of research], edited by Natalia Tikhonova and Konstantin Gorshkov, 80–107. Moscow: Ves' Mir.

Tikhonova, Natalia. 2019. 'Rossiiskiy Sredniy Class v Focuse Ranzyh Teoreticheskih Podhodov: Granitsy, Sostav i Specifika' [The Russian middle class through different theoretical approaches: boundaries, composition and specificity]. Presented at the Conférence franco-russe 'La dynamique des classes moyennes, entre expansion et incertitudes', Moscow, 3 October 2019. Accessed 10 March 2021. https://isp.hse.ru/data/2019/10/04/1541835897/03%20Natalia%20 Tikhinova_03-10-2019_RU.pdf.

Trubek, Amy B. 2008. *The Taste of Place: A cultural journey into terroir*. Berkeley: University of California Press.

Tsing, Anna. 2009. 'Supply chains and the human condition', *Rethinking Marxism* 21: 148–76.

Wegren, Stephen K. 2014. 'The Russian food embargo and food security: Can household production fill the void?', *Eurasian Geography and Economics* 55: 491–513.

Wegren, Stephen K., Alexander M. Nikulin and Irina Trotsuk. 2017. 'The Russian variant of food security', *Problems of Post-Communism* 64: 47–62.

Wegren, Stephen K., Alexander Nikulin and Irina Trotsuk. 2018. *Food Policy and Food Security: Putting food on the Russian table*. Lanham, MD: Lexington Books.

Weiss, Allen. 2011. 'Authenticity', *Gastronomica* 11: 74–7.

Weiss, Brad. 2012. 'Configuring the authentic value of real food: Farm-to-fork, snout-to-tail, and local food movements', *American Ethnologist* 39: 614–26.

Yormirzoev, Mirzobobo, Ramona Teuber and Tongzhe Li. 2019. 'Food quality vs food patriotism: Russian consumers' preferences for cheese after the food import ban', *British Food Journal* 121: 371–85.

Part III
Resistance to domination and empowerment in the economy: An individual perspective

15
Everyday politics of consumption: Why cynical consumers are disappointed citizens – the case of Moscow during the economic crisis of 2014–2017

Regina Resheteeva

Introduction

Consumer grievances – about rising prices and limited choice, for instance – can be experienced as emergencies demanding an immediate response on the behalf of both the government and consumer-citizens (McCormack 2015). General economic instability reinforces citizens' doubts about the legitimacy of both the market order and the political regime that maintains it. According to national surveys over the last two decades, rising prices were named as the most troubling social problem in Russia, consistently beating corruption, unemployment and other popular sources of discontent.[1] Russians interpret consumer experiences as just another facet of politics and evaluate the political system based on their consumer perceptions (Shevchenko 2008). The consumer realm is closely intertwined with political reality: good governments care for their citizen-consumers' well-being and would not let them feel vulnerable and deprived.

Economic grievances and severe restrictions in consumer choices can trigger public discontent and a political outcry (Thompson 1971; Kozminski 1991; Mazurek and Hilton 2007). The readiness of Russians to publicly protest against economic problems and falling standards of living during the 1998 and 2008 crises confirmed this approach.[2] The most recent (2014–17) crisis, however, stands out. During this period indicators of 'protest potential' in relation to economic deprivation have decreased sharply, demonstrating that Russians are not willing to participate in protests on account of the economic downturn. It is possible that the patriotic surge after the annexation of Crimea in 2014 discouraged Russians from protesting (Goode 2016). One may assume that political apathy backed up by the patriotic surge has suppressed anxieties in the consumer sphere. But is it possible that one of the most severe periods of economic turbulence in Russia for the past 20 years had no effect on consumers' subjectivity?[3] Did rising prices and decreasing incomes in 2014–17 really have limited to no impact on ordinary citizens?

There is a growing body of research that breaks down the idea of an apathetic and apolitical Russian society (Erpyleva and Magun 2014). This is possible if we examine events through a different analytical lens and look beyond classical forms of political expression and see how ordinary life contains elements that prompt us to rethink political and social hierarchies. Politicization in a pragmatic politics framework can be viewed as the 'process of linking and aligning one's everyday life with developments in society and politics at large' (Clément and Zhelnina 2020, 145). Consumption is a part of the predictable world of everyday life associated with monotony and organized passivity, but at the same time it is an accessible platform for resistance to the dominant order (Trentmann 2006; 2007). For ordinary citizens the consumer realm is an approachable medium to reflect on the social world and the power ambivalence within it.

Studies explaining consumer behaviour during the 2014–17 crisis in Russia describe a process of consumption simplification (Kotelnikova and Radaev 2017; Mareeva 2017; Kozyreva and Smirnov 2018). Mass surveys show that Russians usually reduce spending in order to get by, buy less, purchase lower-quality products or cheaper alternatives or combine all these strategies. The same coping strategies were observed during the previous economic shocks (1998 and 2008). Even though fixed questionnaires help to detect trends, they fail to capture seemingly trivial interpretations and meanings in everyday life. I want to focus on consumer perception and meaning-making processes because consumer experiences are filtered through various interpretive frameworks (Zerubavel 2009). While focusing on micro-level meaning-making, I acknowledge that interpretive schemes employed in everyday life are shaped by more general cultural meanings.

In the present chapter, I want to show that neither macro-level categories of political protest nor crisis coping can explain a more subtle political rationale in consumers' lifeworlds. Instead, by employing the more flexible framework of pragmatic politics, we can see the intricacies of power ambivalence in consumer perception. I aim to present the 'multidimensional nature of ambivalence' from consumers' perspective and highlight how the state and the market provoke this ambivalence (Hillcoat-Nalletamby and Phillips 2011, 204). How do consumers perceive the connection between daily life experiences and the political and social order? How do consumers rationalize market disturbances during crises? In what ways do political claims and evaluations appear in consumers' daily routines? By using qualitative data, I want to provide insights into the political dimension of consumer experiences during the 2014–17 period and suggest a more general socio-cultural context that shaped those perceptions.

The chapter proceeds in four sections. In the first section I will briefly outline theoretical discussions about the politics of consumption and the analytical benefits of using the culturally specific approach of pragmatic politics. In the following three empirical sections I will start with the perceived political dimension of the economic crisis before explaining the interpretive framework used to make sense of what is happening on the market and then discussing the ambivalence of state involvement. The interpretive schemes are interconnected: reflections on one element of social reality are linked with other interpretations. I will show how consumers lump together meanings about actors at different levels. In the discussion section I will try to bridge the micro-level interpretive schemes with the historical and cultural context that shaped consumer subordination.

Everyday politics of consumption: theoretical underpinnings

A number of social scientists emphasize that consumers use the market as a political arena and define this form of consumer involvement as 'political consumerism' (Shaw et al. 2006; Strømsnes 2009; Micheletti and McFarland 2012; Micheletti and Stolle 2012). This theoretical approach argues that the needs of self-interested consumers can encompass collective goods and political possibilities (Soper 2007; Schudson 2007). Political consumerism is a form of individualized collective action, and purchasing power becomes a tool for restoring social justice without government intervention. Political consumerism is associated with traditional political participation (Micheletti and Stolle 2012; Copeland 2014).

Without the need for external coordination from the authorities, the consumer is able to take responsibility for social change. Recognizing the need to achieve social change or alter the social balance, consumers can act both individually and collectively in their pursuit to contest some system of authority (Handelman and Fischer 2018). Thus, the market provides consumers with the potential for political expression in a creative way. For example, consumers can boycott companies that are suspected of wrongdoing (Friedman 1996). Another popular form of consumer activism is a 'buycott', which is when consumers buy from selected companies in order to reward these firms. However, consumer resistance can seek ideological and cultural change and be directed at more intangible things such as mainstream consumer sensibilities (Kozinets and Handelman 2004; Izberk-Bilgin 2010).

If we specifically look for examples of political consumerism in the Russian context, we can find fitting examples. For instance, at the beginning of 2021 opposition politician Alexey Navalny was sentenced on charges of embezzlement in connection with companies associated with the French cosmetics brand Yves Rocher. Shortly afterwards, consumers who deemed this arrest politically motivated and unjust called for a boycott of this cosmetic company via social media. Manifestations of consumer activism are extremely important in the context of the changing political landscape in Russia. These acts and the rationale for them deserve to be acknowledged and studied. However, this is only the tip of the iceberg: the complex nature of political consumerism cannot be reduced to sporadic acts of consumer activism.

Even though political consumerism captures the changing nature of political expression and civic engagement in the period of late capitalism, it fails to recognize the culturally specific meaning of political action and the institutional embeddedness of the consumer sphere. The theory of political consumerism is based on Western democratic regimes and lacks anthropological accounts of consumer subjectivity. Moreover, prior research on consumer activism explores particular consumer communities or specific ways of achieving their goals and yet ignores ordinary people with their mundane acts of consumption (Handelman and Fischer 2018). Instead, I seek to explain the variety of meaning involved in the everyday politics of consumption.

Firstly, we need to focus on everyday life and the interpretive schemes that consumers use to make sense of market reality. Mundane and seemingly trivial experiences contain within them consumers' ideas about how the economy should work. Even consumer perceptions that experts would consider 'erroneous' can influence consumer reactions and shape the general market order (Swedberg 2018). In order to unpack those meanings, we will employ a pragmatic politics approach. Pragmatic politics emerges when people make political evaluations based on their everyday experiences in their immediate environment (Clément and Zhelnina 2020). By elaborating on consumer perceptions we can detect how people make sense of political reality in consumer matters.

Secondly, we take account of the fact that consumer perceptions to some degree are shaped by collective memory – the schemata by which people understand the past and interpret the present (DiMaggio 1997). Consumer identity is a subject and object of politics in a broad sense (Trentmann 2006; 2007). If we stretch out Karl Polanyi's argument that governments shape markets, we should admit that governments mould consumers as well (Polanyi 2001). Consumers' perceptions of what is just or unjust, acceptable or unacceptable are embedded in social relations and institutions. The development of consumer subjectivity is closely intertwined with the development of the nation state, with the result that national consumer identity reflects local civil norms (Cohen 2004; Trumbull 2006; Bevir and Trentmann 2007; Hilton 2007). That is why in the discussion section we plan to bridge micro-level interpretive schemes and the historical context that produces the cultural matrix of individual consumer meanings.

Data and methodology

Using qualitative methods of analysis, we want to identify the interpretive schemes that ordinary consumers rely on, and the nuances of consumer perception. In the interviews, one can find cultural projections at the macro level: on the basis of personal stories, we can reveal the collective meanings to which the informants appeal.

Data collection and analysis were carried out following the logics of grounded theory (Charmaz 2006). The first stage of the research is the collection and analysis of the in-depth interviews. After that, data collection and analysis are alternated with theoretical comprehension, determining the course of the final conceptualization. Categories and subcategories obtained at the first stage and data analysis were supplemented with subsequent theoretical conceptualization. Recent developments in the field of grounded theory suggest that setting out one's theoretical intuitions at the empirical stage is an advantage, contrary to what the creators of the method believed (Timmermans and Tavory 2012). The main goal of a grounded theory – the formation of new theories – is possible provided the researcher cannot integrate the results obtained into existing theories and therefore is forced to revise them.

The research uses data from 54 in-depth interviews collected in different periods. Initially, the data were collected from May to December 2014, at the beginning of the economic crisis; the second round of data collection was in summer 2015 and the final data gathering round was from October 2016 to March 2017, when the inflation rate slowed down.

The first stage of the analysis was based on 17 interviews, and we developed two central analytical categories – 'not to be deceived' and 'consumer proactive behavior' – and identified subcategories related to the role of the state, the social environment and the quality of goods. Next, we added to the analysis 14 more interviews, gathered in 2016. We refined the existing categories and paid closer attention to how selective savings and calculations were used to maintain informants' well-being in the market. After that, we conducted another round of data collection: 23 additional interviews in 2017. These were more focused interviews, where specific themes were clarified: forms and perceptions of savings and perceptions of state responsibility.

In grounded theory, sample design involves the intention to ensure representativeness not of social groups but of the social meanings that are used by individuals to interpret events in the surrounding world. To select respondents, the theoretically driven snowball sampling technique was used.[4] The informants were recruited through the study authors' social networks. Initially, recruiting informants was based on the snowball technique. However, using only this approach, we risked limiting ourselves only to people of a similar social status. To move beyond the homogeneous group in our social circles, we used multiple entry points into the field and sought to maximize variation in the characteristics of the people whose experiences are represented in the study. Additionally, through the weak ties of the researchers, we tried to reach informants from vulnerable social groups, as well as informants with a high socio-economic status. To obtain a saturated description and reduce the possibility of selection bias associated with snowball sampling, maximum heterogeneity was ensured in other socio-demographic characteristics (informants were aged between 21 and 70 years; 34 informants identified themselves as females and 20 as males).

The analysis of the interviews began with open coding (paragraph by paragraph and line by line of the transcript). Coding reflects emotional assessments, value statements, cause-and-effect relationships and so forth (Saldaña 2015). The next stage of the analysis was selective coding. Comparing interviews and primary categories made it possible to form a continuum of categories and clarify the relationships between them (the stage of axial coding). Continuous categorization is essential for the selection and elaboration of core categories. To structure the coding results, we used situational maps (Clarke 2003), which allowed us to structure the links between categories and subcategories.

Reliving through crisis: forms of powerlessness

In the beginning of the crisis, we detected an acute reaction to the rising prices. Natalia is a young woman working as a brand manager for an international company with a steady income. Our interview took place in December 2014 during the sharp devaluation of the rouble.

> How is it fair that, only a couple months ago, I booked a tour to Courchevel [expensive ski resort in France] and now I should take instant noodles with me in order to get by on my vacation at a luxurious resort? I have instantly become poor and I have absolutely no control over this. They made the decisions [referring to politicians and the annexation of Crimea], but why do I have to suffer?

In the beginning of the crisis, feelings of powerlessness were especially acute for those who had been socialized during the establishment of the market economy and for whom it was their first crisis as a grown-up. The sudden change in their life chances was emotionally articulated by younger people from the middle and upper classes. They described the crisis situation as unjust and unfair. During their life trajectories, they have achieved relative stability and prosperity, but this was crushed by external forces they have no control over. Ordinary things such as travelling, ordering clothes from abroad and buying international products became less affordable or even out of reach almost at once. But all those consumer choices were building blocks for the perception of a 'good life'.

The crisis for young middle-class people in their late 20s and early 30s became a threat to their identity and to a certain extent to their ontological security. The crisis highlighted a perceived sense of powerlessness: they suddenly realized that their lives and well-being can easily be manipulated. If the crisis was perceived as a 'side-effect of political ambitions and mistakes' made by particular actors, the informants described how they blamed officials for the situation. Deprived of their agency, informants expressed great dissatisfaction with government decisions. In line with this reasoning, crisis was an option chosen by those who would not be affected by it, and those who rule the country would not be deprived. Some people expressed their feelings through metaphors of 'being violated by someone in power', meaning that they perceived themselves as expendable instruments in political 'games' that hardly even concern them.

We also traced powerlessness in the narratives of older people, but this powerlessness was of a different nature. They also felt disappointment with rising prices and lowering living standards, but this crisis was just another one in their lifetimes. The interpretation structure of the older generation's narratives is slightly different. Firstly, older people described crises more mildly than younger people. While expressing concern and frustration with the habitual objects of the lifeworld (i.e., product prices and product quality), they normalized this situation with their familiarity with similar situations in the past: 'It happens all the time, nothing new.' This crisis was just another unfortunate turn of events during the course of their lives. In contrast with young people in their late 20s to early 30s, they had lived through structural transformation following the collapse of the Soviet Union and struggled through the transition period with several economic crises. The experience of reliving periods of crisis equipped people with cognitive resilience and the preparedness for things to go down. So, the consumer identities of the older generations have been forged by the routinized uncertainties of everyday life (Shevchenko 2008). Thus, previous hardship experience has created habits of anticipation – a cognitive shield that allows them to navigate crises more steadily. They still feel powerless, but it is not a disarming and disorienting feeling: it is an accustomed state.

States of crisis relatively quickly become the new normality and background idea. During our second round of interviews crisis is rarely mentioned and, in some cases, is not even identified as a source of economic hardship. Everyday life still contains political evaluations and ideas about market functioning, but 'crisis' appears to be more intangible in nature. It was easy for respondents to blame or praise politicians but more difficult for them to grasp the effects of the crisis. In some interviews we traced how respondents used more convenient and acceptable substitutes for 'crisis'. For example, while explaining the current consumer situation or analysing what had changed over the past years, informants referred to the 'usual' or 'natural' rise in prices that happens each year. Others perceived crisis as 'something that happened with dollar/oil prices'.

We do not think that crisis trauma just fades away. Rather it is cognitively costly to stay in a disrupted moment; everyday life requires coherence and predictability. The crisis influenced the situational settings for many people but eventually became part of the new normality to such a degree that it is not even noticeable. This idea that perpetual crisis is a normal state of affairs in the country is widespread: 42 per cent of Russians agree that Russia is always in crisis.[5] It is hard for those who are not experts or do not have special training to make sense of the phenomenon of crisis. It is experienced not as an extraordinary event but as a continuous state of being, part of the surrounding environment.

Cynical consumers and perceived power imbalance

Crisis is a difficult and abstract category to make sense of, but it is easier to label and grasp its consequences. A particularly acute consumer reaction is caused by price rises when they seem hard to justify. For example, Natalia gave the following explanation for the hike in prices. I asked whether she had noticed anything different when casually shopping for necessities. In this small passage she confronts different market actors (international and local producers) and tries to make sense of what is happening. Her reasoning is built around different kinds of products that allow her to navigate rights and wrongs on the market.

> Why should I blame Apple for doubling iPhone prices? They do not care about some distant country and its problems and why should they? They just mechanically reacted to the increase in the currency exchange rate. But I do have questions to nut producers in my local store. Why did they suddenly decide to double the price as well? Do they have international loans or production sites abroad? No, they just pick damn nuts in a Siberian forest, that's all. They have no business operations in dollars. I even looked at the date of production: it was before all this was even happening [meaning the start of economic crisis]. So why should I pay double just because they [nut producers] decided to profit quietly ['*pod shumok*'] from this situation?

Trying to decode the price composition, she feels deceived. If consumers perceive prices as unfair, they will interpret this as opportunistic behaviour on the part of the seller. Unfair prices do not necessarily overlap with expensive prices that consumers cannot afford. In Natalia's case, an iPhone is expensive, but this price change is justifiable. By contrast, nuts are affordable but, even so, their price triggers an emotional reaction and disapproval. In the end, price unfairness is interpreted in the light of the ill intentions of those who set it. So, as it is derived from the behaviour of a market actor, price perception is a judgement tool for ascribing blame.

The moral evaluation of the market itself reflects what a society, or a group, defines as good or bad, legitimate or inappropriate (Fourcade and Healy 2007). In these settings, blunt speculation with prices corresponds with liberal market reasoning but violates social obligations and norms, and so it is criticized by consumers. Enduring circumstances that continuously seem to crush consumers' expectations of fair trade, our interviewees voiced feelings of being vulnerable before the market system, but not in a sense that they could do nothing; rather, they were aware of the power imbalance in favour of sellers. In their perception market players were able to just switch prices without thinking about the consumers' needs.

Accounting for the 'fairness' of the purchase, consumers expect a 'righteous' and 'just' market exchange where each party seeks benevolent and equal relations. Our informants described the behaviour of market players using words such as 'cashing in', 'robbing', 'profiteering' and so on. Basically, in consumers' perceptions sellers have the potential to limit their freedom of choice. In these ambiguous situations, a seller benefits from power asymmetry on the market: they 'seized the opportunity to profit' and 'take advantage when they can'. Crisis was a trauma that happened to all Russians, so in a way consumers expected some sort of compassion from market players and judged those who refused harshly.

Although suspicion was a dominant frame within which to describe sellers' behaviour, the repertoires of critical accounts took different forms. We found that informants with experience of working in sales and accounting expressed their relationship with sellers more mildly – in terms of rivalry. These people acknowledge that the interests of market players and consumers do not align and therefore each party has a right to pursue their own interests. Others in our study articulated more severe forms of opposition and disapproval. The conflictual nature of the relationship between sellers and consumers was most notably expressed by people with a high level of financial prosperity. Poorer respondents felt more vulnerable: they have to struggle to survive and sustain the illusion of well-being. More privileged informants echoed similar sentiments, although it was provoked by a different set of situations. Instead of complaining about food prices in a local shop, they complained about the cost of expensive wine or airplane tickets.

Drawing on Peter Sloterdijk's reflections on 'cynical reason', we suggest the category of 'consumer cynicism', as it captures both the suspicion and the disappointment expressed in the interviews (Sloterdijk 1988). Consumer cynicism is triggered by the lack of transparency in market transactions (different prices for the same product, immeasurable quality of the products, etc.) and/or negative experiences (overpaying, buying bad-quality products, etc.).

The ambivalence of cynicism among consumers stems from simultaneously knowing that you could be deceived and not knowing when it will happen. And yet in our interview data we observe how being prepared to be deceived is naturalized as an integral part of the market realm. In some cases, it can be interpreted in emotional terms, but it was also just taken as a given as to the way things work, without any emotional condemnation. Thus, consumer cynicism is not necessarily a disadvantage but can actually work as a cognitive defence mechanism. Being prepared to be deceived allows consumers to feel protected instinctively.

Adopting a cynical standpoint implies a tension between hegemonic powers and the oppressed (Sloterdijk 1988). In our analysis we see that consumer cynicism entails victimhood. By admitting the immanent possibility for deceit, consumers at the same time perceive themselves as the disadvantaged party in a market transaction. Consumer cynicism reflects power subordination. But this power imbalance does not mean that consumers do not try to challenge this hierarchy. Feeling exposed, consumers in our study equate inaction with surrender. In consumers' perception, if you know the game is rigged, you should act to preserve your status and minimize possible harm. Thus, subordination is far from acceptance and consumer cynicism provokes defensive and creative forms of resistance. This process of 'shifting powers' once again indicates the ambivalence of the perceived consumer position within the market (Hillcoat-Nalletamby and Phillips 2011).

Ambiguities of the state's defence in consumer perception

Previous studies have shown that periods of crisis simply intensify the demand for government protection (Sirotkina and Semenov 2019). But what is the rationale behind this expectation? In our interview data we saw how several analytical steps in the narrative would take a person from discussing something trivial, such as the price of cheese, to reflecting on state responsibility. The government deeply infiltrates the consumer world. References to the state emerged alongside a seller's perceived transgressions. This can partly be explained by consumers' habitual feelings of disappointment and rationalized suspicion that requires the state's attention. But it does not imply that the state is solely regarded as a saviour from market injustice.

Anna, who is an office worker with a relatively low income, evaluates the state's efforts and attitude towards citizens based on mundane consumer experience.

> I trust our government, but I understand that it is not ubiquitous and that I still can encounter bad-quality products. So, I think that the government should launch special raids more frequently in order to control business. If I trust the government, it means that I believe that I can buy proper quality, natural products everywhere. But I doubt that I can. So, it means that I do not fully trust our government.

Note how Anna starts by saying one thing and finishes saying the complete opposite. Trust relationships are fluid, especially if we are talking about abstract entities such as the government. This passage implies that trust in the government has different layers of meaning and is linked to the market (in particular, product quality). Complete trust is associated with full market predictability, and Anna again uses the quality of products as a measurable reference point. In Anna's case negative experiences with the quality of products is sufficient reason to question not only a store's integrity, but also the government's power.

Indeed, the government is perceived as an arbitrator between consumers and market players; the consumers in our research in fact demanded that their interests be defended by a regulator. Our interview data suggest two forms of 'defence': guidance and punishment. Financially deprived informants demanded more radical forms of government involvement, namely, disciplinary inspections aimed at punishing and frightening sellers. Financially stable informants expect transparency from the regulator, allowing them to make their own choices.

Unsatisfying consumer experiences can easily lead to disappointment with state politics and political figures, in particular. However, the simultaneous desire to be protected and the critical evaluation of the state's efforts generate ambivalence. In our interview data we were able to detect two distinct interpretive schemas.

Firstly, consumers' evaluations of the state emerge directly from their reasoning about market players' possible transgressions. From this perspective, the government is deemed a consumer guardian, defending them from sellers' manipulation. Evaluations of the state's efforts could range from disappointment that it does not perform controlling functions to the simple acknowledgement that the state is essential for overall market order and consumer safety. Either way, the state is perceived as a powerful entity that reacts swiftly and smooths tensions. And even dissatisfaction with the work of the government is linked to the belief that the state cares but fails to deliver.

The second interpretive schema is slightly different: consumers link the state directly to the market even without accounting for market players' actions. This type of reasoning is based on the perception that consumer problems are caused by the government's indifference. Here violations by market players are perceived as less serious than the government's failure to take sufficient action. The government has already failed by allowing something like this to happen in the first place. It does not imply the Soviet model of the planned economy, but this reasoning implies that the state has a profound role in ensuring a secure market space and making it predictable for ordinary consumers.

Discussion: institutional roots of consumer subordination

An economic crisis makes a great case study for examining the political dimension of the everyday world of consumers. The pragmatic politics approach assumes that ordinary people are 'rarely either totally politically active or apolitical throughout their entire lives' (Clément and Zhelnina 2020, 145). Any disruption in the social order requires people to repair the breach and provokes an intensive rationalization process on the part of consumers. But these interpretive frameworks have cultural priors. What consumers deem as just or unjust and their predispositions towards the market are embedded in a national institutional context. In addition, consumer identities bear an imprint from the collective past: cultural classifications can direct how consumers feel in the present (Trentmann 2006).

We can assume that habitual suspicion is a structural constraint, forging consumers' identities. The idea that market agents put their own interests above consumers' interests is a social norm. National surveys confirm pervasive distrust on the part of Russians towards business enterprises. In 2019, almost 75 per cent believed that small businesses should not be trusted, and people are even more sceptical about big companies. Further studies confirmed that distrust towards business does not depend on age, education level or even income (Kozyreva and

Smirnov 2017). Scholars argue that trust is a glue that holds society together and reduces uncertainty (Gambetta 1988; Sztompka 1999). However, we argue that habitual suspicion can equally serve as a uniting force. The notion of 'consumer cynicism' allows us to reveal the nuanced ambivalence of consumers' standing and to look beyond the simple dichotomy of trust–distrust.

We also argue that the ambivalence of consumers' perceived position has a broader socio-structural explanation. Consumer–seller antagonism and opposition have a long tradition in the consumer realm in Russia. The disposition of institutionalized trust relations depends upon the cultural and historical context, or, as Luhmann argues, trust is the product of local or national cultural systems (Luhmann 1988). Consumers' suspicion corresponds with the cynical components of Russian culture, inherited from the Soviet period. Although in Soviet times consumer problems were rooted in the state production system,[6] it was against traders as an independent group that ordinary consumers' suspicion was directed. Power asymmetry in favour of the seller was an integral part of the Soviet economy.

The conflict between consumers and sellers becomes a recognizable element of cultural memory. Consumer problems become the object of satire in popular culture, firmly entrenched in normative attitudes. Almost every feature film of the Soviet era contains a depiction of unfair trade as part of everyday life for Soviet people (Fedorova 2014). Films as cultural artefacts capture recognizable events of everyday reality and indicate elements of collective memory.

Consumer vulnerability and subordination in market relations was consolidated in Soviet times. Due to the systematic violation of the terms of exchange, the stigma of guilt was assigned to the seller. A closed consumer system with a fixed distribution of roles was formed: a seller endowed with power, who was both an agent of the state and an independent store entity; consumers who were forced to put up with an uneven distribution of power and were able to respond by making complaints; and a state that cared about global issues and claimed to be an impartial arbiter, a third party.

During the Soviet period the state managed to partially distance itself from consumer attacks by building a system of assistance to 'victims' of the actions of trade workers. Examining consumer complaints, the state played the role of an arbiter, protecting the interests of the consumer. The institutionalization of consumers' dissatisfaction was an important line of political work during the Soviet (Gurova 2006; Randall 2008; Vihavainen 2015) and post-socialist periods (Shevchenko 2008). Official consumer complaints reflected the paternal model of dependence of the citizens on the authorities, which was an organic part of the idea of Soviet societal structure (Bogdanova 2015).

Times have changed, but routine acts of consumption maintain the 'concrete shape of understandings that are profoundly moral and political in their nature' (Shevchenko 2008, 90). We argue that 'consumer cynicism' is a mode framing consumer perceptions of their interactions with key actors in the market. Our work shows that the asymmetry that existed in the market during the Soviet era favouring sellers has not disappeared, despite the shift to the market economy. Even though consumers in Russia now have much more power compared with the Soviet past, they still identify themselves as victims or potentially disadvantaged parties.

This power ambivalence explains why Russian consumers do not boycott or buycott to the same extent and as effectively as in the West but rather look for ways not to be deceived – their proactivity and creativity go in a completely different direction. Again, if we look back, we can trace some of the structural similarities that contribute to understanding consumer cynicism in Russia. In Soviet culture, the trickster – an admired character – employs guile, double-thought, mimicry and cynicism to survive the ordeals of everyday life (Lipovetsky 2010). All these qualities were practical and necessary for ordinary Soviet people, waiting in numerous lines to buy essential products or acquiring goods through informal exchanges (Ledeneva 1998).

Studies in marketing, for example, claim that defensive consumer cynicism should be regarded as a psychological coping strategy to protect oneself from corporate persuasion attempts (Chylinski and Chu 2010; Odou and De Pechpeyrou 2011; Helm et al. 2015; Bertilsson 2015). These institutional features distinguish the consumer cynicism of the Russian consumer from that in the West. But we argue that consumer cynicism is not a local means of resisting excessive persuasion from retailers or advertising clutter. In the Russian context consumer cynicism has a more profound and ontological nature – it stems from power asymmetry in the market with sellers' status quo. Cynical reasoning allows consumers to maintain endurance that encourages them to keep possibilities open and avoid the pitfalls of failure. Oddly, the idea 'I knew it!' grants a feeling of safety and preparedness even in the event of disappointment.

Conclusion

Studies have shown that Russian consumers adjust to crises by simplifying expenditure and relying heavily on state support. In this chapter I tried to problematize these ideas from the perspective of everyday consumer experiences. Instead of focusing on practices, we pay closer attention to consumer perceptions and the interpretive schemes involved in this process. Consumers see abstract things in the mundane things they encounter during their routine life. Changes in prices or product quality can be used as a reference point for political evaluations. This also allows us to trace power ambivalence on the level of everyday life.

Powerlessness associated with the crisis was explained through limited agency and lack of control over the situation. At the same time, we can trace how economic crises gradually become routinized. But that does not mean that crisis displays have become unnoticeable. Individuals use more convenient elements of market reality for sense-making: recounting perceived price injustice and the guilt of market players that manipulate it. Power ambivalence manifests itself here as a form of consumer cynicism. Consumer cynicism captures both disappointments accumulated from previous experiences and suspicion towards new ones. Because of this power dynamic with market agents, consumers in our study indeed expect help from the state. But alongside demand for security comes disappointment with the perception of its absence. Exposure to market risk and preparedness to encounter deceit can be interpreted as the failure of the state to protect its citizens or ensure order. So, consumer cynicism can easily lead to a disavowal of the political realm.

Research limitations

The results of the empirical analysis are based on interviews and surveys of Moscow residents. The consumer experiences of Moscow residents may differ from those of residents of the Russian regions due to differences in living standards. Our sample includes respondents with contrasting socio-economic characteristics. However, the qualitative methodology does not allow us to generalize our findings to the population at large. One of the objectives of qualitative research is to formulate hypotheses based on the data we have at our disposal. The hypotheses that we put forward can be refined and revised based on other data.

Based on the interviews, we cannot make distinctions in relation to different market participants: often in consumer perception there are no clear boundaries between different market actors and business parties. Moreover, the scheme of references depends on the lifeworld of the informants: it was easy for someone to distinguish international companies from domestic producers, manufacturers and distributors, while others noted that the main 'problem' was with the 'entrepreneurs', because they are responsible for products and prices. In some narratives

Notes

1. Levada Center survey. Accessed 20 March 2021. https://www.levada.ru/2020/03/05/samye-ostrye-problemy-4/.
2. Levada Center survey. Accessed 20 March 2021. https://www.levada.ru/2016/09/16/protestnyj-potentsial-4/.
3. The economic crisis, which started in 2014, has posed serious financial challenges for Russians: during the first two years, prices surged by 23.5 per cent and real disposable income fell by 12.7 per cent. Moreover, national surveys have reported that people felt pessimistic about the future.
4. For example, the analysis of interviews showed that the consumer experience is not limited to the economic world alone. Political experiences also arise as a system of references. Through references to the state, the informants built their attitude towards market players. It became clear that the financial situation is not the only differentiating characteristic. Further, we tried to develop the category of 'state (ir)responsibility'. We included people with different forms of economic socialization in the sample, trying to identify breakpoints in consumer experience depending on the perception of state responsibility.
5. Levada Center survey. Accessed 20 March 2021. https://www.levada.ru/2018/09/19/krizis-1998-goda-2/.
6. Soviet consumption had been built under conditions of chronic shortage, manifested to varying degrees throughout the entire Soviet period.

both sellers and manufacturers could be merged into a monolithic group of 'entrepreneurs'.

Acknowledgements

This study was supported by the Program for Basic Research of the National Research University Higher School of Economics (HSE University).

References

Bertilsson, Jon. 2015. 'The cynicism of consumer morality', *Consumption Markets & Culture* 18(5): 447–67.

Bevir, Mark and Frank Trentmann. 2007. 'After modernism: Local reasoning, consumption, and governance'. In *Governance, Consumers and Citizens: Agency and resistance in contemporary politics,* edited by Mark Bevir and Frank Trentmann, 165–90. New York: Palgrave Macmillan.

Bogdanova, Elena. 2015. 'The Soviet consumer – more than just a Soviet man'. In *Communism and Consumerism: The Soviet alternative to the affluent society,* edited by Timo Vihavainen and Elena Bogdanova, 113–38. Leiden and Boston: Brill.

Charmaz, Kathy. 2006. *Constructing Grounded Theory: A practical guide through qualitative analysis.* London: SAGE.

Chylinski, Matthew and Anna Chu. 2010. 'Consumer cynicism: Antecedents and consequences', *European Journal of Marketing* 44(1): 796–837.

Clarke, Adele E. 2003. 'Situational analyses: Grounded theory mapping after the postmodern turn', *Symbolic Interaction* 26(4): 553–76.

Clément, Karine and Anna Zhelnina. 2020. 'Beyond loyalty and dissent: Pragmatic everyday politics in contemporary Russia', *International Journal of Politics, Culture, and Society* 33(2): 143–62.

Cohen, Lizabeth. 2004. 'A consumers' republic: The politics of mass consumption in postwar America', *Journal of Consumer Research* 31(1): 236–9.

Copeland, Lauren. 2014. 'Value change and political action: Postmaterialism, political consumerism, and political participation', *American Politics Research* 42(2): 257–82.

DiMaggio, Paul. 1997. 'Culture and cognition', *Annual Review of Sociology* 23(1): 263–87.

Erpyleva, Svetlana and Artemy Magun. 2014. *The Politics of the 'Apolitical': Citizens movements in Russia, 2012–2013.* Moscow: Novoe literaturnoe obozrenie (in Russian).

Fedorova, Milla. 2014. '"Give me the book of complaints": Complaint in post-Stalin comedy', *Laboratorium: Russian Review of Social Research* 6(3): 80–92.

Fourcade, Marion and Kieran Healy. 2007. 'Moral views of market society', *Annual Review of Sociology* 33: 285–311.

Friedman, Monroe. 1996. 'A positive approach to organized consumer action: The "buycott" as an alternative to the boycott', *Journal of Consumer Policy* 19(4): 439–51.

Gambetta, Diego. 1988. *Trust: Making and breaking cooperative relations.* Oxford: Basil Blackwell.

Goode, J. Paul. 2016. 'Love for the motherland (or why cheese is more patriotic than Crimea)', *Russian Politics* 1(4): 418–49.

Gurova, Olga. 2006. 'Ideology of consumption in Soviet Union: From asceticism to the legitimating of consumer goods', *Anthropology of East Europe Review* 24(2): 91–8.

Handelman, Jay and Eileen Fischer. 2018. 'Contesting understandings of contestation: Rethinking perspectives on activism'. In *The SAGE Handbook of Consumer Culture,* edited by Olga Kravets, Pauline Maclaran, Steven Miles and Alladi Venkatesh, 256–74. London: SAGE.

Helm, Amanda E., Julie Guidry Moulard and Marsha Richins. 2015. 'Consumer cynicism: Developing a scale to measure underlying attitudes influencing marketplace shaping and withdrawal behaviours', *International Journal of Consumer Studies* 39(5): 515–24.

Hillcoat-Nalletamby, Sarah and Judith Phillips. 2011. 'Sociological ambivalence revisited', *Sociology* 45: 202–17.

Hilton, Matthew. 2007. 'Consumers and the state since the Second World War', *Annals of the American Academy of Political and Social Science* 611(1): 66–81.

Izberk-Bilgin, Elif. 2010. 'An interdisciplinary review of resistance to consumption, some marketing interpretations, and future research suggestions', *Consumption, Markets and Culture* 13(3): 299–323.

Kotelnikova, Zoya and Vadim Radaev. 2017. 'Recomposition and levelling of consumption expenditures across four economic shocks in Russia, 1994–2014', *International Journal of Consumer Studies* 41(4): 439–48.

Kozinets, Robert V. and Jay M. Handelman. 2004. 'Adversaries of consumption: Consumer movements, activism, and ideology', *Journal of Consumer Research* 31(3): 691–704.

Kozminski, Andrzej. 1991. 'Consumers in transition from the centrally planned economy to the market economy', *Journal of Consumer Policy* 14: 351–69.

Kozyreva, Polina and Alexandr Smirnov. 2017. 'Business and the population: A lack of trust – reasons and consequences', *Polis: Political Studies* 1(1): 53–69 (in Russian).

Kozyreva, Polina and Alexandr Smirnov. 2018. 'Life in the uncertainty of a crisis society: Experience and expectations', *Sociological Studies* 6(6): 66–78 (in Russian).

Ledeneva, Alena. 1998. *Russia's Economy of Favours: Blat, networking and informal exchange.* Cambridge: Cambridge University Press.

Lipovetsky, Mark. 2010. *Charms of the Cynical Reason: The trickster's transformation in Soviet and post-Soviet culture*. Boston: Academic Studies Press.

Luhmann, Niklas. 1988. 'Familiarity, confidence, trust: Problems and alternatives'. In *Trust: Making and breaking cooperative relations*, edited by Diego Gambetta, 94–107. New York: Basil Blackwell.

Mareeva, Svetlana V. 2017. 'Consumption behavior of middle strata in times of economic crisis', *Journal of Institutional Studies* 9(1): 88–104 (in Russian).

Mazurek, Malgorzata and Matthew Hilton. 2007 'Consumerism, solidarity and communism: Consumer protection and the consumer movement in Poland', *Journal of Contemporary History* 42(2): 315–43.

McCormack, Derek. 2015. 'Governing inflation: Price and atmospheres of emergency', *Theory, Culture & Society* 32(2): 131–54.

Micheletti, Michele and Andrew S. McFarland. 2012. *Creative Participation: Responsibility-taking in the political world*. Boulder, CO: Paradigm.

Micheletti, Michele and Dietlind Stolle. 2012. 'Sustainable citizenship and the new politics of consumption', *Annals of the American Academy of Political and Social Science* 644(1): 88–120.

Odou, Philippe and Pauline De Pechpeyrou. 2011. 'Consumer cynicism: From resistance to anti-consumption in a disenchanted world?', *European Journal of Marketing* 45(11/12): 1799–808. Accessed 16 March 2022. https://doi.org/10.1108/03090561111167432.

Polanyi, Karl. 2001. *The Great Transformation: The political and economic origin of our time*. Boston: Beacon Press.

Randall, Amy E. 2008. *The Soviet Dream World of Retail Trade and Consumption in the 1930s*. Basingstoke: Palgrave Macmillan.

Saldaña, Johnny. 2015. *The Coding Manual for Qualitative Researchers*. Thousand Oaks, CA: SAGE.

Schudson, Michael. 2007. 'Citizens, consumers, and the good society', *Annals of the American Academy of Political and Social Science* 611(1): 236–49.

Shaw, Deirdre, Terry Newholm and Roger Dickinson. 2006. 'Consumption as voting: An exploration of consumer empowerment', *European Journal of Marketing* 40(9/10): 1049–67.

Shevchenko, Olga. 2008. *Crisis and the Everyday in Postsocialist Moscow*. Bloomington: Indiana University Press.

Sirotkina, Elena and Andrey Semenov. 2019. 'Economic crisis and the assessment of public effectiveness: Who bears responsibility for the economic downturn in Russia?', *Journal of Social Policy Studies* 17(2): 191–206 (in Russian).

Sloterdijk, Peter. 1988. *Critique of Cynical Reason*. Minneapolis: University of Minnesota Press.

Soper, Kate. 2007. 'Re-thinking the good life: The citizenship dimension of consumer disaffection with consumerism', *Journal of Consumer Culture* 7(2): 205–29.

Strømsnes, Kristin. 2009. 'Political consumerism: A substitute for or supplement to conventional political participation?', *Journal of Civil Society* 5(3): 303–14.

Swedberg, Richard. 2018. 'Folk economics and its role in Trump's presidential campaign: An exploratory study', *Theory and Society* 47(1): 1–36.

Sztompka, Piotr. 1999. *Trust: A sociological theory*. Cambridge: Cambridge University Press.

Thompson, Edward P. 1971. 'The moral economy of the English crowd in the eighteenth century', *Past & Present* 50: 76–136.

Timmermans, Stefan and Iddo Tavory. 2012. 'Theory construction in qualitative research: From grounded theory to abductive analysis', *Sociological Theory* 30(3): 167–86.

Trentmann, Frank. 2006. 'The modern genealogy of the consumer: Meanings, identities and political synapses'. In *Consuming Cultures, Global Perspectives: Historical trajectories, transnational exchanges*, edited by Frank Trentmann and John Brewer, 19–70. Oxford: Berg Press.

Trentmann, Frank. 2007. 'Citizenship and consumption', *Journal of Consumer Culture* 7(2): 147–58.

Trumbull, Gunnar. 2006. *Consumer Capitalism: Politics, product markets, and firm strategy in France and Germany*. Ithaca, NY: Cornell University Press.

Vihavainen, Timo. 2015. 'Consumerism and the Soviet project'. In *Communism and Consumerism: The Soviet alternative to the affluent society*, edited by Timo Vihavainen and Elena Bogdanova, 28–57. Leiden and Boston: Brill.

Zerubavel, Eviatar. 2009. *Social Mindscapes: An invitation to cognitive sociology*. Cambridge, MA: Harvard University Press.

16
Childbirth with doulas in Moscow: Between empowerment and responsibility

Masha Denisova

Introduction

Since the 1970s there has been a shift towards the de-medicalization of childbirth and a revision of what counts as 'normal' birth in the 'Western' context (McCabe 2016). Childbirth organizations emerged to represent the rights of mothers-to-be and redefine existing biomedical practices of birth (Akrich et al. 2014). Private midwifery centres, lactation specialists and doulas have emerged, while previously underground 'natural' childbirth has become mainstream (Akrich et al. 2014; Torres 2015). Although this approach encourages patient-centricity, some studies of childbirth also underline that 'natural' childbirth services are commonly commercial enterprises and do not necessarily empower women (Fedele 2016; Das 2019). While many studies have been conducted in the Western context, we lack insight into how commercial services around 'natural' birth operate in other cultural and political contexts. The present research explores how doulas, as new childbirth professionals promoting natural birth, support expectant mothers' voices in Russian maternity care.

In Russia, despite several healthcare reforms, childbirth is still largely medicalized and over-bureaucratized. Sociological research demonstrates that Russian public maternity hospitals are dominated by an 'assembly line' service, in which women do not receive proper care and emotional support (Rivkin-Fish 2005; Temkina 2014). Meanwhile, the commercial maternity care sector contributes more to the empowerment of medical professionals and does not facilitate women's active decision-making (Borozdina and Novkunskaya 2020). Therefore, the emergence of doulas might be a response to women's desire to gain more control of childbirth and their bodies. Doulas do not perform any medical manipulations but provide women with informational, emotional and physical support before, during and after delivery. Although doula support is becoming more recognized and is sometimes supported by public healthcare institutions in some countries (McLeish and Redshaw 2018), in Russia, doulas are rather new arrivals to the childbirth profession. Doula services are not institutionalized, meaning doulas are excluded from the Russian healthcare system. However, in practice, they accompany women as birth companions by using a legal loophole. In the present research, I examine relations between doulas and mothers-to-be in different birth situations in Russia: childbirth in public hospitals, childbirth in the commercial healthcare sector and homebirths. I demonstrate that doula support is characterized by several ambivalences: empowerment of mothers-to-be juxtaposed with the issue of responsibility, the indirect exercise of their professional authority and the double-expertise of their support.

The structure of the chapter is as follows. First, I introduce the relevance of doula support in the Western context and in Russia. Next, I present literature on female agency and intensive motherhood to show how mothers' well-informed choices and responsible behaviour have become prescriptive and how those norms are already present in decisions about childbirth. Then, I review sociological studies on Russian maternity care. After discussing research methodology, I explore relations between mothers and doulas by focusing on the topics of mediated agency and shared responsibilities. Finally, I address the issue of ambivalence of doula support and its effects on expectant mothers' empowerment and possible changes in Russian maternity care.

The history and relevance of doula support

Birth doulas are predominantly women who are trained to provide continuous physical, emotional and informational support to other women during pregnancy and childbirth (McLeish and Redshaw 2018, 53). By reviewing research on doulas in different countries, McLeish and Redshaw (2018, 54) show that the contemporary doula movement emerged in North America in the 1970s and derives from traditional childbirth practices, in which other women accompanied a birthing woman. They argue that, having started as grassroots activism, doulas' assistance during birth is now widespread and well-known in the United States, Europe and Australia. Unlike midwives, doulas do not perform any medical manipulations or give medical advice to their clients (McLeish and Redshaw 2018). Instead, they provide women with continuous support and patient-centred care. Many studies show that doulas also promote 'normal' or 'natural' childbirth, which they describe as birth without unnecessary medical interventions (Hunter 2012; McLeish and Redshaw 2018; Torres 2015). Studies conducted in clinical settings show that doula support during birth increases the mothers' positive experience of birth on an emotional level (feeling of empowerment and being in control; increased maternal attachment) and a physical level (reduced medical interventions, increased breastfeeding) (see Hunter 2012, 316; McLeish and Redshaw 2018, 53). Ethnographic research on doulas in the United States shows that they often play the role of a guide and an advocate in birth: doulas help their clients navigate the medical system and encourage positive communication between them and medical staff (Hunter 2012; Torres 2015). In her study, Hunter (2012, 320) argues that intimate relationships between doulas and women distinguish doulas from other healthcare personnel and make them more trusted. In the United States, doula support is often a commercial enterprise, and doulas and their clients are predominantly white middle-class women (Hunter 2012, 318). Although there are grassroots doula organizations, such as black doulas helping black mothers achieve a positive birth experience in racist hospital environments (Lakhani 2019), the dominant US doula practice focuses on a white, middle-class clientele (Kathawa et al. 2021; Lantz et al. 2005).

At the same time, from economic sociology we know that market practices are culturally and historically embedded and hence vary in different contexts (Zelizer 1994). For instance, in England, several doula volunteering projects provide unpaid support for different vulnerable groups of mothers-to-be (McLeish and Redshaw 2018), while in Sweden, a doula project sponsored by the National Public Health Committee has been launched to provide migrant mothers with the support of a doula who is socialized in the same culture as the mother-to-be (Akhavan and Lundgren 2012). In Russia, doulas are a new phenomenon and have not yet been studied. There are several doula communities and certifying organizations in Moscow and St Petersburg, although the doula service is becoming more prominent in the regions. There are 110 doulas registered with the Association of Professional Doulas, a non-governmental organization established in 2015. There are at least two other doula organizations in Moscow that provide certified courses for future doulas. Doula services are provided on a commercial basis, although there are some doula volunteering projects in state maternity hospitals aimed at supporting expectant mothers free of charge. Some maternity hospitals also provide paid doula services or, as they refer to it, psychological support, but this practice is not well established. Studies on Russian public maternity care, as well as numerous media publications, emphasize the systematic mistreatment of women (Litvinova 2018; Ozhiganova 2019; Rodina 2017) and indicate the potentiality of private healthcare to transform childbirth practices to become more patient-oriented (Borozdina 2018; Temkina 2020). The present research explores to what extent childbirth with doula support can be considered an empowering experience for mothers-to-be in the context of Russian maternity care.

'Natural' childbirth: a means of empowerment or another neoliberal ideal?

Since the 1970s, Western feminist and patients' movements against the over-medicalization of birth have embraced the idea of women's resistance. Many childbirth activists emphasize the importance of female agency and resistance to medicalized birth, which portrays women as passive and helpless. In the social sciences, the notion of agency has been traditionally conceptualized as the capacity of setting goals (intentions) based on the experience and resources available for an individual or a group (Ortner 2006; Mahmood 2001). According to anthropologist Sherry Ortner (2006, 136), agency is culturally and historically constructed. By reviewing works of different scholars, she agrees that capacity for agency is inherent in all humans but the forms and expressions of it depend on 'cultural repertoires' and hence vary widely. Research on childbirth further contributed to the conception of agency by showing the collective dimension of childbirth, in which a woman's agency is always mediated by different discourses, technologies and actors (Akrich and Pasveer 2004; Reiger and Dempsey 2006). Many women give birth in hospitals surrounded by various technical devices and medical personnel who intervene in the birthing process. Scholars also emphasize that women's minds and bodies are 'contaminated' by biomedicine that complicates their resistance to over-medicalized births (Akrich and Pasveer 2004; Coxon et al. 2014; Reiger and Dempsey 2006). Biomedicine portrays the female body as an object and pregnancy as a disorder, and hence risky for the mother's and baby's health (Coxon et al. 2014; Lupton and Schmied 2013; Parry 2008; Reiger and Dempsey 2006). It also sees women as lacking agency and the ability to give birth without medical interventions. Research shows that women tend to internalize those discourses and believe they are incapable of giving birth without medical assistance, which complicates their empowerment as patients (Coxon et al. 2014; Lupton and Schmied 2013; Reiger and Dempsey 2006).

The alternative to the biomedical image of birth is the natural childbirth approach that has been promoted and entrenched by childbirth activists and experts. This approach encourages 'normal' birth without unnecessary medical intervention and the active participation of mothers-to-be in decision-making (Parry 2008, 788). Today 'natural' or 'humanistic' perspectives on birth are applied in many Western policies and are encouraged to be followed worldwide (e.g., WHO 2018). Although a 'natural' approach to childbirth embraces the woman's agency and non-medicalized birth, in practice it is not necessarily liberating. As some research underlines, mothers-to-be can be trapped by the ideal of perfect childbirth, which prescribes that a woman is individually responsible for the success of the labour (Das 2019; Fedele 2016). Therefore, failing to achieve a positive experience of childbirth means failing to be a good mother.

To explain how childbirth becomes so central for a mother's sense of self, we should pay closer attention to the culture of neoliberal parenting that highlights mothers' authority and responsibility regarding childcare practices, including childbirth (Faircloth and Gürtin 2018; Hays 1998; Reich 2014). Scholars describe such practices using the umbrella term 'intensive motherhood'. It emphasizes that a woman should invest most of her time, energy and emotional and financial resources in raising her children (Hays 1998; Reich 2014). Intensive motherhood is closely related to the natural parenting approach with a focus on female experience and embodied knowledge (Faircloth and Gürtin 2018, 986). These cultural patterns reflect women's decisions about childbirth, where a woman starts playing the role of a reflexive and informed consumer in the maternity care market. Hence, intensive motherhood is a form of self-governance, meaning that an individual imagines herself as autonomous and responsible for her choices and life (Rose et al. 2006, 90).

In post-Soviet Russia, women are considered the main caregivers for children in the official discourse and social stereotypes. A woman is responsible for raising 'a happy child' and 'a good citizen' no matter what sacrifices it entails (Shpakovskaya 2014, 80). This ideal of motherhood translated by mass media and social media networks is usually supported by the image of a reflexive and competent mother who knows best what her children need (Shpakovskaya 2014, 80). As Susan Gal and Gail Kligman (2012) demonstrate, in post-socialist countries, state-making has been closely associated with the control of human reproduction, something that is also true for post-Soviet Russia. Russian family policy is highly gendered and pronatalist. It is mainly oriented towards increasing population and offering financial support to families with two or more children, while childcare is delegated to mothers only (Chernova 2012, 75). Women are responsible to the state for the reproduction of the nation but are left to tread this path alone (Shpakovskaya 2015, 1584).

Although numerous studies use the concept of intensive motherhood regarding childcare, less is said about how the logic of intensive motherhood penetrates women's perspectives of being 'a good mother' already in childbirth. As media researcher Ranjana Das (2019, 131) points out in her book on motherhood and the digital, 'good birthing, was very much positioned as an individual achievement, an individual responsibility and hence an individual failure when things went wrong'. By exploring British social media on natural and hypno-birth, she concludes that the ideal of 'perfect childbirth' creates unrealistic expectations of birth and the exclusion of mothers who do not fit into this ideal picture. This ideal also portrays childbirth as women's business, a celebration of womanhood, in which high value is prescribed to a large network of women (Das 2019, 89). Doula services seem to perfectly satisfy the demands of the natural childbirth ideal: women helping other women in childbirth, embracing sisterhood and 'essential' femininity. Moreover, doulas' empathy towards 'natural' birth may also contribute to the burden that mothers experience when opting for a medicalized birth. This raises the question as to the position doulas occupy between the ideals of 'natural' birth and empowerment of women.

Entering the maternity care system in Russia

Deeply rooted in the Soviet healthcare system, Russian maternity care is characterized by an 'assembly line' service, strict hierarchical structures and over-medicalization (Rivkin-Fish 2000; 2005; Temkina 2014). Despite several healthcare reforms, scholars characterize contemporary maternity hospitals as highly bureaucratized and incapable of providing women with proper care (Borozdina 2018; Temkina 2014). Medical personnel do not have much autonomy in decision-making, and their medical practice is accompanied by excessive paperwork and high administrative responsibility to medical standards and officials (Borozdina and Novkunskaya 2020; Novkunskaya 2014; Temkina 2014). Moreover, the relationships between obstetricians and midwives are strictly hierarchical: midwives are subordinate to doctors, who independently make decisions and carry the major responsibility (Borozdina 2018, 153). The issue of strong hierarchies is further complicated by other structural problems such as a lack of medical staff and the fact that they are systematically overworked in highly emotional settings (Borozdina 2018; Temkina 2014). Research shows that in the 1990s and the early 2000s, before the commercial services in maternity hospitals had become fully institutionalized, informal payment relations between patients and doctors were perceived by participants as moral correctives to problems inherited from the Soviet healthcare system (Temkina and Rivkin-Fish 2020). As Ledeneva shows in her studies of informal practices in Russia, informality serves as an alternative system of governance to formal constraints, providing actors with pockets of freedom (Ledeneva 2018). While being deprived of proper care in official healthcare provision, women opted for informal practices to exercise their choices and compensate for the structural gaps in healthcare provision.

The composition and possibilities of care are different in the private maternity care sector. Starting from the late 2000s, the schema of 'personal doctor' relationships became official and women were given the chance to choose any maternity hospital (Temkina and Rivkin-Fish 2020). Commercial services provided in state hospitals or private midwifery centres (so-called paid childbirth) allow women to choose medical personnel to assist them in labour and enjoy other facilities such as a private room, bathtub and so on. However, even in the commercial sector, medical professionals assume the main responsibility for decision-making and keep a professional and emotional distance from the client (Borozdina 2018, 161; Temkina 2018). Women, at the same time, acknowledge medical authority and power, delegating the management of delivery to a doctor (Temkina 2018, 222). Together the doctors' paternalistic attitudes and the professional logics of the domination of medical expertise restrict women's freedom of choice.

Unlike midwives and obstetricians, doulas occupy a position outside the hierarchy of the medical system. They come to the hospital as a woman's birth companion, although their service is not fully legalized in Russia, which locates their work in the 'grey zone'. In the maternity hospital, a woman can be accompanied only by a close relative, excluding doulas (St. 51 Federal Law RF No 323 2011). However, in practice, a doula may claim to be a woman's relative and enter the hospital. Since a doula is not part of the medical system, it is possible to imagine that by using doulas' services, women are trying to find new ways to gain more power and protection during childbirth. Despite everything, the fee for doula assistance ranges from 18,000 to 25,000 roubles,[1] that is, several times cheaper than paid contracts with midwives and obstetricians.

Methodology

This chapter is based on two years of research. The first round of research was explanatory and included semi-structured interviews with 13 doulas, conducted in spring 2019, and four women who used doula services during childbirth.[2] I recruited doulas using the snowball technique with several entry points: through personal acquaintances, by attending a conference on childbirth and by contacting members of public doula communities on Facebook directly. This allowed me to diversify the sample by talking to doulas with different professional experience (attending births at home and in hospital, or both) and with those participating in professional doula communities and those working independently. All interviews except two (with doulas from St Petersburg and a town in the Urals) were conducted in Moscow, where the doulas' professional communities are best developed and widespread compared with other Russian cities. The doulas I talked to had specific doula certificates and experience in accompanying childbirth for at least one year. Many doulas had other jobs, which they combined with childbirth assistance. Most of them were registered as individual entrepreneurs and had written contracts with their clients.

The second round involved online interviews (due to COVID-19 restrictions) with 12 women who went through childbirth with doulas in 2018–20. Interviews with mothers were framed as birth narratives (Akrich and Pasveer 2004), in which each of the birth stages was discussed in detail and chronological order. While most informants gave birth in maternity hospitals, two did so at home with a midwife and a doula. I interviewed women who experienced childbirth one time and several times, in public hospitals (by using compulsory medical insurance) and in the commercial healthcare sector (paid contract with a hospital and a doctor/midwife), and from the middle and the working classes. I reconstructed the socio-economic class of my informants based on what type of childbirth they could afford and how they addressed money-related issues. I recruited mothers using the snowball technique by asking doulas I already knew to share with me the contacts of their clients (with their consent) and looking at public Instagram accounts on pregnancy and childbirth. The sample excluded homosexual couples and women with an 'unsuccessful' experience of childbirth with doulas, which I acknowledge as a limitation of the research. Another limitation is geographical: while in Moscow the service of doulas is well developed and well known, in smaller Russian cities the situation is likely to be different (such as fewer paid services and maternity hospitals to choose from).

Doulas mediating the mother's agency in childbirth

The women I interviewed, especially those who had experienced childbirth previously, underlined that giving birth is an unpredictable and barely controlled process. Firstly, it constitutes intensive physical exertion, usually accompanied by pain and a 'half-conscious' state of mind. Secondly, navigating Russian maternity hospitals with their many formal regulations and unspoken rules can be confusing for a woman. Therefore, my informants argued, they opted for the doula's assistance, so she would guide them through both the ambiguous system of maternity care and women's bodies-in-labour. The women I spoke to were not looking for a medical professional but rather for a trusted expert who would support them but not make decisions for them. Before concluding an agreement with a doula on childbirth assistance, women commonly had a face-to-face meeting, which my informants described as 'matching' or 'dating'. After they signed the contract or agreement, the doula and her client stayed in touch until the start of labour so as to allow them to get to know each other and establish close and trusted relations. Some of the mothers I interviewed even called their doula 'a friend' or 'a guardian angel', indicating the intimacy of their relationships and gratitude. In this section, I focus on how doulas assist women in childbirth and mediate their agency and needs in contexts of 'paid' childbirth, childbirth in public hospitals and homebirth.

'Paid' childbirth

Mothers with paid contracts with maternity hospitals emphasized that natural childbirth was the priority for them because 'it's better for the baby's health'; some women even demonized anaesthesia, expressing concern that it could cause long-lasting health complications for their babies. This type of argument presented the choice of natural childbirth as morally justifiable since prioritizing a baby's health already in childbirth makes a woman a good and responsible mother (Das 2019). In the private maternity care sector, a woman enters a consumer role, and hence she has more control over the actions of the medical staff who are expected to provide her with good service. In this case, a doula focuses more on helping a woman bear discomfort and pain by cheering her up and assisting her physically.

> I needed the doula's support in a more psychological way. In case I change my mind and want to inject myself with a bunch of anaesthesia, and I don't want it to happen, there should be a sobering agent as a doula who would tell me why I decided to go for soft childbirth. (Valentina, first childbirth, 'paid' childbirth)

Valentina, who had a paid contract with an obstetrician and a midwife, argued that she wanted a doula to help her have a fully non-medicalized birth. For her, resistance to medical assistance was mostly directed to herself, so she would not end up asking doctors for anaesthesia. She prepared herself to have 'natural' childbirth without any interventions and was not ready 'to give up'. Here, an interesting paradox emerges: giving birth naturally requires extraordinary strength on the part of a woman, extra preparations and extra support. It is not something that can be achieved easily without a strong purpose, knowledge and discipline. 'Coming back to nature' becomes another challenge for contemporary women socialized in a highly medicalized society. For instance, some of my informants believed that attending courses on childbirth and reading books and other sources of information were the only way to understand their bodies and resist the intentions of obstetricians to impose on them the need for medical stimulation. However, this resistance is never easy, especially when medicalization prioritizes medical knowledge over the embodied knowledge of a patient/woman (Torres 2015, 901). Here, a doula's expert knowledge and training served as validation of women's intentions to give birth naturally. For instance, a second-time mother, Oxana, who previously had a C-section, wanted to give birth vaginally even though it was viewed as a difficult procedure by many medical professionals she encountered. So, she signed a contract with an obstetrician who agreed to help with natural birth and a doula who shared her aspirations.

> – The doctors were urging me to have a C-section, but I resisted, because everything was fine with the child, everything was fine with me. And if I had not prepared for childbirth, if I had not known all this, I would have given in. So, if the doctor had

suggested 'a C-section', I would have said 'OK'. I would have believed them blindly without critical analysis, and everything would have ended up not the way I wanted ... At some point, my dilation stopped, and he [the doctor] said that you've been in labour for 10 hours, there's no further dilation, let's have surgery. It seems to me that if I had been alone, I would most likely have agreed, but [the doula] helped me a lot.
– **Did she help you not agree to a C-section? Did you discuss it with her?**
– No, there was no discussion. She patted me on the head and said: 'You can do it.' It was at the level of sensations like silent support. She believed in me, so did I. (Oxana, second childbirth, 'paid' childbirth)

This case provides insight into how a doula's expertise validated Oxana's experiential knowledge (Rabeharisoa et al. 2014, 133). By showing her support, the doula made Oxana's bodily sensations and knowledge legitimate and made them count as a reliable source for decision-making (at least for herself). As previous research on Russian maternity care shows, women's choices are constrained by the unequal distribution of knowledge and the paternalistic culture of the medical profession (Temkina and Rivkin-Fish 2020). Here, a doula enters the 'knowledge wars' in the maternity ward and exercises her power by recognizing women's competence in giving birth and balancing her experiential knowledge with the biomedical knowledge of the obstetrician.

Childbirth in public hospitals

Unlike women who could afford commercial services in childbirth, mothers who gave birth in public hospitals were less persuaded by unmedicalized childbirth; some of them emphasized they wanted 'natural childbirth without going to extremes' such as childbirth without any medical assistance. For them, security in childbirth was of primary importance. Due to the public image of childbirth in Russian state hospitals as abusive and full of 'horror stories' (Litvinova 2018; Rodina 2017), mothers who could not afford a paid contract needed a doula to help prevent negative situations. Women, especially those who had already had a negative experience of childbirth, called their doulas 'advocates in birth', whose presence in the maternity ward disciplined medical personnel. Although a doula had no authority to intervene in the work of medical personnel, she played the role of 'a silent witness'.

According to my informants, a doula continuously monitored the behaviour of medical staff and explained their actions to the woman, mediating between them. Women usually described how polite and professional their doulas acted with medical personnel, even though the tension between doulas and obstetricians sometimes rose to the extreme.

> When the doctor came to do the epidural, he was in a bad mood. He yelled at the entire ward, and I was having contractions, I was feeling bad. With epidural anaesthesia, you need to sit still for half an hour, and during labour, it is quite difficult. The negative atmosphere reigned, they kicked my husband out of the ward and wanted to kick out the doula, but she resisted and said that she wasn't going anywhere. They took her chair and asked: Who is this doula? Why are you here at all? And she didn't leave, she sat on the floor and said that she wasn't going anywhere and would stay there. It was super cool. (Victoria, first childbirth, childbirth in a public hospital)

Here, the doula's indirect exercise of power becomes clear. In Victoria's story, the doula could not directly intervene in the childbirth process and challenge the doctor's actions; however, she exercised her 'power of the weak' by refusing to leave Victoria alone. Therefore, while the doula's presence in childbirth cannot guarantee the absence of unwanted interventions, doulas still can provide 'silent' support to women by demonstrating their compliance with women's choices and opinions.

In the interviews with doulas, I heard many stories of humiliation and medical abuse of their clients, especially during childbirth in public hospitals. When explaining why such situations were widespread, many doulas referred to the insufficiency of the Russian maternity care system, mainly the lack of medical personnel, their long shifts and the over-bureaucratization of clinical practice. Doulas sympathized with how hard the work of medical staff was, especially midwives, who, in their opinion, suffer a lot from burnout, low salaries and the devaluation of their work. At the same time, many doulas insisted that medical professionals can and should revise their daily practices and treat women with more compassion and respect. By assisting women in state hospitals, doulas sought to challenge the culture of humiliation towards women that is part and parcel of the system of domination and control over patients in post-Soviet healthcare (Novkunskaya et al. 2021).

> The doula is here to show that you don't stop being a human once you go to the hospital, you do not stop being a woman with dignity.

> You are still subject to the law on your sexual integrity, even when you are in labour. As my colleague says: 'Why has someone decided that they can put their fingers inside us without our consent during the labour, while outside the context of birth no one would ever do that?' (Lyudmila, doula, psychologist).

According to doulas, their professional mission is not so much about supporting non-medicalized childbirth but rather achieving respectful, women-centred childbirth. While they sympathized with the natural childbirth approach, doulas recognized the importance of medical knowledge and medical authority. In the interviews, they commonly referred to clinical studies that proved the efficiency of 'natural' birth. They also deployed biomedical knowledge themselves when explaining to women what was happening with their bodies-in-labour. Doulas commonly encouraged women to view their bodies from the medical gaze, to use different apps and tests to identify the beginning of childbirth, and to interpret their feelings by means of medical language. The doula's position as a translator between women and medical staff also shows her double-expertise in biomedical and experiential knowledge. This makes doulas' professional competencies blurred and ambivalent. However, I do not consider this a disadvantage but rather see it as a source of potential. Doulas' professional support can be the bridge between a medical birth and natural birth, contributing to the transition to a more careful and women-centred system of maternity care.

Homebirth

I conducted two interviews with mothers who had had extremely negative childbirth experiences in hospital in the past and chose to have homebirths with a doula and a midwife. These women expressed a complete distrust of the healthcare system and questioned the adequacy of clinical practice in state maternity hospitals. Due to their traumatic childbirth experiences, they became involved in alternative medical practices that entrenched further their decisions to have a homebirth. Both women argued that being at home gave them a level of freedom and control in childbirth that could never have been achieved in a hospital setting. Doulas assisted the mothers from the first contractions, providing them with continuous emotional and physical support during and right after labour. One of the mothers explained that the doula followed her wishes, creating a very intimate space between the two, while the midwife intervened only to help her push and deliver the baby. By agreeing to follow women in their aspirations of homebirth, doulas also demonstrate their support of a woman's right to give birth wherever she wants that fits into the framework of 'natural' childbirth.

The birth narratives of these two mothers were characterized by a higher level of autonomy in childbirth compared with other women I spoke with, and their achieved level of agency in homebirth was likely to be higher as well. At the same time, they took much more individual responsibility given that it is illegal in Russia for medical professionals to attend homebirths (Novkunskaya 2014).

Resistance and intentionality correlate with the responsibility women take when they refuse medical interventions. In the literature on (female) agency, the aspect of responsibility is usually overlooked while the authors' attention is mainly dedicated to choices, intentionality and subjectivity (Mahmood 2001; Ortner 2006; Parry 2008). However, I argue that responsibility is the key to understanding the limitations and possibilities of the empowerment of mothers-to-be within biomedical and 'natural' systems of birth. Next, I analyse the responsibilities of women in childbirth, showing how they are enacted, shared and reflected in the doulas' and women's narratives.

Shifting responsibilities of mothers-to-be

The doulas I interviewed did not consult with the women as to what decisions they should make, emphasizing that a woman knows what is better for her. Although a doula does not take responsibility for the 'success' of childbirth, shifting it to the woman and the medical staff, she is responsible for monitoring the settings and providing physical, emotional and informational assistance. My data illustrate how responsibility is shared in childbirth, giving women enough space to play the central role in childbirth. The mothers I talked to emphasized that doulas did not interfere in their choices regarding childbirth: even if the woman decided to go with anaesthesia or other medical intervention that went beyond the ideal of natural birth, the doula supported her. Such non-judgemental behaviour on the part of a doula is a possible response to the pressure facing women to live up to the ideals of a 'good mother' and a 'perfect childbirth' (Das 2019). The doulas' ability to follow the woman's wishes mitigates the burden of responsibility on a mother-to-be, emphasizing that there are no bad choices. In other words, doulas' support can be liberating for mothers-to-be socialized in the 'intensive motherhood' culture.

When we talk about 'intensive motherhood', the socio-economic class of a woman matters, influencing how she prioritizes her needs and responsibilities in childbirth (Temkina and Zdravomyslova 2018, 167). The mothers I interviewed attended courses for pregnant women to study the 'natural' childbirth approach and socialized in online parenting forums and communities on social media, which mostly translate the values of natural parenting and childbirth as morally justifiable. Women with more financial resources could afford a paid contract with a hospital and a doctor, achieving a higher level of comfort and control. Middle- and upper-class women had higher expectations of childbirth and risked bearing heavier individual responsibility. This is because the good birthing ideal implies that childbirth is the individual responsibility of a woman: it is only she who should be responsible for the organization of childbirth or her baby's health (Das 2019, 131). If something goes wrong, it is portrayed as her failure. Hence, the responsibility of a mother-to-be becomes morally weighted.

> In childbirth, you can make many mistakes: do not breathe, but scream, thereby taking oxygen from the baby. These moments which women don't know are, of course, their own problems. A woman must learn this process herself, at least at some basic level. When my doula told me how to breathe, and I realized that it was very valuable information, it can be useful to me. (Kristina, first childbirth, 'paid' childbirth)

Kristina, an upper-class mother, was convinced that only she was primarily responsible for gaining knowledge of the birth process and its successful implementation already in labour. In her case, she gave birth so quickly 'she did not have time to enjoy the process'. The role of a doula here was to help a woman stick to the plan and, in the event that something went wrong, to reassure her she did everything she could.

> At some point, everyone begins to behave like this, and it is normal, it does not mean that you are weak or did not cope. It is just the response of your body to sensations. This helps many women understand that they did not fail this exam, because many define childbirth as an exam, and many have such an uncomfortable feeling that they did something wrong. (Evgeniya, doula, psychologist)

The doulas I spoke to also confirmed that many of their clients were preoccupied with the idea of doing everything right during labour. After childbirth, many mothers wanted to discuss their birthing experiences with the doula to make sure they 'handled it right'. To reassure women, doulas widely refer to the agency of a body that knows better how to endure. One of the doulas even emphasized that a woman's 'mind' is full of fears and anxiety generated by society that prevent her from listening to what her body is telling her during childbirth.

By encouraging mothers-to-be to trust the signals their bodies were sending them, the doulas helped them take an active part in childbirth. Many of the women I interviewed highlighted that they wanted medical professionals to respect their opinions and recognize their bodily sensations and intuition as a basis for decision-making. However, the empowerment of mothers-to-be is complicated by the institutional context of Russian maternity care. The health of a mother and a baby depends heavily on the medical professionals, who traditionally do not enjoy much autonomy in Russia (Temkina 2020, 525). In public maternity care, in which medical staff are also obliged to follow strict medical standards and protocols, it is not easy to fulfil the choices requested by mothers-to-be (Borozdina and Novkunskaya 2020). Despite everything, medical professionals bear the legal consequences if something goes wrong and are officially prohibited from assisting homebirths (Novkunskaya 2014). The institutional precarity of Russian obstetricians and midwives contributes to the constraints on mothers-to-be who want to acquire more power during childbirth. In this sense, doulas provide women with several practical tools that can be viewed as 'the weapons of the weak' in a situation where women do not have much formal power to influence the process and/or organization of birth. Doulas explain to women how to navigate maternity care hospitals, educate them about the childbirth process and teach them how to communicate with medical personnel. This explains the potentiality of doula assistance to empower mothers and challenge the hierarchies in the Russian maternity care system.

Conclusion and discussion

By locating doula services within the cultural context of 'intensive motherhood' and the institutional context of Russian maternity care, this research has contributed to the debates around natural birth, agency and the responsibilities of expectant mothers. The case of doula support in childbirth gives a unique opportunity to see the ambivalence of power in action and its potentiality to bring change in the existing structures of healthcare. Firstly, while encouraging expectant mothers' active participation in the birth and making them trust their bodies, doulas also shift the responsibilities for decisions made to women. As previous research on Russian maternity care shows, 'in the sophisticated professional domain of healthcare, the expectant mother usually does not have enough expertise to actually make informed choices' (Borozdina and Novkunskaya 2019, 449). By recognizing women's embodied knowledge as a valid source of expertise, doulas facilitate mothers' empowerment in the maternity care system. However, this empowerment is juxtaposed by the fact that doulas are not institutionally recognized as childbirth professionals. Instead, they are located in a 'grey zone' of Russian maternity care that causes ambiguity around doula assistance among medical personnel. Moreover, Russian doctors commonly do not enjoy much professional autonomy themselves, which further complicates the situations during childbirth in which mothers-to-be demand more attention to their needs. Hence, the distribution of responsibility between doulas, mothers-to-be and medical professionals is not always transparent and stable and depends a lot on particular childbirth situations.

Secondly, doulas exercise their professional authority by empowering women and extending their control over childbirth but without forcing their clients to align with the doulas' professional expertise and opinion. While not directly intervening in the decision-making of a mother-to-be, doulas exercise the power *indirectly* by sharing their knowledge and encouraging women to make decisions. The close and trusted relationship between a doula and a mother-to-be further contributed to the doulas' ability to support women's agency by *mediating* between a woman and medical staff, between a woman's body and mind.

Thirdly, the nature of doula professional support is ambivalent itself since it is characterized by the double expertise. On the one hand, doulas advocate for 'natural' childbirth and the recognition of women's experiential knowledge; they are agents outside the medical system and are trusted persons to mothers-to-be. On the other hand, doulas still largely rely on biomedical knowledge and clinical evidence, they have an insider perspective on maternity hospitals and medical professionals who share aspirations in 'natural' childbirth, and they are also agents with professional expertise and autonomy. This makes doulas constantly shift between the traditionally incompatible worlds of natural and medicalized birth, market and intimacy.

The ambivalence of doula support stems from the relations between doulas and women, and between doulas and the healthcare system. It is also embedded in the norms around 'natural' childbirth and the 'good' mother. Together it supports the relational vision of ambivalence that exists and evolves within networks of social relations and social structures (Hillcoat-Nallétamby and Phillips 2011). According to Hillcoat-Nallétamby and Phillips (2011), ambivalence can be a source for social change since it provokes negotiations and tensions between actors. In this sense, doula professional support promotes change in the existing hierarchies between mothers-to-be and doctors by facilitating mothers' empowerment. However, it is still not clear to what degree this change is stable and significant at the level of the entire healthcare system. Doulas' professional work and expertise are not fully recognized and institutionalized, which requires them to act informally. They come to the hospital as women's relatives, friends, 'psychologists' or doulas, depending on the particular situation. They do not have a formal right to intervene in medical practice and potentially can be asked to leave a ward at any time. At the same time, doulas' support can still be effective, complementing the official system of maternity care that is unable to provide women with emotional support and principles of shared decision-making between a patient and a doctor. Drawing on the scholarship of informality (Ledeneva 2018; Morris and Polese 2015), we can see how the doula's informal position in the official maternity care system fills its structural gaps, helping the system survive but also potentially changing it. It seems that doulas' support is tolerated by the official healthcare system and occasionally becomes incorporated into the work of the hospital (e.g., doulas' volunteering projects, hospitals hiring doulas).

However, there are still questions that require further exploration: can the informal support offered by doulas undermine the culture of humiliation and raise more awareness of women's needs, or must doula professional work first become institutionalized and recognized to make any improvement in the content of maternity care?

Acknowledgements

I take this opportunity to express my gratitude to the women participating in this research for sharing with me the incredible stories of their childbirth and for the trust they placed in me. This research would not have been possible without the doulas' professional community, people who welcomed me from the beginning of my research explorations. I would also like to thank my supervisors Dr Dorit Geva, Dr Vlad Naumescu and Dr Elena Berdysheva for their support and fruitful conversations through the whole research process.

References

Notes

1 This amounts to around $227–$324 at the exchange rate for autumn 2020.
2 All names of research participants have been changed. The quotations of research participants provided in the text are translated by the author.

Akhavan, Sharareh and Ingela Lundgren. 2012. 'Midwives' experiences of doula support for immigrant women in Sweden: A qualitative study', *Midwifery* 28(1): 80–5.

Akrich, Madeleine, Máire Leane, Celia Roberts and João Arriscado. 2014. 'Practising childbirth activism: A politics of evidence', *BioSocieties* 9: 129–52. Accessed 10 March 2022. https://doi.org/10.1057/biosoc.2014.5.

Akrich, Madeleine and Bernike Pasveer. 2004. 'Embodiment and disembodiment in childbirth narratives', *Body & Society* 10(2–3): 63–84. Accessed 10 March 2022. https://doi.org/10.1177/1357034X04042935.

Borozdina, Ekaterina. 2018. 'Introducing "natural" childbirth in Russian hospitals: Midwives' institutional work'. In *Health, Technologies, and Politics in Post-Soviet Settings*, edited by Olga Zvonareva, Evgeniya Popova and Klasien Horstman, 145–71. Cham: Springer.

Borozdina, Ekaterina and Anastasia Novkunskaya. 2019. 'The patient's perspective on institutional logics in Russian maternity care', *Journal of Social Policy Studies* 17(3): 439–52.

Borozdina, Ekaterina and Anastasiia Novkunskaya. 2020. 'Patient-centered care in Russian maternity hospitals: Introducing a new approach through professionals' agency', *Health: An Interdisciplinary Journal for the Social Study of Health, Illness and Medicine* 26(2): 200–20. Accessed 10 March 2022. https://doi.org/10.1177/1363459320925871.

Chernova, Zhanna. 2012. 'New pronatalism? Family policy in post-Soviet Russia', *Region* 1(1): 75–92.

Coxon, Kirstie, Jane Sandall and Naomi J. Fulop. 2014. 'To what extent are women free to choose where to give birth? How discourses of risk, blame and responsibility influence birth place decisions', *Health, Risk & Society* 16(1): 51–67. Accessed 10 March 2022. https://doi.org/10.1080/13698575.2013.859231.

Das, Ranjana. 2019. *Early Motherhood in Digital Societies: Ideals, anxieties and ties of the perinatal*. Abingdon: Routledge.

Faircloth, Charlotte and Zeynep B. Gürtin. 2018. 'Fertile connections: Thinking across assisted reproductive technologies and parenting culture studies', *Sociology* 52(5): 983–1000. Accessed 10 March 2022. https://doi.org/10.1177/0038038517696219.

Fedele, Anna. 2016. '"Holistic mothers" or "bad mothers"? Challenging biomedical models of the body in Portugal', *Religion and Gender* 6(1): 95–111. Accessed 10 March 2022. https://doi.org/10.18352/rg.10128.

Gal, Susan and Gail Kligman. 2012. *The Politics of Gender After Socialism: A comparative-historical essay*. Princeton: Princeton University Press.

Hays, Sharon. 1998. *The Cultural Contradictions of Motherhood*. New Haven, CT: Yale University Press.

Hillcoat-Nalletamby, Sarah and Judith Phillips. 2011 'Sociological ambivalence revisited', *Sociology* 45(2): 202–17. Accessed 10 March 2022. https://doi.org/10.1177/0038038510394018.

Hunter, Cheryl. 2012. 'Intimate space within institutionalized birth: Women's experiences birthing with doulas', *Anthropology & Medicine* 19(3): 315–26. Accessed 10 March 2022. https://doi.org/10.1080/13648470.2012.692358.

Kathawa, Cosette A., Kavita Shah Arora, Ruth Zielinski and Lisa Kane Low. 2021. 'Perspectives of doulas of color on their role in alleviating racial disparities in birth outcomes: a qualitative study', *Journal of Midwifery and Women's Health* 67(1): 31–8. Accessed 10 March 2022. https://doi.org/10.1111/jmwh.13305.

Lakhani, Nina. 2019. 'America has an infant mortality crisis. Meet the black doulas trying to change that', *The Guardian*, 25 November. Accessed 10 March 2022. https://www.theguardian.com/us-news/2019/nov/25/african-american-doula-collective-mothers-toxic-stress-racism-cleveland-infant-mortality-childbirth.

Lantz, Paula M., Lisa Kane Low, Sanjani Varkey and Robyn L. Watson. 2005. 'Doulas as childbirth paraprofessionals: Results from a national survey', *Women's Health Issues* 15(3): 109–16.

Ledeneva, Alena (ed.). 2018. *The Global Encyclopaedia of Informality, Vol. 1: Understanding Social and Cultural Complexity*. London: UCL Press.

Litvinova, Daria. 2018. 'Labour pains: Mothers speak out about the abuse they receive while giving birth in Russian hospitals', *Index on Censorship* 47(4): 8–10. Accessed 10 March 2022. https://doi.org/10.1177/0306422018819304.

Lupton, Deborah and Virginia Schmied. 2013. 'Splitting bodies/selves: Women's concepts of embodiment at the moment of birth', *Sociology of Health & Illness* 35(6): 828–41. Accessed 10 March 2022. https://doi.org/10.1111/j.1467-9566.2012.01532.x.

Mahmood, Saba. 2001. 'Feminist theory, embodiment, and the docile agent: Some reflections on the Egyptian Islamic revival', *Cultural Anthropology* 16(2): 202–36.

McCabe, Katharine. 2016. 'Mothercraft: Birth work and the making of neoliberal mothers', *Social Science & Medicine* 162: 177–84. Accessed 10 March 2022. https://doi.org/10.1016/j.socscimed.2016.06.021.

McLeish, Jenny and Maggie Redshaw. 2018. 'A qualitative study of volunteer doulas working alongside midwives at births in England: Mothers' and doulas' experiences', *Midwifery* 56: 53–60. Accessed 10 March 2022. http://dx.doi.org/10.1016/j.midw.2017.10.002.

Morris, Jeremy and Abel Polese. 2015. *Informal Economies in Post-Socialist Spaces: Practices, institutions and networks*. Basingstoke: Palgrave Macmillan.

Novkunskaya, Anastasia. 2014. '"Irresponsible" childbirth or contravention of Russian midwifery's norms in homebirth cases', *Journal of Social Policy Studies* 12(3): 353–66.

Novkunskaya, Anastasia, Daria Litvina and Anna Temkina. 2021. 'Pochemu SSSR Konchilsya, a Hamstvo – Net? Sociologi Izuchili Etu Problemu Na Primere Roddomov. I Vot Ih Otvet [Why did the USSR end, but *hamstvo* did not? Sociologists have studied this problem using the example of maternity hospitals. And here is their answer]', *Meduza*, 12 January. Accessed 20 January 2021. https://meduza.io/feature/2021/01/12/pochemu-sssr-konchilsya-a-hamstvo-net.

Ortner, Sherry B. 2006. *Anthropology and Social Theory: Culture, power, and the acting subject*. Durham, NC: Duke University Press.

Ozhiganova, Anna. 2019. '"What do women want": Motives of refusal of maternity hospital in favor of home birth', *Monitoring of Public Opinion: Economic and Social Changes* 2: 263–81. Accessed 10 March 2022. https://doi.org/10.14515/monitoring.2019.2.12.

Parry, Diana. 2008. '"We wanted a birth experience, not a medical experience": Exploring Canadian women's use of midwifery', *Health Care for Women International* 29(8): 784–806. Accessed 10 March 2022. https://doi.org/10.1080/07399330802269451.

Rabeharisoa, Vololona, Tiago Moreira and Madeleine Akrich. 2014. 'Evidence-based activism: Patients', users' and activists' groups in knowledge society', *BioSocieties* 9(2): 111–28. Accessed 10 March 2022. https://doi.org/10.1057/biosoc.2014.2.

Reich, Jennifer A. 2014. 'Neoliberal mothering and vaccine refusal: Imagined gated communities and the privilege of choice', *Gender and Society* 28(5): 679–704. Accessed 10 March 2022. https://doi.org/10.1177/0891243214532711.

Reiger, Kerreen and Rhea Dempsey. 2006. 'Performing birth in a culture of fear: An embodied crisis of late modernity', *Health Sociology Review* 15(4): 364–73. Accessed 10 March 2022. https://doi.org/10.5172/hesr.2006.15.4.364.

Rivkin-Fish, Michele. 2000. 'Health development meets the end of state socialism: Visions of democratization, women's health, and social well-being for contemporary Russia', *Culture, Medicine and Psychiatry* 24: 77–100.

Rivkin-Fish, Michele. 2005. *Women's Health in Post-Soviet Russia: The politics of intervention*. Bloomington and Indianapolis: Indiana University Press.

Rodina, Anna. 2017. 'Kak rozhayut v Rossii. Reportazh "Meduzy" "To, chto proiskhodit v rodovoj, – eto vojna" [How to give birth in Russia. Meduza's report 'What happens in the ward is war']', *Meduza*, 17 July. Accessed 12 February 2020. https://meduza.io/feature/2017/07/17/kak-rozhayut-v-rossii-reportazh-meduzy.

Rose, Nikolas, Pat O'Malley and Mariana Valverde. 2006. 'Governmentality', *Annual Review of Law and Social Science* 2(1): 83–104. Accessed 10 March 2022. https://doi.org/10.1146/annurev.lawsocsci.2.081805.105900.

Shpakovskaya, Larisa. 2014. 'Discourse production of social inequality of maternity', *Women in Russian Society* 2(71): 77–85.

Shpakovskaya, Larisa. 2015. 'How to be a good mother: The case of middle class mothering in Russia', *Europe-Asia Studies* 67(10): 1571–86. Accessed 10 March 2022. https://doi.org/10.1080/09668136.2015.1101210.

'St. 51 Federal Law No. 323-FZ of 21 November 2011 on Basics of Health Protection of the Citizens in the Russian Federation', 2011.

Temkina, Anna. 2014. 'Medicalization of the reproduction and childbirth: A struggle for control', *Journal of Social Policy Studies* 12(3): 321–36.

Temkina, Anna. 2018. 'Budushchaya Mat Kak Issledovatel: Strategii Organizatsii Platnykh Rodov v Rossiyskom Krupnom Gorode' [Mother-to-be as a field researcher: the strategies of private obstetrics provision in urban Russia], *Antropologicheskij Forum* 27: 198–230.

Temkina, Anna. 2020. '"Childbirth is not a car rental" : Mothers and obstetricians negotiating consumer service in Russian commercial maternity care', *Critical Public Health* 30(5): 521–32. Accessed 10 March 2022. https://doi.org/10.1080/09581596.2019.1626004.

Temkina, Anna and Michele Rivkin-Fish. 2020. 'Creating health care consumers: The negotiation of un/official payments, power and trust in Russian maternity care', *Social Theory & Health* 18(4): 340–57. Accessed 10 March 2022. https://doi.org/10.1057/s41285-019-00110-3.

Temkina, Anna and Elena Zdravomyslova. 2018. 'Responsible motherhood, practices of reproductive choice and class construction in contemporary Russia'. In *Gender and Choice After Socialism*, edited by Lynne Attwood, Elisabeth Schimpfössl and Marina Yusupova, 161–86. Cham: Palgrave Macmillan.

Torres, Jennifer M. C. 2015. 'Families, markets, and medicalization: The role of paid support for childbirth and breastfeeding', *Qualitative Health Research* 25(7): 899–911. Accessed 10 March 2022. https://doi.org/10.1177/1049732314553991.

WHO (World Health Organization). 2018. 'Recommendations on intrapartum care for a positive childbirth experience'. Accessed 12 February 2020. https://apps.who.int/iris/bitstream/handle/10665/260178/9789241550215-eng.pdf.

Zelizer, Viviana A. 1994. *Pricing the Priceless Child: The changing social value of children*. Princeton: Princeton University Press.

17
Empowerment of the disempowered: Assessing the impact of young Muscovites through ecological practices

Daria Lebedeva

Introduction

Over the past few decades, the problem of environmental degradation has become particularly significant in global public discourse, with states, international organizations and the general public articulating the urgency of ecological problems (UN Environment 2021). Russia is no exception, as, according to opinion polls, half the population believes that the overall ecological situation in the world – in Russia and especially in their place of residence – is getting worse (FOM 2021). The most recent ecological disasters and catastrophes make the need for environmental action all the more pressing (VCIOM 2019; FOM 2021).

Yet when it comes to caring for themselves and the environment, Russians – unlike the populations of most developed countries – are prone to paternalistic patterns of behaviour. For most Russians, the area of personal responsibility and influence is limited to the family and work (Levada-center 2020). According to opinion polls, 44 per cent of Russians emphasize that state leaders should take the lead in ecological matters, attributing to them the primary role in caring for the environment, while 34 per cent and 10 per cent of Russians accept that responsibility lies with the general public or entrepreneurs, respectively (FOM 2021).

At the macro level, ecological policy remains at the periphery of political and public debate, with discussion of ecological issues constituting a field of power struggles in political, economic and social domains (Yanitsky 2011; Human Rights Watch 2017). Experts claim that the prospects for ecological modernization are still quite limited, while the government's declared ecological and sustainability goals are vague and tokenistic, following the former industrial logic (Potapov 2020). The implementation of environmental policy lags behind what individuals believe needs to be done to care for the environment and does not meet the population's expectations, even though Russia has ratified a number of international programmes and agreements (*Rossijskaya gazeta* 2020).

The state's weak engagement with the ecological agenda frames the latter as unimportant to citizens, a state of affairs that is exacerbated by the poorly developed infrastructure and low ecological culture and consciousness of the population. All this prevents the population from really engaging in pro-environmental activities. Environmental practices therefore seem controversial and marginal, as there is a gap between individuals' attitudes towards ecological activity and the meanings society attaches to it, between the global social discourse on ecological issues and the real implementation of pro-environmental policies in Russia.

Nevertheless, some Russians do take a proactive stance towards caring for the environment, despite the ambivalence of social meanings attached to the agenda. According to opinion polls, the sector of society that is most ecologically active is young people aged between 18 and 30 (VCIOM 2019). They also express high anxiety about the environment and passionately bring up environmental issues in public debates (UN Environment Programme 2019; Gudkov et al. 2020).

Taking account of the ambiguous lines of responsibility for ecological activity in present-day Russia, this study investigates why young people still engage in everyday ecological practices, despite environmentalism being a peripheral issue in relation to the dominant political agenda. The research is guided by the following research questions: how do proactive and ecologically responsible young Muscovites justify their everyday engagement in individual ecological practices, and what motivates them to actively care for the environment? Does the ecological agenda become, for them, a field of power struggle and a means of alternative political representation? Do young people, by engaging in ecological practices, become empowered, taking a stance against the official rhetoric?

In this study, ecological practices refer to an individual's conscious actions, aimed at interacting with the natural environment for its conservation and sustainability (Dunlap and Catton 1979; Stern 2000; Hargreaves 2011). We rely on the interpretative paradigm of social analysis and focus on how individuals mark and enact particular practices that have a preserving effect on the environment. This approach captures the whole spectrum of everyday practices which are usually taken for granted by individuals, looks behind the formal representations of care for the environment and reveals how these practices are legitimized (Volkov and Kharkhordin 2008, 22).

The chapter is divided into four sections: it begins with a brief description of the theoretical framework of the research, before outlining the research methodology (justification of the chosen methodology, data collection and analysis technique, sampling and recruitment). The results of the empirical stage of the study are presented in the third section. Finally, the results are conceptualized and discussed, and the limitations as well as the possible directions for further research are outlined.

Theoretical framework

In modern society, relations between the people and the natural environment have become acute, giving rise to a gradual shift in human values, from the anthropocentric mindset of consumerism and the technological mastery of people over nature (the 'human exceptionalism paradigm') to the biocentric ideology of the balance between nature and human activity – the 'new environmental paradigm' (Dunlap and Catton 1979). Post-materialist values are also considered to be a significant precondition for the manifestation of environmental concern by individuals (Inglehart 1995).

The link between pro-environmental values and behaviour was suggested by Stern (2000) in the 'values-beliefs-norm' theory. Motivations that encourage individuals to have a positive attitude towards the environment imply a complex of (1) biospheric, (2) altruistic and (3) egoistic values. Individual pro-environmental behaviour is an output of multiple coexisting motifs. They include attitudes (knowledge, emotions and intentions), non-ecological motifs (including market-based drivers) and institutional conditions (Kollmuss and Agyeman 2002) and should be considered collectively.

According to the interpretative risk paradigm (Gavrilov 2007), risk perception is socially constructed. Public discourse on environmental issues (what problems are being raised, what knowledge on the problem is being disseminated and what the interests of the various actors with regard to this problem are) determines how they are perceived. At the societal level, environmental concerns mark how significant the issue is in the social order in terms of how (dys)functional it is for the system. The ecological agenda constitutes a political question due to the fact that particular issues are discussed and others are silenced (Dake 1992). Hence, environmental concerns serve as a means of social control, prescribing peoples' specific attitudes towards the environment and encouraging them to act accordingly. As Douglas highlights, 'taken too much at face value, such fears [of pollution] tend to mask other wrongs and dangers' (Douglas 1975, 215).

Accordingly, environmental governance has gradually shifted from direct enforcement to a discourse of proactivity, of institutionalized 'active citizenship' (Buttel 2003; Shamir 2008). The discourse of responsibilization produces a particular social actor: the 'reflexive subject' is individualized and proactive, making decisions rooted in her/his personal interest. The mechanism of 'green governmentality' is implemented in the form of 'simple solutions' (Soneryd and Uggla 2015). They encourage individuals to engage in everyday practices, linking behaviour to personally significant aspects of their lives and emphasizing the value of proactivity.

In modern market societies, ecological consumption becomes a significant means of engaging in pro-environmental behaviour (Welch and Warde 2010). Patterns of 'green consumption' (such as rejection of consumerism, minimizing consumption and waste, choosing certain brands, sharing economy, and boycotting particular goods or brands) give individuals a voice and an opportunity to personally influence the ecological agenda. Through their economic behaviour, consumers acquire the status of 'citizen-consumers', expressing their personal beliefs, attitudes and position in the social structure.

Power relations produce ambivalence for those who have limited access to resources and status; the more rigid the social structure, the more challenging it is for the powerless to express themselves (Room 1976). Their intentions are ambivalent, oscillating between the need to obey the dominant mode of power and the will to resist it in order to realize their aspirations.

However, power itself should be conceptualized in the broad sense (Haugaard 2012; Ledyaev 2019). Apart from traditional 'power over' as a mechanism to force individuals to obey, actors might also manifest their will and identity (Haugaard 2012). This dimension of power is expressed as 'emancipatory, giving capacity to action' (Haugaard 2015, 147). Furthermore, as individuals collectively engage with significant agendas, they jointly exercise 'power with', acting in concert with others (Haugaard 2015). This framework consolidates the different conceptualizations of power relations.

Accordingly, ecological activity – understood here as a set of an individual's pro-environmental attitudes and activities – constitutes an ecological lifestyle, which organizes eco-friendly dispositions, tastes and practices into an integral eco-habitus (Carfagna et al. 2014) and engages socially excluded groups (Rudel et al. 2011).

However, the rethinking and criticism of the 'green choice' policy shows that the latter exaggerates the impact of individual action on the environmental agenda. It shifts a large share of the responsibility for market failures and environmental policy decisions to individuals (Maniates 2001; Evans et al. 2017). The 'green choice' is a responsibilization mechanism, but it should be actively supported by the state. Responsibility is shared among social actors who occupy their niche in environmental discourse and collective action (Rudel et al. 2011; Karlsson 2012).

The coexistence of different motivations as well as the ambivalence and distribution of power in the field may create contradictions and clashes in individuals' understanding of their activities (Ledeneva 2014). However, justifications for ecological practices might not contradict but rather complement each other, together fostering pro-environmental activity and redefining power in the field.

Data and methods

To identify the justifications that young people ascribe to their everyday ecological practices, qualitative methodology was applied. The choice of the methodological framework is justified by the focus on the way justifications unfold in everyday experience and how they are interpreted by individuals (Charmaz 2006). While previous sociological work on the issue of pro-environmental attitudes and behaviour is very diverse, little attention has been paid to individuals' personal arguments for their pro-environmental engagement (Kollmuss and Agyeman 2002).

We conducted in-depth semi-structured interviews with young Moscow citizens aged between 16 and 30 who were engaged in environmental activities in their everyday lives. The minimum age threshold of 16 years is associated with the methodological norm of not collecting data from minors, while 30 is considered the upper threshold for 'youth' in the latest research in the field of youth studies in Russia (Sedova 2016; Gudkov et al. 2020), although this is a matter of academic debate (Omelchenko 2020). By focusing, in particular, on young people with pronounced pro-environmental attitudes, we assume that they can be considered a more progressive sector of the population and become a driving force for ecological engagement (Sedova 2016).

The basic assumptions of the study is that environmentally oriented young people's concern for the environment and personal engagement in ecological practices are essential components of their modern lifestyles and identities (Spaargaren 2003; Rudel et al. 2011). Young people are, probably, largely concerned about environmental degradation as a violation of moral norms and a threat to their future life chances and perspectives. For young people, the ecological domain could become a field in which they can exhibit personal proactivity and responsibility (Nartova 2019). Thus, we assume that ecological activity establishes a field of symbolic power struggle, in which young people can declare care for the environment as a significant public issue and manifest their personal interests, attitudes and citizenship (Soneryd and Uggla 2015). For young people who are suspicious of the official political space and who are basically excluded from it, the ecological niche constitutes a means of political participation and representation.

To examine the implicit justifications of daily ecological activity, the data collection and analysis were performed in line with the grounded theory tradition (Strauss and Corbin 1990; Charmaz 2006). According to this strategy, theoretical sampling was applied as it is an effective means for the researcher to develop research questions according to category saturation from the empirical data (Charmaz 2006). For the initial sampling we used characteristics such as the range of ecological practices (such as waste separation, zero waste and volunteering in ecological organizations) and residence in Moscow (as Moscow is highly heterogeneous in terms of the quality of the environment).

To recruit participants, we used social networks such as Vkontakte and Facebook. As a starting point to recruit individuals involved in ecological practices, we reviewed public posts and discussions on ecological topics, in public pages and groups. We also browsed groups dedicated to the regions of Moscow. In order to avoid the systematic bias of capturing the justifications of successful practices, performed by people active on social networks, participants were also recruited from the acquaintances of the initial informants. At the stage of recruitment, the individuals were asked about the practices they actually performed in order to specify the intensity and type of ecological activity carried out.

Additionally, people of other age cohorts, ecologically indifferent individuals and experts in the sphere of environmental public administration were included. Combining the recruitment strategies was beneficial for the results of the study, allowing us to compare discourses on environmental issues.

As a result, 25 interviews were conducted. Table 17.1 presents the core information about the respondents in the final sample.

In line with grounded theory methodology, the data analysis aims to develop a conceptual framework of the social phenomenon. The narratives were coded in several iterative stages, moving from *in vivo* codes to categories and concepts (Strauss and Corbin 1990). The coding was carried out manually, using MS Word software. Field notes (memos) were collected during the interviews and used afterwards as additional sources of insight and illustration and to help structure the analysis (Charmaz 2006). Overall, we suggest enriching and broadening the theory on the justifications of ecological practices of individuals within their daily experience, as follows.

Results

The results show that young people find themselves in the ambivalent context of performing pro-environmental practices. On the one hand, they feel the urgency of tackling environmental problems and have an interest in making a personal contribution to pro-ecological activity; on the other hand, they perceive the lack of support from the state, which depreciates their beliefs and practical attempts. Moreover, ecological practices themselves are ambivalent in the daily experience of young people. On the one hand, they are politically neutral, justified as morally loaded caring for the environment or pragmatically as ensuring future well-being. On the other, since young environmentally conscious Muscovites have limited capacity to express civic and particularly ecological demands and publicly promote their interests in the current dominant political field, simple everyday practices become a form of empowerment – the civil representation of the officially powerless. The results of our research show that environmentalism is a political issue and young people use pro-environmental arguments to formulate general civic demands. In their everyday ecological practices, individuals take personal responsibility for the global and their own personal futures, claim moral principles and defend their civil and political positions.

Table 17.1 Characteristics of the respondents

No	Name	Gender	Age	Occupation	Place of residence	Engagement in ecological activity
1	Daria	f	18	BA student, economics; employed	Kuzminki	Occasionally engaged in waste sorting and zero waste consumption; pronounced ecological mindset
2	Michail	m	22	MA student; freelance at web-dev	Fili-Davydkovo	Actively engaged in waste sorting; popularizes the topic on social media
3	Vlada 1	f	21	BA student, economics	Troparevo	Actively engaged in waste sorting and zero waste consumption; active pro-environmental concern
4	Kirill	m	34	Expert, PhD ecology; worked at the national project 'Ecology'	–	Apart from professional activity: occasionally engaged in waste sorting and popularization on social media
5	Angelina	f	21	BA student, sociology	Moscow region, Odintsovo	Occasionally engaged in waste sorting and the consumption of eco brands
6	Daniil	m	30	Self-employed teacher; BA in finance	Presnensky	Occasionally engaged in health-related practices; no proactive attitude
7	Lena	f	20	BA student, journalism	Nearest Moscow region	Actively engaged in waste sorting, occasionally in zero waste consumption; moderate ecological mindset
8	Ksenya 1	f	23	MA student, PR; employed teacher	Dynamo	Occasionally engaged in waste sorting and zero waste consumption; pronounced ecological mindset and concern
9	Alexandra	f	20	BA student; employed	Nagatinsky Backwater	Rarely engaged in practices, occasionally waste sorting and consumption of eco brands; no ecological mindset or concern

No	Name	Gender	Age	Occupation	Place of residence	Engagement in ecological activity
10	Dina	f	23	BA in sociology; employed	Marina Roscha	Rarely engaged in practices, occasionally waste sorting and consumption of eco brands; poor ecological mindset
11	Ilya	m	23	MA student, philology; self-employed	Timiryazevsky	Actively engaged in waste sorting and zero waste consumption daily; vegetarian; volunteer in an eco-project; pronounced ecological and civil responsibility
12	Vasiliy	m	18	BA student, aircraft; employed	Severnoe Tushino	Occasionally engaged in waste sorting and zero waste consumption; moderate ecological attitudes
13	Danil	m	20	BA student, management; employed	Putilkovo	Occasionally engaged in waste sorting and consumption of eco brands; pronounced ecological and civic position
14	Beata	f	20	BA student, ecology	Chertanovo South	Actively engaged in waste sorting; eco activist; vegan; member of a student eco organization; pronounced ecological and civil responsibility
15	Libov' Alexeevna	f	65	Pensioner	Zapadnoye Degunino	Occasionally engaged in waste sorting, ecology as neatness; low level of ecological attitudes
16	Lubov' Vasilievna	f	76	Pensioner	Troitsk	Not engaged in practices, ecology as neatness; no ecological mindset
17	Katya	f	18	School, 11th grade	South Butovo	Actively engaged in waste sorting and zero waste consumption; pronounced ecological mindset
18	Vladimir	m	22	MA student, chemistry; employed	Odintsovo	Actively engaged in waste sorting, occasionally in zero waste consumption; records a podcast about ecology; pronounced ecological mindset

No	Name	Gender	Age	Occupation	Place of residence	Engagement in ecological activity
19	Sergey	m	22	BA student, international relations	Odintsovo	Occasionally engaged in waste sorting and zero waste consumption; records a podcast about ecology; pronounced ecological concern
20	Vlada 2	f	22	BA student	Troparevo	Actively engaged in waste sorting, occasionally in zero waste consumption; pronounced ecological reflexivity
21	Ksenya 2	f	25	MA; employed, artist	Sokol	Occasionally engaged in waste sorting, actively in zero waste consumption; pronounced ecological reflexivity and anxiety
22	Oksana	f	21	BA student; eco-volunteer	–	Actively engaged in waste sorting and zero waste consumption; founded the eco club in university; volunteer; pronounced ecological reflexivity and civic responsibility
23	Yulia	f	24	Employed	Zhulebino	Occasionally engaged in waste sorting, actively in zero waste consumption; moderate ecological responsibility; pronounced ecological and health anxiety
24	Anastasia	f	29	MA in ecology, ecological expertise	–	Actively engaged in waste sorting and zero waste consumption; works in ecological expertise; has an eco-blog; pronounced ecological and civic responsibility
25	Ksenya 3	f	30	Employed in finance	Kapotnya	Actively engaged in zero waste consumption; participates in neighbourhood clean-up; pronounced civic responsibility, ecological and health anxiety

Environmental concern: 'now or never'

The data show that young people reflect on the environmental issues they 'see around them', with a particular emphasis on environmental degradation, its unpredictability and its negative impact on human life.

> It would be better if this does not continue. We are now familiar with the problems. Now or never. It is better to start now, little by little, than later, when you'd have to use harsher measures that you do not even want to think about. (Interview 9)

The level of anxiety is different for young people; they can even be quite rational about it. However, we suggest that for them, environmental concern is an important life principle. It relates strongly to their futures as young people, aspiring for better life chances and personal success, and their ambition and proactivity prompt them to respond to the ecological agenda and to be willing to act pro-environmentally.

> It seems to me that in 20 years everything will be very bad with the environment. It will be similar to China and there will be smog, probably everywhere. And people will pay for clean air. (Interview 1)

Participation in ecological practices, at the same time, is a response to the negative changes taking place 'here and now'. It is a mechanism of coping with the current threats to their personal life chances (such as quality of life, health, well-being and access to resources), safety and ontological security.

Young people primarily aim to take practical steps to care for the environment they live in, which is close to their locality and day-to-day private lives. Yet, in comparison with older generations, they seem to have a broader understanding of 'the place' they associate with and for which they are responsible. It stretches from their backyard to the district, the city and even the planet.

> It is such thinking, it seems to me, when you think: 'Oh, that's it, I will rid the whole world of plastic!' – this is not normal. This means that a person will not do anything. Another thing is that I will rid my own yard from plastic – this is a normal situation. And a person will really achieve this, and it will be very cool. (Interview 11)

'The support is minimal': contradictions in the experience of young people

Young people emphasize the perceived indifference of older people to the environmental agenda. Older generations, according to the narratives of young people, 'are stewing in their own issues and problems' and do not pay attention to potential threats until they actually affect them. As young people personally engage in ecological activity and attempt 'to reduce their impact on nature', they feel that their efforts are devalued by older 'stubborn, passive' individuals. This ignorance is considered extremely unjust, while taking 'real' action to care for the environment is perceived as progressive and 'simply right'.

> You are sitting in your beautiful cozy little world, and the landfills are far away, it does not concern you. You do not see the air. Therefore, a significant part of the population does not care. People do not see the environment in mega-cities, they do not care. (Interview 4)

Young people are more likely to argue against the state's discrediting of the agenda. As the state is a more powerful and wealthy actor, young people expect it to assume responsibility and implement the environmental agenda. However, it is not seen as a real priority for the Russian state either in the present or in the near future.

> In our country, the state itself is not very fond of talking about ecology. Many of our landfills belong to quite influential and wealthy people associated with the current government, the ruling power in Russia. It is not really profitable to talk about ecology in Russia. Therefore, the creation of infrastructure will take more time. (Interview 2)

This affects their attitude towards officials. As pointed out in the narratives, young people are mistrustful and sceptical of the way state-imposed environmental measures and infrastructures are legitimized.

> It is difficult to hold out for a state that does nothing at all. It should do a little bit. Especially to the public. At least it relieves tension a little bit. But I would really like to have a waste separation system like the one in Singapore. (Interview 21)

Thus, young people face the ambivalent social and political context of performing care for the environment. Interestingly, even though the youth's pro-environmental attitudes are embedded in equivocal and de-motivating politics and state infrastructure, this does not prevent young people from engaging in ecological activity entirely. Ultimately, they tend to express proactive attitudes in opposition to the passivity of 'the ordinary people' and the state, paternalism or external enforcement. Those who are ready to take pro-environmental steps feel ambivalence in the contradictions between their internal proactivity and external constrains associated with ecological activity.

> And this eternal contradiction of the laws to each other. No matter how strange it may sound. When people talk about environmental friendliness, and then try to prohibit the minimization of packaging. And you sit there and think: 'Well, somehow strange … This is not how it works!' And you sit and wonder frankly. Therefore, everything should start with activists, and trust in the state system will appear when these activists interact with what they [deputies] really prescribe. (Interview 22)

Why do young people still engage in everyday ecological practices? What motivates them, and how do they justify it to themselves and to others? The results show that, by becoming engaged in ecological activity as an important personal and social agenda, young people become empowered, contrary to the dominant intention to keep them powerless and subordinate (literally and symbolically) within the social structure. And this ambivalence generated by the powerful empowers young people in the domain of everyday civic self-expression.

> Well, generally speaking, I have always been somehow sensitive to some unfair things that are happening in the world. Probably, it nudged me to ecological problems and motivated me to think about how I could change this. (Interview 3)

'A simple man' in the care for the environment

Young people believe in the 'greening' of society globally and to some extent in Russia. For them, ecological practices are either a set of 'marginalized' practices of the 'green fanatics' (as described in the discourses about eco-activism) or a privileged activity (since zero waste goods are generally more expensive). They believe that ecological issues are gradually becoming an everyday matter in contemporary society, which is not performed 'on the barricades' but is integrated into the ordinary course of life.

At present, it is a moral imperative and social norm to reflect upon the fact that 'we are not alone on this planet'. In this social order towards which younger people are oriented, pro-environmental activity is perceived as 'absolutely normal practice' not only at the level of value declarations but also as an everyday habit and a part of public discussion. Caring for the environment is regarded as a duty of and at the same time an opportunity for 'ordinary people'.

> And people cannot even think that, firstly, they are really significant in ecology, it is not just some beautiful slogans, right? But they are really significant, they can really do something, that one drop in the sea is already cool ... (Interview 8)

For young people, the responsibility of each individual towards the environment and the attempts to make a positive contribution to protecting it (or at least minimizing the negative impacts) have become a marker of 'a good person' in modern society. This modern social actor is depicted as one who appreciates the environment and follows the principles of personal responsibility 'for oneself and for the space around' in their everyday lives. As the empirical data suggest, being responsible is crucial for young people and their interaction with the world.

> You are the master – you are responsible. It is not that someone else is responsible, but you are also responsible. You are an active participant. That is, your role, it is also significant ... And if you, as an irresponsible consumer, simply consume and do not give a basis for the future, then ... I think it is irresponsible, and such people have problems not only with the environment and waste disposal, but with everything. (Interview 13)

Their understanding of what it means to be 'the master' is framed by the phrase 'my planet is me', marking a shift from reckless consumerism and wasteful predatory destruction to neatness, consciousness in daily decisions and activities. Interestingly, they express the components of biocentric value orientations (Dunlap and Catton 1979) and post-materialism (Inglehart 1995), while simultaneously maintaining the anthropocentrism framework. Moreover, such orientation is not solely pragmatic (for instance, the desire to live in a clean environment or minimize future climate risks) and economically rational (namely, saving water or electricity in the home) but represents morality and social justice (Stern 2000). The discussion of ecological issues ultimately refers to human rights and dignity, questioning what a decent environment is and how people should act in order to achieve it.

> Well, a person influences it [the state of the environment] and constantly worsens it. Accordingly, one can influence it in the opposite direction, improve it. At least when we stop turning a blind eye to problems and start talking about them, paying attention, express the attitude that we care ... I mean, we are aware that we need to sleep more, to eat well, to move – this is, probably, more inherent in us, it is more talked about. But that we must take care of the environment too – well ... But in fact we must send inquiries about the quality of water, demand to measure its quality in the laboratory, or think about what kind of air we have in our city. (Interview 24)

'Not to be passive in this world'

Young people are not harsh on themselves and others in being environmentally engaged since they believe in the 'small solutions theory' as a means to achieve the eco-friendly lifestyle. Importantly, the responsibility is seen not as a burden but as an opportunity to be a 'civilized citizen' and 'a good person'.

> And at some point, something clicks in your head, and you think: 'Is everything really so bad? Do I need to do it?' But then you come back to reality and you realize that: 'Well, yes, it needs to be done, because if not me, then who?' (Interview 7)

'Elementary, simple practices' are an individualized tactic of managing ecological problems, making ecological activity a habit and embedding it in one's daily routine. 'Simple solutions' seem to be a more worthy and effective strategy 'than doing nothing' and passively witnessing the unfolding of the environmental crisis. By making a 'small but personal contribution' to protect the environment, young people emphasize their intrinsic personal interest in the environmental agenda, to attempt to make a personal contribution 'to help the environment' or at least try to feel engaged.

> Because being a couch expert and saying that everything is so bad, but doing nothing is generally the worst thing that can happen. (Interview 17)

Ecological attitudes, values or emotions are essential, but the principle 'you are what you do, not what you say' is fundamental in relation to the environment. For young people, ecological practices become a crucial indicator of one's mindfulness, as they expect other people and themselves to 'do at least something'.

> It was kind of romantic, yes. Then I realized that this is a big problem, and this problem needs to be solved, right? And it is in our hands – whether to solve this problem or not … (Interview 1)

Embedded in the context of capitalist economic systems, consumption is a powerful framework, anchored to the idea of sustainability and 'being green' (Chappells and Trentmann 2015; Welch and Warde 2015). Within everyday ecological activity, young people engage in zero waste consumption, upcycling or the sharing economy (Spaargaren 2003; Chappells and Trentmann 2015). Their 'green choice' in the everyday domain becomes a tactic of opposition to violent environmental destruction and passivity in relation to the ecological crisis.

> My sister, for example, asked me to buy bananas. She is like, 'Buy the ones in the packaging'. Haha, hell no! I will never buy bananas in packaging! I told her: 'Are you serious? Why? Oh, why?' Or there is an orange or something like this, that they try to put into an extra plastic bag. Well, why? This worldview, I do not know … Maybe, it is such short-term thinking, ignorance to what you leave behind. (Interview 23)

In pro-environmental discussions and activity, young people not only ask themselves 'What kind of person am I?' but also 'What kind of environment do I want to see around me?' Here we recognize the paradigm of the actor in modernity, who works on the 'self as a reflexive project' (Giddens 1991). In personal ecological actions, which are elementary yet meaningful, actors constitute the 'self', approaching the desired ideal of a modern person and citizen, and define who they are for themselves and others. Here, the 'internal' ambivalence of pro-environmental activity of the youth can be identified. On the one hand, as was mentioned above, young people depoliticize ecological practices since they are available for everyone and represent the modern social morality. At the same time, the narratives suggest that the civil dimension is also inherent to pro-environmental activity.

> I would call it the 'attribute of a decent person'. That is, a conscious person who understands what he is doing and why. Everyone sees it in their own way, what a decent person is, but usually this person is good. And if you are good, then you must in some sense be responsible for the environment. And every person wants to be good. I think that precisely this concern for the environment should be such a basic concept of goodness. (Interview 18)

The worldview of self-management and empowerment, specific to young people, seems to be applicable to ecological activity as well. It becomes a pragmatic act of investing in their future and at the same time gives them the space to be proactive in shaping their personal life courses and the social order around them. Hence, pro-environmental behaviour shapes the proactive subject since one acquires agency in promoting the ecological agenda.

'Find like-minded people'

As 'no man is an island', young people seek individualization but not atomization in ecological activity: they try to be independently responsible, while relating to the community around eco-friendly activity. On a macro-scale, private practices make societal changes cumulatively. Given the importance of individual contributions, the latter are conceived as 'part of the overall picture, a fraction of the whole' of environmental protection.

> This [engagement in waste sorting] gives you confidence, the hope that you do it for a reason, that it helps. And it helps not only you, but also other people, and this also helps our country and the planet. (Interview 7)

The ecological domain is a field of symbolic struggles in which actors distance themselves from 'non-ecological' people. However, the ideal eco-friendly social order, depicted by young people, is 'organically supported' by all social actors: the public, influencers, businesses and the state. All actors are foreseen to be in dialogue with each other and responsive to ecological issues.

> And everything should be in balance. But in such a balance that they interact without harming the planet, the object on which they are working. Now, if the object – the planet – will feel better from this kind of interaction, then it is a good thing. (Interview 8)

Ecological participation becomes for young people a means to engender solidarity by becoming symbolically integrated into the eco-community and being 'part of something bigger'.

Discussion and conclusions

At present young people have limited resources and channels to express their political and environmental concerns. This study explains how they justify their ecological engagement via socio-political activity. Drawing on interviews with ecologically oriented young people from Moscow, we suggest that everyday ecological practices are understood by them as enacted in an ambivalent social environment (the 'external' ambivalence). Moreover, daily ecological activity is ambivalent itself, being both a politically neutral moral issue and at the same time an actively politicized field of civic and political representation for young people.

Our results are consistent with previous studies which suggest that everyday ecological activity is embedded in the concept of a proactive, individualized and responsible citizen (Welch and Warde 2010; Soneryd and Uggla 2015), while personal engagement enables individuals to enact the pro-environmental social order they yearn for. The results go in line with the studies, showing that young people uphold the idea of personal success and opportunity (Matza 2010). Due to these values they are extremely concerned about environmental problems as an unpredictable yet serious risk to the global and, importantly, their own personal futures. The narratives of young people illustrate that they have a 'pessimistic attitude, but it includes hope for the future'. The importance of practical involvement seems to be a crucial insight of the study, highlighting the contribution of the individual to improving the ecological domain and taking charge of the global and their own personal futures, life chances and prosperity. In addition, young people demonstrate a gradual shift in their value and citizenship orientations, expressing components of biocentric (Dunlap and Catton 1979) and post-materialistic (Inglehart 1995) attitudes, demanding civic activity as part of their personal contribution to positive social changes (Rudel et al. 2011; Nartova 2019).

The 'implicit' ambivalence of ecological practices exhibited by young people is depicted by the fact that they appeal to a moral norm of 'a simple man' distanced from the current controversial politics, and at the same time to citizen participation. At first sight, these justifications, rooted in moral values or pragmatic considerations, are apolitical. However, the ecological domain becomes politicized as, in the perceptions of young people, the state distances itself from the environmental issue. But for young people, caring for the environment is framed as a significant issue, and they prioritize their intrinsic personal pro-environmental choices in opposition to both paternalism and external enforcement. Remaining 'ordinary citizens', they support their personal claims and express their values and attitudes (Spaargaren 2003; Haugaard 2012), consequently reshaping power relations in the ecological domain. For them, ecological practices become tools for their civic and political representation and empowerment in the ambivalent social position between external resistance to the state agenda and internal pro-environmental attitudes. In this case, 'power' should be conceptualized as the capacity for action: 'power to' as emancipation, rather than 'power over' as dominance over other individuals or coercion (Haugaard 2015; Ledyaev 2019). More broadly, young people make political decisions by their everyday actions (Eliasoph 1998), being explicitly apolitical and at the same time acquiring power in trying to change the world around them, hence managing the 'implicit' ambivalence of ecological practices.

Furthermore, pro-environmental engagement allows ecologically concerned young people to take part in significant social activity (Spaargaren 2003; Welch and Warde 2015), rooted in expressing citizenship, collectively preserving the world and changing it for the better. Actors exercise 'power with' as the ability to act in accordance with others and discuss the issue with them (Haugaard 2015). Remaining a highly politicized field of power struggles, for young people ecological activity constitutes a space of communication and civil collaboration.

To conclude, young people make use of the 'implicit' ambivalence of ecological practices and their understandings since, even without making an explicit political statement, they express their desire for a particular type of civic engagement and citizenship, in contrast to the present distrust of official political discourse. Pro-environmental activity becomes a tool of civic empowerment and representation for young people. We argue that it is through ecological activity that young people communicate their political claims, namely, their demand for justice and the right to a decent quality of life as a manifestation of socio-democratic values (Gudkov et al. 2020). Furthermore, this has the potential to establish local grassroots communities and movements, indicating a redistribution of power dispositions.

The example of proactive young people suggests that the imaginary representations of the eco-friendly social order can become the basis for real social changes (subject to the relevant efforts and support). Based on socially shared expectations, individuals structure their activity, thereby investing in foreseen 'imagined futures' (Beckert 2013). An important task of social researchers will be to study the vector of these changes and the subsequent dynamics of power in the field.

It is worth noting that the empowerment revealed in the interviews is not entirely straightforward, as young people still express contradictory attitudes towards ecological engagement. This stems from the fact that environmental responsibility has to be shared among social actors, while the 'politics of choice' approach exaggerates the reflexivity and autonomy of individual actors (Maniates 2001; Welch and Warde 2015).

Young people recognize the limitations of their agency in protecting the environment through personal actions only. Even though they perceive eco-friendly activity as an intrinsic interest, and while environmental responsibility 'does not kill you, but encourages you to keep going and strive', at some point caring for the environment becomes a duty in the negative sense of a burden. Ecological activity is seen by young people as resistance to the state (namely, to its ecological ignorance and passivity), but they still hope that the authorities will eventually follow a pro-environmental path and so all actors will act in accordance.

Ecological activity also turns out to be functionally ambivalent in its implicit meanings for young people, simultaneously constraining and empowering, assigning actors the obligation to protect the environment and maintain their engagement (Ledeneva 2014). We suggest that the particular focus on how multiple justifications and modes of power coexist, shaping the transitional yet specific patterns in ecological engagement, is productive for fostering the pro-environmental agenda and activity, relevant for the Russian institutional setting.

The ambiguity of personal responsibility exhibited by young people might also stem from the peculiar socio-cultural Russian context. In the case of young Muscovites, a combination of values and patterns from Soviet, contemporary Russian and Western models is probably captured (Yanitsky 2011). The study primarily refers to the context of the modern market society, capturing the deliberate actions of individuals who attempt to assume responsibility for the environment. They are not motivated by the economic deficit or limited market options, which would be the case with older people who experienced the Soviet economic system.

Limitations

Since we rely on the narratives of young, ecologically oriented people, the results of the study might represent a pretty optimistic picture of personal pro-environmental behaviour. Young people tend to idealize eco-friendly activity. Still, it indicates a gradual shift towards the civic dimension of pro-environmental engagement and concerns. To ensure a more thorough analysis, we deliberately limited the scope of our research to proactive and ecologically responsible young Moscow residents.

Furthermore, young people do not always reflect on the meanings of ecological practices within their daily routines. Occasionally during the fieldwork, they failed to articulate their attitudes towards daily forms of activity. This highlights the problem of the answers given, or implicit meanings which eluded the research.

Due to the ethnographic framework of the research, we intentionally accepted the perspectives of the individuals and did not attempt to depict 'objective' ecological engagement. Additional experts from the field of ecology, climate studies, biology as well as political science in the sphere of ecological regulation could make a significant contribution to understanding the field and counterbalance the ideal-typical understanding of caring for the environment, translated by the young people.

As for the perspective of this study, we did not capture the macro context of the ecological activity and did not pay detailed attention to the perspectives of other social actors. The power dynamics in the field require further research, unpacking the whole spectrum of power relations between multiple institutional actors and the ways they frame, articulate and negotiate the environmental agenda.

Acknowledgements

Support from the Basic Research Program of the HSE University is gratefully acknowledged. The author is indebted to the members of the Laboratory for Studies in Economic Sociology, HSE and the participants of the International workshop 'The varieties of power in the economy' (HSE, Moscow, Russia, 3–4 July, 2020), for useful discussions, help with this manuscript, and support.

References

Beckert, Jens. 2013. 'Imagined futures: Fictional expectations in the economy', *Theory and Society* 42: 219–40.
Buttel, Frederick H. 2003. 'Environmental sociology and the explanation of environmental reform', *Organization Environment* 16: 306–44.
Carfagna, Lindsey B., Emilie A. Dubois, Connor Fitzmaurice, Monique Y. Ouimette, Juliet B. Schor, Margaret Willis and Thomas Laidley. 2014. 'An emerging eco-habitus: The reconfiguration of high cultural capital practices among ethical consumers', *Journal of Consumer Culture* 14: 158–78.
Chappells, Heather and Frank Trentmann. 2015. 'Sustainable consumption in history: Ideas, resources and practices'. In *Handbook of Research on Sustainable Consumption*, edited by Lucia A. Reisch and John Thøgersen, 51–69. Cheltenham: Edward Elgar.
Charmaz, Kathy. 2006. *Constructing Grounded Theory: A practical guide through qualitative analysis*. London: SAGE.
Dake, Karl. 1992. 'Myths of nature: Culture and the social construction of risk', *Journal of Social Issues* 48: 21–37.
Douglas, Mary. 1975. *Implicit Meanings: Selected essays in anthropology*. London: Routledge.
Dunlap, Riley E. and William R. Catton, Jr. 1979. 'Environmental sociology', *Annual Review of Sociology* 5: 243–73.
Eliasoph, Nina. 1998. *Avoiding Politics: How Americans produce apathy in everyday life*. Cambridge: Cambridge University Press.
Evans, David, Daniel Welch and Joanne Swaffield. 2017. 'Constructing and mobilizing "the consumer": Responsibility, consumption and the politics of sustainability', *Environment and Planning A* 49: 1396–412.
FOM. 2021. 'Ecology: general situation and acute problems'. Accessed 5 March 2022. https://fom.ru/Obraz-zhizni/14659.
Gavrilov, Kirill A. 2007. 'Sociological approach to risk analysis', *Sociologicheskiy jurnal* [Sociological journal] 3: 40–58.
Giddens, Anthony. 1991. *Modernity and Self-Identity: Self and society in the late modern age*. Stanford, CA: Stanford University Press.
Gudkov, Lev, Natalia Zorkaya, Ekaterina Kochergina, Karina Pipiya and Alexandra Ryseva. 2020. 'Russia's "Generation Z": Attitudes and values'. Friedrich-Ebert-Stiftung. Accessed 9 March 2021. http://library.fes.de/pdf-files/bueros/moskau/16134.pdf.
Hargreaves, Tom. 2011. 'Practice-ing behaviour change: Applying social practice theory to pro-environmental behaviour change', *Journal of Consumer Culture* 11: 79–99.
Haugaard, Mark. 2012. 'Rethinking the four dimensions of power: Domination and empowerment', *Journal of Political Power* 5: 33–54.
Haugaard, Mark. 2015. 'Concerted power over', *Constellations: An International Journal of Critical and Democratic Theory* 22: 147–58.
Human Rights Watch. 2017. 'Russia: "Year of Ecology" a sham'. 21 November. Accessed 9 March 2021. https://www.hrw.org/news/2017/11/21/russia-year-ecology-sham.
Inglehart, Ronald. 1995. 'Public support for environmental protection: Objective problems and subjective values in 43 societies', *PS: Political Science & Politics* 28: 57–72.
Karlsson, Rasmus. 2012. 'Individual guilt or collective progressive action? Challenging the strategic potential of environmental citizenship theory', *Environmental Values* 21: 459–74.
Kollmuss, Anja and Julian Agyeman. 2002. 'Mind the gap: Why do people act environmentally and what are the barriers to pro-environmental behavior?', *Environmental Education Research* 8: 239–60.
Ledeneva, Alena. 2014. 'The ambivalence of blurred boundaries: Where informality stops and corruption begins?', *RFIEA Perspectives* 12: 19–22.

Ledyaev, Valeriy G. 2019. 'Conceptual analysis of power: Problems and modern trends', *Politicheskaya nauka* [Political science] 3: 14–29.

Levada-center. 2020. 'Responsibility and influence'. Accessed 9 March 2021. https://www.levada.ru/2020/10/13/chuvstvo-otvetstvennosti/.

Maniates, Michael F. 2001. 'Individualization: Plant a tree, buy a bike, save the world?', *Global Environmental Politics* 1: 31–52.

Matza, Tomas. 2010. '"Good individualism"? Psychology, ethics, and neoliberalism in postsocialist Russia', *American Ethnologist* 39: 804–18.

Nartova, Nadezda A. 2019. 'Citizenship as understood by St. Petersburg young people and their parents', *Sociologicheckiye issledovaniya* [Sociological research] 12: 38–47.

Omelchenko, Elena. (ed.) 2020. *Youth in the City: Cultures, scenes and solidarities*. Moscow: Izd. Dom Vysshej shkoly ekonomiki.

Potapov, Victor. 2020. 'Why 17 Sustainable Development Goals are reduced to global warming', *Regnum*, 4 June. Accessed 9 March 2021. https://regnum.ru/news/polit/2972668.html.

Room, Robin. 1976. 'Ambivalence as a sociological explanation: The case of cultural explanations of alcohol problems', *American Sociological Review* 41(6): 1047–65.

Rossijskaya gazeta. 2020. 'Russia has set a course for the development of a "green" economy', 21 July. Accessed 9 March 2021. https://rg.ru/2020/07/21/rossiia-vziala-kurs-na-razvitie-zelenoj-ekonomiki.html.

Rudel, Thomas K., J. Timmons Roberts and Joann Carmin. 2011. 'Political economy of the environment', *Annual Review of Sociology* 37: 221–38.

Sedova, Natalia N. 2016. 'Life goals and strategies of Russians: The context of passionarity', *Sociologicheskij zhurnal* [Sociological journal] 22: 73–91.

Shamir, Ronen. 2008. 'The age of responsibilization: On market-embedded morality', *Economy and Society* 37: 1–19.

Soneryd, Linda and Ylva Uggla. 2015. 'Green governmentality and responsibilization: New forms of governance and responses to "consumer responsibility"', *Environmental Politics* 24: 913–31.

Spaargaren, Gert. 2003. 'Sustainable consumption: A theoretical and environmental policy perspective', *Society and Natural Resources* 16: 687–701.

Stern, Paul C. 2000. 'New environmental theories: Toward a coherent theory of environmentally significant behavior', *Journal of Social Issues* 56: 407–24.

Strauss, Anselm and Juliet M. Corbin. 1990. *Basics of Qualitative Research: Grounded theory procedures and techniques*. London: SAGE.

UN Environment. 2021. 'About UN Environment Programme'. Accessed 9 March 2021. https://www.unenvironment.org/about-un-environment.

UN Environment Programme. 2019. 'Thundering youth call on power to act now'. Accessed 9 March 2021. https://www.unep.org/news-and-stories/story/thundering-youth-call-power-act-now.

VCIOM. 2019. 'Care for the environment: We want, but cannot?'. Accessed 9 March 2021. https://infographics.wciom.ru/theme-archive/society/religion-lifestyle/moral-relations/article/zabota-ob-okruzhajushchei-srede-khotim-no-ne-mozhem.html.

Volkov, Vadim and Oleg Kharkhordin. 2008. *Theory of Practices*. St Petersburg: EU in St Petersburg.

Welch, Daniel and Alan Warde. 2015. 'Theories of practice and sustainable consumption'. In *Handbook of Research on Sustainable Consumption*, edited by Lucia A. Reisch and John Thøgersen, 84–100. Cheltenham: Edward Elgar.

Yanitsky, Oleg. 2011. *Eco-Modernization of Russia: Theory, practice, perspective*. Moscow: Institut sociologii RAN.

Index

academic excellence 238–42, 248, 250, 252–3
agreement violation 147, 152, 161–3, 166, 158–9, 161
Altbach, Philip 237
ambiguity xxi, xxii, 2, 239, 337, 361
ambivalence (definition) xx–xxii, 2, 102, 284
ambivalence of power xxii–xxiii, 5–6, 9, 41, 54, 77, 78, 93–6, 123–5, 140–1, 146–7, 150, 167–8, 186, 191, 208–9, 212, 239–40, 245, 258, 264, 276, 303–4, 316–17, 336, 346
ambivalence of authenticity 281
ambivalence of capital 58
ambivalence of doula support 322, 337
ambivalence of ecological practices 360
ambivalence of exchange relationships 119
ambivalence of inter-firm ties 103
ambivalence of innovations 83, 93
ambivalence of resource rent 54
embedded ambivalence 80, 82, 93, 96
social and cultural ambivalence xxiii, 80, 173, 218
sociological ambivalence xx–xxii
source of ambivalence 2, 3, 238
types / patterns of ambivalence xxiii–xxiv, 3
 functional ambivalence (double deed) xxiii, 3, 124, 132, 141
 motivational ambivalence (double purpose) 3, 7, 123, 125, 140, 234
 normative ambivalence (double standards) xxiii, 3, 9, 239
 substantive ambivalence (double thinking / doublethink) xxiii, 3, 239, 293
Appadurai, Arjun 294
Arnstein, Sherry 174
authoritarian state 1, 5–6, 94, 276
authority
 enforcement authorities 225–6, 229, 230–1, 233
 private authority 188, 191, 194, 205, 212
 professional authority 10, 322, 337
 state authorities 166, 261, 263
authenticity 9, 280–4, 287–8, 290–3

Bauman, Zygmunt xxi, 3, 284
Beckert, Jens 288
Bengtsson, Bo 172
Bleuler, Eugen xx, 2
Bogdanova, Elena 294
Bohr, Niels xxii–xxiii
Bourdieu, Pierre 290

Callon, Michel 175–7
capitalism xviii, 1, 5, 16, 22, 24, 33, 44, 58–9, 77–8, 263, 274, 282, 284, 293, 305

channel relationships 102–3, 106, 112, 116–17
Chayanov, Alexandr 64
checks and balances 15, 19, 21–2
complexity xviii, xx, xxii–xxiv, 3, 4, 176
consumer cynicism 10, 312, 315–17
contract infringement 7, 104, 107, 111–12, 115–19
counterfeit products 8, 9, 217–18, 223–8, 232
Crozier, Michel 123

diffusion of innovations 79–80, 84–5, 90–1, 93–4
digital platforms 8, 146–7, 149, 151, 167
Dobbin, Frank 4
Douglas, Mary 345
Douglass, John 242
Durkheim, Emile 83, 94

ecological activity 343, 346–8, 353–4, 356–62
ecological practices 343, 346–8, 352, 354, 357–60
economic freedom 15, 18–19, 22, 25–6, 32
economic governance 6, 15, 26–7, 29, 32, 33
Einstein, Albert xxii
empowerment/disempowerment 8, 10, 174, 192, 198, 207, 209, 211, 322–3, 325–6, 334, 336–8, 348, 358, 360–1
enforcement
 external enforcement 354, 360
 law / contract enforcement 88, 90–1, 93–4, 167, 219–20
environmental policy 343, 346
Etzione, Amitai 80

Fadeeva, Olga 64, 76
Foucault, Michel 10, 92, 264
freelance contracting 8, 149–50, 155, 166
Freud, Sigmund 2

Giddens, Anthony 3–4
gig economy 8, 146, 149, 168
global rankings 237–40, 243
Gustafson, Thane 46

Hajda, Jan 173
Halpern, Paul xxii
Haugaard, Mark 5
Hazelkorn, Ellen 237
Hillcoat-Nalletamby, Sarah 338
Hirschman, Albert 131
homogenization 9, 240, 243–5
housing renovations 8, 173
Hults, David R. 49, 51

import substitution 271, 280, 285–6, 291
informality 126, 130, 146–7, 150–1, 153–4, 166–7, 275, 327–8
intellectual property rights 1, 9, 217–18, 220, 223, 227
intensive motherhood 322, 325–6, 334–6

Johns, Adrian 219
Jones Luong, Paulina 45
Jung, Jiwook 4

Karpik, Lucien 175

Latour, Bruno 175, 177
Ledeneva, Alena 3, 275, 293, 327
legitimacy
    cognitive legitimacy 262
    contested / partial legitimacy 7, 86–7, 94, 96
external legitimacy 238–9, 243
legitimacy of innovation 84–6
moral legitimacy 7, 85–7, 93–4
    political legitimacy 23, 86
pragmatic legitimacy 7, 85–7, 93–4
    social legitimacy 14, 219, 232
liberal democracy 19–22, 26
Luhmann, Niklas 315
Lukes, Steven 4

Mahdavi, Paasha 42–3
Malinowski, Bronislaw xx
Marginson, Simon 237
market (definition) 280, 289, 298
    consumer markets 1, 117, 119, 227
    food markets 58, 286
    global markets 81, 190, 209
    housing markets 172–3
    labour markets 8, 82, 146–51, 154, 167
    local markets 1, 71, 173, 218, 228
market actors/agents/players 3, 10, 74, 171, 175–6, 189, 263, 281–2, 286, 310–11, 313–14, 317–18
market campaigns 192–3, 209, 211–12
market economy 6, 10, 15–17, 19–21, 26, 32–3, 51, 67, 270, 308, 316
market regulation 7, 50
market-oriented / economic reforms 14–16, 22–5, 27–8, 30–1, 33, 45–6, 50, 58, 60, 63, 67, 75, 150, 266
    pharmaceutical markets 265–6, 268, 270
Markus, Stanislav 220
McLeish, Jenny 322
Merton, Robert xx, xxi, 239, 284–
Mintzberg, Henry 140
Morrison, Kevin 43

natural childbirth 321, 323, 325–6, 329–31, 333–5, 337
Nefedova, Tatyana 63

opportunism 103–4, 119, 149, 166, 185
inter-firm opportunism 7, 103–5, 107, 109–12, 115–19
opportunistic behaviour 103, 105–6, 109, 111–12, 114, 118–19, 147, 310

oscillating behaviour xviii, xxi, 2–3
Osnowitz, Debra 149

Parsons, Talcott 4
Petkova, Iva 85
Polanska, Dominika 174
Polanyi, Karl 306
political consumerism 304–5
power (definition) 4–5, 123, 360
    abusive power 7–8, 19–21, 103–4, 117–19, 124–6, 128–30, 140
    asymmetry of power 106, 129–30, 311, 315–16
    balance/imbalance of power 124–5, 132, 140–1, 177, 311–12
    bargaining power 7, 106, 108–9, 111–12, 115–19
    centralization/decentralization 6–7, 62, 188
    definitional power 9, 262–4, 274–5
    distribution of power 5, 41, 53, 62, 64–5, 77, 315, 346
    economic power 1, 5, 33, 41, 61, 71, 77, 226
    managerial power 8, 123, 125–6, 140
    market power 7, 103–4, 106, 117–18, 293
    negative power 126
    platform power 151
    political power 6, 15–16, 21–2, 24–6, 32–3, 50, 535, 104, 109, 225
    power dynamics 188, 191, 193–4, 203, 211–12, 362
    powerful / powerless actors 4, 7, 10, 96, 201, 262, 276
    power for/over/together 8, 192, 198, 203, 205, 208–9, 212, 234, 345–6, 360
    powerlessness 308–9, 317
    power relations 4–5, 58–60, 65, 73, 77, 80, 102, 122–3, 125, 128, 140–1, 167, 171, 245, 262, 264, 345–6, 360, 362
    power struggles xxiv, 7, 60, 191–3, 201–3, 208–12, 343, 347, 360
    unilateral power 10
Pozanenko, Artemy 63, 78
public goods 15, 20, 44, 51–2, 172, 227, 258

Radaev, Vadim 7, 125
Readings, Bill 241
Redshaw, Maggie 322
regional models of rural communities
    mixed economy 64–5, 73, 76
    roadside economy 64–6, 69–71, 73, 77
    symbiotic economy 6, 63–5, 71, 73, 77
    unipolar economy 64–5, 74–6
relational conflict 103–5, 107, 111–12, 115–18
relational/embedded exchange 105, 116
rentier state 36–7, 53
rent-seeking 6, 21, 32
resistance xxi, 3, 7, 23, 52, 60, 66, 80, 104, 106, 118, 125, 303, 305, 312, 324, 330, 334, 360–1
resource curse xxiv, 6, 36–7, 44, 52–5
Rodgers, William 148

Schmitt, Carl 83–4
Schrödinger, Erwin xxii
Scott, James 61

Shanin, Theodor 62, 64
sistema 272, 274–5, 286, 293
Smelser, Neil 141
Sorokin, Pitirim xx
Stenberg, Jenny 174–5, 177, 180–1
strategic positioning of universities 9, 238–40, 243–5, 247–9, 252–3, 257–8
sustainability standards 8, 188, 205, 211

Tepper, Bennett 126, 129, 133
transition 14–17, 22–4, 31–3, 45, 59, 220, 233, 243, 270, 309, 333

uncertainty xxi, xxii, 80, 105, 116, 123, 176, 179, 257, 315
    quality uncertainty 175–6

valuation/evaluation 119, 130, 135, 138, 173–6, 180, 207, 225, 258, 263, 265, 281–2, 284, 287–9, 291, 304, 306, 309, 311, 313–14, 317
voice strategies 8, 125, 140–1
Vorbrugg, Alexandr 60

Weaver, Warren xxiv
Weber, Max xx, 4, 83, 123, 233
Wolf, Christian 43

Lightning Source UK Ltd.
Milton Keynes UK
UKHW021438180722
406019UK00017B/198